"Bully for the Band!"

"Bully for the Band!"

The Civil War Letters and Diary of Four Brothers in the 10th Vermont Infantry Band

CHARLES GEORGE, HERBERT GEORGE,
JERE GEORGE *and* OSMAN GEORGE

Edited by James A. Davis

McFarland & Company, Inc., Publishers
Jefferson, North Carolina, and London

Library of Congress Cataloguing-in-Publication Data

"Bully for the band!" : the Civil War letters and diary of four
    brothers in the 10th Vermont Infantry band / Charles George,
    Herbert George, Jere George and Osman George; edited by
    James A. Davis.
            p.   cm.
        Includes bibliographical references and index.

    ISBN 978-0-7864-6686-3
    softcover : acid free paper ∞

        1. United States. Army. Vermont Infantry Regiment, 10th
    (1862–1865)   2. United States — History — Civil War, 1861–1865
    — Music and the war — Sources.   3. Military music — United
    States — History and criticism —19th century — Sources.   4.United
    States — History — Civil War, 1861–1865 — Personal narratives.
    5. Vermont — History — Civil War, 1861–1865 — Personal narratives.
    6. United States — History — Civil War, 1861–1865 — Regimental
    histories.   7. Vermont — History — Civil War, 1861–1865 —
    Regimental histories.   8. Soldiers — Vermont — Corespondence.
    I. Davis, James A. (James Andrew), 1962–
    E533.510th .B85 2012
    973.7' 443 — dc23   2011050861

British Library cataloguing data are available

Front cover images: *background* sheet music for *Dixie*; Civil War
military infantry drum (courtesy Military & Historical Image Bank,
www.historicalimagebank.com); bugle © 2012 Shutterstock

Manufactured in the United States of America

McFarland & Company, Inc., Publishers
  Box 611, Jefferson, North Carolina 28640
    www.mcfarlandpub.com

To my parents,
Rose and Don Davis,
with deepest gratitude for everything
—*J.A.D.*

Table of Contents

"The 10th Vermont in Dixie"

There is a gallant regiment
    Which is called the 10th Vermont
Composed of men who are as good
    As anyone might want;
And coming from a State where snow
    In depth, comes several feet,
It is not strange they drink down here
    Where there is no snow to eat!

This regiment is divided in three parts,
    You'll understand;
In "Battle Line"—with center,
    And a "wing" on either hand,
Along the old Potomac—and you
    Need not think it strange
If they would, instead of eating snow
    Just take a drink, for change.

The "right" is at Monocacy
    In command of Captain Frost,
Whitesford is where the "center" is,
    And where old Stuart crossed,
And, of course, he riled the water
    So those here and those below
Sent to Monocacy for their drink—
    All for the want of snow.

The "left" at Conrad's Ferry,
    Major Chandler is the Peer,
Colonel Henry at the "center"
    Colonel Jewet, Brigadier;
Now officers and men I know
    Would rather stand retreat,
Then say they would refuse a drink,
    Where there is no snow to eat.

But this I'll say in candor
    Of these Green Mountain boys,
There are none who can excel them much
    Whom Uncle Sam employs;
And 'tis natural for a man to drink
    To keep out cold or heat
Especially in a country
    Where there is no snow to eat.

This song was included in a letter from Daniel W. Ware to Edward A. Wardner from April 20, 1863, while the 10th Vermont was stationed at Camp Heintzelman near the Potomac River. The song was apparently composed in gratitude by a soldier for whom members of the 10th Vermont purchased whiskey in nearby Monocacy. (Frederick County Civil War Centennial, *To Commemorate the 100th Anniversary of the Battle of Monocacy: The Battle That Saved Washington* [Frederick, MD: Frederick County Civil War Centennial, 1964], 41.)

Acknowledgments

I am indebted to many people for their help in bringing the words of Charles, Jere, Osman, and J. Herbert George to life. To the staff of Reed Library, State University of New York at Fredonia — Janet, Linda, Barb, and everyone else — I simply cannot say enough. From tracking down and obtaining obscure materials to fixing microfilm readers, your help made this project a reality. I know that I could not have done it without you.

Paul A. Carnahan and Marjorie Strong of the Vermont Historical Society Library were wonderful, and I was fortunate to benefit from their friendly and informed help. I am also grateful to Rick Baker and Richard Sommers of the United States Army Military History Institute, Carlisle, Pennsylvania, for sharing their amazing knowledge of the collection, pointing me in directions I had not considered, and making the institute a comfortable place to work. My gratitude also to Pat Andersen of the Montgomery County Historical Society, Maryland, and Brigette Kamsler of the Historical Society of Frederick County, Maryland, for their friendly assistance in obtaining materials. Thanks also to the staffs of the Manuscript Division, Library of Congress (Washington, D.C.) and the Manuscripts and Special Collections, New York State Library (Albany).

Kelly Nolan, military archivist, Vermont Military Records Project shared her invaluable knowledge of materials and facilitated access to the collection. Betsy Kelty and Angela Hallock of Records and Research, Department of Buildings and General Services, Middlesex, Vermont, provided friendly support while I worked in their holdings. James LaMonda offered his research talents and helped to track down supplemental materials at the Middlesex facility as well. Assistance was also provided by Heather Turner of the Pearce Museum, Navarro College (Corsicana, Texas); Dara Flinn of the Woodson Research Center, Rice University (Houston, Texas); Patty Cooper, executive director of the Historic Medley District, Inc. (Poolesville, Maryland); Jordan

Goffin of the Rhode Island Historical Society (Providence); and the staff of the Special Collections department, Bailey-Howe Library of the University of Vermont. Thanks are due to Susan Ginter Watson, archives director, University of Wisconsin–River Falls Area Research Center, for her help in locating resources and uncovering additional materials useful in this project. Reta Sanford of the Pierce County Historical Association was very helpful in answering questions and providing useful information.

A number of my students at SUNY Fredonia contributed to this work as well. Kasey Polito, Dennis Repino and Erin Meissner read portions of the manuscript and offered useful comments; Ashley Carlino willingly helped track down and order a ridiculous amount of material; and Jillian Ellis tackled the imposing task of double-checking the final edit of Herbert's letters. I'm also grateful to Jeremy Linden of the Image Permanence Institute (Rochester, New York) for many stimulating conversations and assistance while trying to decipher illegible images.

I am indebted to Linda Mitchell, Dick Phillips, and Vonnie George, descendants of the George brothers, for sharing materials with me and giving their blessing to this project. I am grateful to Judy McIntyre for responding to my genealogical queries, and sharing her own information as well as friendly conversations. Gail McLaughlin also offered genealogical information on the George brothers.

I am grateful to the State University of New York at Fredonia for providing a much needed sabbatical and financial support through a Scholarly Incentive Award. Thanks are also due to the campus Professional Development Committee for their generous support through Individual Development Awards of the New York State–United University Professions Joint Labor-Management Committee. Encouragement was also provided by many colleagues, including Hazel F. Dicken-Garcia (University of Minnesota), Randall Allred (Brigham Young University–Hawaii), and Michael Schaefer (University of Central Arkansas). Thanks are due to my colleagues at SUNY Fredonia — Paul Murphy, Gordon Root, and Michael Markham — for their patience with my often distracted company, and my gratitude to Ralph Locke (Eastman School of Music) and Evan Bonds (University of North Carolina–Chapel Hill) for years of support and encouraging me to see this project through to the end. As for introducing me to the J. Herbert George Collection, my lasting gratitude to Jeremy Smith (University of Colorado). And my deepest thanks to my wonderful wife, Jennifer Alhart Davis, whose patient support allowed me to see this project through to the end.

Introduction

Civil War Musicians Charles, Jere, Osman and Herbert George

The town also had suffered fearful ravages from war, and now a Union army was marching through its streets, every band and every drum corps playing the stirring but to southern ears hateful air, "John Brown's body lies mouldering in the grave," and we may anticipate our narrative to say that whenever our army or any part of it have occasion to pass through this town, the bands always struck up this air, as if to taunt the inhabitants with the memory of their victim, and played it from one limit of the town to the other. So John Brown was revenged![1]

Such a dramatic image is a familiar part of American Civil War narratives, whether written by those who participated in the conflict or by later historians trying to recapture the spirit of this tumultuous time. Music was an omnipresent part of Civil War America; "Taps," "Dixie," and "Battle Hymn of the Republic" remain defining elements as much as the Confederate battle flag, Fort Sumter, or generals Grant and Lee. It is impossible to revisit this time without encountering music, be it the casual songs shared among friends to the marches of regimental bands. Yet who were these music makers who brought their art into this bloody conflict? Certainly theirs is a story worth telling. General Robert E. Lee agreed, when he stated: "I don't believe we can have an army without music."[2]

Music was found at all times and locations during the war, in the streets and at home, on the march and in camp. From the outset of the war to today music has been seen as capturing the spirit of the participants and embodying cultural issues that were central to the conflict.[3] Certainly music was an integral part of the soldiers' lives; a day did not go by without hearing the commanding call of the bugle at "Reveille," the patriotic tunes of brass bands on parade, the martial airs of the fife while marching, and the reassuring songs from around the campfire at night. Countless soldiers referred to the benefits that music provided and it would be difficult to overstate its impact. As Elisha Hunt Rhodes of the 2nd Rhode Island Infantry remarked: "I am much favored by the musical talent of the Army. Well, it makes this life pleasant and even enjoyable, and we are better men and soldiers for cultivating a taste for fine things."[4]

Though many enlisted men were talented musicians and played for their comrades on whatever instruments were at hand, the real treats for soldiers on campaign were performances by the regimental and brigade brass bands. During the first half of the nineteenth century bands were the dominant instrumental ensemble in America. Brass and wind bands were used in most every possible performance setting, including parades, dances, and indoor and outdoor concerts. Band literature reflected this versatility, so much so that a typical concert program could include waltzes, popular tunes, patriotic works, marches, and transcriptions of orchestral and operatic music.[5] This music — what musician Charles Benton drolly referred to as "music rations" — affected the troops on innumerable levels.[6] Certainly it was entertaining, softening many a lonely and cold night for troops who were longing for home. Band music also provided stimulation for weary troops on the march, motivation before and during combat, and relief for the wounded after battle. Such was the power of music that some officers felt the need to censor their musicians; according to S. Millet Thompson of the 13th New Hampshire, officers forbade the performance of "pathetic" or "plaintive" tunes "lest they serve to dispirit and unnerve our suffering men."[7]

Most band musicians saw themselves as contributing their best to the war effort, knowing that their music was of vital importance to their fellow troops. The majority of soldiers greatly appreciated the presence of musicians in the ranks and the special gift that they shared. According to one member of the 24th Massachusetts Infantry: "I don't know that we should have done without our band."[8] A small number of officers and soldiers found the bands to be useless, a view often directed toward any noncombatants attached to the army. There was some justification for this attitude; certain band members avoided combat situations at all costs, while others probably contributed little beyond occasional musical performances. But this was not the case for all Civil War musicians. Enlisted musicians worked hard and shared many of the dangers faced by their comrades in the ranks. Field musicians suffered significant losses when compared to average enlistees, while certain bandsmen performed well in combat situations when the opportunity arose. Some musicians were even awarded this country's highest military decoration, the Congressional Medal of Honor, for their heroic performance in combat. Certainly enough musicians gave the last full measure of devotion; the first soldier lost in combat for the 87th Pennsylvania Infantry was Daniel H. Carnes, the drummer of Company I, while bugler Joseph H. Law was the last battlefield casualty for the 148th Pennsylvania. [9]

To read the letters and diary of Charles, Jere, Osman, and Herbert George is an extraordinary way to experience a musician's life during the Civil War as they performed every duty imaginable for army musicians. This included working in the two primary roles available for enlisted musicians: field musician and band member. Field musicians included the drummer, fifer and bugler. Drums were the standard instrument for communicating orders and establishing marching tempos in European armies, and American military units had adopted their use when formed in the previous century. Tradition held that the fife served to transmit orders as well as play tunes for official functions in the infantry, while the bugle did the same for the cavalry. Bugles were a more capable instrument in the field and quickly supplanted fifes in infantry regiments, though the fife remained active in the drum corps (formed from the regiment's field musicians), performing tunes while marching or during guard mounting and dress parade.

Unidentified Union drum corps with a principal musician (or drum major), two fifers, and drummers (National Archives and Records Administration).

Though drummer boys, fifers, and buglers are often portrayed as colorful accouterments to the combat soldiers, they were integral to the running of the army.[10] Field musicians were responsible for playing the "beats" (camp calls specific to certain hours) that ordered the soldiers' day, pulling them out of their bunks in the morning ("Reveille"), sending them out to work or drill, calling them in for meals, then returning them to their tents at night ("Tattoo"). There were special calls, such as "Church" on Sundays, as well as calls to summon specific officers for particular duties. All told this was no small task as the average number of beats per day was eighteen and could rise higher depending upon the type of unit or commanding officer.[11] In fighting situations field musicians were also called upon to play combat calls, such as "Fix Bayonet," "Quick Time," and "Cease Firing." It was performing these duties that led to the wounding or death of so many musicians. Necessity demanded that orderly or principal musicians remained close to the commanding officer during combat and consequently in positions of increased danger.[12] In addition, the ubiquitous specter of sickness haunted musicians as much as other soldiers. So life as a Civil War musician was no easy task, and death and illness took a toll on the enlisted musicians. The 2nd Minnesota Infantry had 11 drummers when first mustered; by January of 1863, there were only two remaining.[13]

The role of a band musician was quite different from that of their fellows in the drum corps. This was due in large part to the variable presence of bands throughout the war. At the onset of war it seemed that every regiment was fronted by a band. Military musicians parading in front of proud volunteers suited the idealized vision of war held by so many nineteenth-century Americans. Apparently the federal government was guilty of such visions as well, given the number of musicians detailed during the formation of volunteer units. According to General Order 15 of 4 May 1861 each infantry company would have two musicians (a drummer and fifer or bugler) and each cavalry squadron would have two buglers. Each infantry regiment was allowed two principal musicians (in charge of the company field musicians) and 24 musicians for a band, while cavalry regiments could have two principal musicians and 16 musicians for a band.[14] A report by the United State Sanitary Commission noted that bands were found in about three quarters of the regiments visited in the Army of the Potomac at the end of 1861; historian Kenneth Olson speculated that the total number of bandsmen in the Army of the Potomac alone could have been over 2,500.[15] Such enlistment allotments created an abundance of musical riches, yet by the end of that year both sides realized that the war would not be a brief and glorious affair and that each army needed to reevaluate the viability of having so many military musicians. Concern that some were using the band to avoid serving in the ranks led

General George McClellan to order his inspector generals to examine the bands and "discharge all men mustered therewith who are not musicians."[16]

The cost of supporting so many bands was prohibitive as well. Benjamin Larned, paymaster general of the Union Army, raised this point to Senator Henry Wilson of Massachusetts: "The bands (regimental) are, in my opinion, far more ornamental than useful, and should be abolished. This would be a saving of about $5,000,000."[17] Enlistment shortages and escalating costs finally led to an official attempt to reduce the number of bands in the Union Army. According to General Order 91 of 2 October 1861: "No bands for volunteer regiments will in future be mustered into service, and vacancies that may hereafter occur in bands now in service will not be filled. All members of bands now in service that are not musicians will be discharged upon receipt of this order by their respective regimental commanders."[18] The following year Congress passed Public Act 165, transmitted to the army in General Order 91 of 29 July 1862, which abolished regimental bands and recommended brigade bands in their place.[19] On 9 August 1862 the adjutant general's office informed all commanding generals:

> Have all volunteer regimental bands in your command mustered out of service at once. Enlisted men detached from companies to serve in said bands will not be mustered out. They will return to their companies. Not enlisted as musicians, they cannot be discharged as such. Each brigade is now allowed a band of sixteen musicians, with same pay and allowances as now provided for regimental bands, except leader, who will receive $45 per month with allowances of quartermaster-sergeant. With their own consent, musicians of regimental bands may be transferred on present enlistment to brigade bands, at discretion of brigade commanders.[20]

This decision was met with disapproval by many:

> Another matter, where Congress would do well to pause, is the discharge of regimental bands. Those who advocate this cannot have an idea of their value among soldiers. I do not know anything particular of the science or practice of music ... but I see the effects of a good band, like ours, continually. It scatters the dismal part of camp life; gives new spirit to the men jaded by or on a march; wakes up their enthusiasm. Could you see our men, when, of an evening, our band comes out and plays its sweet stirring music, you would say, if retrenchment must come, let it be somewhere else. Let Congress lay an income tax of ten per cent., if it will, on officers, while men at home pay but three — as a reward for patriotic sacrifices; but let the men have their music.[21]

Bands cost a great deal, but their worth to the troops was inestimable. Despite decrees from on high and the dismissal of countless ensembles, many regiments insisted on having a band and went to surprising lengths to insure that they had one. The men of the 24th Michigan Infantry of the vaunted

Iron Brigade chose to send home fifers and drummers in order to retain their band.[22] Of course, if a ranking officer was fond of music then there was little chance that a band would be dismissed. Fortunate bandsmen were detailed to division, corps, or army headquarters, where they were excused all duties but that of performing for their commander; in some cases a band was attached to a specific commanding officer and would follow him depending on his appointments.[23]

So regardless of official efforts to curtail their numbers, new musical ensembles continued to appear even up to the war's final years; the 33rd Iowa Infantry welcomed a new brass band to their brigade as late as September of 1864, while the 17th Connecticut formed a "string band" in middle of the same year.[24] The 10th Vermont was one of many units to form a band after General Order 91 of 1862 had been issued, as was the 87th Pennsylvania, a unit that would join the 10th Vermont in a brigade in spring of 1864. Charles E. Gotwalt of the 87th Pennsylvania summed up his regiment's feelings about their band:

> Before reaching Beverly, at Clarksburg, the band (The York Springgarden) was discharged. Previously each regiment had a band but this was too great an expense to the government; so thereafter only one band to a Brigade was allowed by the Government. As the Regiment wanted a band, one was detailed from the ranks. The instruments were purchased from the sum of $1200.00 raised by the officers of the Regiment for the equipment of the band.[25]

Official sanction was not required to form a brass band; a regiment or brigade could have an ensemble if the men were willing to fund the band and support the musicians' efforts. This included buying instruments and music as well as relieving the players of various soldierly duties so they could rehearse. Many regiments collected money from officers — and in some cases the enlisted men — to purchase instruments.[26] Some of the more affluent regiments hired professional bands, though by 1863 most of these ensembles had either returned home or been integrated into the ranks. Other regiments would cull their own companies for capable musicians, often drawing on the field musicians first, as was the case with the 10th Vermont and 87th Pennsylvania, but not hesitating to pull enlisted men should they show talent. The number of players in a regimental or brigade band was fluid by default of the environment. Band members could get sick, wounded or captured, or their term of enlistment might end. In April 1865 Herbert George numbered his band at sixteen, which was the accepted number for a brigade band as proscribed in General Order 91 of 1862.

The responsibilities of regimental band members could be less onerous than those of other enlisted men.[27] The band's primary duties were to perform

Band of the 48th New York Infantry at Fort Pulaski, Georgia, from 1863. Members of the drum corps can be seen in the back (Massachusetts Commandery Military Order of the Loyal Legion and the U.S. Army Military History Institute).

at dress parade, guard mounting, and review, and to lead the regiment in parades. Like all soldiers they were required to look after themselves in terms of building shelters, cooking, and other necessities. Some bandsmen were detailed for guard duty or assigned to police the camp, just like ordinary soldiers.[28] Yet their need to rehearse and perform often kept them from the drilling and work duties that occupied much of the average soldier's time. Release from such mundane tasks did not mean that bandsmen suffered from a surplus of free time. Most bands rehearsed at least once a day when in camp. Bands were constantly engaged to perform, whether as part of their officially prescribed duties or in informal concerts for the troops and serenades for the officers. According to Union general Robert McAllister there was "plenty of this kind of music. We hear it all hours of the day while in camp."[29] Bands also performed for special events such as the arrival or departure of commanding officers or visiting dignitaries. At times brass bands were called upon to play music of a more social nature, entertaining civilians or providing dance music for the occasional ball. Bands also performed at hospitals, offering emotional support for captive but grateful audiences of wounded soldiers. So many performance demands could oblige a band to give a lengthy performance every day, and sometimes twice a day, especially when the regiment was in permanent camp. Units that did not possess a band would solicit the talents of nearby ensembles, as when the band of the 7th Wisconsin played a review for the 19th Indiana after that regiment's band had been sent home.[30]

Bandsmen and field musicians were usually not required to fight in combat situations. Field musicians who did not have musical duties during a battle were given the dangerous but necessary assignment as stretcher-bearers, helping to remove the wounded from the field. At the battle of Antietam, musician Ludolph Longhenry of the 7th Wisconsin discovered just how harrowing an experience this could be: "Many shells and even canisters exploded all around me but not a splinter hit me. One soldier I saw lost half his head and one leg torn off by a shell."[31] Band members were ordinarily stationed behind the lines and designated to assist the surgeons. This could include fetching water, cleaning the surgeon's tools, or the grisly task of restraining soldiers during amputation.[32] Many felt that this was not the best use of musicians: "In another order I think that he [Gen. Meade] has made a mistake; viz: in ordering all the musicians down to the hospital as nurses, cooks, and the like. We have little enough music in the army as it is, while a good tooter may be worthless as a nurse or cook."[33] Band members who did not serve as hospital orderlies could be called upon to assist those soldiers engaged in the fighting by carrying ammunition, helping to move artillery pieces, constructing fortifications, and removing the wounded from the battlefield. Occasionally bandsmen were called upon to use their musical talents on the battlefield. Some clever officers would use their bands as part of tactical deceptions, trying to mislead their enemy in terms of the size, location, and intention of their troops. In rare instances bands could be found at the front line of battle, playing music in the hopes of inspiring their comrades.[34] Musicians were also called upon for more traditional soldierly duties; picket duty was something no one could escape, and a field musician was necessary at guard posts to give advanced notice should the pickets have a hostile encounter.

Even when being kept from the line of combat, musicians still ran the risk of being wounded and killed by stray fire, or even being taken prisoner. During the Battle of Williamsburg, May 5, 1862, musicians of the 33rd New York were assigned to the ambulance corps, but when moving the wounded they found that they had moved straight into a skirmish with Rebel soldiers.[35] And the sickness that decimated Union and Confederate camps made no distinction between musicians and combat soldiers. Burdick A. Stewart, leader of Stewart's Brigade Band attached to the 10th Massachusetts Infantry, died fairly shortly after rejoining his regiment at Brandy Station, presumably of illness.[36] Of the thirty-one men who either enlisted as musicians or performed in the band of the 10th Vermont, six would not live to see the end of the war.

This was the volatile world in which Charles, Osman and Herbert George found themselves beginning in the fall of 1862, and where brother Jere would join them two years later. The George brothers were born and raised in the small town of Newbury in east central Vermont alongside the Connecticut River. The George family had been farmers in the region for generations; grandfather James George (1775–1839) was a soldier in the War of 1812, then raised stock and crops in New Hampshire and Vermont. Jeremiah Nourse (1777–1857), the George brothers' maternal grandfather, was a highly respected farmer in the area, and their grandmother Ruth Bayley Nourse (1790–1862) came from one of the oldest families of Newbury. The brothers' uncle, Charles Harvey George (1796–1851) was a farmer in Newbury, and also married into the Bayley family. The George brothers' father was James George (1804–1882), a farmer and drover who had moved with his family from Topsham, Vermont in the 1820s. In Newbury he met and married Maria Nourse (1809–1890), a Newbury native. Apparently James failed as a drover and the family faced difficult times, so Maria's parents granted acreage for a farm to the couple that was subsequently sold so they could purchase land in Newbury. Here they settled in to raise a family. James and Maria had seven children: Ann Marie (b. 1829), Charles Harvey (1831–1914), Ruth Nourse (b. 1834), Jeremiah Nourse (1837–1887), Osman C. B. (1840–1863), James Herbert (1843–1925), and Emma Sophia (b. 1848).[37]

James George's intemperate habits made him a poor provider, leaving Maria to work the land with the help of the children while also taking on washing and house cleaning jobs in the neighborhood. Despite the financial strain, Charles, Jere, Osman and Herbert seem to have been relatively content as children, receiving a "good common school education" at the Newberry Seminary while pitching in around the farm.[38] All the siblings were devoted to each other, and the brothers — particularly Osman and Herbert — seem to have been particularly close to their mother. The letters that survive reveal an intimate and compassionate relationship between all of the brothers and sisters. They seemed genuinely found of each other, sharing personal feelings as well as playful teasing.

James George appears to have contributed little to the family's situation, having lost his job as a drover and turned to drink. One neighbor referred to him as a "burden to the family."[39] It is possible that there were some difficulties in the relationships between the children and their father, as Charles, Jeremiah, and Herbert all left home at a relatively early age and lived some distance from Newbury. In the request filed by Maria George for her son Osman's pension, one witness asserted that what money James George made "went to his own support and the maintenance of his intemperate habits. He gambled only when he drank."[40] Throughout the war Herbert plaintively asked for letters from his father, with little result it would seem. One glimpse of the father's behavior is found in Jere's diary entry of 11 September 1864, as he is departing for the army: "My heart was touched when Father bid me 'good bye' for I noticed that as he added 'May the Lord bless you and be with you' his voice trembled and he turned silently away. I knew that he realized that he was parting with a son, whom I know he loves, with only a war chance of ever seeing him again…. It seems as though I never loved him better than I have during my two visits this summer. He seems to overflow with goodness. Not that he is any more so than Mother, for she was always so. I notice it more in him because he was *not* so when I visited home last summer." Despite his inability to support the family, James George seems to have given his children a sense of duty and a musical upbringing. All four of the George sons enlisted in the army, and each of them performed as musicians.

Charles followed the family tradition by becoming a farmer in the region near Newbury and starting his own family. Charles married Ellen Maria Peach (1837–1931), a native of Newbury, on 15 October 1856. The young couple had two children: Nellie (b. 1857) and Arabella (b. 1858), but only Nellie survived past childhood. Charles' world revolved around his wife and daughter, and while times were probably tight he seemed to have been fulfilled and content with his life. Charles' unflagging devotion to his small family was the force that sustained him through what would be the most trying years of his life.

Jeremiah served as Newbury's first telegraph operator, a skill that he shared with his younger brother Herbert. He eventually moved to New Hampshire and then Massachusetts where he seems to have held a variety of jobs (including working in a tailor's shop right before enlisting), a pattern that remained with him for the majority of his life. Life was not easy for Jere according to a letter he sent to brother Charles: "Herbert says I owe you a letter," he admitted in a letter of March 31, 1862. "Things have been so 'tuff' with me that I am thin as a rail & most as thin as two rails. They say I am very poor & look more like having consumption than Lucretia does, '*howsomever*' I can blow a big blast yet with my old lung bellows." Though employed as a telegraph operator, the money was not good, and Jere suffered from doubts of his future as well as his financial plight: "I am like a man lost in the woods. I have been hunting & trying to find my way out for years, but go which way I will I can't find the way out & am still wandering from place to place still hoping to get sight of a happy future in this world. Confused and confounded I roam, trying to *see out* but am as far in the woods as ever.

A portrait of Charles and Ellie George from 1897 (private collection).

Still I have some courage. You have been in the woods a long time too, and have *seen out* several times but it was only a small opening which led to a denser forest." Jere quickly countered the somber tone of his confession with a jab at his poetic style: "Ha, ha, wont you laugh now at my originality?" Jere then recalls fond memories of life in Newbury with a mixture of humor and melancholy, and signs off with greetings for his other siblings.[41] Jere's emotional disclosures side-by-side with witty comments perfectly captured the open and supportive relationship shared by the siblings.

Osman was the only brother who remained in Newbury after coming of age, assisting his parents around their farm. Prior to leaving for the war Osman informed a neighbor of his "intention of remaining at home with his father and mother and taking care of them." Plans were made for Osman to buy a small stretch of land alongside his parents' plot with the hope of enlarging his family's estate. In spite of his father's troubling condition, Osman "was willing and expected to stay at home with him, and help carry on and improve the place."[42] Whether it was the chance to earn a soldier's pay or to be with his brothers in war, Osman left his parents to enlist in the 10th Vermont. It quickly became apparent that he was poorly suited to life as a soldier, and Osman's sufferings proved to be the most arduous trial that the George family faced during the war.

Herbert in particular had a fair amount of musical experience prior to the war, owning his own cornet, band uniform, and an impressive collection of band music. Newbury locals described him as a "musician from the cradle."[43] Newbury had a cornet band, organized in 1857 or 1858, and Herbert was possibly a founding member, playing the B♭ cornet for the ensemble at age fifteen. The director of this band was Henry W. Bailey, a community leader who joined the Third Vermont Infantry as bandmaster. Despite his apparent talents, Herbert sought other means to support himself. His brother Jere had been the first telegraph operator in Newbury, and Herbert trained to replace him. When he came of age Herbert moved to Greenfield, Massachusetts, and was there employed working the telegraph. Like so many other young men of the time, the outbreak of war lead Herbert to return home to join the war effort.

Charles, Jere, Osman, and Herbert George personified much of what it meant to be young men from rural New England during the Civil War. Their small town upbringing and farming sensibilities permeated their letters. For Jere and Herbert, any potential provincialism was somewhat counterbalanced by their experiences outside of their hometown of Newbury, especially the time spent in Massachusetts. And while Charles may not have seen as much of New England as Jere and Herbert, his experience running a farm provided a pragmatic stability that made him a solid and unflappable soldier. All four brothers were fairly well educated, experienced in music, strong in their faith, and committed to their families. In these ways they reflected the time and region in which they were raised, embodying those qualities that historian Howard Coffin saw as defining Vermont's Civil War soldiers:

> They went well prepared, sons of large, close families on self-sufficient farms where each person had tasks, was accountable, yet where cooperation was essential. Educated in one-room schools under close supervision, they learned the essentials, including history. Fun was self-made, and most learned early to shoot, to tramp the hills looking for deer and squirrels. On Sundays, most everyone worshipped in their faith, be it in church or around the kitchen table, where mother or father got out the Bible. Beliefs were firm; death was part of life and could come on the wings of angels. The Vermont that took its part in the Civil War produced young people who understood duty and hard work, who could walk forever and shoot straight. And they lacked street smarts, clever ways of getting out of things that should be done.[44]

A portrait of "Prof." J. Herbert George from after the war (E. M. Haynes, *A History of the Tenth Regiment, Vt. Vols,* 2d ed. [Rutland, VT: The Tuttle Company, 1894], 438).

In so many ways Charles, Jere, Osman and Herbert George endeavored to fulfill their distinctive roles during the American Civil War. Charles went into the war feeling a duty to his young family at home as well as a responsibility for his younger brothers beside him. Perhaps his age allowed him a more realistic perspective on what he had volunteered for; Charles managed to remain optimistic throughout the war and did not let the tragedy surrounding him change his view of his family, his country, or his God. Yet this strength was sorely tested, given the nightmares that seemed to plague Charles, especially towards the end of the war. Charles enjoyed his time with the band, believing their music to be beneficial to the troops, yet it is his service to the wounded that seemed to have made the biggest impact on Charles.[45]

Jere entered the war late and brought with him a less tarnished view of life at the front. This would quickly change, and Jere's thoughts would turn to understanding the human turmoil that surrounded him. Jere was the most spiritually inclined of all the George brothers. He was very religious and devoted to a Christian lifestyle, something that would be tested when he eventually enlisted. Jere was also inclined to consider the world from a philosophical or even poetic perspective. Whereas Charles remained focused on his family, and Herbert would be swept up with his music, Jere tended to spend his time pondering the chaos around him, looking for deeper meanings. While all the brothers were artistic, it was in Jere's writings that an aesthetic perspective was particularly apparent. Here is how Jere described the shelling around Petersburg in 1865: "The heavy gunboat pieces put in the deep bass notes to the loudest pieces of music I ever heard or expect to hear. For three hours such cannonading was probably never heard before on land. Sometimes a continuous roar like deep heavy thunder. It was grand and majestic in the extreme."[46] All three brothers were particularly attuned to the impressions and sensations of military life — they *hear* and *feel* the war as much as the *see* it.

For Herbert, music defined his army experience. Herbert served in most every capacity possible for a musician, and often went beyond the basic requirements of his service to bring music where it might do the most good. He approached his duties with the utmost seriousness, and gladly accepted added responsibility whenever it was placed on him. He worked tirelessly, and grew both as a person and as a musician. For Herbert the war proved to be a coming of age, and it was a different, certainly wiser young man that was to return home to Vermont in the summer of 1865.

Yet one brother did not return home. Charles, Jere, and Herbert were profoundly changed by their experiences during the war, but the suffering of their brother Osman ensured that the war left an indelibly personal and heartrending mark on the entire George family. Not even the surrender of the Army of Northern Virginia at Appomattox Court House and the triumphant parade through the streets of Burlington could erase the pain of the loss. For the George brothers, as with so many Americans, the war would stand as a family tragedy as much as it was a national crisis.

Throughout this book editorial introductions and interpolations by the editor are in italics. — J.A.D.

CHAPTER 1

September to December 1862

Enlistment; Military District of Washington; Offutts Crossroads; and Poolesville, Maryland

In July 1862, following President Lincoln's call for 300,000 troops, Governor Frederick Holbrook of Vermont announced the formation of two new regiments, including the 10th Vermont Volunteer Infantry, Colonel Albert B. Jewett commanding.[1] *Since the inception of the war Vermont had been eager to provide what troops it could, so when Secretary of War Stanton wired on June 26, the state was ready. The response was overwhelming and the regiment filled up with "unexampled rapidity."*[2] *From July 10 to August 15 companies for the new regiment were gathered from all over the state, including St. Johnsbury, Waterbury, Rutland, Burlington, and Bennington. The staff officers included Colonel Jewett, Lieutenant-Colonel John H. Edson, Major William W. Henry, Adjutant Wyllys Lyman, Quartermaster Alonzo B. Valentine, Surgeon Willard A. Child, and Chaplain Edwin M. Haynes.*

Included in the list of new recruits were two brothers from the small town of Newberry, Vermont: Charles and Osman George. Charles, age 31 at enlistment, was a lean 5' 4", with brown hair and blue eyes; Osman, age 22, was similar in size but possessed a somewhat more frail constitution. They joined Company G of the 10th Vermont Infantry that formed in Bradford on August 12 under the command of Captain George B. Damon, also a native of Newbury. Eventually ten companies, a total of 1016 officers and men, gathered at Camp Washburn in Brattleboro and were mustered into service September 1. It was here that a third member of the family, Herbert George, caught up with his brothers, and "while there he was seized with an ardent desire to 'go with the boys,' and he enlisted as fifer in the company where his brothers were."[3] *The young Herbert was a healthy*

18 years old and described himself as 5′ 4″ of slight build, light complexion, blue eyes and brown hair.

The new regiment began basic training in company and regimental drills. Supplies were brought in for the men and each soldier soon received the basic kit, including old muskets of dubious quality. The regiment was fortunate to receive even these, for the state of Vermont was ill equipped for war and had delayed preparations for some time. The outdated guns were eventually replaced with better weapons, including new Springfield rifles for two companies, but only after numerous protests by Jewett and his superiors.[4]

From Charles:

Brattleboro, Vermont
August 20, 1862

My dearest Ellie:

Another day has rolled around and I will write the usual amount of passing events. Yesterday I was detailed for special duty. Osman was on guard and has just got in. About 12 are detailed for guard and 2 for special duty every day. Guards are on duty 2 hours on and 4 hours off. My first duty was to put up barrels for men to stand on that were in the guard house — many were in for missing the guard — one of them would not get on to his post and they made him carry a block of wood for 2 hours. We had to march them to their posts. The next was to punish 7 men for refusing to do duty by making them carry blocks of wood.

Those that are not on duty (guard) are not required to go out on drill, so last night I went out and saw them drill. The first battalion drill we have had. I tell you it was splendid to see 1000 men all armed and equipped — the Colonel is front commanding. Our company officers are all green. The captain and our 2 Lieuts are greener than half the privates. The two sergeants are the only ones acquainted with the tactics. I can go through all the movements I have been though so far. Our Company thus far bears the name of being the steadiest. The steady ones prevail and that keeps the rest down — not one has yet been in the guard house.

I shall not be home under 2 or 3 weeks — they don't give but 3 furloughs a day and they are taken up a good ways ahead, but they favor the married men. I want to go home even more before seeing the rebels. The talk is now that we shall stay here for some time yet. (Thursday) — Herbert has just come in and is now going to the examining Sergeant. We are signing our allotments today. (Friday the 22nd) — I have just signed the allotment roll for 10 dollars per moth to go to you. I will send this letter by Herbert.

Your ever loving husband, Charlie.

The raw volunteers were excited to be part of their new regiment, naively "ready and anxious to push forward to action."[5] *There was no band attached to the regiment when it was mustered, so the new soldiers filled the air with all kinds of melodious sounds. Oscar Waite of Company I described what he heard: "First Sabbath in camp. I write this among all manner of confusion and all sorts of noises. Some boys are reading aloud from the Bible; others are singing hymns; others are singing 'John Brown's Body,' and still others 'Dixie,' with now and then a French song and a few oaths mixed in, while a fife in the next tent is playing 'Yankee Doodle.'"*[6] *Many of the recruits found military life to be more of a challenge than they had first imagined. Willard Thayer of Company B wrote to his wife at home of the difficulties some of the troops faced, describing how some men almost fainted while*

Wartime portrait of Col. Albert B. Jewett, first commander of the 10th Vermont Infantry (Roger D. Hunt Collection at the U.S. Army Military History Institute).

drilling.[7] *As with so many volunteer regiments, the men were unrealistic in the gear they collected for their new life in the army. Officers brought tables, stools, and fine mattresses, intending to take these into the field, while Captain Edwin B. Frost of Company A donated a collection of 200 books for the regiment. Burdened as it was with so much unnecessary equipment, the 10th Vermont was fortunate to receive a stationary posting for the first year of their service.*[8] *Major events were swirling around the men from Vermont and they anxiously followed the news as the fighting drew near.*

September 6, 1862, the 10th Vermont received marching orders and set out for Washington, D.C. The Vermonters piled onto trains for the first stage of their journey, passing through Springfield, Massachusetts, to New Haven, Connecticut. There they boarded the steamer Continental *and arrived early Sunday morning in New York City. After breakfast ashore they again climbed aboard the transport, sailing down the harbor to Perth Amboy, New Jersey. The men were transferred to dirty freight cars and continued their southerly journey. The Vermonters were warmly received in both Baltimore and Philadelphia—"such cheers never was heard as they gave for the bully green mountain boys"—and arrived at the nation's*

88136

The barracks at Brattleboro, Vermont, where Charles, Osman, and Herbert George enlisted in the 10th Vermont Infantry (National Archives through the Vermont Historical Society).

capital on September 8.[9] *The following morning the troops marched to the southern edge of town and were assigned a site at Camp Chase on Arlington Heights overlooking the Potomac. It was an exciting time for the regiment, surrounded by thousands of soldiers from countless states. Colonel Jewett described the muster as "covering this country with new Regts. getting them in so thick there we can hardly find room to drill."*[10] *There were plenty of opportunities to hear stories from veterans of previous campaigns, especially those involved in the recent debacle of Second Bull Run.*

From Charles:

Camp Chase
September 11, 1862

Dearest Ellie: I will now tell you where I am — being about 5 miles southwest of Washington and 2 miles south of the Potomac — in fact I am in "Dixie." The Capitol is in sight by gong 40 rods — it is a great building. I went up to it soon after I wrote the last letter and around it as much as allowed. It is such a magnificent building it would be an awful loss to have the rebels destroy it. The rest of the city is less beautiful — in fact I call it a rather "scrubby" city. We marched from there on Tuesday P.M.— 5 miles in the heat of the day with all of our rig on — as much as ⅓ of the regiment fell out of the ranks and came straggling along hours afterwards.

Tell father's folks they needn't worry about Osman, he kept to the ranks and then took hold and helped clear land and put up tents and came out all right. But "Charlie" did not come out all right the next day. I did not feel at all fatigued when I arrived here — felt as though I could do 10 more hours so I took hold and worked hard carrying tents etc and then took hold and helped set them up and wasn't aware that I was overdoing till I went to bed and was so tired I couldn't eat. In the night I woke threatened hard with fever — got myself covered up nice and warm and threw it off, but had an awful headache the next day.

Herbert came in all right — he hired his knapsack carried. The Orderly tried to get me out again today but precious little work I did do yesterday, but today I felt as well as ever. Have just been to the store and bought one pie, 15¢, 2 onions, 4¢, and ½ lb of cheese, 6¢. The cheese I threw away....

The first cavalry is only about 2 miles from here. They water their horses directly in front of our camp. Saw L. Burnett yesterday — he thinks we have a hard time before us and all the troops are discouraged (keep this from your father) since the battle of Bull run. We have camp rumors that Jackson is wanted and again that he is in Pennsylvania or that they are fighting at chain bridges. The rebel pickets are around us most every day — some are caught and brought in as prisoners. Last night we were ordered to be in readiness — arms and equipment all ready for a moment's warning — but don't be alarmed, Washington can never be taken — it is guarded by about 200 forts and troops innumerable. It is thought there is nearly 200,000 troops about here so don't worry about me. I am fast becoming a soldier. The dread of battle is never away. We are told by old soldiers to throw away our knapsacks saying that we will sooner or later be on the march.

Following the devastating Union loss at the Second Battle of Bull Run on August 28–30, Confederate general Robert E. Lee took advantage of his victory and pushed his army north. The first week of September he sent the Army of Northern Virginia up through Leesburg and across the Potomac, arriving in Frederick, Maryland, on September 9. General George B. McClellan, recently reinstated as commander of the Army of the Potomac, cautiously moved his massive army towards Lee. The resulting Battle of Antietam was a Union victory, though at an extremely high cost to both sides; September 17, 1862, became the bloodiest day of the entire war.

Eager to join the Union initiative, the George brothers and their comrades were disappointed when on September 14 they were ordered up the Potomac to guard various locations on the Maryland side, stretching a distance of ten miles from Seneca Creek to Edwards Ferry. This location was a natural first assignment for a new unit, and many regiments were to get their initial taste of army service in the defense of Washington along the banks of the Potomac.[11] This was also the first extended march for the regiment, and the lack of experience showed as the 10th Vermont managed only six miles on the first day. Herbert and Osman certainly found the march exhausting, perhaps even more than the other soldiers, as the drum corps was placed at the front of the regiment to play music during the march. It was not until September 17 that the weary and footsore soldiers arrived at their assigned positions along the Potomac. Regimental headquarters was established in the center of the line at Pleasant's Meadows, and Company G was placed on the left flank and formed pickets around Edwards Ferry. The combination of a new lifestyle and the extended march took its toll on Herbert George. By the end of the week he was laid low by sickness, enough so that he was placed into an ambulance and sent to a nearby hospital. To make matters worse, a surgeon at the hospital accused Herbert of stealing blankets, the first of many occurrences that led the George brothers to have little respect for the medical staff.[12]

Two letters from Charles:

Saturday, September 20, 1862

My darling Ellie: I have just got around to write to you. It is about 10:30 P.M. and I have been busy till now. It took me till 9:00 to make Herbert some gruel. Had to go a mile and a half after flour and milk — the latter was sour at that! Herbert is pretty sick. I left him on the lock yesterday real sick — he was in a private house — he came to camp about 5 P.M. completely beat out, just in time to see the surgeon. Poor fellow, he was so fatigued and pleased to see the surgeon and get to camp that he threw himself down on the blanket and cried. The surgeon left him some powders and I think he is some better — fever not so high.

Lieut. Blodget is very kind — gave up his berth to Herbert and gave me a chance to sleep near him. Besides that he was good to him himself by wrapping him up in a blanket and doing everything he could to make comfortable. Blodget is a first rate man. I like him better and better the more I get acquainted with him. The night we were called out so suddenly we were surprised how cool and collected he was, carefully surveying the ground and as calm as an old General.

Last Sunday I went to Sabbath School — he was our teacher and Lieut. Newton was the teacher of another class, so you can see what kind of officers

The first photograph shows Confederate troops marching west on East Patrick Street in Frederick, Maryland, on September 12, 1862. A few months ago it had been blue uniforms crowding the streets of Frederick, such as these Union troops on North Market Street celebrating Washington's Birthday on February 22, 1862 (courtesy Historical Society of Frederick County, Maryland).

we are under. He advised us to have prayer in out tents and we have done so since when we could in ours. Today I am excused from duty to take care of Herbert. Osman is well and so are all the Company but two — I am among friends and what is still better, brothers. All are good and kind but none will stick by like brothers. It is truly said about us soldiers that our families worry about us more than we worry about ourselves....

(Sunday Morning) — We moved last night down to the lock or rather a hill back from the canal. There is a rifle pit built by General Banks last year and built in the form of a cross or plus sign with holes to shoot through. It is built of oak logs 12 inches thick with a ditch around it.

I think our Company could hold 2 regiments. Where we were before we were completely penned up between the river and canal and could not beat a retreat. Herbert is still sick — I carried him up the hill on my back. We are going to try to get him into a private house and Gitchel [*Getchell*], the drummer will take care of him.

Lock #22

September 25, 1862

My dearest Ellie: Once more I find an opportunity to write. I have been very busy lately, taking care of Herbert, poor fellow, he has gone to the hospital now. I stayed by him as long as I could. We got him a chance to be in a private house on the lock and pretty soon we had another sick man to take care of— Rowel by name. Gitchel, the drummer, and Osman and I took care of them till Tuesday night. Herbert had a good bed, had just eaten his gruel when the surgeon came down and ordered them to the hospital 7 miles away. The Lieuts and Sgts were very much displeased with the order. Martin said that had he been there they never would have been suffered to go, but he got them into a boat as comfortable as could be under the circumstances and moved them up to the next lock — 2½ miles.

Herbert had not been able to sit up any for 3 or 4 days, he had a species of fever and ague. He is the most pleasant and patient person I ever saw to take care of— he never complained. When we got to the lock we had 5 or 6 miles to go in an ambulance. I went with them and laid down with them — and such a ride! — you can't imagine — the roughest roads you ever saw part of the way through fields — wild mules — one of them unmanageable and the carriage not very easy. Down hill they would run in spite of the driver. The poor sick boys rolling from side to side — they kept very calm, but sometimes I thought they would die before they got there. But they lived through it and got there about 11:00 P.M. — dark as it could be

Now for the hospital: a tent about 12 feet square with 8 cots made by driving 4 crotched sticks in the ground — two poles on each side and a strip nailed across and hay spread over the top comprised the bed. The only clothing was what they brought —1 rubber blanket, 1 woolen ditto and one overcoat. I could not but compare it with the comfortable quarters we had left and had traveled so far in the dark of night to find the one he now occupied — but he took it calm and very patiently and strange to say did not appear any the worse for the journey. I went there without leave from anyone but was received with good favor by the surgeon and was approved for by our Lieut. When I got back he said he was very glad I went with the boys. The nurses (male) were very good. After giving up my blanket and seeing they were well cared for I went to seek lodgings. A nurse took me to a cavalry camp and there after talking about an hour with a drunken cavalry man I laid down on a couple of rails on the floor and with nothing to think of but my noisy cavalry man, brothers in the hospital and a thousand other things I fell asleep. As the fire lowered down I crawled up closer to the fire as it was cold without my blanket, but the cavalry man got up swearing because I let the fire go down. At length morning came, men began to crawl from under their blankets and I went to see how Herbert was and found both of them better. When the surgeon came in — No. 1, next to Herbert had to be moved — suspected he had a contageous disease — No. 2, (Herbert) has had fever and diarrhea — Surgeon gave him more quinine — No. 3, has got the typhoid fever — No. 4, has been out of his head, — No. 5, getting better — surgeon thinks he can soon join his Company. — No. 6, feels better, but has a pain in his side — surgeon prescribes a blister — No. 7, says he feels better, but has a sore tongue — No. 8 (Rowell) feels some better. This was all a sad sight and I felt sorry for the boys. I went off after making arrangements about blankets etc. for the boys — I went to the Col. For a pass but was told I could go without one — "just tell the pickets how it was and they will pass you," but I found it pretty difficulty to get by some of the pickets — was stopped once as much as an hour, but finally got through and arrived about 2:00 P.M., every one inquiring about Herbert — they all like him — the surgeon seemed to be rather partial to him. I have written this expecting you to send or get it to father's folks. I think of you so often with love.

From Herbert:

Camp of Co G near Potomac
(Maryland side) Oct 1st/62

Dear folks at home

If you rec'd Osmans letter no doubt you are very anxious to hear from me — I have had a kinder hard time but not so hard as some of the poor sick soldiers of our company — I had a fever but not very severe — it was sort of chill fever, a touch of the Ague.... We left Camp Chase Va on Sunday night the 14th (two weeks ago last Sunday I believe) at five oclock with knap sacks on our backs and traveled up to the Aquiduct bridge across the Potomac. Crossed there over into Georgetown and resting here a lot of artillery got arranged in front of us to march. We went <u>on on</u> backs aching awfully stopping only a minute once in a while or so to rest — as soon as we would halt every man would lay down on his back immy. It made no difference to us whether it was mud or grass — I would drop as quick as tho I was shot all most when we stopped for a minute. At eleven o'clock we turned in to a field and spread one blanket on the ground, lay down & put the other over us, then to sleep in just one minute. Got up in the morning all wet with the dew. Lame & Sore we shouldered knapsacks again after making a breakfast on raw ham & hard crackers. "Forward drum corps," Drum Major would say every little while.... After dinner the regt all but Co B & G went up the river — Charley fixed a tent out of our rubber blankets & we went to bed that night feeling pretty well — I had eaten a good many apples during the day and about twelve oclock that night I was taken with a terrible griping in my bowells — I never was in such pain in my life. I awoke Charley & he got me some thorougher and I got better but it rained during the night & I got some wet & didn't feel very smart in the morning. Some time in the forenoon we were ordered down the river then down on the towpath about ten miles & left 8 pickets then we hiked back up the river leaving pickets along side the river. My drummer & my self volunteered to go up & stand picket in a rifle pit up on a high hill (I am in the same pit now). I was quite unwell we stayed there the day & at night. I was quite unwell — went down to the lock on the canal & had a dunk. I was chilly & took some pills — I stuck it thro till Friday. The surgeon did not come to see me at all — I walked up to head quarters Co G about ¾ of a mile. The surgeon was there but just going [off]. I was so weak I could not stand Charley was there and I lay down on his blankets. Surgeon give me powder & left some saying he would see me the next day. Lieut Blodgett give me his bed & I lay quite comfortable. The next day Lt Blodgett moved his quarters up here to this rifle pit. They carried me up & the surgeon did not come to see me at all. Sunday Charley took me down to the house at the lock. They offered me a good bed upstairs. Charley was detailed to take care of me & he took the best of care of me too. I could not sleep on the bed it was so soft. I ached all night awfully. I was feverish and sick.... I was taken up in a boat to the next lock above here (2 miles) & there took the ambulance. Arrived at the hospital about eleven. I forgot to state that another fellow of our Co was sick with me at the house & was taken with me to the hospital. We two filled up the house. My bed was some poles fixed up with pieces of boards put across & hay put on then put on my rubber blanket on the hay. Lay down pull woolen blanket over me. Charley went back in the morning. We had not yet received our knapsacks so I didn't have my overcoat. I was cold part of the time. The 2nd night one fellow from Co. C died. They took him to the Wash [hospital] (Going to send him home). Well I got a lot better & Saturday PM I went into a little side tent to stay at ... and after I had been on my couch a little while Surgeon came in & accused me of stealing 2 or 3 blankets from the other boys!!! I denied it & he told me not to lie to him — After scolding me pretty hard he went away. I couldnt understand it. Next morning he pitched in to me again about it. I commenced to tell him that I was a different fellow from that & had said these words "I was brought up." He cut me short & said, "Was brought up to steal blankets yes." He used me very mean on the whole He is the most hard hearted fellow I ever saw. They all hate him in the worst way. Before I came away he found out that I did not <u>steal</u> any blankets. Well Sunday morning he said I was discharged from the hospital. I was so weak I could hardly walk but was awful glad to get away. Came down in the ambulance but sat on the seat all the way.... We have reading & prayer in our company every night, it seems good to tell you, & then we have a lyceum in our company. It makes it seem home like. I tell you when I was the sickest I thought of home pretty often. I wanted to see mother. In fact I wished I was home not [to return] again. I was real home sick.... We have got a mean chaplain, he aint any more of a minister than I am. He did not come in to the hospital & talk with us at all while I was there. He was in once & left a few papers. I am quite sure he did not say a word to that man that died. The Poor fellow was out of his head & spose it wouldnt of done any good but Chaplain has not preached a sermon since he came into the regt. I never heard him make a prayer. He will smoke his pipe & take things easy. But our 1st Lieut Bludgett is a real good man he prays with us every night. 2nd Lt is a Christian too. Capt has not yet come out to join us. Expect him soon....

From your Son & Brother

Herbert

9 P.M. 2nd — Our drummer has gone after grapes & I just beat the drum for company drill (what is left here). Aint I getting smart? There are any quantity of peaches & grapes toeing here. We make sauce & jelly or some do. Has Henry Bailey got home yet? How is C. Little? My respects to all at home.

Feeling like real soldiers in their crisp uniforms the men approached their new duties with callow seriousness. Despite their earnestness the men had received shockingly little training, and anxieties ran high with each report of an enemy incursion. Sometimes their raw eagerness led to some rather humorous encounters Willard Thayer of Company B described one such moment:

> *Company G is stationed a mile and half below us. Their pickets got a little frightened and suppose they see a boat. They hailed it and it minded nothing about them. They fired into it and called out their company and company B started and formed into line and marched about half a mile when the word came back to them that it was a mess of rocks that they was a firing into.*[13]

Aside from one report of an enemy assault on October 5 that pulled many companies into battle formation, the regiment saw no action here. According to one participant, the "enemy assault" was no more threatening than the pile of rocks that had recently assualted Company G. What was thought to be enemy troops were spotted across the river, and Major Chandler was called. He summoned artillery to handle the situation: "Quickly those guns were unlimbered and shot after shot went screeching across the river. The column on the opposite side was soon scattered; at just about that time it was discovered that instead of rebels, the six-pounders had been shelling a negro funeral procession."[14]

These days spent along the Potomac were filled with constant drilling, and men like Oscar Waite began to adapt to their strictly regulated life: "company drill at nine; battalion drill from ten to twelve, A.M.; company drill from three to five P.M., and then dress parade."[15] *The troops were anxious for a combat posting and various rumors spread through the camp as to where they might be posted. Recent activity in the Western Theatre led many of the newer regiments in the Army of the Potomac to believe that they would be stationed in Texas, an option that Herbert and some other members of the regiment found agreeable.*[16] *A journey south was not to be, as the regiment was assigned to Brigadier General Cuvier Grover's Brigade, Military District of Washington. October 11 the various companies were gathered together and the regiment was brigaded with the 39th Massachusetts, 23rd Maine, and 14th New Hampshire. A central camp was formed at Seneca Creek, an unhealthy location much too close to a swamp. Not only was Herbert still recovering from his illness, but brothers Charles and Osman were now sick enough that the three of them were left behind to follow the regiment as best as they could. Herbert and Charles were to recover soon enough, though for Osman this was the beginning of a long and constant struggle to regain his health.*

From Osman:

Camp Newton
October 7th 1862

Dear Mother

As I have some good news to tell you I must write. Last Friday we moved again we are now not far from two & half miles from our old camp which was named Camp Blodgett in honor of our first Lieu. This our present camp is in honor of our 2nd Lieu. it is a very pleasant place considering our situation. Our regt at least half of it are near here so that we have battallion drill with knapsacks which is not very easy, but I must write my good news. Herbert wrote I believe that we had meetings last conducted by Lieu. B. Sunday last we had one which was conducted as follows. First singing next prayer, singing & then a lecture read by Lieu. Newton & by [Beecher] which was good & read as well as Geoff. King could have done had he been here. After that we had our second meeting during which nearly every eye was wet with tears as for myself I could not keep the tears from running down my cheeks as our second sargeant Martin who has been very rough made up his mind to lead a different life and as he spoke of his mother with sobs and tears flowing like rain I could not but say to myself that God is in our midst. After a few more had spoken a chance was given for all who desired interest in the prayers of others and who wished live better lives to rise. Nearly all who were there stood up. In the evening we had another meeting at which time some eight or ten started by speaking some were backsliders. Some of them you know at least one who was Edwin Tuttle. Another James Hadlock, a cousin to the Hadlock girls. After all had spoken who desired too there is another chance given to all who meant to live better to rise and some near all that were there rose up. Our first Corp. Leavit a backslider spoke his determination to be on the lords side. I just wish you could have been here to witness the proceedings. Today I was speaking with Lieu. B he said he thought there were at least twenty conversions Sunday. I hear they will hold out even say we are going to have another meeting tonight. I am glad that we can have meetings with out the aid of our chaplain who has not visited our Co to my knowledge since we left Brattleboro. I believe though he came round & gave some papers to the boys. So you can judge what sort of chaplain we have got. I have never seen him with out a cigar in his mouth yet. I should like to have a request made in the class or prayer meeting for all to pray for Co. G. 10th Vt. Vols. I will write about the meeting we are to have tonight tomorrow if I get time. Since the meetings begun there has not been more than one fifth of the profane words used as there were before. I feel myself honored by being a member of company G.... Write soon, from your son,

Osman

From Charles:

Camp Newton
October 8, 1862

Dear Ellie — last night I was sick — had a dizziness in the head and how I wanted you to bring me water, coffee or something — but am better today.

After taking 4 pills I volunteered for picket duty to get rid of the drilling. I tell you we drill pretty hard—double quick a great deal. While on picket guard I can take it very easy—sitting down al the while—just keep our eyes peeled. McKellops has just brought along 30 or 40 little fishes from 3 to 4 inches long—he caught them in his hands. We shall have them for supper. Tonight we want to catch some eels _if we can_. It is not really tedious acting on picket guard on this river—it is very wide and all we have to do is to prevent a crossing or give the alarm and I don't think they will attempt to cross—they would have to start wit several thousand men to accomplish their objective, which would be to destroy the lock and capture the commissary stores.

The next thing, you will want to know about the health of the Company—Well, Osman is better and Herbert is getting along slow but sure—he will get well if nothing further befalls him. Yesterday at one time we were all three on the sick list and Herbert was the smartest of the lot.

(Thursday 12 noon)—I am again seated in our little tent that we three brothers have made. Yesterday our Lieut. Col. Was deprived of his Commission on account of drunkenness—(he is not always drunk, according to his reports). We also had marching orders—report is that we are to cross the river at Edwards, and help take Leesburg, Virginia. That is where Col. Baker was killed and so many drowned over a year ago—but we are here still and no indication of moving. One of Company K boys shot off all the toes on one foot while cleaning his gun this morning....

(Saturday morning—Headquarters of V 10th regiment)—I find myself beneath a rude tent made last night by George and Co.—it has rained most of this time yet we are pretty dry. The next day after I commenced this letter we had orders to march but after going about 40 rods we were ordered back to spend the night. Osman came in sick from picket duty so we were all sick together. Next morning 9 of us started with blankets, haversacks and canteens for headquarters (5 miles). Osman and I were better and carried Herbert's things—arrived about 3:30 P.M. Osman and Herbert were used up so I had to go into the woods, cut my timber and frame it and build a house. Osman helped what he was able to do and more—he was sick again all night and is now. I have had night sweats for 3 or 4 nights—don't know what is the matter with me.

(Saturday 4:00 P.M.)—have been taking vitriol, camphor and quinine today. Osman is in the hospital—Herbert is still improving....

Upon rejoining the regiment the George brothers immediately engaged in a familiar pastime of soldiers, that of building a small shelter to live in, what

The 4th Vermont Infantry was one of the lucky regiments that had a band when formed. Unfortunately for the regiment, the ensemble was mustered out in August 1862 (courtesy Vermont Historical Society).

Herbert affectionately described as a "pig pen." Sickness apparently did not keep Herbert from performing his musical duties admirably, for beginning on October 16 he refers to himself as "Sergeant Fifer." Though there was no such official designation, it probably reflected his being raised to chief fifer, a position that made him responsible for all the regiment's fifers. Another musical change at this time came from one of the regiments that had joined the 10th Vermont in their new posting. Dan Barker of Barre described it:

> *I have just been down to the canal to hear a brass band that belonged to the 14th N. H. Reg. they have just come out here they are a very healthy looking set of men, you had better believe that the Boys Sckedadeled for the canal in a hurry when they heard the band, it is as good a band as I ever heard I believe, they left Concord about one week ago. The Boys thought that it sounded a little like old Vermont.*[17]

The enthusiasm generated by the New Hampshire band undoubtedly led Colonel Jewett and his officers to consider forming a band of their own. The George brothers would have been ardent supporters, though concern for Osman's unstable condition restrained their enthusiasm. Herbert and Charles grew increasingly

disgusted with Surgeon Childs and his seeming indifference to Osman's plight;
Herbert also had little respect for the drum major and began to assume more and
more of the regiment's musical duties.

Though relatively far from the action, tensions ran high as word spread that
the notorious Confederate cavalry commander J.E.B. Stuart had embarked upon
one of his infamous rides and was in the vicinity.[18] Stuart and his troopers left
Williamsport, Maryland on October 10, reaching Chambersburg, Pennsylvania,
where they appropriated supplies and burned what they could not take. The fol-
lowing day Stuart turned back south into Maryland, passing through Hyattstown
and reaching the Potomac at White's Ford. Word was sent to Colonel Jewett that
Stuart was heading toward the mouth of the Monocacy River, so Jewett mustered
his troops and quickly moved to intercept. The Federal troops stationed at White's
Ford put up minimal resistance and Stuart's men successfully crossed into Virginia
with Union infantry hot on their heels.[19] The men from Vermont were spared an
encounter with the flamboyant general, and it would remain some time before
they would see any combat.

Two letters from Herbert:

Camp on the Potomac, Senaca Creek Md
Oct. 14th 1862

Dear Father

I have just about half an hour to write you a letter in and I will try to
write all I can. The last time we wrote we expected to march you know "ie"
if you have got the letter. Well we did march Thursday five miles up the river
& as Charley & Osman were about sick we all stayed behind that night &
went up the next day very slow. Our knap sacks were carried. Well Saturday
night we had orders to march back again and the whole regt came together
here at Senaca Creek. We expected to have a fight here & so we were called
in together to be ready for any enemy. There is some artilery here with us.
Have not seen any rebels yet. Osman has been quite sick he was in the hospital
a day or two, but is with us now in our pen. We have to build a house every
time we move & that is pretty often. We havent had any tents since we left
Camp Chase Va. Each party builds his own house. We build one large enough
for us three. This time we (Charley & I) built a log house or <u>pen</u> rather. It
looks like a <u>pig pen</u>. We split the logs open & so the inside is all nice &
straight. It is only four logs high & then a roof put on & covered with our
rubber blankets. Charley done most all the work. I only brought light stuff
down from the woods. It is quite a house the best in the Co. We may get a
chance to sleep in it one night & we may have marching orders tonight. Our
house has not been completed more than 20 minutes & it will be too bad if

we cant sleep in it one night. We may stay here two or three weeks. I am pretty well now but am weak yet. I go out on duty & fife as tho I was as well as ever. I commenced to do duty yesterday & played at dress parade last night. Was out at reveille this morning. I am gaining now because I am getting my appetite back. Can eat now with some relish. Live on the same the rest do now only we buy some molasses to eat with our bread. Now is the first time our regt has been together since we left Va. It seems good to be together once more. There are a good many sick in our company & in most every Co. Some cannot muster much more than half their co. fit for duty. We have three drummers sick & one or two fifers. I am thankful that I was not left on the sick bed. When I am sick I am <u>home</u> <u>sick</u> too & when I am well I feel like staying till the war is over. I dont care how soon the <u>hateful</u> business is settled now. The quicker the better it will suit me I aint homesick at all but still I want <u>peace</u> to be declared before next spring & then I would like to <u>go</u> <u>home</u>. I can't read a letter from home or from any of our folks without the <u>tears</u> <u>coming</u>. When I read Ruths letters the tears come the fastest. I can hardly read them aloud. I cannot even look at the name of any of you without a sigh some way or other. Capt Damon arrived yesterday & we got all the things mother sent & all the letters all safe. Thank you all for it. The cough drops will be needed & the pills too for I have been very costive. We are all getting along well. I must go & play for drill immy will write again soon. Please write me a letter yourself

From Herbert

In haste Oct. 16th After all my hurry I was too late for the mail. The post Master had just gone & the mail wont go again till Saturday so can write so more. Osman is getting better slowly Charles is not very well but is on duty. I have been doing rather too much lately & am not very well today. Got excused from duty by Drum Major. If I am kinder better tomorrow I shall have to go it. What used me up the most was Day before yesterday on battalion drill they <u>double</u> <u>quicked</u> it about 15 rods & the drum corps was with the colors & I run about 8 rods I guess & my strength all left me I fell out & sat down. I was so beat out that I sighed about two minutes & couldn't help it. As soon as I could walk I went to Drum Major & he excused me the rest of the day. The trouble was you see I haint got my strength yet & tired out easy. We are still here — had the fun of sleeping in our house two nights.... Don't work too hard this winter Be of good cheer. If it be the will of the Lord we shall come home some time. I have so many to write to that I cant write to often, will as often as I can we haint had any mail for a week expect it to night. The reason we haven't had it is on account of the rebel raid between here and Washington or some where I don't know where it is or was. Please send us a paper once in a while & some of you write often for a letter from home is worth a <u>hundred</u> <u>dollars</u>. You write me one when you get time or take time. <u>Please</u> <u>do</u>. Love to all our folks & respects to the neighbors.

Your own son,
Herbert
Searg't fifer
Co G 10th Vt
<u>Ahem</u>
Don't direct letters that way leave off the seargt fifer
Ha, ha. Guess I feel pretty well.

Camp on the Potomac Senaca Creek Md
Oct 22 1862

Dear mother

I rec'd Emma's letter soon after I wrote to father & was very glad to get it. I should feel pretty well now if I hadn't got the diarea. I have had it about a week now but not half so severe as some of our boys have it. I have a colic most all the time. I dont eat hardly anything, drink tea & eat soda crackers, buy them at the little store here at the lock. 15 cts per pound (32 in a "lb") they are better for me than the rations we draw. I have not drawn one quarter of my rations for the last month don't think. They dont feed us very well some times when I dont have any thing that is fit to eat I wish I was home again. It is cold & windy here now & I cant keep warm in no way play warm nights but today my fingers have been so cold that I cant fife worth a cent & it is as much as I can do to write. We are all in our old tents once more & it seems good to have them too. We took down our log house & made it two logs high the bigness of the tents & then put the tent on top of them. That makes the tent higher & more convenient. There are five of us in it. Fuller (the one that was sick) Charley & I are the only ones in at present, all writing using our knee for a table. If it wasn't so inconvenient for us to write I should write twice as often. If we dont write often you must for a letter from home is worth everything to us poor soldier boys. I should like one or two every day but if you will write every week I would like it very much. Osman is quite well now, is out to work some where, goes out on dress parade. He is not entirely well for he has the head ache considerable. He, Charley & I have all got the ague slightly. Charley was out on picket last night & says he had a severe chill in the night & then was as feverish as could be. He did not go on any beat at all. There was enough so that he didn't have to do any thing. Lucky for him as he was sick. I dont have a chill only about once a week now.

Take quinin when I have one. have taken a lot of cyanne pepper for the diarea, dont know but it will stop it for it is not so bad as it was. I guess half the regt have got it. There are about two hundred sick in the regt, 150 any way and I should think more likely 200, some a little sick & a good many real sick. I played at two funerals last week, or one was last Sunday. Both died from Co K. Two have been sent home that died since we came into this part of the country. one from Co C and one from Co H.... Dont send <u>any</u> box by express until I tell you to for we have no way to get it where we are now. Wish we were at Washington then we could get boxes easy enough — Emma I would make you a ring out of a peach stone if I could get one but peaches are "played out" perhaps I can find one by & by. I have got to go & play at battalion drill now. Good by for this time. More anon. From your son

Herbert

From Charles:

Camp on the Potomac
October 25, 1862

I write to you today with a heavy heart — I am disgusted with the head officers of this regiment — they have no feeling for the poor soldier, nothing less than a surgeon excites their sympathy — it is real maddening to go up to the surgeons tent when the sick men are called out to hear surgeon Childs talk — yesterday morning I gave up and went with the rest. He began with bringing down the greatest mess of threats and hard talk because there were so many men sick — talked as thought they had no right to be sick — said they all ought to die — but his list will continue to increase just as long as he manages his way. When he came to prescribe, some he would send back and mark "duty," others, give medicine and mark "duty" — and to all was as cross as a bear. But our Company is a little better off — Surgeon Clark prescribes for us — he is more of a man — when it came my turn I told him I had got the fever and ague and he marked me "quarters" and gave me some powders, but this morning he was close to Childs and I was marked "duty" — had to go out on drill this forenoon and felt so weak I could hardly carry my gun. I asked the Captain to be excused but, no, it was against the Col's orders and he could not excuse men — they must keep in the ranks until they fell from exhaustion and be carried off by two men — that is the way they kill men out here. I don't see any chance for a man's life if he is sick.

   I don't know what will become of me, but if the chills will let me alone I will get my strength in a few days, but every one makes me weaker. When Clark felt my pulse I told him it was as high as that all the time and Childs spoke up and wanted to know what right I had to feel my pulse — I didn't know anything about such things. When we marched from Camp Chase he followed in the rear to pick up the sick and made them walk when they were unable and actually struck his bayonet in some because they didn't get up and march. — Oh! soldiering will do pretty well for well men, but the sick!! but we look on the bright side — have had 3 or 4 frosts and that kills the ague, perhaps I wont have it much more.

The 14th New Hampshire regiment is here, they have a band. I can hear the big drums now. We heard cannons firing south of here this forenoon. Well, I must go and fix up something for supper — we buy butter for 40¢ a lb, bread for 10¢ a loaf....

The beginning of November found the regiment continuing to settle into their new lives as soldiers. Charles continued to look after his brothers as both Herbert and Osman slowly recovered. Domestic duties also occupied the George brothers as they sought to improve their living conditions while fighting off the sickness that haunted the regiment. The brothers continued to improve on their tent, look for good food when possible, and plead for more letters from home. As the cold weather set in Charles suffered on picket duty and Herbert began to ask for clothes from home as well as food. The rumors that the brigade would be sent to Texas increasingly concerned the men, though Herbert admitted that at least the weather would be warmer there.

Two letters from Herbert:

Camp on the Potomac Senaca Creek
Nov. 1st/62

My dear mother & all the rest

As Osman has been writing home I will write a letter by candle light this evening. You can't guess what we had for supper tonight. We had <u>bread</u> and milk. Didn't we smack it down. I went a mile last Thursday & got some flour. 5½ lbs. Paid 20 cts for it & Charley made just as good minute pudding as you can make out of it that night. at the same time I got the flour I got a quart of milk too. The pudding lasted till Friday noon & Friday night Charley made a <u>soup</u>. Had fresh beef & potato cut up & hard bread. put in some black pepper & thickened it up with flour. It was <u>awful good</u>. We feel a great deal better when we have something that is fit to eat. You must send us a little black pepper in you letters. There has been a great deal of sickness in our regt since we came here. Last Sunday we buried three. The next day two & the next day one. None have died since then I believe. There has been three sent home. I believe one from Co. H & C & I think one other one. One that died last Sunday was our best fifer or full as good as any. He stood next to me in the Drum Corps.... If it wasn't for my cold I should feel pretty smart now. Don't feel home sick any when I feel so well. We don't like our Drum Major very well & there aint hardly any one in the regt that does, he don't come up to the mark. I heard that Col said he hated him. He (Major) thinks he will get promoted before long, expects a commission. I should'nt wonder if the Drum Corps played out before long. If it does I suppose I shall have to take a bugle. So they say. I aint very particular but am afraid that I should not stand it long to blow one for they don't blow so easy as my cornet.... Tell Em that I can't get time to make a ring. Some way my time is all taken up. I don't laze round any, hardly lay down to rest through the day. Either fifeing or cooking or something else. Can't find time to write any letters to any of my friends that I promised to. We have heard cannonading all day off to the Northwest, don't know where it can be. Hope the rebels will get whipped where ever it is. I suppose you knew that I was 19 didn't you! Quite an old boy for your youngest. I have lost about 15 lbs since I enlisted. Weigh 105 now, should think by that that I was growing poor. I feel as though I had. It looks as though it would rain tomorrow, hope it won't blow as it did a week ago. We haint had a letter from home since your & Em wrote, mailed Oct. 22nd, hope to get one next mail. Azro is tough as a nut, has grown fat & tall since he enlisted. He is thickening up just like Henry — He has had good living & I haint all the time. Thats the difference. I suppose the mail goes out in the morning, so I will have my letter ready. My respects to all the good folks. Charley has been writing Ruth — All pretty smart only Osman is weak & unfit for drill — Good night home,

From Herbert

Camp on the Potomac Senaca Creek
Nov 5th/62

Dear folks at home

    We rec'd a letter the other day mailed the 30th ult. I believe. Was glad to get it as we always are, and I suppose you are just as anxious to get word from us often as we are from you. I suppose we shall winter here without any doubt, unless the rebels drive us off. We are all fixing up for winter. Build logs up about 4 feet high and then put the tent top of that. We went off yesterday & confisticated some boards for a floor & for shelves &c. Got them off from an old canal boat. We calculate to have things as comfortable as possible. Now if you & Mr. McKinstryes folks send us a box of stuff (& Ellen) we want something to wear & something to eat. If you have not sent any thing by mail yet then send us (Osman & I) an under shirt a piece. Send me a pair of footings, two or three pocket handkerchiefs, a neck tie or two, a good pair of scissors. Osman lost his. Perhaps some thread & a little yarn. Osman says he wants two under shirts & two pocket hdkfs. We want dark colored shirts. He wants a pair of draws, <u>the right size</u>, & a pair of wristers. Guess thats 'bout <u>all</u> for clothing unless you think of something you think we need. I can't wear gloves & play my fife, taint got any here either. Now for something to eat. Some pickle, tea, dried berries dried apple, <u>Sure</u>, want some butter if you can send it and a dozen eggs if possible. Some black pepper. No saleratus as we can get it here, have got some now want <u>green</u> tea. Can you send some jelly of some kind or am I sending for more stuff than you can get into a box of such size as will be of little trouble or expensive rather! I'd like a <u>cake</u> of <u>maple sugar</u>, 5 or 6 of them, bottle of cough drops anyway. Mother cant you send some of your good dough nuts & have them <u>warm</u> when they get here so I can smell em? Wish I had some fresh lamb and a pumpkin pie would taste good but I cant have it this year. Dont know but I'd better have a pair of mittens and then when I'm playing I can put 'em in my pocket, guess better send a pair. One thing more. I want an <u>awful good long</u> letter. Em you tell French & Greene to write, & Hen Bayley & all the rest of the folks, <u>girls</u> and all. I'd write to <u>everybody</u> most if I had time but I <u>haint</u>....

Your little soldier boy

J. Herbert

It is reported that our regt is going to Texas with Genl Banks. Don't think we shall go my self!! It is so cold I can't fife very well most froze my fingers this P.M. at dress parade

From Osman:

Headquarters 10th Regt Vt Vols
In camp on the Potomac Nov 5th 1862

Dear folks at home,

Again I improve a few moments in writing to those at home. Since I wrote last my health has improved very much but it comes quite hard to drill in battalion drill now. Last Monday I went on picket & being a cold windy day and a pretty cold night I caught cold. I did not have to go out but twice & then only as a guard in a grocerie store which was the most comfortable place I had in the night. I slept in our little tents & from twelve till morning my feet were what I used to call plaguy cold. It is uncertain where we may stay this winter if we stay here. I am going to have some warm clothing for I shall certainly need them at least when on picket duty. Azro says that arrangements have been made so that we can get boxes and he is going to send home. I thought we had better all send together. If we do so we shall send pretty soon perhaps now. [We] will for such things as we need & you can put some other things in, which you think best. I cannot write much more now for I have got to drill. Will mail a soon as I can get time.

Nov. 6th — As there is no drill this forenoon I will try & finish my letter.... I feel a great deal better about the farm ... than I have since we left the old place. I see nothing now to prevent at least a comfortable living & if I am spaired to return home with C. & H. we can once more live in peace. Yesterday on whole a skirmish drill, which takes only half of the company. Our second Lieut. asked the reserve how many wished that they were at home. [Not] one volunteered to raise his hand. All seem anxious to have the war close & then all would lay their arms down & shout for Vt. If I was as well I have been part or most of the time since I came out here could join right into it & enjoy the drills. To day all seem to be busy fixing up their tents for winter quarters. But we know not how long we may stay here. I am not very particular where we stay if we stay in one place. It will be hard some nights on picket duty. But if we have suitable clothing I guess we can stand it. We are losing men almost every day. Perhaps not quite as often but there has been between fifteen & twenty deaths in the regt. Perhaps there would have been as many at home in same number of men. It is cold today. The weather changes very often but we have not had but a few rainy days. Suppose that will come soon now & then the picket boys will have to take it, for then will be the time I shall need the oiled cloth or something to keep my hands dry. I shall want a pair of good pants before spring. I have a pair of shoes besides my boots but for picket duty I can not get along with shoes. I am some cold & the fire is going out. I will not write any more now.

In a hurry,

Osman

The regiment continued to guard strategic points in the area, which meant plenty of time for drilling. Such activities grew all the more unpleasant as winter set in, leading most of the soldiers to complain incessantly of the snow and cold. Not surprisingly Herbert complained about playing his fife outside, though at least he was regaining his health. The same could not be said for Osman, and then it was Charles' turn to catch a cold. This month also saw a number of changes and promotions in the regiment. On November 11 Colonel Davis of the 39th Massachusetts replaced General Grover as brigade commander, and soon thereafter Colonel Jewett replaced Colonel Davis. Lieutenant Colonel Edson resigned and Major Henry was promoted to lieutenant colonel and oversaw temporary command of

Officers and soldiers of the 10th Vermont Infantry from 1862. Front row, from left: LTC Wyllys Lyman; 2nd Lt. Edward P. Farr, Co. E; Maj. Lucius T. Hunt; Capt. John A. Sheldon, Co. C; 1st Lt. George E. Davis, Co. D; 2nd Lt. Ezekiel T. Johnson. Back row, from left: Unknown, Unknown wearing hospital steward's chevrons; Comm. Sgt. Austin Fuller; 2nd Lt. Lucian D. Thompson, Co. B; 1st Sgt. Silas H. Lewis, Co. D; Pvt. Leonard R. Foster, Co. B. (U.S. Army Military History Institute).

the regiment. Captain Charles G. Chandler of Co. I was also promoted, replacing Henry as major.

Not all changes were the result of promotion, however. Though the 10th Vermont had yet to see combat, the men were learning to accept losses from their ranks as deadly sickness swept through the regiment. The first soldier to die from the 10th Vermont was Charles H. Dayton of Company C, on September 26; too soon others would follow. At one point five men from the regiment were to die in one day.[20] The 14th New Jersey Infantry, a unit that would share most of their service with the 10th Vermont, lost seventy-five men in nine months while camped nearby at the Monocacy River.[21] The 10th Vermont averaged between eighty and ninety men on the sick list between November 1862 and January 1863.[22] Such losses meant that the drum corps was continually called upon to perform one of *their saddest tasks, that of performing the "Dead March" as a lost comrade was laid to rest.*

    From Herbert:

Bayleys Cross roads
Headquarters of the
Brigade 7 miles south
of Senaca Creek
Nov 13th 7–30 PM/62

Dear Parents & sister

    We left our comfortable winter quarters (as we supposed) this AM at 10 o'clock & marched here to headqrts. Five regts here: VT, NH, Me, Mass & RI cavalry I believe — There is a telegraph line runs past here but no office very near. Charley was left at Seneca to guard some baggage &c will be along by & by. Osman is here but not very well. His legs are swollen badly & face bloated like Charley Littles. He got his knap sack carried & equipments. I had mine carried too but we have not got them yet. Won't be here till tomorrow. We have to beg blankets tonight & have no over coats either. Guess we can get along for we have got in to the Sergeants tent tonight. It is reported that we have got to go to Texas & guess it is <u>so</u>. This brigade is going & that's what we are called together for. Our Post Master said it was a <u>sure</u> <u>thing</u> for he saw the order on dispatch. We may not go but it looks like it now sure, so much like it that if you have not sent the box, <u>don't send</u> it at present. If it is on the way perhaps we shall get it but if it is not I think it is not best to send it till we know where we are going to stop. You can send little things by mail as much as you choose. Osman got a letter the other day from you, it was day before yesterday you was going to some thing by mail but didn't because the PM didn't know about the postage. If we go to Texas it will be warm & we shall not need the shirts so much.... I should enjoy going to Texas I think if I know I should be tough & return again to my dear home. I mean to be true to my country & my God where ever I go but its a hard place to live a christian. My health is better now than Charleys or Osmans either. Charley has an awful cough that I'm afraid he wont get over. His head feels bad & he is unfit to do duty but cant help it. I wish he could go home for I do think his cough is dangerous. Perhaps he will get over it soon, hope he will & Osman too. You see I dont have to go on guard or picket, thats what makes the boys sick I believe. I'll write again as soon as I find out what we are going to do....

From Herbert

From November 13 through December 21 the regiment was shifted to nearby Offutts Crossroads. Though sickness followed (including a bout of typhoid that took twenty-five lives), living conditions began to improve and life in "Camp Grover" became more tolerable. As winter snows set in the soldiers entertained themselves as best they could. The men played games (including "foot-ball"), officers hosted their wives, and everyone managed to celebrate Thanksgiving in respectable style given their situation, including Timothy Messer of Company H: "I went to a bakery and bought some cookies, aples and very nice doughnuts for my thanksgiving we had no drill that day and thought of you a great many times."[23] In an effort to bolster the men's spirits, Colonel Jewett and Lieutenant Colonel Henry purchased a pig, greased it, and turned it loose amidst the men, with the winning hog-catchers being allowed to eat the unlucky porker.

Musicians contributed to the celebrations as only they could, and now, as for the rest of the war, music became a primary means of emotional support and spiritual recuperation for the soldiers. The distinct pleasure the soldiers took from hearing the music of bands transcended any other form of entertainment. According to Tabor Parcher of Company B: "They have a brigade band here in this brigade & I tell you that w have some nice music it is the place for me to enjoy myself...."[24] For Philip Arsino, Company F, the music brought back memories of home: "wea have a Brass ban in our brigade it plays evry day and evening it seames like old times to here it play it is most time for dress praid that is the last thing wea have to doe half pass fore."[25] Those without music certainly felt its loss. One soldier of the 14th New Jersey, a regiment with no band, complained that "Christmas and New Years were very dull, and passed off very quietly in camp."[26] Other members of the same regiment built a performance hall above a guardhouse in Frederick where the troops enjoyed performances by members of their regiment as well as other units.[27]

Amidst the entertainments Herbert and Charles fought colds and coughs intermittently, while poor Osman's condition continued to decline. By now all the men were anxious to establish winter quarters as the weather continued to worsen. Herbert still complained heartily of playing the camp calls outside in the cold, while Charles' stints on picket duty kept him from shaking his cold. Rumors continued to circle the camp as to where the regiment might get stationed, and the troops were increasingly anxious to see action. The highlight for every soldier at this time was the box from home, filled with treasured food, winter clothes, and the concerns of loved ones at home.

Two letters from Herbert:

Camp Grover <u>Offuts</u> crossroads (instead of <u>Bayleys</u>)
November 27/62

Dear father and the rest

We are still here and all alive. We got a letter dated the 22nd & C. got one today dated the 23rd mailed the 24th. We are awful glad that you have started a box. Hope it will get here safe before we leave. We have made up winter quarters again, bound to be comfortable while that we shall not stay long. Some say that we shall march between now and next Sunday. They say too that we may stay two or three weeks but go before long sure pop. One report is that we go to Washington and then to Point of Rock up above Poolsville, another to Texas another South Carolina. Cant tell nothing about where we shall go may go may be possible we shall remain here a month or two yet.... It is cold windy weather here now, go to the fire to warm & <u>burn</u> our faces & freeze our backs cant get both sides warm at a time no way. Lay cold nights too some times. I didn't sleep hardly any last night I was so cold. "O who wouldnt be a soldier" is what the boys say. Ive got pretty well smoked through. There is always a ring round the fire & if I happen to get on the smokey side, have to <u>take it</u> or take the cold. It's kinder tough to not have any house to go in to when we get so cold. My fingers were so numb when I got through playing at dress parade to night that I could hardly hold my fife, but I dont complain any. got used to it so that I can put up with most any-thing. It would seem hard for you or any of the boys at N to go out to the barn & sleep with only one blanket over them but I'd like as warm a place as our hay to sleep in this winter. Dont know what place we may get yet, perhaps not as good as this & perhaps better. Guess I shall <u>stood</u> it any way Wish Osman was as tough as I am. He is quite sick yet with dysantery & diarrhea, but rather think he is on the gain. Charley is better than he was, guess he will come out all right. O. will if he dont have to drill too much before he is able they made him drill this AM when I really pitied him he looked so pale. He has been up round most of the time today & done more than he has any day for a long time hope he will continue to gain till he gets tough again. I am cold now & shall have to go & warm me, it is almost time for tattoo. Pretty cold night I tell you. We are pleased to hear you making so well on your pelts — "Bully for you." Make all you can so I can have some when I get home.

With much respect

Herbert

Camp Grover Offutts Crossroads Md

Dec. 6th/62

Dear mother

Spose you've been looking for a letter from us for several days & haint got any. Well what you going to do about it? Keep looking & you'll get one when it gets there ... you see we've been so busy since we got our **BOX** that we could'nt do any thing but <u>eat</u>! We got the box all "OK" last Tuesday night. Every thing came safe. The cover was off the pickle can & some of the pickle was on the shirts but no damage done. I tell you our clothing does us a heap of good just now. My under shirt feels so good that I would'nt take a four dollar bill for it. Every thing sent was acceptable I assure you.... We had a good time last Thursday. They greased a pig & let the Regt chase him. Two men caught him at the same time & both claimed the poor pig. Col. told them he should be divided between them. He was cut in two cooked & eat up before night. Then they had a foot race $3, 2 & 1.00 prizes. A fellow in our Co got the 1.00 prize — The fellows that caught the pig got their clothes greased up so that they had to go & draw another suit. I didn't run in either case. The officers of this Co. done well by us. They sent off & got 18 chickens & some butter, & we had a tip top Thanksgiving supper. Just as good as we could wish — And then they got us some molasses & we had a candy pull in the evening. Think our officers done better by us than any of the others did by their Companies. There is about four inches of snow on the ground now quite cold & windy today. I cant play much this weather, fingers wont stand it. If I had a pair of black kid gloves <u>lined</u> dont know but I could play in them. Perhaps I shall send to Jere for a pair by & by. Will see how I stand it first. I can eat all I can get now. My appetite is better than it has been for a long time as good as it was when I was 12 & worked on our old farm. Wish I had some of the good apples we used to raise out there in our old orchard. Osman is gett'ng pretty smart again. Not well but a good deal better than he was. C. is better too. O I guess we shall all get tough again in time and all turn up sound in old Beanfield yet. What a joyfull meeting it will be if we three all arrive home safe after the war is over — But we may not see home again either of us. Jere wrote me that if I was at home I could have a good chance telegraphing on the new line from Lawrence to the White Mountains via Manchester.... You wont know me if I stay here three years & then go home. I shall be 21 you know. I weigh 111½ lbs now — <u>on the gain</u>, Osman weighs 113 & Charley 119 — Azro weighs about 130 — He has grown <u>awfully</u> — I have got to go this cold PM & play for a funeral. Two lay dead at the hospital. I'm playing for a funeral every day now for three days I believe — 9 have died since we came to this camp. One from our Co. His body was sent home. There is only one in our Co now that is very sick. He was taken to the hospital this morning. I will write some more to Emma tomorrow — Got a letter from A.M. the other day & one from Ruth. No more now.

From Herbert

From Charles:

December 11, 1862

Darling, what I would not give to have you sit by my side and see what I see. You would see Herbert leading his drum corps out to practice. I am on guard today and am sitting by the guard tents — its about 10:30 A.M. and warm enough to write comfortably without gloves on. We are having a thaw and most of the snow is off the ground, but to the subject in front — I see men riding horseback, Companies drilling, guards walking their beats, one decent looking house with miserable outbuilding — a few old huts and a two-story frame house that looks as though it might have been a good house 75 years ago. — through the fields a few scattering posts that have been stripped of their rails by the soldiers — some shocks of corn not yet husked and in the background woods of chestnut and pine and now I see our army wagons coming laden with provisions, express boxes etc. — they have been to the canal or landing as we call it....

(December 12 — continuing) — Turning around you would have seen our regiment's tents sticking up high with the officer's tents in the rear and the hospital at the left. Still further to the front is the New Hampshire 14th — a little to the right the Mass. 39th and Maine 23rd and the cavalry — oh joyful news!!! when peace is declared and we are on our way home!! ... (Saturday evening) — have just come in from meeting — I feel first rate — have some cough — the sweet flag is very good, the hemlock essence is first rate — the brandy, Osman and I "take a little occasionly" about a teaspoon full at a time when we are cold or wet or have taken cold (or think we are going to). Don't you think we are intemperate? Guess you'll have to send us some more by about next August — I don't believe will last longer than that.... Roll call is just over and we must not burn up our candle for we have to pay 5¢ a piece for all the extra ones we use. Osman and Battles have just finished a game of checkers and now to bunk we go. Good night.

(Sunday noon) — I slept fairly well last night having a little straw between us and the rails. Just as we all got ready to go to sleep a witty fellow in the tent, name of Abbott began to sing and tell stories and got us all laughing — we could not hold in — it was a pleasant note on which to go to sleep.

I don't believe I have described the inside of our tent — The door is at the left as you go in and swings against the side of the tent leaving a straight road to the furnace, which is right opposite and in the corner. On the right are two tiers of double bunks which leaves about 3½ ft by 5 ft long in the clear, but we make all the room we can by making a place for everything. We keep them on our berths and hung up around — we have a cupboard over the stove and throw our wood into the <u>lower berth</u> — we get along fine. All the trouble is that Osman is so particular it makes it rather unpleasant sometimes.

There were perpetual rumors of enemy activity as well as false alarms, and the troops were occasionally mustered for scouting missions or battle, though nothing more than minor skirmishing was the result. December 21 the regiment was once again moved, this time to Poolesville, Maryland, with various companies assigned to adjacent locations including White's Ford and Monocacy. Company G was posted to duty at Conrad's Ferry, and here they remained through the winter and into the spring. On the evening of their arrival men of the regiment were quickly mustered to repel a small band of Confederates who were attempting to cross the river.[28] *Such minor engagements only frustrated the men of the 10th Vermont, and some expressed concerned that the war seemed to be passing them by.*

From Charles:

Poolsville
December 22, 1862

Now, Ellie dear, where do you suppose I am? At 10:00 A.M. yesterday we were at Orfuths Cross Roads and now at 5 o'clock this morning am writing this by the light of a camp fire in the woods about ½ mile from Poolsville and 18 miles from camp — didn't we do well? But you don't know how tired we were — we were ordered Saturday evening at 8 o'clock to be ready to march next morning at 9:00, then came a hustle packing knapsacks, consulting what to carry and such work — slept an hour or two had a good breakfast and were on the march soon after. About 25 or 30 were left behind including Osman. We bid him good bye and left for parts unknown. Our captain was all around during the march inquiring how the men were standing it and sometimes carrying a gun for a man — sometimes a knapsack or getting a ride for a weaker one, and more than once I saw him put his hand under a knapsack to ease the load on their shoulders. Lieut. Newton also carried something to releave some one all the way.

The day was extremely cold and clear, the ground frozen hard and did not thaw any, but our load was heavy and they marched so fast we got lame. When we reached Poolsville and were ordered to rest we all dropped at the side of the road tired! tired! and lame!, lame! Rested about ten minutes and were ordered to the woods about ½ mile away, where we are now and you never saw so crippled a set of men — you would have thought your husband was at least 75 or 80 years old and everybody was just about the same — didn't know hardly which leg to favor most, but Co. G put it though and I believe not a man fell out while on the march.

December 29, 1866² Camp on the Potomac ... I am here on guard again and a "right smart" pleasant day it is. Osman and I are on together. 8 privates, 1 Sergeant and 1 Corporal are sitting around a small fire with three sides surrounded with rails to break the wind — the south side being open; here we stay 16 hours out of 24 — the other 8 hours we are on guard. It froze quite a little last night and we took turns during the night to keep the fire going....

(December 30) — It is time for us to be relieved by the new guard but circumstances alter cases you know — Last night was quite an eventful night — White's cavalry was seen crossing the river (the same that took some of our cavalry at Poolsville about a month ago). Our 8 Companies were drawn up in line about 1 A.M. Company B went down to the river while the cavalry were running their horses without mercy to their poor beasts carrying dispatches and making observations — the women (there were 8 in the three Companies) all went to neighbor White's and the captain's things were packed. The Colonel had the men drawn up in line at Headquarters ready — a little later our 8 Companies went down to the river and soon on came 8 Companies of the 39th Mass. from Poolsville with artillery. The prospect looked fair for a battle — a sharp lookout was kept during the night. This morning our Companies have come back but Co. B have orders to take one day's rations and cross the river. We may have a fight today — if they do I shall be in it, as the new guards are being detailed and we shall be relieved of guard duty.

We are all quite fat — Osman says I look 5 years younger than when I enlisted — my clothes are too small — I eat my rations and help the boys eat theirs. Herbert's cheeks stick out like a striped squirrel's, but Osman looks like a shark....

CHAPTER 2

January to June 1863

Poolesville, Maryland

The small town of Poolesville, Maryland, "leapt into the front pages of many Northern newspapers" with the unfolding of the Civil War.[1] Located near a number of fords on the Potomac and roughly halfway between Washington and Harpers Ferry, West Virginia, Poolesville was considered important enough to be occupied by Union forces for the entire war. It functioned not only as a line of defense against enemy incursions from Virginia, but also as a vital communication link between the government in Washington and Union forces in the field. While stationed in this bucolic setting Herbert George's life became increasingly busy, as on January 3 he was appointed acting drum major. The previous drum major, Russell Fisk, was discharged, either because there had been no authority for his appointment as a non-commissioned officer or (as Hebert implied) he was less than capable in his efforts.[2] Now Herbert was officially responsible for training and leading the drum corps, and he took to his new duties with dedication and enthusiasm. Though the increase in responsibility meant more work, the new job had certain advantages, as Herbert was no longer required to go out on picket duty. Yet Charles noted that Herbert still continued to fulfill his other duties as field musician. On January 5 another member of the regiment was promoted, as Colonel Jewett officially took command of the brigade, a position he would hold until the regiment joined the Army of the Potomac. Charles George took advantage of his free time to compose a few lines of poetry for his beloved Ellie, a pastime he would continue throughout the war.

From Charles:

January 1, 1863

Another year passed and another on the way and may God grant it may be a happy one to us. The last few days have been rather eventful — the rebel cavalry

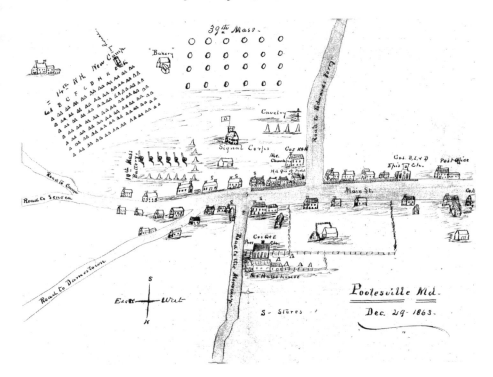

Hand-drawn map by John W. Sturtevant of the 14th New Hampshire Infantry showing the camps of his regiment, the 39th Massachusetts Infantry, and other units stationed in and around Poolesville, Maryland, in December 1862 (the original is mislabeled) (courtesy Historic Medley District, Inc.).

have been crossing the river, — the islands are covered with rebels and wagon trains moving there — signal lights seen in many places and on both shores, but the storm is abated and the rebels disappeared and <u>not a gun fired</u>!

Our Company has been on picket duty — all of them at once so that the camp was left destitute of privates fit for duty. I was on duty yesterday and commenced this letter in the prettiest little grove you ever saw — our post was on the top of a tree on top of a hill — the wind blew cold up there so that we could not stay more than two minutes — there were three of us besides the Corporal — (Osman, Ezro and I). Ezro volunteered because there was no other well enough in our camp. From the top of the tree could be seen the river turning around the bend as marked on the map — and the island where Baker's troops crossed onto — Balls bluff where the troops climbed the hill — thousands of acres covered with woodland in spots; nice buildings surrounded by the usual amount of negro huts and old barns; steeples of meeting houses sticking up as if to show that the inhabitants were once civilized — spots of corn stalks and grain to show that they intended to eat something, but alas for the men — not a stir could be seen, not a wagon or scarsely a dumb beast. In the night I looked in vain for signals or even a camp fire....

(January 3, 1863)

> How pleasant is Saturday night,
> When we've tried all week to be good.
> Have not spoken a word but what was right
> And obliged every one that we could —

but how few can answer to the 3 last lines — many answer to the first. Tonight seems certainly the most pleasant of any since I came south. We have our tent banked up or nearly so, got the door all hung and have a good fire with a seat in front occupied by us three brothers — all alone and each writing letters. Our things are picked up and "in their places" — have our water all ready for a good bath in the morning. We have not washed for some time....

Bully for Vermont tent and Co. G. We have got two Contrabands in our Company — taken by the Captain himself. They came to the shore and waved their hats at our pickets who invited them to cross, but they found the current too strong and retreated. The Captain then got permission from the Major to go after them — and so he did.

They took an early start on the emancipation proclamation — they are about 16 years old — bright and smart — have on the rebel uniform — new grey cloth and better cloth than our clothes are made from. They came from the rebel army.

You ask for my miniature — but I have not seen one since I left Camp Chase. If I could get it taken I would do it quick. I would write you some poetry but cannot seem to settle my mind to it. I am more than common absent minded — at least so in talk — words come out wrong end to, and sometimes sideways. Have not been troubled with "night mares" much but when I do they have to shake me pretty hard to scare her away. But what about the war?...

(Monday, 3:00 A.M.) — On picket again — this time on the river. Yesterday we had inspection and then went on guard, used up the entire forenoon. We have to work lively to get ready for inspection by ten-gun to clean — clothes to brush — wash all over — knapsack to pack — haversack to arrange — boots to black etc. I am out of stamps — this will take the last I have and I have one partly written to Jere. By order from our Major, Herbert was appointed Drum Major of this detachment.

From Herbert:

Conrads Ferry
Jan 3rd'63

Dear folks at home

Its about time I was writing home I guess so here goes a few lines. We have just got our new house up and a stove in it all comfortable again so that we can sit down & write with some comfort. It is now fifteen minutes to seven P.M. with a bayonet for a candle stick we three <u>George boys</u> are writing letters.... Some one wraps at the door —

It was the Captain. You cant guess what he wanted. He wanted to know if I could read telegraphing by sound. Gen'l Davis at Poolsville wants an operator & I would go if I could read Morse by sound. I could have the chance immediately but I cant go it by sound. Could if they used Bains alphabet. Cap'n talked as though I might get the chance and take on paper untill I had practice enough to read by sound. He wanted to know if I would like to go. Told him I would, so if they cant do any better perhaps I shall go. My pay would be considerable more. Gov't operators get $60.00 per month I believe. Well I dont spose I shall go for they want sound oprs and may find one some where. At dress parade to night general order number 5 and it was an appointment, appointing J. H. George acting <u>Drum Major</u> for this detachment of the 10th Vt. By order of Charles G. Chandler, Major commanding detachment. Ahem wasnt that awful? To tell the truth I have had charge of all the music ever since I went to Brattleboro. Drum Major dont know anything about music and left it all to me. I might as well be Drum Major of the Regt. Our officers think I ought to be too. I dont think I am hardly competant to fulfill the post but still I could do better than our present Drum Major does or my name aint Herbert....

Osman is very poor cant bear to look at him hardly still he is ever so much better than he was. If he had his flesh back he would be OK again. We dont have any drilling here, nothing but picketing and he will fat now on rest. The picketing is not so bad as it might be if there is any fighting going on I am in for it. Can fight better with a gun than the fife. I used to drill some at Camp Grover with the Co. Our drummer had a gun too & went with the Co after the rebs. C & O were on picket that night so they were not with us. The last time they were on picket they were on at the look out where they have to climb up a large tree & stand about 30 feet from the ground. Can look all around over in Va but cant stand it more than 15 minutes at a time it is so cold — After Tattoo — Ha, ha, ha, O ho, ho, ho. Well there if we haint had a laugh — The boys outdoors are mimmicing every kind of animals and just as natural as possible. O if we haint had a laugh I'll give up. A regular jolly old time they are having. You'd laugh till you couldn't stand to hear em. Well guess I've grow'd half an inch on it. We have good times here once in a while. If we dont get shot or get sick we shall be all hunky. Dont know as we shall see any fighting but may any day. Dont think the war is progressing very fast. If it is "I cant see it" the war will never be settled by fighting in my estimation. They will fight as long they can & then compromise. Might as well compromise first as last. Whats the use to fiddle along in the way they have for two years most. "I cant see it" ... I was invited to the Majors tent to play on a flute New Years night had a good time....

Yours Truly

J. Herbert

We expected a brush with the rebs the other night. The Co's were called up about midnight & stood an hour ready for em. I went and got a gun & some equipments from one that was sick & fell in to the ranks with the rest. I was in for it you see. Well we went to bed again with gun beside us ready at a moments warning — at six in the morning we were called again & went down to the river & got into a rifle pit & waited till nine or ten oclock but the rebs didnt dare cross so we lost the fun. I still keep my gun

By the beginning of the New Year the men of the 10th Vermont had learned the daily routine of a soldier's life. Henry Burnham of Company G described it thus: "The following is the order of exercises first reveille at sunrise camp police directly after, coffee half an hour after roll call, drill from 6 to 7, breakfast 7½ surgeons call & guard mount at 9, drill from 10 to 11 dinner 12½, drill from 3 until 4½ supper 5½, retreat at sunset (& in fair weather dress parade half an hour before retreat) tatoo 8½ taps at nine."[3] The troops were comfortable with the drill after three months in the service of their country, and many were pleased with the camaraderie shared by the men. There was still frustration surrounding the regiment's outdated guns, as the promised Springfields had yet to arrive.[4] The men from Vermont were kept busy at a variety of duties, much to Charles' frustration, yet it was food and not fighting that occupied their minds the most.
    From Herbert:

Conrads Ferry
Jan 16th/63

Dear folks at home

Got a letter from you this morning and concluding to have another box come. I will write to day — Charley has written to Ellen for one and Azro has written for one, all to come in one box the same as the first box you sent. We want some considerable dried apple and some green ones, some more sausage and lot of cheese little butter and some more sugar. Couldnt you get some dried beef and send? Might send some fish. Try and get some more pickles they go good with hard tack and pork. If you should send any have the cans soddered up tight. We have got an express man now for this regt and boxes will be forwarded in immy after arriving in Washington so things will not spoil before reaching us. If you choose you can send a chicken stuffed, it will keep good and mince pie will keep, doughnuts will keep if they are not put in warm ginger bread too, and I should think a big loaf of brown bread would keep if put in when perfectly cold. Osman wants some medicine to take for strengthening and some cough drops. Dont send any liquor. Guess we'll have a little pepper and I want a pint dipper. Put in my band cap just as it is, and my old cornet mouthpiece.... C. is on picket today. O. is asleep in the tent with me. He was on picket last night. Poor fellow he is pretty much tired out this morning. C. was sick yesterday and not very well this morning. I wanted to go on picket for him but orderly couldn't let me, said it wouldnt do for me to leave being Drum Major. It wouldnt but I wanted to go. Osman was detailed to help load wood yesterday & I took his place as it was only for an hour or two. I washed yesterday too. I am getting to be quite a worker. Two weeks ago I washed six shirts four prs draws five prs footings and a dozen or so of little things quite a wash. I have to scuffle with some of the boys every day. Generally with the sergeants. I can handle Azro if he is the heaviest. Every body says "How fat you are" well I hope I shall grow fat till I weigh 150—father I wish you would send me a light axe, one that will weigh about three lbs. We need one awfully and I want three cornered file—Send what you think we want and send immy—We expect to move to Poolsville next Monday—Please number your letters and we will then we can see how many get lost this is number two for 1863 no more for now

From Herbert

Where is fathers letter?

January and February offered a mix of weather for the troops. On clear days the men would drill, whereas the frequent rain and snowstorms kept the men sequestered in their tents.[5] Food remained a primary concern, making Herbert and Charles extremely appreciative of a series of boxes from home. Any rural area was strongly impacted by the presence of troops, and the area around Poolesville was no exception. Food was often scarce, as soldiers foraging for both crops and livestock along with the breakdown of transportation systems and commercial opportunities forced many small communities to rely solely on their own already depleted resources. Still, the troops ate well enough, or at least enough to keep most of the men happy, according to William White of Company I: "fresh beef, once or twice a week, beans, peas, pork, potatoes, and once & sometimes twice a week, rice, salt, bread occasionally, good coffee for breakfast & tea for supper."[6] *Apparently Herbert ate well—by the end of January he claimed to be up to 135, a gain of thirty pounds since November!*

From Herbert:

Conrads Ferry
Jan 29th 1863

Dear folks at home

A Mr Bartlett from Wells River is here to see his son & leaves camp today. He will carry a small bundle for me & so I am going to send my slippers & in them 4 hard tacks. Just one ration, so you can see what we live on. 4 of them for each meal. Just try one of them & see how you like it, be careful & not break your teeth. Azro & I went to Poolsville day before yesterday and had our likeness's taken together. I send it to you & you can let Mr McK's folks have it half the time. Azro paid for half of it. It is not taken very well but the best we could get. It is too dark but you can see by it how fat I am & it is solid fat too. Azro & I both weigh in the same notch —135 — aint I fat tho? Can't hardly see out of my eyes I am so fat — Ha, ha, ha. We steped in to the saloon & had our pictures taken just as we was without fixing up any, pants tucked into our boot legs & boots all mud. Please send it to A.M. & tell her to send it to Ruth & Ruth send it to Jere & Jere send it back to you again, so they can all see <u>how I look</u>. I shall send it by mail instead of Bartlett. We have got from eight to ten inches of <u>snow</u> this morning. Came yesterday & last night. Awful cold. All pretty well. Write often. Tell me how you like the hard tacks — Father — please write me your promised letter. I'll whip you when I get home if you dont. I'm most as heavy as you are now & shall be as tall by & by. I'm the heaviest of the 4 boys now — <u>Ahem</u>! Well good morning to you all —

In haste
From Herbert

P.S. — The bundle sent by Mr. Bartlett will be left at the depot in care of Mr. Gould. This letter will probably reach you before he gets home. The paper around the slippers is the Bennington Banner — read the piece from the 10th in it.

Herbert

Evenings were passed with letter writing, card games, and other forms of entertainment. It may be at this point that the brothers saw the possibility for forming a band, or Herbert may simply have been preparing for his upcoming

*role as regimental bugler, for he wrote home and asked that his cornet mouthpiece
be sent. Herbert and Charles grew hopeful when Osman's condition seemed to
improve, but a cold caught while on picket duty incapacitated him once again,
and by February 8 the brothers had arranged for Osman to live in a local house.*

Two letters from Herbert:

Conrads Ferry Maryland
Feb. 8th 1863

Dear folks at home

It has been some time since I have written to you so I will write this P.M.
It is very warm and pleasant today. We have had considerable snow here within
the last two weeks. In all I think there has about a foot fell. It has not all left
yet but will soon be gone. One while it was so cold that water would freeze
in a pail in two minutes time quite hard. Osman was put on picket after his
two weeks were up and he caught a severe cold on top of one he had and it
took him <u>all down</u> again so that he could not do any thing. I went to the
Major and talked with him about his going off to a private house to stay. He
had no objections if the Surgeon thought best. Then I went to the Surgeon
and talked with him and after a day or two he said he would not object as he
(Osman) would not be able to do duty for a long time. Well then I went up

Conrad's Ferry, Maryland, on the Potomac River, where Company G of the 10th
Vermont was stationed for the winter of 1862–1863 (Frank Leslie, *Famous Leaders
and Battle Scenes of the Civil War* [New York: Mrs. Frank Leslie, 1896], 263,
retrieved January 1, 2010, from http://etc.usf.edu/clipart/11300/11321/conrad_
ferry_11321.htm).

on the hill East of here and got him a chance to board with a Mr. White. Mrs. White is a very nice woman young, pretty, and good. They are not Secesh I know & they will do the best they can for Osman. I got the leave of absence for him yesterday & got a man to take him up with a team. Saw him comfortably sitting on a chair before a fireplace in a pleasant sitting room and he really had a smile on his face, a thing I had not seen on him for a long long time. The Surgeon says he has got the Bronchitis quite bad, and it is not likely that he will be able to do any duty in the Company again.... I wish he was at home poor fellow, then he might get well again. He will have to pay $3.00 per week for his board and you will have to send some money immy to him. Money will be nothing if he can only get better. Charley is detailed for the present as a carpenter and don't do any military duty. He is as fat as can be, awful fat just like me. I spect I shall weigh 140 very soon if I don't now. How I wish you could see me with my cheeks sticking out as they do. I am going to bugling in a few days, bugle & fife both — I sent some things home by Capn's wife the other day, she will give you a call some day & tell you how I am &c.... From your Herbert

Tuesday morning 10th

Good for me for I got my box last night and had to pay only 10 cts — Bully — Every thing was nice — nothing spoiled pies all good. O, we shall fat now. C & J but poor Osman is not here to enjoy it. He is up to Whites yet and don't gain any. He can hardly speak aloud. I shall carry up his medicine and dried berries, candy &c, &c. Am afraid he is going into the consumption. Wish he could go home now. I'm going to do my best to get him discharged. He will never do for this country & this life. I shall do all I can for him but you must send me some money to do with. His diarrhea is no better. We are awful grateful for the box and will try and not hurt ourselves eating. I have sent for my cornet can have it carried when we march and I want it to play on badly. Write soon and tell me what to do for Osman.

In haste from
Herbert

From Charles:

Conrad's Ferry
February 12, 1863

I'll spend a few minutes with you — Today is quite warm — the snow has left and it is quite muddy. I am still working on the stockade. I want to go to Poolsville to have my miniature taken — am making a locket to out it in of laurel root about as large as a watch — but haven't any silver to make the hinges or fastenings — there are no coins. I wish you would send out some 3 or 5 or 10¢ pieces. Herbert makes pipes and sells them for 50¢ a piece. Osman had the choice by the surgeon, of staying where he is (at Whites) or going to the hospital — of course he will stay there. He thinks he will get his discharge before long — he is very hoarse, but able to wait on himself. Herbert continues tough and blows the calls now on the bugle — don't know whether he gets any extra pay or not. He got a pass which read, "Please pass fifer, bugler, drummer, and musician generally, whose name is George and also his brother Charles G. who is also a musician — a private in my Company, to return at dress parade" and signed it Captain Commanding in big letters. — on the whole it looked rather laughable.

We had a sham battle last Friday. The battalion was drawn up in line of battle and fired their pieces as though they were in battle. The Major ordered them at the fort and they came up the hill double quick and filed in single file and all around until the stockade was filled. The Major ordered them to ready, aim, and pick your man and aim low — fire! And if the old stockade didn't ring — (200 muskets at the same time). Herbert had to keep with the Major to repeat the orders on the bugle. They had to load and fire on the march — there were several accidents — though not serious. I was on duty at the stockade so did not participate.

From Herbert:

> Conrads Ferry
> Feby 12th 1863

Dear folks at home

I have just been up on the hill to see Osman and he had a letter written to you and Jere. I brot them down and will write some in them — I think Osman is some better than he was when he went up there but he is far from being well. He will never be able to do picket duty again I don't think. Unless he can get a chance where he can be spared from picket he will have to go home or lay sick here. I shall try and see what I can do towards getting him a place or getting him discharged — He looks very pale and thin. I feel just as though I would give all I own, all I am worth to get him home safe — Wouldn't I like to take him home and then come back again? All but the coming back. Well I'm perfectly contented now. Happy as a clam I sound the Camp Calls on the bugle now. Commenced yesterday, like it well —

C & I are enjoying the box highly. We can take care of all the corn & apple too I guess. We are awfull grateful for all the nice things, will repay you some time — I hope to get a letter from you next mail. Father if you don't write to me & tell me how you like the pipe I shall begin to scold. I have made three pipes like it since I sent that one to you and sold them for 50 cts apiece nothing but the bowl. I don't furnish stubs to them. Just whittle out the bowl & get 50 cts for all I can make. Have engaged to make three or four more. Making money aint I?

Well I must close this letter.

Much love to all

In haste

From

Herbert

Though fast becoming familiar with camp life and picket duty, the 10th Vermont and their brigade were still untested in combat. This led to a certain amount of scorn from veterans who had little respect for well-supplied troops safe in their camps around Washington. Certainly there was some justification for such teasing, as the troops around Poolesville suffered more from the snow and cold than from any Confederates, though the men of Vermont seemed to cope well with the weather as well as the teasing.[7] The men were not immune to the various rumors and reports that drifted through camp, and the Vermonters were stunned at the news of the Union defeat at Fredericksburg the previous month. Though eager for action the 10th Vermont was in many ways fortunate to remain posted to the defense of Washington and kept from the slaughter in Virginia.

Osman's condition deteriorated to such a degree that he was moved to a local hospital. Charles and Herbert were anxious to have their brother discharged, but the bureaucracy—and, according to Herbert, the regimental surgeon—moved indolently, and the brothers grew increasingly concerned. Already the medical infrastructures of both the North and South were sorely taxed. The escalating severity of the combat meant increased (and more vicious) casualties in need of care, and illness continued to prey on the soldiers. In nearby Frederick, Maryland, the January census of wounded and ailing at the United States General Hospital averaged between 300 and 500 men.[8] Fellow Vermonters of the 11th Infantry stationed at nearby Fort Totten suffered a lethal run of measles and smallpox.[9] Both Herbert and Charles believed the best thing for Osman would be to return to Newbury, but it would be some time before any of the George brothers would see their hometown.

From Herbert:

Conrads Ferry
Feby 22nd/63

Dear folks at home

You say you like to get my letters so I will write as often as I can conveniently. Osman has left Whites and gone to the hospital, went day before yesterday.... He was at Whites two weeks lacking one day and they charged only $5.00 — Reasonable wasn't it? They done some washing for him too. You need not send any more money at present. Wait till I see what is going to be done — I think that if father should come out here and put the <u>thing through</u> he could get him discharged. It takes so long for a discharge to get round unless there is some one to put it through that he might die before he got it.... In many cases the father of a sick soldier has done so. I think I shall talk with the Surgeon and if he thinks it advisable for father to come I shall send for him sure pop. I would be willing if necessary to let him have all my bounty money to defray the expenses of coming out, and should be <u>tickled</u> half to pieces to see him. Don't know as the Surgeon will do any thing about it. Will see and if I should send for father he must come. It snows and blows hard — been snowing ever since last night About ten on — well about eight inches of snow on the ground now pretty camping out such weather ain't it?... Charley has got through carpentering. he was at work cutting port holes in a stockade on a hill about 1/4 of a mile from here. We had a <u>sham</u> fight the other day all passed off well, had a good time I bugled for the skirmishers. I am bugler for this Detachment. Sound the camp calls on the bugle instead of the drum, play the fife too. Our Chaplain does not show himself here at all. Charley aint very <u>blue</u> we are too fat to have the blues. He would like to go home well enough — so would *I*. There haint I answered all your questions? I wish I was in the Cavalry as bugler then shouldn't have any more to do than I do now and shouldn't have to carry my knap sack but guess I can't get transferred.... Well write as often as you can and father must write some once in a while.— <u>A stormy day</u>

Affectionately yours
Herbert

   From Charles:

Conrad's Ferry
February 25, 1863

I'm with you again, Ellie — I have been making some new ink and thought I would try it a little — It has snowed and been very cold. Monday I went on picket again — you'd laughed to see our four — I being the largest you can imagine our sizes! — One man recently froze both his feet, but with my new feetings, good think boots, drawers, 2 pairs of pants, 2 shirts, 2 coats and cap and gloves and comforter with thick woolen blanket over my shoulders I manage by walking my beat pretty fast to keep from being frost bitten. The Company is now drilling in the streets under the Sergeant Martin — we all like him better than Newton. Last night someone brought in a circular written

by a man in the convalescent camp at Alexandria. It is enough to make ones
blood run cold to think of the abuse we have got to go through....

Herbert has made Emma a present of a photograph album — cost $5.00.
He has been having some fun with her. I will tell you: Emma writes letters
sometimes and puts them in the "Comfort Bags" that got to soldiers. Herbert
knew her assumed name and wrote her a letter disguising his hand. He succeeded in getting a reply, which was all he wanted. It was a splendid letter —
one that a brother might feel proud of— he answered in his own name. I don't
know how it came out.

*The month of March proved to be more temperate for the members of the
10th Vermont; pleasant weather meant more company and regimental drilling
(including some practice skirmishing), though there were many days where the
troops were free to fill their time as they saw fit.[10] The constant petitioning by
Charles and Herbert finally paid off when Osman was granted a rare furlough
to spend a short time recuperating in Vermont. Charles celebrated this time of
optimism with more poetry for his wife.*

From Charles:

Conrad's Ferry
March 11, 1863

As there is no drill and no news I will write about that which is nearest
my heart, love —

> Oh! how my heart for thee doth yearn,
>   My soul doth in me leap
> The blood within my veins doth burn
>   With love sincere and deep.
>
>   Could you but read my thoughts entire
>   And see the visual orbs
>   While viewing what I most admire
>   In Dixie's land of snobs.
>
> Methinks thine eyes would moisture fast
>   Thine heart might leap within
> And thou wouldst think of days gone past
>   When bliss did reign supreme.
>
>   Thy picture, love, is what I mean
>   Naught else doth please mine eye
>   Elsewhere, not here, <u>lest thou be seen</u>
>   But better times, bye and bye!

The war will soon be over, love
  The end each day draws near
Seven months recorded now above
  Since I enlisted here.

      Another five will run the race
        And join the other soon
      Perhaps rebellion's burial place
        Ere then will need a tomb.

What joys! What cheers! What hope! What life
  Will greet the closing scene
Of all this quarrel, wrath and strife
  'Twill seem as but a dream.

      Take courage, love, May God's right hand
        Assist us through the mud
      And through the snares of Satan's Band
        With laurels brave and good.

So patient love — in faith I trust
  'Tis right for us to be
A time apart, no doubt tis best
  There's good times yet for <u>we</u>.

      But after all, I can but ask
        The time would soon draw near
      That we each other's arms should clasp
        The ones we hold so dear —

Guess you'll think I'm crazy — but I "ain't." Spring is coming — Osman is going home. Our orderly thinks and expects a promotion to take the captaincy of a Negro regiment — wish I could go with him and be orderly or something else — I am a great friend to the negroes. It is strange in seeing the differences of opinion about them being fit for soldiers. The fact is, probably, that some have courage and some do not. One circumstance I will relate: Last year while the rebels were throwing shell over here, one Negro "Perry" on seeing a shell strike nearby ran to pick up the pieces out of curiosity, said, "he didn't think two would be likely to strike the same place" — another, "Jim," ran away being afraid just as most would do.

Herbert has got his cornet from Boston — we had some things come with it — nuts, figs, dates etc., 3 song books and various other things. We have to toe the mark pretty close here, I tell you — tonight I went out to roll call with my blouse on and had to come back after my coat — thereby being ¼ of a minute late — for penalty had to do about 15 minutes extra duty — two others were served the same.

From Herbert:

1863
Conrads Ferry Md 29th

Dear brother Osman

I got your letter this morning all OK 5.00 all right and I rec'd the other 5.00 sent some time ago by mother. So I have paid Seymour all up. I paid for the horse $1.00 and consequently have one dollar of your money. Credit it on the book which will make your account $2.20 instead of 3.20. I believe thats it. I am glad you got home safe hope you will have a chance to remain some time and dont you come back here again till you are well. They shall keep up the respect that the 10th Vt are 9 months men dont see it but wish it was so! Charley is on picket today is on at the lower stockade the last place you were on. Tell Em that Ill write to her some time before soon. Cant you work it so & not have to come back at all? Do your best any how. We dont want to see you back here again. I'll bet you all had a good time when you first got home. How I should like to go home & stay a few days how I cant afford it and I shall not take a furlough for 3 years if I have as good health as I now have. I am in an awful hurry for fear the mail will go out before I get this letter in. Miss [Fink] has sent all my things to Jere bully for me. I expected she would keep them. Had letter from Jere the last mail. Well do the best can to stay at home

no more now
in haste
Your brother
Herbert

Increased activity by Confederate scouts across the Potomac led to some concern among the Union commanders that a sortie into Maryland was forthcoming. By the beginning of April the troops stationed around Poolesville were being distributed throughout the area in an effort to block any possible incursions from Virginia. On April 12 Company G received orders to prepare for a march, and the men believed they would soon see combat. Yet by April 19 the outlying companies of the 10th Vermont had been recalled to Poolesville for a peaceful stay at Camp Heintzelman, named for the general currently commanding the XXII Corps. Here the regiment continued to enjoy a time of calm, though there was a brief scuffle at nearby Seneca Lock with elements of General E.B. Stuart's command on June 11.

This stay at Poolesville was probably the most pleasant time for the regiment during the entire course of the war. Officers resorted to a popular pastime, the evening sing. Surgeon Rutherford described one such night: "After dinner we had a high old sing — Capt Frost acting as leader — Mrs. Childe took part and such a sings is not often found."[11] Such musical activities had a profound impact on

Union Forces on Main Street, Poolesville, Maryland (courtesy Montgomery County Historical Society, Rockville, Maryland).

officers and enlisted men alike, bringing consolation to many of the homesick soldiers. As Henry Burnham confided: "We had a very good singing. the Brigade Surgeons wife is here she sung it is about the first time I have heard a females voice in singing since I left home."[12] *On April 13 the officers were also able to participate in a special entertainment, that of a military ball.*[13] *Herbert, Charles and their comrades spoke fondly of the locals, though sometimes it seemed that the residents of Poolesville were as pleased to see Confederate troops as they were the men from the Union.*[14] *Any good spirits were held in check by the discouraging reports coming from the front, as news of the setbacks in the Shenandoah Valley in April and rumors of the Union losses at the Battle of Chancellorsville in May drifted into camp.*

Two letters from Charles:

Conrad's Ferry
April 3, 1863

My darling Ellie:— Time still flies and so do the letters but the bullets don't very fast just now but very soon I think they will take fiery wings and light upon the rebellion with an overwhelming weight — I am almost persuaded to believe the war will close satisfactorily before many months. The rebels have about exhausted their supplies of, and means of supplies of, men. Thus far they have been able to meet us with an equal number of men, but if we raise another large army they cannot meet it and besides, we are slowly but surely closing them in. Osman got back safe last night — could not get a place to stay there. Our company drew several barrels of flour a few days ago, we have it raw and cook it ourselves. I started some yeast right off— it has not got to be very good yet, but we have made bread twice out of it. The first loaf was made of clear water, <u>rather</u> heavy!— the next was made of my sour dough — it did not rise very much. Today I made some biscuits, they were pretty good — light enough for <u>soldiers</u> — the boys thought they were nice. I think it two or three days I can beat the lot on break making. Herbert went to White's today and got some sour milk — I shall stir up a cake tonight — guess I know how to do that. Osman did not bring any money — I owe 85¢ for topping my boots and have got only 20¢.

I have been amusing myself lately playing chess — it is a very pretty game — there are 3 sets of chess men in the Company. I am enjoying (?) a toothache — face was swelled up some this morning.

(Sunday P.M.) — Last night was the roughest I have seen in Maryland and morning found about 6 inches of snow with wind almost a hurricane. It stopped snowing about 10 A.M. and we have carried off in boxes and tubs the snow in the streets so it will be dry when the sun comes up....

Conrad's Ferry
April 8, 1863

Ellie, you are in my thoughts — Last Monday we all went up to Head Quarters and exchanged our muskets for rifles. I like them much better than the muskets — I presume we shall now be going to the front now that we have our rifles. The rifles are light and so are the cartridges — they are old guns fixed over....

(Wednesday) —... Herbert has gone to one of the neighbors to play — all he gets is a good supper. I have got to be quite a chess player —find it a good thing for recreation and rest for the brains. They have games of ball every day but I am too old to learn.

(Sunday Morning) — I received your letter, Ellie dear and will answer it after telling you the news — we have got marching orders. — Yes! Ellie we are going — going somewhere but nobody knows where, but it is generally believed that it is not to Poolsville. We are to take 3 days rations in our haversacks and 4 days rations on the teams — so it seems we are going some distance. Conjectures very — some think it is to be Harpers Ferry — some Washington and others think Fairfax Court House. At any rate I think we shall go into the field some where and bid good-bye to Conrad's Ferry with its camp of huts where we have passed the winter. Goodbye to the playground where old and young have mingled together in childhood play and good-bye to the parade ground that every night has seen the soldiers called into line. And what shall be our next place of observation? Surely we are like a thistle blown whither-so-ever the wind wills. Today we have battalion inspection — in about 30 minute the whole detachment will have knapsacks strapped upon their backs and everything read — or supposed to be — for a march. That is the understanding at every inspection, but this time it will be pretty near the reality.

From Herbert:

Conrads Ferry Md.
Apl 12th/63

Dear sister Emma

I must write just a word to you to day. We have marching orders with 7 days rations, 3 days in our haversacks and 4 on teams. I suppose we are going to the front. We are going in to the field soon where with nothing but little fly tents carried by our selves and the line officers have the same and can carry only one small vallise. The field and staff officers are to have only 3 wall tents between them. I suppose we are to see some fighting soon. We march tomorrow at 9 o'clock I suppose. I have left everything that was not necessary to have with Mrs. White. I put them all into my cornet box and carried it up to her to day. She says she will take good care of them till I call for them. I wish I could leave my over coat there but that would not be <u>military</u>. I shall throw it away if it is so heavy that I can't carry it and <u>keep up</u>. I hope we shall not have to go more than 20 miles a day. Well such is the life of the soldier. Osman will go into the hospital and may have to go to some genl hospital at Washington. I hope he will not have to walk much. He is no better. Don't see why there couldn't of been some way for him to of staid in Vt some where. I don't know as I shall stand it to travel I am so <u>fat</u>. Mrs. White gave me & Azro a good dinner to day. She is a good woman and awful pretty. Azro is in the ranks, he was not court martialed. He has thrown away considerable clothing. Charley & I have been making biscuits most all day. Our Co drew flour and cooked our own bread for the last ten days. I can make as good biscuit as you can. We have yeast to make them with just as light as can be. We got your letter to day with the needle book &c.. &c..

Yes I have written to Miss Beane. Don't expect an answer. I will write again as soon as we halt any where.

No more now
Affect your brother
Herbert

From Charles:

Conrad's Ferry
April 18, 1863

(Sunday) — Dear Ellie — I will try to write a little more now — as you see we are still here impatiently waiting orders to march. Last night at "Tattoo" we had the order to have "Reveille" at 5:00 A.M. and breakfast at 5:30 A.M. — Accordingly, at 5:00 A.M. our guns were all stacked in the street, knapsacks packed and lying with the guns, haversacks and canteens on our backs and here we have been waiting till now — (1:00 P.M.) — for orders to start. The tents, stoves and cooking things are on the wagons and on the road. Understand we are to go to Poolsville — the order to go into the field having been, for the present, countermanded....

(Headquarters of Brigade — Poolsville — Sunday morning) — Last night found us here after a march of 55 miles — and to begin where I left off — some of the boys put the kitten into the stove so she is with us yet. We waited at Conrads till we were relieved by two companies of the Maine regiment at most 5:00 P.M. Then we had a fine march — did not hurry so fast as we always have before, for the reason that we had Herbert to lead off instead of Fiske, the old Drum Major. On arriving we found all the tents up but ours, which being "fly tents" we found our selves homeless. Other tents of men being selfish about taking us in, we very independently put our flys up and slept well. Our situation is a splendid one on a slight elevation of land sloping off on all sides.

There are 6 companies of our regiment — 5 of the New Hampshire; 5 of the Cavalry and 6 pieces of artillery. (The calvary are Michigan.) Everyone seemed proud of Herbert's bugling and wished he would be "Bugler and Drum Major." This morning he was called up by the Adjutant and put in command of the Drum Corps and Chief Bugler Captain Dilingham gave him a bugle and said he wanted to hear it filled up. The boys seemed very pleased to hear him sound it — Herbert is an excellent bugler!

Herbert pursued his musical duties with a passion, rehearsing his drum corps and leading the field musicians. Charles proudly drew attention to Herbert's blossoming talent and the pleasure the men took in his abilities. On May 1 Herbert was rewarded for his efforts and officially promoted to principal musician of the 10th Vermont Infantry.[15] This position placed him in charge of all the regiment's fifers, drummers, and buglers, and he was responsible for rehearsing and leading the drum corps. Apparently Hebert's new rank also brought new duties that were not musical in nature. May 10 he was placed in charge of the guard taking some Confederate prisoners to Washington. Ever the musician, Herbert took advantage of the trip to purchase new fifes, drums and music, and even managed to tour the capital.

Two letters from Charles:

May 1, 1863

My darling — I wish you could be here to enjoy this beautiful spring day with me! The rumor still keeps up that we are nine-months men, but I dare not indulge in such expectation too much. The Maine regiment is out the 10th of June. There will probably be a change in our situation on or before that time — hope we shall get to Vermont. Yesterday I was on Camp Guard duty — glad it is over — had rather be on picket every other day than camp guard once a week. Let me sum up the duties of a Camp Guard and see how you would like it. In the first place: guard mounting at 9 A.M. in which we have to stand with knapsacks, haversacks etc — same as in marching, then hold them for inspection of arms beating off by the music etc, after which we are marched to the adjutants tent and then to the guard tents, where we have to stand till every man's name (45) is written down before we are allowed to take off our load. We walk steadily the remainder of the 2 hours, not allowed to sit down or converse with any one, keep a sharp lookout all around, salute officers according to rank and carry the gun in just certain positions, remembering to bring it to a shoulder at the end of the beat and about face according to rules of the "school of the soldier." Nor is this all — the officer of the day must be saluted by all at the guard tent no matter what we are doing, whether eating, reading or sleeping. When the officer of the day is seen approaching all have to fall in, according to number and present arms and the Sentinel on the Post must challenge the "Grand rounds" in the night for the countersign and any slight variation from just such a form causes him to get a blowing-up. Hang the Military! I'd rather see a whole company of rebels coming than to see the "Grand rounds." But its all for the Union as the boys say and does so much towards putting down the rebellion.... Herbert has got the bass drum rigged up, but there is another man that was reduced from a corporal last winter on purpose to play it at his own request — it makes a great addition to the music. Herbert has a man to spell him with the bugle so that he can go away occasionally. He has a standing pass to go and come at pleasure. He goes to Poolesville and plays on the piano with a pretty little girl — shouldn't wonder if he fell in love yet!

Camp Hientzleman
May 13, 1863

Dearest Ellie — I am thinking of you — We do not get any more news about going home in June, but we shall evidently move somewhere about that time for the Quartermaster has had orders to draw no more rations clothing than what will last this month — perhaps we shall go to Richmond then.... Osman has been ordered back to the Company. The Colonel thought there were too many men detailed so all that can be spared are ordered back.

(Thursday) — Herbert has returned from Washington and brought some new fifes, drums, etc. The drum corps is improving since Herbert got the command. He had a fine present of a bugle costing about $20.00 presented by the officers of Conrad's Ferry — also a flageolette presented by Company G, worth about $8.00.

(Friday) — weather fine — drilling is a pleasure. We will drill 3½ hours a day — the regiment is improving very fast — guess we could fight the rebels <u>right smart</u> now. — I cannot write very well, there is so much confusion around here — talking, playing cards etc. — will wait until it is more quiet (later) — I will tell you what a good time we had drilling today. Captain Damon took us out at the usual hour — 10 A.M. — drilled us a while on the parade ground, then took us into a swamp covered with stumps, tree-tops, brush etc. — went though the Company movements with the greatest of mirth and pleasure for all — it was so novel and he was so good natured that it was a real treat — he then marched us in two ranks and part of the way in one about three fourths of a mile across wheat fields, over fences and then a piece of woods where we stacked arms and had the remainder of the hour to pick "posies" and dress ourselves in green bushes — we were not allowed to wear them into Camp, however — Captain Damon did not think it would be exactly military. I tell you we have got a good Captain — he is growing in favor more and more with the boys every day.

Today I have done a washing — quite a job done! They talk strongly of getting up a band in this regiment — Herbert will probably be the leader — I shall try a bass or alto horn if they have a band — my lips are not good for blowing a high toned one. Herbert thinks I could blow bass well enough. News is very scarce my dear — nothing has been heard from Hooker since a week ago yesterday.

Good bye for now dear Ellie.

From Osman:

Camp Heintzelman near Poolesville Md.
May 17th 1863

Dear parents and sister —

This is a beautiful day. It is the first time I have done any guard since Feb. 1st which was [Sun. That must] be my luck to be on duty when there is no drilling to do but we have to furnish a heavy guard ... and more in five days or so. I am [at 5] which is at the jail house. We have four prisoners & two privates. I have to go with them if they wish to leave for any thing. It is the first time I have done such duty. Two of them were brought in to day. I think from Conrads where we were.... I was mistaken they came from Monocacy.... The Capt. is jolly good at [drill].... I believe if we are in battle he would prove himself to be no coward.... I can not think of any more now. One thing that is I think Azro is not what he [wants] to be, he is Chaplains waiter. He has also learned to use cards in simple games.... I will if asked the question after I get home, that I am not a handler of cards, but few in the rgmt can say the same, not a game have I played.... Please write.

Affc.

Osman

From Herbert:

May 18

I must write a little this morning and tell you of my experience during the past week or so. I have been down to Washington (32 miles) on a <u>bust.</u> I wanted to purchase a new drum and two new fifes & some music so I got a chance to go a week ago (day before) yesterday. Went as a guard over some rebel prisoners that we took here. I acted as corporal over the guard and had to sit up all night and relieve the guard. There were 3 privates & a Serg't over us. Went on a canal boat arrived there the next day (Sunday) at 2 o'clock P.M. After delivering up our prisoners to the Provost Marshal we scouted round the city road all round in the horse cars throug Wash — & Georgetown. Visited the Navy yard saw all the big <u>guns</u>. Saw any amount of poor wounded men just in

William H. Headley [Hoadley], Co. C, 10th Vermont. Hoadley was a field musician but did not perform with the band (U.S. Army Military History Institute).

from Fredericksburg. Saw nearly a whole regt of rebel prisoners taken there, mostly North Carolineans & Georgians, looked rather rough. Saw Tompson Baxter of the 39th Mass.

Then came some news that Charles, Osman, and Herbert were thrilled to hear—the regiment had finally decided to form a band. By the beginning of June a subscription among the soldiers and officers had raised $150.00, so Herbert once again visited Washington to purchase instruments.[16] Some of the regiment's field musicians formed the core of the ensemble, able or willing musicians such as Charles were culled from the ranks, and Herbert was designated bandleader (though he continued to perform as a bugler). Many of these players would eventually be officially detailed as band members and leave their respective companies to mess and tent as a unit. The soldiers were excited at the prospect of having music, and many shared their enthusiasm in letters home: "They are getting up a brass band in the Regiment & they have not got so as to play any yet" wrote Henry Burnham of Company G to his sister.[17] The membership of the band was fluid at best, as various players came and went due to illness, death or other reasons. In September there were fourteen players in the band, though membership would grow to at least sixteen musicians at times.[18] After the war Hebert gave the following roster:

Norman Puffer enlisted at the age of 14 as a drummer with the 2nd Vermont Infantry. He then reenlisted as a drummer for Company E, 10th Vermont Infantry, where he also became a member of the band (E. M. Haynes, *A History of the Tenth Regiment, Vt. Vols,* 2d ed. [Rutland, VT: The Tuttle Company, 1894], 442).

E♭ Cornet—J. H. George, W. W. Munsell
B♭ Cornet—Warren McClure, Chas. H. Green
E♭ Altos—Nathan Hamilton, E. J. Foster, R. W. Wells
B♭ Tenors—L. M. Kent, Will Clark, J. N. George
B♭ Bass—J. H. Goldsmith
E♭ Bass—Richard Moon, Dan Barker, W. W. Garvin
Drums—N. M. Puffer, O. C. B. George, D. B. Sexton
Cymbals—Delos Stewart[19]

Apparently Herbert's assignment as bandleader precluded his

leading the drum corps as well, and Richard Moon of Company E was soon pro-
moted to drum major and placed in charge of this ensemble.[20] *Herbert, Charles*
and Osman were fortunate throughout their enlistments to be attached to units
that were commanded by officers who supported music. Despite the release of Gen-
eral Order 91 of July 1862 dismissing regimental bands, the George brothers and
their comrades were surrounded by band music. By the end of the war four of the
five regiments brigaded together could boast musical ensembles.[21]

Three letters from Charles:

May 27, 1863

Monday morning six from each Company were detailed to go to Edward's
Ferry, about 4 miles — to throw up breast-works. I was among the number
and glad was I to find some way to get out of camp and see the country. At
6 A.M. our squadron of 36 men was ready to march with 2 day's rations, guns
and blankets. Sergeant Powers from Company KI, Corporal Beale from B and
Lieut. Newton from G made up the fatigue party. The morning was cool and
cloudy and we made a quick march without getting warm — arriving at the
Ferry we found Company D and one section of the Battery situated on a con-
ical hill overlooking the Ferry and a great extent of land in Virginia....

(Later) — I will tell you some news. Herbert is getting up a Cornet Band
with the help of Colonel Henry. Herbert is to be the leader — the regiment
buys the instruments. If everything works favorable I shall play an Alto Horn.
We shall be detailed out of the Company for that purpose. The pay will be
the same as now, but I believe I'd rather do it. Hope it will work. I have got
over being homesick, but I did have strong intentions of applying for
furlough — especially when I learned you were sick. Please Ellie get well
soon....

Osman fails under every day's duty and I don't know what will become
of him — he is discouraged — wishes he could go to the front — says he had
rather be killed by a bullet than by inches here. I went to the dispensary today
for some physic — saw Surgeon Childs and found him very sympathetic —
quite a change from what he used to be — but they say he has altered a great
deal.

May 30, 1863

Dearest Ellie — once more I can write a few words to you. Yesterday I washed
my dress coat and blouse. I ripped the lining out of the coat, it was so torn
I could not mend it, also it is much cooler and looks just as well. Many of the
boys have drawn new coats when the old one was better than mine is now. My
feetings are good yet as I keep them well darned. My pants are good yet —
the only holes are where I stuck the knife through when I cut my leg. The

leg soon healed up but the hole still grew larger! The Cavalry Band are just leaving.

Sunday — While the rest are out for inspection I will write some to my darling. Herbert was regularly promoted to Chief Musician last night. His rank is now the same as Quartermaster Sergeant being one of the non-commissioned staff. His pay is the same, which is the same as Orderly Sergeant, or $21 per month, which with $7 makes $28 a month. He does not belong to this Company now, but tents with the non-commissioned staff. News comes rather slow from Vicksburg — if Grant takes the City then rebellion must fall soon — no news about moving yet.

Monday — Nine months have passed away and one fourth of my time served out. I have got the "blues" again. I miss you terribly. I see not the least ray of hope in peace being declared this year. The nine-months men will soon be gone then there will be the brunt of battle to fall upon a few old worn-out soldiers — they have been so slow about calling out the draft men it makes me almost rebel! If they would prosecute the war with some vigor I could have courage, but they must be so slow about everything.

June 5, 1863

My Ellie, here I am again. I have been out after shade trees, which are very essential here. The Quartermaster sends out the teams and a squad of men and we had to go about 3 miles to find the trees — the trees are pine. We have two in front of our tent.

Last night a cavalry man and Harry the Scout (as he is called) came into camp in a hurry having been fired upon 10 or 15 times — some balls coming real close. It would be nothing strange if we are attacked here by cavalry — our detailed men are being returned to their companies every day. In our Company, first Osman came back, next E. McKillips, teamster, next D. Seymour, wagoner and so on — one of them will come to our tent. Did I tell you about the little drummer boy of Company B? You may remember him, his name is Foster — apparently about 16 yrs old — beardless, with face as smooth as a girl — small — good looking and decidedly a feminine look, which gives rise to the name "Nellie," which he goes by and answers to. Herbert calls him his girl and often you might see him sitting in his lap. It is real amusing to see Corporal Martin put on an act with "Nellie." He (the drummer) has plenty of wit and plays the girl part well.

Sunday — Herbert has returned today from Washington having faithfully performed his business. He is growing poor under so much care — I am afraid he is taking too much of his portion onto himself. Shortly after his return Captain Damon made him a present of a coat which cost probably $12 or $15 and is not very much worn. His wife sewed on some chevrons which he got at Washington so that he comes out with a nice outfit and looks pretty well. He is now making all preparations for the Cornet Band. The 10 Companies are getting up a subscription — the Adjutant is looking after it and when the amount is raised Herbert will go again to Washington and on his return the instruments will be ready to toot. I have chosen to play and Alto Horn — Osman is going to take Herbert's place as musician in Company G — not as a fifer, but as drummer — he is using all his spare time practicing and will be soon detailed to that work. Bully for Herbert!! He made me a present of his old dress coat, which is worth as much now as mine was when I drew it — he also gave me his cap so that in spite of my obstinancy in not drawing new clothes I am pretty well dressed!

From Herbert:

> Col. A. B. Jewett's 10th Regiment Vermont Vols.
> Camp Heintzelman
> June 7th 1863

Dear folks at home

Why dont some of you write more letters? I think I know Em is going to school & has no time & Mother has all the work to do at home & father wont write. Isn't that it? Well now we dont get half the letters either from home or from our sisters and brothers that other boys get. And I have not written to A. M. or Ruth as often as I used to. Jere writes oftener than the rest. I was in Washington most all of last week. It is about 35 miles or so some say 40 from here. I went down to get some band caps for the Drum Corp a drum & some clothing for myself got in there.... My new cap has got almost a dollars worth of gold lace on it. O My. Well now. We have been paid off again paid last Wednesday — no Thursday and I got only 4.00 & so must have part of my allotment. Please send me $10.00 as soon as you can and I want you to send me a pair of boots too.... I have not got moved from Co G yet but shall have a large tent with the Sergt Major in a few days. We are getting up a band here and I am to lead it.... I started it myself & worked round till I got the Cols consent to buy the instruments. I got $150.00 signed by subscription yesterday and calculate to get enough this week to buy them. I want some of our old pieces to play and will write a letter to Hen Bayley or Bailey for some music will you please hand it to Hen, or Bailey? I shall have Charley playing and Osman too think Osman the Base drum & Charley solo alto. Charley will learn easy. Most of the players that I shall have have played in some band a few have not. I dont want to lead it because I am not competant

to lead a band but Col says I must so never mind I'll do the best I can. We are much pleased with your picture mother & want fathers. Well dont think of more to write this time. Answer immy. With much love from
Herbert

P.S. Direct the express as follows
J. H. George
Principal Musician
10th Regt Vt Vols
Washington D. C.

P.S. again. Hand this other letter to Hen Bayley if he is in town. I want him to send me some music in the same express with my boots. Have him send it sure in my bag with boots. Let him know when send you know. Osman is on guard & C too. Very dry here. Need rain bad

No more
Herbert

While caught up in the excitement of forming a new band, Herbert, Charles and their fellow musicians still had plenty of military duties to occupy their time. As part of the regiment's preparations the surgeons began to drill those who would be under their command during battle. Most musicians found themselves in these exercises, learning new and demanding skills that would save countless lives in the near future. Surgeon Rutherford offered a description of the exercises:

> This is done by taking the Hospital attendance with the ambulances and a good supply of bandages lint &c. for draping wounds out into a large field and then play as in having a battle. I have with me some 10 or 12 soldiers to play the wounded men, some in one part of the body some in another. One will drop, two or 3 nurses will take him up lay him on a stretcher and carry him out of the way of shot.[22]

It was a trying time for Herbert. Though excited at the formation of a band, he was inundated with work (including a visit to Washington to pick up instruments), and Charles feared that he was working too hard.

Three letters from Charles:

Camp Hientzleman
June 18, 1863

No doubt you are concerned about us but we have not yet see a reb in arms, but are constantly on the alert. I believe I left off with our being under orders and expecting an attack. But the rebs not coming here to fight we took off our equipments at ten o'clock.

Yesterday we had the same thing all over again with two days rations in our haversacks. We were almost certain of going to Washington, but did not.

Last night about midnight we were called out again on another alarm and stood in line of battle two hours, when we again went to quarters. This morning the same thing again and here we are at break of day — We are still under marching orders. Herbert has returned — brought three new instruments — one is for me (if I can play) — a very pretty alto horn.

June 19, 1863

I find it is less tiresome to drill than to lie around doing nothing — and the drill will be dispensed with as long as we are under marching orders. There seems to be pretty stirring times around here and it would not be strange if we were drawn into a fight somewhere. Our troops are gathering in this vicinity — 1200 cavalry at Manassas. Last night our regiment donated a portion of our rations to them, they had been without food for 24 hours.

I heard the 1st Vermont Brigade were opposite Edward's Ferry. I will not attempt to tell of the movements of the various troops about here as the reports are more or less reliable than they are in the newspapers. Accounts are good for Vicksburg. Osman continues tough — Herbert is well but grows poor under so much business. I don't believe there is another man in the regiment that could have got up the band — but he has got himself in favor with all the officers — has got their consent and assistance — they hunted up the instruments and players. I have tried several instruments and find it will be impossible to play a small one like Herberts. The larger the instrument the easier I can play — but the bass takes too much wind so I took what is called a "Baritone." This is probably the last time I shall go on guard as the detail (band) will be made right away. While I sit here writing I can hear the cannons booming in more than one direction — times are very stirring out here just now.

June 20, 1863

My darling — Another day has passed and we remain under marching orders. Last night was made notable by the appearance of a Telegraph Corps in our Camp. They came well fitted out with everything necessary and this morning at 7 o'clock they were just hitching the wire on the first post — at 9 o'clock they were out of sight. They dig the holes and take the poles in the woods ad travel at the astonishing rate of 12 miles a day. They are running a line from here to Leesburg, Virginia where we have a large force now.

It is useless to talk of our going to the front for the front has come to us. Herbert has got all the instruments now for the band and the players picked out and the adjutant has their names. My instrument hangs in the tent — I have played some on it. Think I can learn. Osman will beat the bass drum. We shall be excused from other duties from after tonight. The detail will be postponed on account of our rations. There is no preparation as yet for them and we can draw from our Companies till after the detail — then we shall draw rations and mess by ourselves. Guess we shall live some better — may mate (one with a similar instrument) has been cook for the officers since he came out here.

Got a letter from Jere today — I'll send it along with this letter. Strange to say, some people here have not yet come to their senses! I saw yesterday a man bet $50 that we would go home as nine-months men and another one today wanted to bet $100 the same way — I think many will be disappointed.

(Sunday) — A cool, cloudy but pleasant day, but not so pleasant for some judging from the cannonading we can hear apparently about 20 miles away. When it first started it was quite slow but has increased so 30 reports a minute are heard. There must be some desperate fighting there and it would not be strange if we were engaged in it soon — or before it is over anyway. I have no desire to be under fire but would do all I could to help the poor fellows who are there fighting. Every little while there is a lull and then it commences again in earnest. They are evidently changing positions for better — or for worse! We don't know what to expect now — I will write again as soon as I can, Ellie.

While the soldiers drilled, the loyal citizens of Maryland and Pennsylvania grew uneasy. The first week of May had seen the routing of the Army of the Potomac under General Hooker at Chancellorsville, and the demoralized Yankees had been forced to withdraw. Lee once again seized the opportunity and began to push his army north. By early June Confederate forces were moving northwest into the Shenandoah Valley, steadily advancing while the Union army shadowed them to the east. A close watch was kept along the Potomac, and tensions ran high in the units stationed in Maryland. Prentiss Scribner of Company B wondered if they had enough troops to stop a Confederate incursion, and the Vermonters were often ordered to sleep with their cartridge belts on and their weapons close at hand. [23] *Before the end of the month Confederate forces had crossed the Potomac at Shepherdstown and Williamsport and pushed as far north as Mechanicsburg, Pennsylvania. The months of waiting finally came to an end for the men of the 10th Vermont when they received orders to pack up and join the Army of the Potomac.*

CHAPTER 3

June to December 1863

Pursuit of Lee; Bristoe Campaign; Mine Run Campaign; and Brandy Station

On 22 June 1863 the 10th Vermont Infantry received orders to relocate to Harpers Ferry, a rail junction seen by many as critical to the defense of Washington as well as necessary for control of the Shenandoah Valley. As the regiment was unsure of its ultimate destination, the band members were told to leave their instruments behind. Company musicians returned to their respective units while other band members retrieved their guns and rejoined the ranks.

From Charles:

June 25, 1863 — on the march.

We left camp, Ellie, last night at 5 P.M. — marched to [Monocacy] and camped over night — started again at daylight and at noon found ourselves well on the way to Harpers Ferry. Though we have had orders for some time it came rather abrupt at last. We were out practicing in the woods when a messenger notified us to report at once and prepare to march. It appears that Colonel Jewett has a dispatch from General Hooker to report with the Brigade to Harpers Ferry, West Virginia. He telegraphed to Camp Hientzleman to know whether to go or not and was ordered to go, The Maine regiment, whose time is out the 29th had to go too. At 5 o'clock the long dark line was on the move — we took our rubber and wool blankets — the rest in the knapsacks were carried by teams to some place — I don't know where. The Band instruments were left and we were obliged to carry a gun. Osman, however goes as Company Musician and does not carry a gun.

Arriving on June 26 the regiment spent four soggy days clinging to the steep slopes of Maryland Heights. The evening of their arrival the men were allocated

"Guard Mount in the Camp of the 1st Mass. Vol. Opposite the rebel position on the Potomac near Budds Ferry," a sketch from 1861 by Alfred Waud showing the band marching in front of the troops (Library of Congress).

a narrow, flat portion on the rise, then were moved to the summit and forced to camp on the windy incline. Despite such challenging terrain and weather, many regimental musicians were kept busy. According to a member of the 14th New Jersey: "There are three or four splendid brass bands here, one just opposite our camp — distant not more than a hundred yards and every evening we have a grand serenade from them."[1]

June 27 saw a profound change in the high command of the Army of the Potomac. Joe Hooker was relieved of command after the disaster at Chancellorsville and Major General George Meade was appointed commander of the Army of the Potomac. At this point the 10th Vermont was officially transferred to Major General William H. French's command of the VIII Army Corps. Following the loss at Chancellorsville, Lee had again pushed north, hoping to threaten the area surrounding Washington and perhaps speed up the end of the war. The Army of Northern Virginia and the Army of the Potomac began a tense pas de deux that would culminate in the Battle of Gettysburg. Concern over the nearness of the Army of Northern Virginia and the intentions of its commanding general led President Lincoln and General Halleck (general in chief and military advisor to the president) to press for the security of the capital. By June 30 the George brothers' regiment was on its way to Frederick, Maryland, where they joined with other regiments of their new assignment: the 151st New York, 14th New Jersey, and for a brief time, the 6th New York Heavy Artillery. General William Morris took command of the brigade, now officially the 1st Brigade, 3rd Division (French), III Corps (Sickles).[2] Joining a new, larger command meant that the men from Vermont were once more surrounded by martial music, and while the George brothers did not have their instruments to play, they still "marched to the music of all the bands in the Division amidst the waving flags and handkerchiefs."[3]

On July 2 the 10th Vermont and soldiers from the 14th Massachusetts and 10th Massachusetts Battery were sent to Monocacy Junction, Maryland, to guard a critical railroad bridge from marauding elements of Lee's army. Little did the men realize that they would return to this site in almost exactly a year for one of the most difficult battles of their careers. French's troops were to guard the rear and flank of Meade's army as it moved into Pennsylvania. If Meade should catch and defeat Lee, then French was in a position to strike Lee's line of retreat; if Lee were to win the upcoming engagement, then French could fall back to Washington to ensure the safety of the capital.[4] Due to this defensive posting the 10th Vermont did not participate in the Battle of Gettysburg the first week of July, though as it turned out, the regiment had been recalled in time to

General William H. Morris took command of the 1st Brigade, 3rd Division, III Corps in June of 1863 (National Archives and Records Administration).

join in the pursuit of Lee's defeated troops. Perhaps the possibility of combat led to heightened tensions, for the normally good-natured Charles had an altercation with an officer, an incident he would remember angrily for the rest of the war.

From Charles:

Monocacy Junction
July 4th, 1863

Hello again — we are here ordered to hold the railroad bridge, which was once destroyed by the rebels. I suppose you are thinking your soldier boy is at Gettysburg, but instead I am here. This was an iron bridge and took the rebs 3 days to destroy it — it is now built of wood.

Being close to the river the opportunity to go in swimming is being taken advantage of by the boys, being the first we have had. Our knapsacks I guess are burned and the Band instruments with them and I expect that

Bugbee left in charge of the commissary stores is taken prisoner. Most of my things I could not carry on the march and I suppose they are lost. My health is good now. I wish you would send some tea in every letter till I tell you not to. They don't draw tea when we are scouting around and I can't drink coffee. I have gotten to be quite a tea drinker and would sometimes give 25¢ for just a cup — but money won't buy it — our rations are rather hard to eat being hard-tack and coffee for breakfast, dinner and supper with a little pork for dinner — so you see my meals are mostly hard-tack and water.

I received a little abuse from Captain Damon on the first day's march from the Heights that I shall not forget for sometime. The road was very muddy and raining all the time. In passing mud holes in the road the men would sometimes slow up and after passing the holes would take their usual going. The rear of the regiment would be then far behind and in order to close ranks must increase the gait. The head of the regiment marched very fast which of course made it hard for the rear. At one time we were traveling as fast as we could — were all out of breath and tired. We did not "double quick" but took a very fast walk. Damon ordered us to close up — I did not change the step but walked as fast as I could — he ordered me to "double quick." I was too much out of breath and told him I could not, that I was gong at the rate of 4 miles an hour and that was enough. Says he, G — d — you, you can double quick and you will and he came at me with his sword — caught me by the back and struck me with it. I did not change step until he pushed me and then not any farther than his push. If he had struck me a second time I should have turned on him — an officer has no right to strike a private. Don't worry though, Ellie.

The 10th Vermont was shifted to Crampton's Gap near South Mountain and here they stood guard over captured supply wagons and prisoners. On July 5 units of the regiment took charge of approximately 1,000 prisoners previously held by the 14th New Jersey and escorted the captives to nearby Baltimore.[5] These were the first Confederate troops that many of the men from the 10th Vermont had seen.

On July 8 Major General French was officially placed in command of the III Corps as a result of an injury to General Sickles at Gettysburg; Brigadier General Washington L. Elliott was placed in charge of the 3rd Division, and General Morris retained command of the 1st Brigade. The III Corps moved through Turner's Gap to Boonsboro, near Antietam Creek, staying there for a few days while awaiting the order to attack. It was a miserable time for those soldiers unused to campaigning in the field, for they had marched without supplies and the nights were cold and wet.[6] The attitude of the other troops towards the fresh units did little to boost the Vermonters' confidence. As a member of the V Corps described:

We marched through the gap (Turner's) in South Mountain, chaffing most unmerci-
fully a part of Schenk's or French's Corps, which had just come from Baltimore and,
lining the road as we passed, were cheering for this and for that corps of the Army of
the Potomac. Their uniforms were new, their buttons bright, their knapsacks var-
nished, and paper collars predominated. We were ragged, dirty, shoeless, hatless and
blackened by a month's steady marching. Envious of their newness our bummers vig-
orously shelled them with cork and hardbread.[7]

On Sunday, July 12, the brigade prepared for an attack, maneuvering in front of the gap though no battle was forthcoming. When the order to move forward finally did come on July 14 it was to find deserted enemy camps. The men could not understand why they had sat for two days in sight of the enemy then allowed them to escape. Unfortunately these troops would experience such frustration many times before their service was over.

The members of the newly formed brigade had yet to bond into a cohesive unit, so teasing, and sometimes friction, arose between regiments. A member of the 151st New York told of losing his shoes on the march from South Mountain: "So we quietly walked over where the 10th Vt. regiment was soundly sleeping and Frank [Winans] helped himself to a pair of shoes that some Cooky Vermonter had left beside him, and handed them to me. I found marching easier the next day, but I always felt a bit sorry for the man from Vermont."[8] Unfortunately this discord could lead to hard feelings, and at least one member of the 151st New York felt that the men from Vermont were largely to blame: "It was a current report at that time that the 10th Vt. and 14th N. J. were continually quarreling, and getting in fistfights and keeping up a racket generally. By placing the 151st N.Y. in the center it kept peace in the Brigade. The 10th Vt. men were great on trading, and peddling all kinds of truck when in camp, and were not very well liked by the rest of the Brigade."[9]

From Charles:

July 14, 1863 About 10 A.M.

This morning we were ordered to roll call about 4:30 to be ready to move at 5:00 A.M. Osman and I had time to make a cup of tea and eat our hard-tack before we started — marched about three quarters of a mile where we now are in line of battle — the rebel pickets are within a mile — we have a good position, but whether we are to act on the offensive or defensive I know not, but judge the latter. No firing has been heard today yet.

3:00 P.M. (in pursuit of the rebels) — we started about 1 oclock towards the front — passed the rebel earthworks about 2 P.M. — they left in the night. All along the road we came through their old camping ground with the camp fires still smoking. We are in the woods now and by the side of me is where some officers camped and left their canvas. Some skirmishing has been going on today — I am afraid Lee is getting across the river.

Osman's feet trouble him very much — the march here was very fast and very warm. I carried his gun part of the way and his haversack part way. Herbert carrying his blanket on his horse — he owns part of a horse. I am tough as a bear and have an excellent appetite. I believe I could carry my load 40 miles — don't think of getting tired or having sore feet....

<u>Wednesday Morning</u> — Well! — General Lee has got away after all! but we have taken a lot of his rear. I suppose that the North will blow about his getting away, but I tell it is hard for one man to surround another in an open field — and it is difficult to find out their position too. I heard a man from the 6th corps, 1st Vermont Brigade say that if we had made an attack Monday we should have gotten whipped for they had all the advantage. I believe the best and most has been done that could be — We march immediately....

Osman fell out on this march but has since come up — 24 others fell out from this Company — all have come up now — some from other Companies fell out and died — rather tough — and we march again soon.

The 3rd Division then moved on to Sharpsburg on July 15, a grueling march as the heat had become nearly unbearable. Countless soldiers fell out of the ranks, unable to maintain the pace in such oppressive weather. The men were given only a brief rest before they were ordered south into the Loudon Valley. The regiment crossed both the Potomac and Shenandoah rivers on July 17, eventually arriving outside of Warrenton, Virginia. While the rest of the brigade moved to Ashby Gap, the 10th Vermont was ordered to Piedmont Station where it was detailed to guard the III Corps' ammunition train. Though in hearing distance of the fight a few miles away at Manassas Gap, the 10th Vermont was again kept from combat; while waiting for the column of wagons to pass, some of the regiment even managed to grab a nap.[10] *Though struggling with the difficulties of forced marches and life in the field, the new brigade had yet to experience a fight. In fact, Simon Cummings of the 151st New York noted that his regiment had still not lost a man in combat.*[11] *Some time later the men were to learn that Meade had ordered the III Corps to fall upon Lee's rear, but French was overly cautious and only his 1st Division engaged the enemy. This did little to improve the reputation of the III Corps as a fighting unit, as soldiers from other corps were disgusted with French's failure to support the assault. With no prospect of joining the fight in front of them, the men from Vermont managed to entertain themselves as best they could. Some enterprising soldiers came across a beehive while out foraging, and upon returning placed the hive on the stomach of a sleeping captain, "making business quite lively in that neighborhood shortly afterwards."*[12] *Other less fortunate soldiers, such as the musicians, were detailed to the ambulance corps; Herbert even came under fire while helping to remove the wounded from the field.*[13]

Two letters from Charles:

> Camp near Maryland Heights
> Friday, July 17, 1863

I will take a little pleasure this rainy morning in writing to you, my dear. I have just finished my breakfast of fried pork and fried hard-tack and a cup of tea. Osman and I are tenting alone — eat alone and have things all our own way. I think that more than one half of this Company have thrown away their woolen blankets and many of them have no fly tents. I find that upon trial that I was not wrong in saying before I enlisted that the marching and fatigue would be nothing to me, for while others are throwing away their blankets and extra cartridges to lessen the weight, I feel perfectly well and fresh under 60 rounds of cartridges, the heaviest wool blanket in the Company and a fly tent besides carrying rations more than is actually needed (for fear of what may happen) and also carry Osman's gun part of the way. I am tough!...

<u>Saturday, 2:00 P.M.</u> — We broke camp last night about 6 oclock and marched till 12 oclock and such a time you never saw — went about 8 miles (I should think we march from the Valley to Sandy Hook) then went up the Potomac to Harper's Ferry and of all the mud!!!! you can't imagine worse. It was 4 or 5 inches deep and like thin pudding. The column moved so slowly — (not over a mile an hour) it was tiresome holding our load so long and in the night made it worse. Crossed the river at the place where the railroad bridge was when we were there before — but it was not there now — has been destroyed. We marched up the street a piece and turned to the left. Herbert fell here, went into a deserted house and stayed all night — did not overtake us till we were well on our march today. We crossed the Shenandoah River, passed around Linden Heights and kept on in a southerly direction — after crossing the Shenandoah the road was rough and muddy and Osman fell out so tired and his feet so sore he could hardly step. When I went (to <u>bed</u> I was going to say but will call it <u>grass</u>) I could not help feeling concerned about him — the night was cool and he had no blanket, but I went to sleep and forgot all my troubles till daylight. I endured the march without fatigue — Osman came in in the night but could not find our regiment so camped with the 106th New York in our Brigade — he came along inquiring for Company G just as I got up. I went immediately for water and was getting our breakfast when the order came to be ready to march in half an hour, but it was nearly an hour before we started. I cooked our beefsteak (we draw fresh beef part of the time — the cattle are driven around with the army) and had time to eat

it. On the march my only trouble is to pity Osman — I carry his gun some of the time to ease him but my load is rather heavy and I can't carry everything. We marched today, I think south and about 8 miles. I don't know where we are nor where we are going, but guess we shall get somewhere sometime — probably Richmond is where we are going....

Upperville, Virginia
July 21, 1863

I have just sent off a letter without its being finished — we marched day before yesterday about 8 miles and had a little novelty in the course of the day. In the forenoon we rested by a nice house — good orchard etc. and while the rest were filling their sacks with plunder I went to the orchard for some apples — got enough for some sauce and what was better, caught a half grown chicken — dressed it in less than 2 minutes and put it in my haversack — that was allright, but the sequel was the funniest in the afternoon. The boys were all going blackberrying so I took some canteens to go after water and went a little farther for berries — just as I was returning along came the provost guard and took in 50 to the Provost Marshall — 15 from our Company — most of them had had permission from their Company Captain to be berrying but that was no account — we had a sergeant from our Company and 2 other sergeants all under arrest. Our orders were to "stay there until further orders" and "live on our blackberries" or in other words, go hungry until further orders. At night the provost sent for our blankets — Osman brought mine and in it rolled up I found fried bacon and my chicken and hard-tack all ready to eat. Osman had fixed it — thus I ate the fruits of my forenoon's work under arrest, for supper. Some of the boys had no supper.

In the morning we had orders to roll up our blankets and go to our Companies with the guard for our equipments — it was about 5 oclock — the regiment was gone but we found the things all there in a stack. Colonel Jewett was mad about our arrest and told the Captains not to touch our guns — if they put his men under arrest they must see that they had their guns. If the Provost had not been a good fellow we should not have got them even so.

We were kept in the rear of the whole corps through the whole day's march and until late that night before being released and ordered back to our Companies. We styled ourselves the "<u>Blackberry Brigade</u>." At noon I got permission from the Provost to go after water, in going I passed through a blackberry field where I picked what I wanted to eat in about 15 minutes — they were good....

On July 26 the 10th Vermont and their division moved through Warrenton with bands playing Union music, including the "Star-Spangled Banner" and

Joining with the Army of the Potomac meant that Herbert and his brothers would get the chance to hear other ensembles, such as the band of the 8th U.S. Infantry shown here at headquarters near Fairfax Court House, Virginia, in June 1863 (Library of Congress).

"Yankee Doodle," much to the consternation of the remaining locals.[14] *The regiment was given five days respite outside of Warrenton where the men gratefully made camp and rested from their exhausting march. It had been a demanding ordeal, with the previously stationary Vermonters learning the harsh realities of life on the march.*[15] *The troops felt that they had performed well as the newest members of the III Corps, though General Elliott felt otherwise, complaining that the division — especially the 1st Brigade — was obviously "unaccustomed to marching."*[16] *This may or may not have been the case, for even veterans toughened by earlier campaigns found time to complain about the severity of the recent marches.*

Following the protracted retreat from Gettysburg Lee eventually set his army in a relatively secure position on the south side of the Rappahannock River near Culpeper, Virginia. Meade, cautious as to how to proceed, placed his army along the opposite bank, a ten-mile stretch from Sulphur Springs in the north to Rappahannock Station on the Orange and Alexandria Railroad. The 10th Vermont took up a defensive position at Routt's Hill, about two miles south of Sulphur Springs, on August 1. According to one historian, the regiment experienced a first here: "On the 14th Sergeant Martin of company G, while on picket, shot a guerrilla who was aiming his gun at one of the Union pickets. This was the first shot fired at the enemy by a member of the regiment, but not the last."[17] *For Vermonters such as William White of Company I, recent events had drawn attention to the distressing horrors of war: "I have seen a great deal of suffering & destitution caused by this war. More than I ever expected to see before I enlisted, and more than I hope I shall ever see again."*[18]

Early in August Meade sent cavalry in force across the Rappahannock to gauge Lee's strength and deployment, resulting in over a week of skirmishing, though no general engagement ensued. The III Corps stayed in position on the right of the Union line, allowing the 10th Vermont five recuperative weeks to heal the sick and wounded and to replace lost equipment. Many of the sick who had been sent to hospitals in Washington rejoined the regiment, including Osman George, and officers traveled north to recruit new men for the unit. Remarkably Osman had not been granted either an extended furlough or discharge and was now required to move with the regiment. At one point he dropped behind during a march and was missing for a few days. Needless to say his health continued to decline. Recruits for the entire brigade arrived and each regiment returned to near full strength: the 10th Vermont and 151st New York, around 900 men each; 14th New Jersey, 800, and the 6th New York Artillery, 1,100.[19]

From Charles:

Camp near the Rappahannock
August 19, 1863

I am again permitted to inform you of my welfare! The days and weeks pass by rapidly with little change in our affairs. We still occupy the same ground were we first camped, yet other troops are on the move. I know that some grand scheme is being wrought out and being kept a secret....

Thursday.... A few days ago I went over to the hospital to watch with the sick at night and learned for the first time that blankets were not furnished in the hospitals at the front. Some were there with nothing to cover them — others had shelter tents for blankets — a few had good woolen blankets. I found one fellow from Company D with no covering and lying where the night winds and damp air blew in on him — he even had no blouse. I asked permission of the nurse to go to his captain to ask for one, which I got and the fellow slept that night as thought he hadn't slept for a week. Others lay with their bare feet exposed and no pains taken to cover them up. While I was there I tried to make them comfortable. One young man from Company C died at 10:00 P.M. Three died from the same regiment the same day. I helped lay him out — closed his eyes and as I brushed back his hair I could not help thinking of those who would mourn his death. How different from a Corps where kind and willing hands are near. His coarse pants and shirt, as all are dressed, with his blouse under his head, was all that was done for him.

Our instruments have come so that we shall now commence practicing again. This is probably the last time I shall go on picket duty for a long time, for he3rbert says that Colonel Henry said that of they got the instruments again he should hold on to them. Herbert has been so busy copying music for the band for the past week or two that has grown poor. Kent, one of the Band men has a hatchet which I shall carry part of the time and will have it to use. Osman and I have just bought a can of milk — it will last a week.

Saturday — Yesterday was such a busy day I couldn't get time to write any, so will begin back. On arriving in camp we were very busy looking over mails and drawing rations. A little before noon Herbert came in and had Osman and myself and Kent detailed for the Band. He wanted us to report directly to his quarters, which we did and from there a short distance away from camp we set up our tents. I like our new place first rate — away from the camp and bustle and in a cool place. We have put up our tent so as to have it 8 × 12 feet — have been into the woods and cut little poles for a bed-stead — they make a good bed — bend enough to make them lie easy. We build them about 18 inches from the ground which makes a good seat besides plenty of room underneath for storage. Herbert still keeps his tent with the officers so as to be handy to blow the bugle calls.

Today Colonel Henry being temporarily in command of the brigade, left the regiment in command of Captain Saulsbury, who being the worse for liquor ordered Herbert to move his tent to the "rear" — he has accordingly moved here with the rest of use. I shouldn't wonder if Colonel Henry would order him back. Herbert says he expects Saulsbury will order us back to our Companies. We are not excused from Company duty entirely — keep our guns yet and shall have to attend dress parades and inspections until we can play so as to answer for duty as a Band. If we are ordered to march before that time comes, our instruments will be packed again in the box and we carry our guns and when we stop again go to practicing. If we gain as fast as we have in just the first day we can playing in 2 weeks. I now have Herbert's old horn — the same that he had at Newbury. I think I can never be a good player, but can manage my part (2nd B flat Cornet) well enough I guess. We have just got a lot of mail from last June — thanks for the tea....

Indeed, the band's instruments had finally caught up with the regiment, so practice began immediately, much to the delight of the regiment. Timothy Messer of Company H announced: "We have got a brass band in this regiment now the players were selected out of this regiment, they have twelve brass pieces, they play on dress-peraid &c &c."[20] Apparently the budding ensemble was still in need of building their repertory, at least according to Henry Burnham of Company G: "We have got a brass band in our Regt they have not got so they can play much yet."[21] Herbert was once again knee-deep in his duties as bandleader, which now included finding new music for his band. He often wrote home for pieces or arranged the music himself. The men of the regiment were grateful for the music, if somewhat cautious in their praise. As Tabor Parcher of Company B wrote: "I must say a word about our band it consists of 14 members out of the regt they play first rait for the time that they have been a practicing."[22] *Perhaps the new group was taking longer to come together than Herbert would have preferred; as Henry Burnham ingeniously noted: "Our band has got so that it plays some they have been out on dress parade twice they play very well for new beginners."*[23] *Regardless of the capabilities of the new ensemble, on September 1 the band was officially detailed for duty.*

From Charles:

Camp near Gum Springs, Virginia
September 1, 1863

Just one third of my time is served now — only two years longer to live in cloth houses — two years longer to grind hard-tack — two years more to live under military commanders and away from my dear wife and child.... We have not yet reported as a Band as yet but will run the risk of it soon to get rid of carrying our guns. Today we practiced marching and playing — I make rather green work of it yet, but shall learn after a while.

An old negro, the picture of hard times and hard usage made his appearance at our place of rendezvous while playing today — he lived not very far away and came to hear us play. He described the country about and conditions, deplorable indeed, — starvation stares them in the face. His master was in the Southern Army and his mistress had nothing to eat. She applied to General French and he told her if she would take the oath of allegiance he would furnish her with food, but she would not and will have to take from her slaves only what the soldiers give them. This is only a sample of the suffering condition in which the Confederacy have run themselves — <u>Let them starve or surrender!</u>

4:00 P.M. — While practicing today Lieut. Hill came down with orders from Colonel Henry for us to turn our guns and equipments over to our Captains and report for duty as a Band. <u>Bully for the Band</u>! We have now got rid of our guns. I have had one to carry most 13 months. I don't know but what I'll be lonesome without one — I have kept it bright all the time — very few have had better looking guns.

The boys all through the Company are down on Osman — they think he is old maidish and <u>thinks</u> he is sicker than he is — the Band boys think the same. He does not come up to Herbert's expectations as a drummer. He will not stand it I think to drum. I wish he was at home. I have to bear a great deal and if I get a little out of patience with him he thinks it is a terrible thing.

<u>Sunday, September 6, 1863</u> — I will add a little more today to my list of

scribblings — we have undergone the ceremony of inspection this forenoon — played several pieces and were complimented by General Morris when he inspected us — not on our appearance, but on the music. Herbert has sent to Jere for uniform caps — I don't know what our coats will be.

We are prospering finely. Yesterday we had a grand review of the three army Corps by General Meade. Our band was honored by being the brigade band in preference to the New York band with its 10 or 11 months practice. Before night we were complimented by General Elliott and he advised Surgeon Childs to have us fitted out for a Brigade Band. Our regiment being the first in the Brigade and the Brigade the first in the Division we had the honor of leading the troops into the field. In fact the field was entirely clear when we entered at the head of our regiment and just in rear of the General and Staff, so we had the privilege of seeing all the troops come in. It was an entirely new thing to Herbert to know his place, but the General Morris was always on hand to tell him where and when and how, and he made not a mistake!

The arrival and disposal of the troops as they came I was the grandest sight I ever saw. The first Division as they emerged from the woods formed in columns by Division (which is two Companies marching abreast) led by one of the most splendid drum Corps ever known, consisting of 40 drums all playing. The second Division also had one large drum Corps (32). They were in place of a Band. Other Brigades had either bands or drum Corps.

After they were all placed, the announcement of General Meade's coming was given by the firing of guns. The reviewing of the troops by him as he rode through the brigades accompanied by his Staff was magnificent. At the approach of each Band (or head of the Brigade) they "struck up" "Hail to the Chief" so that the tune was played entirely though the whole ceremony — as fast as one Band got through with it the next took it up. After the ceremony they marched by columns past the General, each Band playing what they chose as they marched until they were opposite the General, then turning out and playing until the entire Brigade had passed. It was tough on our lips, being all green at it, but we lived O.K.

General Meade is a little guy and a very good looking officer. General French I have described before as being red-faced and anything but pleasant looking. General Elliott is about the size of John E. Chamberlain — General Morris is a man all over — good looking — pretty appearing and pleasant, yet very piercing eyes. I wish his eyes were not quite so keen when he viewed our Band for my shirt was a little dirty. Everyone likes him — he is smart and shrewd. I wouldn't wonder if he is promoted soon. The staff officers were a smart looking lot of men....

For Meade's review on September 7 the troops of Elliott's 3rd Division turned out in newly acquired uniforms. This no doubt caused resentment with the other troops, and as a result the division first heard the nickname "French's Pets."[24] *Such teasing was probably immaterial for Herbert, Charles, and Osman as it was their band that was selected to play for the review. The proud bandsmen found that their new duties occupied a surprising amount of time. There was constant practice, playing for the daily rituals of guard mounting and dress parade, and the occasional required appearance at drills, reviews, and inspections.*[25] *On free evenings the band might serenade a commanding officer, though if that officer offered whiskey as payment, the results could be comical. Osman's precarious health had apparently become a strain on the brothers, however, and Charles in particular began exhibiting signs of frustration.*

Two letters from Charles:

Wednesday, September 9, 1863

Everything all right! We are improving finely in the Band — all we lack is music and I guess we shall have some soon. I have no other news to write except that Osman is not liked in the Band — he is so <u>old maidish</u> that I have

Members of the band of the 4th Vermont Infantry pose with their instruments behind them. The time spent living and playing together led most bands to become tight-knit units within the regiment or brigade (courtesy Vermont Historical Society).

all I can do to get along with him. If he were not a brother and sick I would not bear with him as I do. Herbert is very willing to leave him for me to look after.

I had my hair cut short and side whiskers cut off.

Saturday — You speak of my having more leisure time now that we have the Band, but it is not so, as we have scarcely any time to idle. When the regiment goes on drill we must go too and play occasionally — also to dress parades — then we practice 3 or 4 hours besides playing for tattoo and serenades etc. Night before last we went with Major Chandler and several line officers to serenade Colonel Stoughton (of sharpshooters). The Major treated before we started and the Colonel treated twice and then we went to the other Colonel to serenade and were treated again and by this time one third of the Band was drunk — one third knew they had had enough and one third were strictly temporate. The cymbal player occupied the whole road, sometimes both sides and sometimes the ground!

Osman has been ordered to his Company by Colonel Jewett.

Camp near Gum Springs, Virginia
September 11, 1863

Dearest Ellie — I am afraid that it will not be that I can get away on furlough at all now being a member of the Band. I shall have to stick by, but never mind, the war will be over some time and I can go home then and stay.

It is much easier on me being with the Band than it was with the Company. Being excused from military duty and the difference in the weight of my horn and gun and equipments (more than 20 lbs) is great on the march — and again being off by ourselves is more comfortable. No roll calls to attend can go and come where and when we please — only look out for the patrol.

Now to describe our little party — to begin with, our leader, J. H. George is the idol of the party — no one pretends to contradict him or show any signs of dissatisfaction, but take everything he says as "law and gospel" and it is always said pleasantly too. He looks very wise, in fact, so much care has changed his looks very much — he is perceptive and comprehensive too. The 2nd E Flat player is about 5 ft 8 inches — single and good looking; the 1st B Flat man is about my size — a little taller and skinnier — about 25, married 4 months before enlisting. The 2nd B Flat is your humble servant. We four constitute the front rank — Herbert on the right and I on the left. The 1st Alto is about 5' 10" — heavy proportioned, with whiskers — good natured and very agreeable. He is 2nd Chief Musician in the regiment acting as leader of the Drum Corps and Band in case of Herbert's nascence. He is a married man about 36 years old. Richard (Dick) Moon by name.

The 2nd Alto — a short fellow about 17 years old — drummer of Company F and a regular case for fun. 1st Baritone is a young man, medium size who was reduced by his request from a corporal on purpose to join the Band — so you see a position with the Band is preferable to that of a Corporal. — 2nd Baritone, L. M. Kent of Bradford about my size — 36 years old — has a wife and 4 children. — 1st Bass is W. Garvin — Bass Drummer in the Drum Corps — large, stout young man about 21— and married — was reduced from corporal last winter at his own request, purpose to beat the drum. 2nd E Flat Bass, J. H. Goldsmith also married; Cymbal player, a young fellow 178 years old from Company I — the captains waiter. This fellow is a regular wag — Norman Puffer, tenor drummer — is sergeant drummer in the drum corps, is 16 years old and as good a looking fellow as you can find in Vermont — a joker and full of un. The next and last of the Band is the Bass Drummer (that is Osman) I have only one more to describe and that is our cook E. A. Colby from Company D — about 28, married and has a family.

We all improve very rapidly. I can play with ease now what I could not play a week ago. Herbert does not have to drill me alone as he does some of the others.

(Sunday) — A year ago today we were on the march going towards heavy cannonading at South Mountain. I little thought that a whole year would pass without our seeing a battle, but so it is and now it seems as thought it was a natural consequence that we should escape going into action, but 24 hours may not pass before we see fire! Today for the first time in a month has the quietness been broken by firing in the direction of the enemy — not very rapid as yet, but increasing fast. I shouldn't wonder if we had marching orders soon.

Though the Army of the Potomac and the Army of Northern Virginia were separated by no more than a river, neither commander seemed eager to start a brawl. Events in the Western Theater had forced both Lee and Meade to send valuable troops to Tennessee, and both commanders feared the impact such a loss of troops would have on their fighting effectiveness. Pressure from Washington and favorable scouting reports eventually led Meade to begin deploying, and by the second week of September Meade's cavalry had pushed the Confederates out of Culpeper. By September 15 the rest of the Army of the Potomac was moving forward, so the George brothers and their brigade were sent southwest towards the Rapidan. Morris' brigade managed to get lost for some hours but finally crossed the Rappahannock River at Freeman's Ford and camped for the night. The next day the march resumed and the troops arrived about two miles outside of Culpeper.

From Herbert:

Camp near Culpeper Va
Sept 21st/63

Dear Mother.

Guess I'll write a few lines & send in Osmans letter. We are encamped in a rich planters garden a mile or two below Culpeper. To get here we had to march some I tell you. Forded the Rappahanock where the water was up to our waist allmost & the current was very swift. Forded the So. Branch of the Rappahanock. Marched all day without Eating & till half past 8 o'clock in evening. Came through what was once a splendid country. Large plantations with nigger houses on em. The Army of the Potomac is now in line of battle but we may not fight any. May move any time. Band prospers well. We acted as Brigade Band on Genl Review the 8th inst. Music complimented by sev'l Genls. I have arranged 3 pieces to play & they go well. I have written to H W Bailey Esq abt that state pay & got an answer. He sent me a new <u>blank</u> order to be filled out & sent to him so that he can hold it. Am going to draw my alloted pay here after this & then send it home as I want it. Have just been paid off again. Jere seems to think that father cannot account for all my money. Don't let him sell the colt anyhow & then I'll save that if all the rest is last. I have made up my mind to write to him & have you give it to him. When he is sober if he ever is — well no more now. Send on our shirts as soon as you get them ready.

Herbert

The intended offensive across the Rapidan failed to materialize, so the 10th Vermont remained encamped at Culpeper till early October. It was a stressful time for the Vermonters as the daily routine of drill took on a more somber note with the threat of combat looming over them. According to William Thayer of Company B: "It is pretty hard now. We drill some 2 1/2 hours a day besides some policing such as cleaning up the ground and fixing our tents, brushing up equipment & gun. But I had rather be back where we was last winter." [26] *While the drilling may have been intense, the men still had their music. In fact, the close proximity of the two giant armies allowed some soldiers to enjoy the music of their opponent's bands, as when Thomas Galwey of the 8th Ohio relaxed to a sunset concert of "'Dixie,' 'The Bonnie Blue Flag,' 'My Maryland,' and other Southern airs" by a Confederate band.* [27]

From Charles:

Camp near Culpeper, Va.
September 24, 1863

I am again at my favorite amusement. I think my letters would make quite a volume. I know they are full of nonsense for there is surely nothing here worth writing about. We are expecting to march soon and I shouldn't wonder if this letter was finished a long ways from here. Yesterday we played on Brigade Dress Paraded — our Band playing down and the New York playing back to camp. It was the longest stretch we ever had, but we were acknowledged ahead of the New York Band by everyone. "Bully for us!" I like my place first rate — the more I play the better I like it. I am writing on the Bass Drum and Herbert is writing on it too. He is writing for another horn and a new bass drum — we are going to have a tip-top band bye and bye.

Our hard-tacks are not very good now — they are wormy — we talk some of driving them instead of carrying them.

Sunday, September 27, 1863 — We are still at Culpeper — rumors are that the 2nd and 12th Corps have gone to reinforce Rosecrans — if so, there probably will be no offensive movements here. We have just received 5 new pieces of music, which makes 21 in all. We can play all but 3 of them. Herbert wants me to take the Solo B Flat — he says I can play better than the one that plays it now. I had rather not take it, but will if he insists. I had rather be a good second than a poor 1st. We have the praise of being a good band now playing about as well as the old band that have been playing 2 or 3 years. The beauty and credit of it is all owing to Herbert — he is the best soprano player I ever heard. Osman is worse again — has a sour stomach, mouth and throat — he is pretty much discouraged. Herbert has arranged for him to learn to bugle. How long we can keep the officers from letting him alone I don't know. We had to have a new bass drummer — Osman could not fill the bill. He is as old maidish as ever!

October 2, 1863 — Good morning Ellie! I have just got up — have mended a hole in my feetings and can now write a little as it is still early — few are up. It is raining and quite warm. Herbert has changed my part — I now have the 1st B Flat, which is much harder to follow — runs now with the air much more.

October 3, 1863 — I am improving fast in my playing. We have some excellent pieces of music such as "Yankee Doodle," "Star Spangled Banner," "Hail to the Chief," "Hail Columbia," "Gift Polka," "Fitz Clarence Waltz," "Twilight Dews" and a "Quick Step" of Herberts own composing etc. etc. 23 in all.

From Herbert:

Camp near Culpepper Va
Oct 4th/63

Dear Mother

Rec'd a letter from you to night or Osman did and I wish to answer it now when I have time and a chance. One thing I wish to speak about & that is that 2 months allotted pay that you did not get last winter. I dont think you will ever get it, for Ellen did not get hers and Charley wrote to the State treasury about it and got an answer saying it had been delivered to her. Now we know that She has not rec'd it. I want you to write or have father write to the State treasurer about it and find out <u>immy</u>. And I'll [bet] a four dollar bill nine feet [long] that you will never get it. And thats why I wish to draw it all here. We are all three of us going to break up the allotment C & O have done so to day & I shall as soon as our Adjt can attend to it. $40.00 ($20.00 each) gone to pot I'll guarentee. I dont seem to care much if all my money gets lost if the war would only end, but that wont end it. Please write to the treasurer soon and see what he says I kinder pity Gen Morse, poor fellow, wish he would come out and play with me in my band. I hear that Soph Bailey is about to get married, is she yet? Hope she will be satisfied with her man. I've got sore eyes quite sore what am I going to do with them! they itch awfully & ache. Cant open them in the morning hardly. Hope they will get better soon. Band prospers nicely. We serenaded Gen'l Elliot our Division commander last night at midnight. He has been ordered to report to Gen'l Rosecrans for duty in active service and left us this morning. We gave him among the several pieces the song "Ever of thee I'm fondly dreaming" He is a good man & an excellent officer beloved by officers & men. We dont like to loose him but he is going where he will more good perhaps. Our band can play 23 pieces of music now & have been playing only a month. Oh by the way Jere is 26 tomorrow. <u>Eld back</u>. It has been very plesant today.

No more now
From Herbert

From Charles, the same day:

Camp near Culpepper
October 4, 1863

Ellie dear, I guess I shall abandon writing this — on one side I hear the groans of a suffering soldier in the hospital and on the other Chaplain preaching — guess I'll go to meeting — —

Yesterday was a hard day for my lips — we did a good deal of playing during the day practicing, Dress Parade, Tattoo and by that time my lips had a hole cut into them by the mouthpiece. In thinking back over my letters I fear I have said more about our Band than you care to hear, but it is foremost in my mind right now and there isn't much of anything else going on, and I do want to talk to you as often as I can.

At about 11 P.M. last night we were called upon to serenade General Elliott, he having a few hours before received orders to report to General Rosecrans. The Pennsylvania 78th Band had been playing all the evening and had got pretty drunk and we were called upon to relieve them! Herbert hated to go because we were all in a crippled condition and the bass drummer had failed to show up and one of our men was sick, but there was no excuse for us not to go. We felt much relieved on arriving to be escorted by General Morris' Aide (a pretty little fellow). We took our stand if front of and facing the General's quarters. He was quietly seated at the door of his tent and all around him were sitting and standing representatives from nearly every regiment in his division. Speeches were called for from Captain such-a-one or Lieut. so-and-so. The Band playing between speeches. After playing 4 or 5 pieces and giving good satisfaction generally, we retired. Liquor was passed around to us twice — all drank but Herbert and I. Herbert resists all temptations of a demoralizing character. Not a Sunday has passed without his being urged to go and practice with the band, but he says not unless he is ordered to do so.

He gives me much encouragement about playing. If I continue getting a lip as I have done so far it will be much easier. You don't know what "getting a lip" means? As one practices ones lips become strong and tough and finally they become hard enough so they do not become sore. Mine are some sore today....

Much to the disappointment of the men from Vermont, General Elliot was ordered west to join Rosecrans and the Army of the Cumberland, so Herbert, Charles, Osman and the band offered a serenade to their departing commander. Elliot was replaced by Brigadier General Joseph B. Carr.[28] As the cold of winter drew closer the men began building more permanent shelters. Local fences and barns quickly disappeared as the soldiers gathered whatever they could find for what they envisioned to be a lengthy stay. Unfortunately this was not to be, as Lee and Meade, for once closely matched in numbers, began maneuvering in search of a tactical advantage. The aggressive Lee decided to take the fight to his opponent, and on October 6 he began shifting his forces north and east in an effort to flank the Army of the Potomac.

On October 10 the 10th Vermont was ordered to make ready for battle. The band, fourteen members strong by now, was ordered to remain with the surgeons and follow at the rear of the army. To their surprise the troops were ordered north, not south, and managed only three miles before bivouacking. After crossing the Rappahannock the following morning the troops returned to their earlier position on the north bank of the river. Over the next few days the entire army was to pull

*back in a general redeployment towards Centreville, very close to where they had
started the campaign four months previously. Both the van and rear guard of
French's III Corps encountered the enemy on the move, yet the brunt of the fighting
was to fall on the II Corps. Throughout the Bristoe Campaign the 10th Vermont
was near the action, yet once again what combat occurred did not directly involve
the regiment. Other units from their brigade had contact with the enemy; the 14th
New Jersey had forty men taken prisoner, and the 106th New York, acting as rear
guard for the brigade, was nearly cut off from the army and escaped only after
fierce fighting. The 10th Vermont would have a brief encounter with a small enemy
detachment near McLean's Ford along Bull Run—site of the first major engagement of the war—though the result was a skirmish at best.[29]*

*Following General A. P. Hill's repulse at the battle of Bristoe Station on
October 14, Lee headed south once again, followed closely by the Army of the
Potomac. Members of the 10th Vermont spent much of this time repairing railroads
destroyed by the fleeing Confederates. The George brothers were also confronted
for the first time with one of the most unpleasant tasks facing musicians, that of
helping the wounded off the field and assisting the surgeons in the field hospitals.
The unbelievable carnage that sullied the battlefield shocked the young men from
Vermont. Philip Arsino of Company F offered an unsettling description: "all of
our wonded are here I see wone fellow have his two arms taken off what doe you
think of that and some had thair leggs & wone arm taken of that is the first
wonded that I have seen it made me think of home."[30]*

From Herbert:

Camp at Union Mills Va
Oct 18th 1863

Dear folks at home

Long ere this reaches you the news of the late movement of the army of
the Potomac will reach you by telegraph & Express. "We 3" are all safe as yet
no wounds nor anything of the kind We have seen the flash of the enemies
guns, had shells burst within a few rods of us, heard the rattle of Musketry,
the roar of cannon close on our rear for two or three days, seen wounded men
born off the field on stretchers, some dead, some being buried, some having
their legs & arms sawed off. (amputated) by the Surgeons. Skedaddled all the
way from Culpepper here, forded the Rappahanock So & North branches.
Broad Run, Bull Run, &c. &c. and not a man killed out of the 10th Vt and
only one wounded with shell — Our Division was not in any engagement with
the rebs. Our Corps was not used much in the fight the 2nd had quite a hard
time & the 5th. Our 1st Division had several killed.... We do not expect to
stay here but a short time. It depends upon the movement of the enemy. We

shall get our express next time they bring it to the Regt. Genl Sickles with but <u>one</u> <u>leg</u> arrived here yesterday to take command of our corps. He can ride a horse by having his <u>stub</u> strapped to the saddle. <u>My</u> <u>band</u> was ordered to Corps Head Quarters yesterday at half past one PM to play for his reception and dinner. We went and played the Gen'l in and played till he got through dinner. Don't it a little strange that the 10th Vt Band should be selected from all the old bands to play upon such an occassion! I was astonished. We are getting up a <u>name</u>, play pretty well for green ones — Poor Osman is not with us. He was not able to march and so went with the ambulance Corps. He road all the way and is now with the ambulances about a mile from here. He is no so well as usual. Pretty sick the Surgeons begin to talk of discharging him Brigade surgeons & all say he is not good for any thing. He is very poor, diarhea no better chronic. Some time when I have time I will write the particulars about our march no time now. We get no mail now have not since we moved from Culpeper.

(In haste)
From Herbert

By October 27 the brigade was back at Catlett's Station and detailed to guard headquarters. Herbert proudly claimed that the reason for this assignment was that the command staff wanted the 10th Vermont around due to the quality of his band! Though combat between the men in blue and gray had come to a standstill, battles continued to rage between Charles, Herbert, and the surgeons. Though Osman had been in a hospital in Maryland, the regimental surgeon required that he travel with the regiment. This obviously exacerbated his already precarious health, and finally, after incessant pestering, permission was granted for Osman to be moved back to a Washington hospital. The continual concern for their brother, combined with the experience of a campaign in the field (including the grisly sights of the field hospitals), were potentially overwhelming circumstances for any young men. Yet both Herbert and Charles remained dedicated to their tasks and surprisingly positive if more somber in their correspondence.
From Herbert:

Camp near Catletts Station Va
Oct 27th 1863

Dear folks at home

If you have read the papers lately undoubtedly you know what the latest movements of the Army of the Potomac have been. Our Corps is around here and the others are out near Warrenton & all around here. We are waiting for the railroad to be repaired.... Osman is still with us he is a little better but ought to go to Washington or rather he ought to be discharged. Our head Surgeon Childs thinks that he is not sick but <u>playing off</u> and scolds at him awfully. Tells him that he is lazy, helpless <u>good for nothing fellow</u>! but Ass't surgeon Clark does not think though and excuses him from all duty and gives him a pass to ride in the ambulance when we march. He has also tried his best to get Osman off to Washington or discharged but cant do any thing as long as Childs has command. He says that he shall keep on him to get him off to Washington into the invalid Corps. We went into camp about a mile and a half from here when we first came into this vicinity and had orders to fix up quarters to stay at least 10 days. Our Brigade was detailed for Corps Head Qr's guard and it was all on account of the regt having a good <u>band</u> that we should serve on guard as long the troops staid in this vicinity so we took hold and worked hard two days fixing up comfortable quarters building stone fire places & stockading with logs & boards and staid in them first <u>one</u> night. Had to move at 7 oclock in the morning. It was reported that the rebs were crossing the Rappahannock & we had to form a line of battle. The night before we left our good quarters. Surgeon gave Osman orders to be ready at 5 oclock in the morning with one day rations to go to Washington into general hospital. He told me to be sure and have him ready. O how glad we all were. Osman was feeling very good about it & we began to make arrangements about his box &c. &c. Well in the morning we had him ready and when the ambulance came for the sick no order came for him to go. Charles went to see the Surgeon about it and what was our disappointment on learning that Surgeon Childs had countermanded the order sending Osman to Washington!! <u>How Mean</u>. Well we marched at 7 you know & left him to get along the best he could. It so happened that we did not go over 2 miles and he came up with us [before night we] pitched tents and went too bed but I had just turned over to drop to sleep when orders came. Come boys, wake up, pack knapsacks, strike tents & fall in in <u>two minutes</u>.... Well nothing to be done with Osman but leave him. We marched about 3 miles and in line of battle for the night spread our blankets & lay down with out putting up our little tents that was last night. We are now on the same ground and Osman came up a little while ago he road here in ambulance.... We have no overcoats & it is awful cold weather. Freeze one side & toast the other at the rail fire. No good quarters to go into. We are suffering now if we ever did. All got a cold, my nose runs [water] all the time to tell the truth we are having a pretty hard time. Suffering for our Country Ha. ha. ha. But never mind laugh it off—I am not low spir-ited by any means. Only 4 mo's longer & we are at the top of the ladder and then will begin to come down. I'll serve my time out then the gov't can just go to _____ I shant be there. I shall go right home <u>smartly</u> good time coming by and by never mind I have not seen any thing of that level dont know where the sixth Corps is now. I'm cold and cant write any more now. With much love from Herbert

The events of August and September had left Meade feeling cautious. Though he could claim a notable victory against Lee at Gettysburg, Meade felt that he had been outperformed during the Bristoe Campaign. While tempted to establish winter quarters on the north side of the Rappahannock, Meade instead succumbed to pressure from Washington for a movement against the Army of Northern Virginia.[31] *On November 7 Meade split his army in two and launched his assault. General Sedgwick with the V and VI Corps moved against Rappahannock Station. Lee had arrayed the majority of his troops behind the Rappahannock except for a small force at Rappahannock Station, left there to give Lee a fortified bridgehead should he choose to go on the offensive. Herbert, Charles, and the men of the III Corps, still under the command of General French, moved a few miles south to Kelly's Ford. Here they placed a pontoon bridge and managed to cross despite heavy fire from the enemy. The 3rd Division, III Corps was placed at the front and prepared for battle, though no engagement followed for the moment. The 10th Vermont was removed from the advancing front and placed in support of a battery of the 2nd Connecticut Heavy Artillery. The men from Vermont felt that they finally had been part of a battle, albeit from a distance.*

Following numerous breakthroughs along the Confederate line the Union forces then pushed the Army of Northern Virginia past Brandy Station and Culpeper to the banks of the Rapidan. Herbert, Charles and some companions hiked over the previous day's battlefield where the sight of dead Confederates had a grim impact on the Vermonters. Pursuit was hampered by the onset of bad weather and by November 9 Lee had crossed the river and fortified his position along the banks of the Rapidan and Mine Run rivers. Much to the frustration of the Federal troops, the men encamped and waited for supplies. It was an exasperating time for the George brothers and other band members as well, as the anticipation of battle left little time for the band to rehearse or perform. Still, the men would have their music, and various musicians continued to fill the evening air with music of all kinds.

From Charles:

Brandy Station
November 9, 1863

Well, Ellie, I have to report to you that we have been about as near being in a battle as I care to be! Saturday morning the bugle began to blow about 3:00 A.M. At 6:00 o'clock the troops began to move. The 1st Corps being ahead of us, we did not start until about 7:00 o'clock. The 2nd division being back on the railroad. Where we are going we know not, but as usual some one is smart enough to guess after a few miles travel, and Kelly's Ford rang through the ranks. We marched very fast — rushing ahead at the rate of 3 or 4 miles an hour. About noon, within a short distance of the river, cannonading was heard ahead which showed that we had run into the rebs!...

We lay down on the sandy beach of the Rappahannock till morning. In the morning I went and saw the holes made in the brick mill and store by our big guns — also saw a rebel sergeant dead on the field. Afterwards I learned that one of our boys ordered him to halt and surrender three different times, but he was fool enough to keep on running, so he got a ball put into the spine and died instantly. He was a smart looking fellow about 35 years old. Our prisoners buried him as we marched by. Another was found dead from loss of blood — his leg being shot off below the knee. In another field it was said the dead lay quite thick!

We crossed the river on pontoons. Orders were received to march at daylight! We again had a hurried march of 5 or 6 miles to the railroad where a line of battle was formed and skirmishers sent out. The rebels were in sight on the hills. We lay there about an hour when orders were received to take a building which was about a mile off and in which were rebels. Pretty soon our battery opened up on them — we could see the house and see some of the shells burst — pretty soon the showed us a battery to the left of the house and a number of shells were thrown towards us with no damage done. Pretty soon after, some cavalry showed themselves on our right — 2 or 3 shells were thrown towards them, the last of which burst directly over them. The way they skedaddled wasn't slow! We saw no more of them.

Next came orders for us to advance towards the house — we passed the house and where they had their battery, but came to a halt pretty soon afterwards, for they had made another stand — some shells were thrown towards us, one of which burst within 20 rods and a piece of the shell came whizzing over our heads!

Suddenly, the 6th Corps flag was seen coming up till their advance reached us — and what do you think? — The Advance was the Vermont brigade! And the second in the lead so that the 10th and the 2nd joined together. The 3rd was to the rear of the brigade and I did not see them. The 5th Corps is right here with us. I should have said we moved just before dark into the woods and lay last night in line of battle. The cannonading ceased at dark. It is about 10:00 P.M. now and nothing doing yet. I have given up cooking — send me a fourth pound of tea by mail.
As ever your loving Charlie

Osman started with the Company with his gun — fell before he had gone

20 rods. We haven't heard from him since. Herbert is not quite so tough as usual — and as usual, I am tough!

From Herbert:

Camp near Brandy Station Va.
Nov 10th 1863

Dear folks at home,

I'm awful cold but must write a little to you so to be ready for the mail. We are on the march again you probably know by this time. We are "right" on our Fall Campain! After the rebs double quick. make em run too every time. We left camp near Warrenton Junct last Saturday morning at sun rise and advanced to Kelly's Ford where we had a fight with the rebs, not our Brigade though for as luck would have it our Brigade was on the reserve. The Sharp Shooters and batteries kept driving the rebs out of the woods. We could see the reb sharp shooters & ours shoot at each other every time one showed his head a above the rifle pits. Shells were fired from where we stood and the rebs retreated smartly. This was first at night, and we laid our pontoons & crossed at 10 o'clock PM. In the morning (Sunday) we had a chance to look over some of the dead rebels that lay around us. One (a sergeant) lay dead close to where we camped, a lot of prisoners were in line under guard near us too. The prisoners of our regt buried the reb sergt, dug a hole in the ground & laid him in & covered him up just as you would a dead horse. but could do no other way. All the dead rebs near us were buried by us. The prisoners taken said they had much rather be taken prisoners than fight this fall. They were a fine looking lot of men, well clothed & rationed. We marched on towards Brandy Station but had not gone far before we ran in to the enemy. We began to shell & they did the same. One piece of shell came near hitting Lt. Col Henry. Some burst near us. How they whistled through the air. I never heard any shells sing before. Our Division was in the advance of the whole & our Brigade in advance of the division & our regt in advance of the Brigade so we had a pretty good chance to see the rebels run. They made the dust fly I tell you & they run into the 6th Corps & caught Jessie too. They retreated to Culpepper & we advanced to Brandy Station. Encamped in the woods that night & all day Monday till just night when just as we had got all fixed to go to bed by a good fire. Pack up was the hated order. Then the Col sang out "George," "blow the assembly." Away we went in the dark through the brush and out into the open field on rising ground not over two miles or hardly that where the wind blew hard & O so cold & not a might of wood & here we staid all night. (last night) Now wasnt it mean to take us away from our big warm fires in the woods and put us in such a place! We went back to the edge of the woods & brought some green wood & made out to get up a fire, but could not set up our fly tents for we had no stakes for a frame & the wind blew so hard, & I had no over coat but wore my blanket over me — we spread our blankets & lay down but it was too cold for me to sleep — It <u>snow'd</u> some in the night & the wind blew right through our blankets. Slept some however & in the morning my blanket was white with frost. Got breakfast & some more wood & after a long while had a good fire going. That was this morning & we have remained here all day only moved about 25 rods to get a better position & put up tents. Beaufords division of Cavalry left here this P.M. for Culpepper suppose after he routs the enemy we will go too, & I hope we shall follow them clear into Richmond. I'm ready and willing to march to Richmond if we can whip the rebs right up nice & clean....

November 14 the 10th Vermont was sent out to demonstrate towards Culpeper, marching through mud for a few days before returning to their camp near Brandy Station. The Vermonters remained alert, however, sensing that another offensive was near at hand. Somehow Herbert managed to continue rehearsing his band, boasting that the band "gets along so fast that we have got out of music to practise have sent for some to day."[32] After gathering intelligence and resupplying his troops, Meade and his generals laid out a plan for dislodging Lee and possibly destroying his army. Warren's II Corps would cross at Germanna Ford and proceed to Robertson's Tavern at Locust Grove. French's III Corps would cover the Federal right flank, crossing at Jacob's Ford and hooking up with the II Corps at the tavern. The VI Corps would support the III, and the I and V Corps would cross at Culpeper Mine Ford four miles downriver from Germanna and converge on Robertson's Tavern as well. It was a complex plan largely dependent on timing: the success of each corps' movement relied on the others with little margin for error. Originally targeted for November 24, heavy rains forced a postponement for two days.

From Herbert:

Camp near Culpepper Va
November 22nd 1863

Dear folks at home

Such a splendid day we are having down here to day. I must write home.... While we are in camp I feel just as well contented as I ever did at home but when we are on the march and I get awful tired and can't stop to rest I feel a little ugly. Some times we are not allowed to get anything to eat in all day and then have to get up at 4 o'clock in the morning and get our breakfast in the dark. Then is the time when a soldier will curse the rebellion.

But for all this I am glad I am here and that I came when I did for now I am not there to be <u>drafted</u> and then my time is all most half up. I have not heard a word from Osman yet feel very anxious to know where he is. There is no way to find out but to wait patiently for him to write or till something comes to light. Shall hope for the best. I am better than I was. Charles & I are both in pretty good health. I got those gloves you sent last night or night before last I guess it was. Did I send for <u>Kid</u>? If I did it was a mistake. I thought I wrote for thin buck-skin. Buck-skin is what I wanted. These are not fit for the Army and will not be very warm. Am sorry you sent Kid but never mind. I'll keep them for fancy purposes. I suppose you thought I could not play in buck-skin but I can if they are not too thick. My cornet is not like a fife and I do not play the fife at all now.... If I should be lucky enough to get a furlough next winter should want to go home with decent clothes on, don't want to wear any home out of the <u>field</u> for they will be **lousey**. The ground here is covered with old clothes & lice & no man can keep them off only by picking them off when they <u>bite</u>. If we take off any of our clothing nights we have to hitch them to a steak or they will crawl off where we can't find them. We can drive a pair of pants or a shirt any where with a little patience. Some of the largest ones are a little ugley and we have to use a <u>biting machine</u>. Just so with our wormy hard tack. When we fill up our haversacks we have to be carefull to put the string over a stump or something to keep them from running away haversack and all <u>Ahem</u>! What do you think of that? Ha. ha. ha. Well such is the life of a soldier.... I've got a horrid pen and guess will stop writing for this time. Do I write often enough? I like to get letters from home & spose you like to hear from me often. Father where is that promised letter of yours? Please write to me.

With a son's Respect
J. Herbert

From Charles:

Brandy Station
November 24, 1863

Well, darling Ellie, here I am again — We are on the backward move. After lying still all day yesterday waiting orders to move we got them just at dark and instead of going forward as we expected we went back towards Brandy Station, where we arrived about midnight and for the first time encamped in our old quarters, but some changed — all the lumber, poles, etc carried off and fireplaces torn down. It rained through the night some as well as this morning.

All provisions are being carried back towards Washington Where our destination is we know not. I think General Meade a cautious and sure man and wherever he strikes he will fetch something. The Army of the Potomac is in good condition, spirits and healthy — it is also large enough to meet anything the rebels have got. A man in the Division commissary Dept. says from records showing the number of rations issued, this Corps has 20,000 men and that the 2nd and 6th are larger than this, which makes 60,000 in these three Corps. Then there is the 1st, and 5th, which will make at the least calculation, 90,000 — the 11th and 12th being the Tennessee department. I know the rebel army must be small. Now I think <u>Richmond must come</u>. We were to march at 7:00 A.M., but it is now 10 oclock and we are waiting orders, and I feel as everyone else, anxious to push on!

Herbert and I get along finely together — not a word or thought except pleasant and peaceable. Last night just before we got orders to <u>pack up</u>, we were preparing to go and serenade General Morris. We gave that up and instead played some of our best pieces for the regiment — it suited them first rate — they cheered us good! We can beat the New York Band all out — we play 4 pieces they could never learn because the hardness of execution. We now play at least 30 different pieces.

On Thanksgiving Day, November 26, Meade began his Mine Run Campaign. It was an arduous time as the men of the 10th Vermont experienced the difficulties of campaigning with short rations and unpleasant weather. Complicated orders and misled troops ultimately caused Meade's plan to fail, though the 10th Vermont was to see its first real combat, what the regimental historian referred to as "a baptism of fire."[33]

At 7:00 on the morning of November 26 the troops began to move out. Bands were ordered not to play to help keep the army's movement a secret.[34] The VI Corps under Sedgwick was to follow the III Corps across Rapidan first thing in the morning, yet when the VI showed up, French's corps had not broken camp. This was but the first of many missteps French would make before the campaign was ended.[35] There were numerous delays at the Rapidan as the III Corps pressed over Jacob's Mills, and the crossing was not completed until around 4:00 P.M. French was then ordered to push south and hook up with Warren's II Corps at Robertson's Tavern. Problems continued to plague the Union troops as the 2nd Division (under Brigadier General Henry Prince), the lead unit of the III Corps, marched the wrong direction. Once this became apparent the men were forced to counter-march back to the river and bivouac for the night.[36] The following morning the III Corps headed towards Robertson's Tavern where they were to hook up with the remainder of the Union Army already moving into place. Again they experienced delays, this time when confusion arose as to which direction to take at a fork in the road. Unfortunately this series of setbacks allowed the Confederates to redeploy in reaction to Meade's move, and French was shocked to find Major General Johnson's division of Ewell's corps in his way. So just north of Robertson's Tavern, on the property of the Widow Morris, the Union troops were placed in line of battle.[37]

By noon skirmishing had become heavy and French chose to throw an entire division into battle. By 2:00 Carr's 3rd Division was ordered to support Prince's division, and the men of Morris' brigade, including the 10th Vermont, found themselves on the front line at a place known as Locust Grove near Payne's Farm. Confederate general Johnson had no way of knowing that he faced the entire III Corps, so he chose to push his division into battle. Morris' 1st Brigade took the right of the line, with Kiefer's brigade in the center and Smith's brigade on the left. No doubt intimidated by the upcoming battle, Charles, Herbert and their fellows received some backhanded motivation from their comrades in the other corps, according to a member of the 14th New Jersey:

> *We were called by the other divisions of the corps, Gen. French's pets, as they thought he favored us more than the rest, he being the former commander of the 3rd division. The 1st division, commanded by Gen. Birney, was in the rear of the 3rd division. When they were told we were to charge the enemy, the men of the 1st division exclaimed, "What! send French's pets in there? they can't fight." The General hearing them, in his blunt manner remarked, "We'll see if they can't fight. Move forward, boys."*[38]

The men of the 10th Vermont found themselves in the center of the brigade's line of battle, with the 151st New York on their right and the 14th New Jersey on their left. According to Kiefer, commanding the 3rd Division, 2nd Brigade, the troops took some time to get into position as a result of the dense trees.[39] *The Confederate troops occupied a good defensive position upon a small hill, with some men behind a fence and others in trees on the far side of Payne's Farm.*[40] *Around 3:00 the long awaited order was given and the 10th Vermont charged. Captain Darrah led Company D in front of the regiment, successfully driving the Rebel skirmishers from their positions. The fighting was brisk, but the men of Vermont, New York and New Jersey persevered, eventually forcing the Confederates away from their line and securing the fence on the crest of the hill. Many of the soldiers, including Company B of the 10th Vermont and two companies of the 14th New Jersey, continued their pursuit past the fence and found themselves separated from the brigade; after briefly holding this position, they retreated back to the recently taken line. Many of the soldiers stood their ground until their ammunition ran out.*[41]

Surgeon Joseph Rutherford described the heavy amount of firing during the fight: "So thick was the shot that it did not seem possible for a man to hold up his hand without its being hit."[42] *Some musicians found themselves in serious danger as they attended to the wounded both on and off the field. One observer watched as a cannon ball "smashed to pieces two innocent stretcher-bearers close by who were carrying off a wounded man who was insensible."*[43] *The injured man proved to be Lieutenant Henry Kingsley of Company F, 10th Vermont; it was not until after the battle that he was removed from the field. Other musicians from the brigade found how dangerous helping the wounded could be: "[Private] Darrow narrowly escaped with his life from the field. He was carrying a stretcher accompanied by J. Fitzgerald, of the band, and while looking for wounded, suddenly came upon the enemy secreted in a thick under-brush, and was suddenly greeted with a volley from the enemy. Fitzgerald fell wounded and Darrow's escape was miraculous indeed, but he came out unscratched."*[44] *Seth A. Birdsall, a musician with the 151st New York, was seriously wounded at Payne's Farm, and was eventually discharged as a result of this injury.*[45] *Charles and Herbert were fortunate in that their band was ordered to the rear to assist the surgeons. In their eagerness to obey this command some musicians left their instruments at the battlefield, and Herbert was forced to carry a number of them back with him. Miscommunication about the band's actions led to serious confrontations between Herbert and Colonel Jewett after the battle.*

There were a number of counterattacks by the Confederate forces and at times the men resorted to bayonets, but the 1st Brigade refused to move, and the Confederates eventually retired to the safety of the trees.[46] *At one point the members of the 151st New York found themselves attacked by the vaunted Stonewall Brigade and, though flanked at one point, managed to reform their line and seize their previous position.*[47] *Evening fell and the brigade was eventually replaced by the 141st Pennsylvania and other units under Birney's command.*[48]

Colonel Jewett was rightfully proud of his unit's performance: "My loss was heavy, about one-sixth of my command having been killed or wounded, but my regiment has sustained the reputation already established by our brave Green Mountain boys."[49] *Unfortunately commendations from higher up were not to be found; the 14th New Jersey was cited for its performance by General Morris, and General Carr commended both Morris and Colonel Truex of the 14th in his official report.*[50] *Though the Battle of Payne's Farm was not considered a major engagement, Morris' brigade paid heavily, with the 10th Vermont taking the highest losses of the brigade: nine killed and fifty-eight wounded. Captain Dillingham of Company B, who had been assigned to General Morris' staff, was taken prisoner. All told the 3rd Division lost around 1,000 men. The Confederates suffered as well; a member of the 33rd Virginia claimed that his brigade lost at least 450 killed or wounded.*[51] *The casualties were a shock to those new to the savagery of fighting, and Herbert and Charles were troubled by what they saw on the field and in the hospitals.*

From Charles:

On the battle field
November 30, 1863

Yesterday nothing was done in the way of fighting — troops were placed in good positions, but concluded to delay the attack until this morning.

The rebels could be seen plainly throwing up breast works — could see their batteries and see our skirmishers advancing. Last night we drew 2 days rations. This morning at an early hour all were up and ready to move. We were a few rods from the regiment in the woods and the whole brigade moved off and left us. We soon followed — struck the plank road about an hour before day light and concluded to wait till light before going any further, but we employed our time profitably by tearing up some old drawers, shirts and bed sheets into bandages for which we were complimented by Colonel Jewett and Surgeon Rutherford.

Tuesday Morning — At the appearance of light yesterday morning we followed on after the brigade and came up to it about sunrise drawn up in line of battle at the rear of the other two brigades just at the edge of a dense pine woods. At about 8 o'clock the balls opened and such cannonading I never heard before — 75 to 80 per minute — a continual roar. We were within one half mile of the enemy — all at once a sharp musketry occurred by our skirmishers being surprised by the rebs — some balls came where we were so we moved farther back and established a hospital before we built a fire. The wounded came in — 2 on stretchers and one alone — the two were from one Company of the 87th Penn. I made myself useful in building fires, bringing water etc. Our bandages came in handy as the hospital knapsack was left on the battle field of Friday....

When the 10th Vermont made a charge yelling with all their might and such a volley of musketry as we hard then, I had never heard before. This was rather the commencement of the battle — all before had been carried on by the skirmish line. The order was given for them to charge to a fence at the edge of the woods and hold that position — the rebs being on the opposite side of the field. This they all did, but one Major misunderstood the order and ordered them to charge over the fence — they did so pouring into the rebs who were about half way across the field and only 5 or 6 rods off. The fire, according to rebel accounts, was terribly destructive. We drove them back to the woods, but our exposure was so great that a retreat was inevitable. As soon as we saw them coming back, the way we skedaddled wasn't slow! I had just taken my horn off my neck and laid it down. I came off and left it, but brought everything else. Herbert came off the place with 5 horns, including one of the New York band's. I went in company with Munsell, the bass drummer, helping to carry the drum part of the way while he helped carry a stretcher with a wounded man....

We passed through a small field — the shells burst all around us, but we were spared — on we went following the hospital surgeons and nurses who were hunting for a place to stop and operate. Dark overtook us and quarters were established. The Band arrived all at the same time. Fires were lighted and the wounded were attended to as fast as we could — I worked as hard as I could till 10 P.M....

I built a separate fire for the wounded, washed and dressed them as well as I could. I learn that two of <u>Company G</u> were killed and 11 wounded. Colonel Jewett proved himself worthy of his position — two of the color bearers were killed — about 15 killed and 75 wounded in one regiment. Charley Haynes and Corporal Fulham were killed from our Company. Yesterday morning we joined our regiment on the march towards Fredericksburg.

Further particulars of Friday's fight shows 2 killed and 10 wounded from our Company — most of all on the charge <u>over</u> the fence. It was a most gallant and daring charge. Only two of the New York Band were wounded — one fell into the hands of the rebs, but was retaken immediately after. They lost two horns and the bass drum — we came off very fortunate for we all came through safe and with all of our instruments. Musicians are never supposed to go up so near the firing line as we were — we were ordered back by the Provost as soon as he saw us. But don't think we ran from <u>cowardice for we did not</u>. I went because the rest did and we thought from appearances our forces were being driven back. Our supporting column was about 15 rods back and it was our intention to get in the rear, where I supposed the Surgeon would establish another hospital. When we got there the Provost ordered us back to the Division Hospital.

It seems almost a miracle that none of us got hit. The balls were as thick as hail stones. Herbert said that to him it seemed that there was only just room for him to go between them!

Yesterday was expected to be a big battle, but there was only skirmishing. The balls have not opened yet this morning. Cold!!! Cold!!! Good bye, my dear.

The soldiers of the George brothers' brigade were oddly elated, having passed their trial by fire and managed a victory of sorts. Herbert was first surprised, then angered, when after the fight at Payne's Farm Colonel Jewett confronted him and accused him and the band of running from the battle. Despite protestations that he was ordered to withdraw, Jewett remained indignant, and Herbert eventually took his case to the brigade commander, General Morris. Morris (as well as the division surgeon) supported Herbert, but it was some time before Herbert and

Colonel Jewett would reconcile their differences. The regiment withdrew from the field and eventually arrived at Robertson's Tavern. The following day the 10th Vermont and the rest of the corps reformed with the bulk of Meade's army and followed Lee to the Mine Run River. Meade himself reconnoitered his advance lines only to discover that Lee had withdrawn, so once again the Army of the Potomac gave chase, finding the Confederates in fortified positions behind the Mine Run River. The 10th Vermont was sent from one side of the Union line to another, at one point forming a line of battle beneath the Rebel works, though they were not called upon to attack. At times the Vermonters were close enough to hear their opponents singing and talking across the line.

The temperature plummeted and both Northern and Southern soldiers suffered from exposure. Some remote pickets were found dead in the morning because of the cold.[52] Nerves were tight as it became apparent that Meade was planning on attacking the strong fortifications, and at one point Morris was told to prepare his brigade for an assault on the enemy's batteries. Following some skirmishing and two planned but unfulfilled assaults on the well-entrenched Confederates, the Union Army pulled back over the Rapidan.[53] By the time Lee decided on an attack of his own, he was surprised to find the Army of the Potomac gone. Meade had ordered a silent withdrawal; the 10th Vermont, having been on picket duty, now functioned as rear guard and was the last unit to cross the river on December 2. The regiment marched to Brandy Station and entered winter quarters, there to remain for many months.

From Herbert:

Camp near Brandy Station Va.
Dec 6th 1863

Dear folks at home

I suppose that you are looking anxiously for a letter from me about these times. Here we are all O.K. Charlie and I. No bones broken no wounds. The 10th Vt has been in one battle (The battle of Locust Grove) and lost 13 men killed and some 70 wounded I believe. Our Brigade behaved very bravely, made a charge & drove the rebs before them. Our band was in the rear with the Surgeons carrying wounded from the field. Surgeon Rutherford of our regt had charge of us and when the bullets began to whistle about our ears he leaped upon his horse & skedaddled bidding us to follow him farther to the rear. We retreated back to Division hospital and there we band boys worked all night upon the wounded. Division Surgeon told us we ought not to have gone in to the field at all but stay with him and assist the wounded. Our Col gave me the tallest **damming** I ever had for leaving the field when I did. But I was under the Surgeon and he gave us orders to retreat back out

of danger so we could work on the wounded without being exposed. So I was not to blame. The Col is mad and says he shall break up the band and send us all back to the ranks says he shall put me into the ranks but he aint big enough to do it. I enlisted as a musician & he cant make me carry a gun. He called me a <u>coward</u>. A cowardly miserable low lived **<u>Skunk</u>**. Said the same as to say he should have me court martialed for cowardice. But he can't do all these things. We done our duty on the battlefield and done more than any other musicians in the Corps. You see Col is mad because he cant have command of us in a battle. He thinks he can but Surgeon has charge of the musicians. He says he shall put it in the papers how the 10th Vt Band <u>run</u> and deserted the wounded on the field. <u>hump</u> let him put it there if he wants to. The 10th Vt Band all brought off wounded men from the field. I never took such a <u>cursing</u> and never was called such names as our Col called me, but <u>he was</u> <u>drunk</u> when I had the talk with him so I must make allowance for that. Gen'l Morris will make Brigade band out of ours & the 151st N.Y. Band together if Jewett puts us into the ranks. I had a talk with the Gen'l about it yesterday. He will do so anyway I guess. I could shoot Col Jewett easily he has abused me so. You don't know anything abt it. But enough of this.... It is pretty cold campaigning it now — I have no time to write the particulars of the marches & battle this time will when I get time. Co G. lost two killed and 13 wounded. Capt Co B is missing. Have heard from Osman. Glad he is in hospital at Washington. For Thanksgiving supper I had raw salt pork & hard tack and cold water. We were on the march left here & crossed the Rapidan that day. Will write again soon. No more now.
From Herbert

From Charles, on the same day:

Camp near Brandy Station
December 6, 1863

I am lonesome — I want to go home — <u>when will this cruel war be over?</u> One thing that makes me feel a little sad is the prospect of our band being broken up. Colonel Jewett is no man for music and has always acted as though he is trying to find something against us. General Morris favors the consolidation of the New York Band and ours — also the New York Colonel agrees. Herbert and the New York Band leader concur, but Jewett gave Herbert a big blowing up saying we were no good and ran from the battlefield — there was no chance for any discussion. The New York men were more unfortunate than we, as their stretcher bearers were many of them wounded, while we were spared — furthermore of any blame should be put anywhere it should be on the surgeons under whose orders we were. We worked all night taking care of the wounded and I cannot think of anything we could have done different or better.

General Morris is all right and I think he will take it into his own hands if necessary in spite of Colonel Jewett, as he seems very much displeased at Jewett's conduct with Herbert.

Now about the retreat etc. — Last Monday morning a general attack was expected, our Division reinforced General Warren, but a close examination of the enemy works showed it impracticable to make an attack. You will read in the papers of the advance of the skirmishers on the left at Mine Run. We assisted in taking care of the wounded at that place, being again at the front — we were the only Band on the field, too. The New York Band were ordered back by the Division Surgeons. Monday night we marched back to our old position and lay there till Tuesday night. Our regiment then went on picket. The Band and some others were ordered to carry their supplies to them (fresh beef). It was a hard job! By some mistake of the commissary one Company was missed and for that Jewett charged Herbert with keeping it and dividing it up amongst us. I wonder if he thinks there is no hereafter after the war is over when we have a right to speak!

Well, we started just at dark and marched full 25 miles before morning. We got cut off by artillery, mud and wagon trains and darkness scattered us and I finally found myself alone at the head of the Division supposing myself in the rear of one brigade. I hastened on, passing it. I kept on towards Brandy Station and arrived there a quarter of an hour <u>ahead</u> of the brigade. It was three quarters of an hour before any of the rest of the Band got in — they came in, one and two at a time. Herbert did not get in till 3:00 A.M.. Everyone seems well played out. I can outmarch any man in the Band by several miles.

Day before yesterday we moved to about 2 miles from Brandy Station into an old rebel camp — the stockade timber being divided up among the Companies — today building is going on briskly. I received your letter containing the thread, but there's one letter back yet I'm sure. Its very cold writing without any fire — I think I'll have to stop for now, my dear —

Charles and Herbert were relieved to have survived their first combat and to have settled into winter quarters at Brandy Station, but their happiness was quickly tempered when they received the grievous news of their brother Osman's death in Washington. Herbert hoped for a furlough to return to Vermont for his brother's funeral, but a recent order by General Meade severely limited the number of leaves granted, so he was unable to visit home until March of the following year. Both brothers took the loss as well as could be expected, yet Charles and

Herbert remained sensitive to their brother's absence for the rest of the war and never stopped referring fondly to his memory.
From Herbert:

Camp near Brandy Station Va
Dec 15th 1863

Dear Father and mother

It has been some little time since I have written home and you must be looking anxiously for a letter from me. I suppose you have heard the sad news of Osmans death in Washington. I did not hear of it till the official report came to the commanding officer of Co. G. I was very much surprised when Lieut Thompson of Co G told me he was dead. If you have not heard of it he died the 2nd day of this month, at Carver hospital [Ward 49] and that is all I know about it. I know nothing about the circumstances of his death. Wish I knew if he left any word of any kind and think I shall write to the Surgeon in charge of the hospital about it. Osman wrote to me after he got there and I was feeling very glad that he had got to a hospital hoping that he would get well soon when the sad news reached me of his death. Co. G. officers feel very bad about it and have been giving the Surgeons a dressing, even the Col asked them what they thought about his case now. They dont say much about it. Well, he is now where no one can harm him. I trust he is happy in Heaven. The express has come and I gave his medicine to some of my band boys that had the diarhea and it helped one, the other is pretty sick yet not able to do duty. The boots I have got on my feet they fit me well. Osman could not have worn them if he had had them before he died, one of them is almost too small for me. The shirts Charles took and will pay for them. I took both pairs of socks, and the other little things. Osman was owing me some borrowed money so I will take the boots and if father has his property I will settle with him. I will also take his colt to match mine rather than have it sold. We have just got fixed up for winter, got a log house 10 feet square covered with our little shelter tents sew'd together.... We first finished the table & chimney tonight and <u>now</u>! Oh dear me we have got to <u>move move move move</u>. fush all to fiddle sticks ... I have come to the conclusion that a soldier in the army of the Potomac is to have <u>no more</u> enjoyments. They mean to keep them on the tramp all the time. To night is the first time I have had good accomodations for writing since I left Camp Heintzleman Md and I'm going to write all night so to get all the good out of it I can. I must close this letter though for the mail goes out in a few minutes & I must <u>blow</u> Tatto on my bugle too in less than 15 minutes. We are living tip top now for soldiers, we draw for rations, soft bread beans, potatoes, onions turnips rice & molasses beef &c. Cant find fault with our grub now but must hurry for the march more soon

From Herbert

Grateful for the chance to relax, the men began to build lodgings for the winter. The Vermonters were placed near the house of the well-known statesman John Minor Botts, a comfortable campground recently occupied by Southern soldiers. The men sought to brighten their small homes with covers and drawings from popular magazines of the day. The onset of the Christmas holiday brought celebrations and performances, and Herbert, Charles and the band played often for the men. Such performances could be challenging given the weather; John Ryno of the 126th New York noted that his band's instruments froze one morning during guard mounting.[54] *Herbert also took advantage of the time to rehearse his band more frequently, so the band's repertory increased dramatically. At one point the band added a comic element to the holiday spirit by mounting mules and joining the officers for visits to the other regiments. Certainly such celebrations were welcome for the homesick soldiers. The 10th Vermont and the rest of the 1st Brigade had shed blood now, experiencing both the elation of victory and the sorrow of lost comrades.*

From Charles:

December 27, 1863
Camp near Brandy Station

Though I am comfortable and need nothing to make my body comfortable in life, but I do get lonesome and want to see my family and my wonderful wife.

We have eaten up most of the eatables that came in the express box. I have divided with Herbert,— he is going to have a pound of tea come with Hamilton's box so we will have enough to last all winter. You wonder if my face does not lengthen under the hardship of war — I don't know as it does. I keep my flesh fairly well, but you would hardly know me with these long whiskers.

The Colonel is absent now and the regiment is in command of major Chandler. Herbert is going to try for a furlough — when I see a chance I shall try for one, but as only one from a Company can go at a time my chance is extremely small.

The Company G officers are against the Band, so I expect no favors from them — You spoke of Osman's death. Mr. Bryant learned nothing — only he died with chronic diarrhea. They probably won't move his body. Father takes his death very hard.—

From Herbert:

Camp near Brandy Station Va
December 30th 1863

Dear Father

It has been some time since I have written to you or mother and I now steal a few minutes in which I will try and get a letter written. I have been so busy lately leading my band and learning new pieces to play that I have not written to any body or hardly read the news. We did not move as we expected to do when I wrote last and I was <u>so</u> glad we did not for we were fixed up so good. My tent is large enough so that the whole band except the drums can get into it and play when it is cold. We practise every day, Sundays excepted and can play 39 pieces of music, learned 9 since we came to this camp after the battle over the Rapadan. But I have to work pretty hard to play the solo all the time for my solo Cornet player is sick in the hospital and has been ever since we came here is getting better slowly however and I hope to get some help from him soon.... Poor Osman has gone to rest. I think of him very often and every time I look back and say to my self, Well I done all I could for him. I favored him all I possibly could. Argued with the Surgeons time & time and again. Tried to have them send him off long ago but Mr. Childs would not listen to me but Dr. Clark would and now Clark is so mad at the other Surgeons that he has a good mind to resign, but I think he will be head Surgeon in our regt yet. Hope he will. Well let us hope that Osman has gone to Heaven, and remember that the Lord doeth all things well. Do not be discouraged father. Cheer up! I will take Osmans place on the farm if I am spared to return to you. Keep up good spirits take good care of the colts and farm for <u>me</u>, I'm coming when this Cruel War is <u>over</u>. I would not desert and go to Canada for all the green backs Gov't ever issued if I knew I should not get caught on the way. They have put a stop to all furloughs for the present and that makes me a little <u>mad</u> for I was intending to go home this winter on 15 days furlough but <u>cant</u> now Well let em went when my 3 years are out then I'll go any how. I am enjoying very good health this winter & so is Charley. It is pretty warm now and rainy. Awfull muddy. You will never know what mud is till you travel the army roads through Va. Ankle deep. <u>Knee</u> <u>deep</u>. **<u>Waist</u>** **<u>deep</u>**. **<u>In</u>** **<u>all</u>** **<u>over</u>**!!! [*triple underlined*].... We had a gay old time here Christmas day. All our officers got <u>mules</u> to ride and they had a big time. Maj commanded the squad and he would give off all kinds of commands you know, some times he would laugh so that he could not speak. The mules were all <u>poor</u> as crows & ugly, some got thrown & Some got <u>hurt</u>. Maj got thrown once. Our band played for them and we marched at the head of the column through the brigade stopping at the head quarters of each regt had funny speeches &c, &c. O, such a funny time as we all had. Maj said I had got to ride a <u>mule</u> <u>too</u>, so I got one & got a saddle on to him, but he was so ugly I could do nothing with him, he would jump & kick & run so. I told Maj how he acted & he let me go on foot. You would have laughed I know if you had seen us. Genl Morse calls me over to his quarters frequently and gives me lessons in <u>music</u> he is a splendid musician He will make Brigade band of us by & by I guess, says he will if he can and have our officers satisfied. If he does my <u>pay</u> as <u>leader</u> will be $45.00 per month pretty good aint it. Hope he will brigade us. Well good night my sheet is full. Please write to me

Herbert

CHAPTER 4

January to May 1864

Winter Quarters, Brandy Station; The Wilderness; and Spotsylvania

From Charles:

> Brandy Station
> January 2, 1864

Another year has passed, my love, and another "on the wing." I hope this one will carry me to Vermont, and you!

Today is stinging cold and windy, but I have done my washing including myself. Our fireplace smokes a little today. Yesterday Herbert and I took a tramp through the mud to the 6th Corps. I went to the 3rd regiment and found George Peach. I do not think their quarters are as good as ours — they will have a long ways to go for wood by Spring. One regiment the 122 Penn went past on their way home while we were there. Many of the boys are re-enlisting. Did not see anyone else I knew. Herbert put in his time with the Band talking with their leader. On our way back we called to see Mr. Bryant, but he was absent.

Our regiment was mustered in for pay last Thursday. We had 15 new recruits a few days ago.

General Morris is in command of the 2nd Division now, their General being home on furlough. I think if he does not leave our Division that in 6 weeks time we will be mustered as a Brigade Band at their pay. Our line officers are mostly in favor and I guess the field and staff officers will not object.

I expect Colonel Henry is expected back soon. They have stopped giving furloughs in this regiment. Lieut. Barber got a dispatch the other day telling of the death of his child and could not go home.

It is very cold and I can hardly write. Yesterday we built a rousing fire in our fireplace and set it aflame, but we put it out quickly.

The beginning of 1864 found the 10th Vermont Regiment enjoying an excellent campsite outside of Brandy Station, Virginia. The band took advantage of this rare period of calm to practice and perform for their fortunate comrades. The men from Vermont also enjoyed comparatively fine lodgings, having taken over huts constructed by the Rebels when they had been camped at the same location. Though uncomfortably close to the Army of Northern Virginia, there were basically no hostile encounters at this time, and at worst the Vermonters were called upon for picket duty. Fatigue had taken its toll and the 10th Vermont and other regiments posted extremely large sick lists.[1] Fresh recruits were brought in for many of the regiments. Upward of twenty new men joined each company and the 10th Vermont was returned to a semblance of fighting strength.[2] Also at this time came some of the first furloughs for the regiment, but only a few men were able to take advantage of this rare opportunity.[3] For others it was a time of visits from home, and the 10th Vermont hosted many officers' wives, creating a festive atmosphere in camp.[4] Christmas and New Year's Day were celebrated in what style could be arranged. The band of the 10th Vermont, as well as the bands of other regiments, contributed as only they could, according to Lieutenant Abbott of Company D: "I was awakened long before daylight by the band serenading the birth of the New Year."[5]
From Herbert:

Camp 10th Vt Infty Near Brandy Station Virginia
Jan 9th 1864

Dear father and mother.

I got a good long letter from <u>mother</u> last night and was glad to get it to for had not read one from any body since 1864 came in. It was the longest letter I have rec'd from home in a good while, two whole sheets. Then you got every thing ready for <u>my</u> <u>reception</u> with Poor O's remains did you? Well

I wish it could not of <u>have</u> been so, but no, they won't let me go home at all now. Orders from Army Head Quarters <u>now</u> are that <u>no</u> furloughs are to be given to any one, neither sick nor dying. All those sent in from our regt came back <u>disapproved</u>. So I am up a stump about going home. I have a good mind to be mad about it for I did want to see old Newbury this winter and all the folks up on the hill you know. Suppose our chamber looks pretty well but I wont probably have a chance to see it till Sept 1865 — Then if Im alive and well guess I'll just give you a call. I feel just as though I could. Strike Genl Mead for issuing such orders about furloughs. I won't play for him if he don't do better. What's to hinder a poor <u>soger</u> from going home in the winter while the army is lying still? There will be more deserters by no furloughs being given than there would be if they could all go. Hang it I feel real vexed because I can't go.... About that little <u>testament</u>. It was lost with the rest of my things in my knap sack and I wrote to Ruth for another one and she sent it to me by mail, a real nice one. I do not wholly neglect my bible but shall have to confess that I write, & read, & study <u>music</u> more than any thing else. It's no lazy job to instruct a young band especially when the instructor does not understand it any too well him self. My table is covered with music all the time & every few minutes <u>rap</u>. <u>rap</u>. <u>rap</u>. "Come in." In comes a band boy. Well Herb, can you tell me what <u>that</u> means or how do you play <u>that</u> or will you please take my horn and play that strain and a thousand other questions, which I take pleasure in answering or doing. Evenings when it is warm enough we go out and play. Practise twice a day unless it's awful cold. So you see I have enough to do, but can find time to read too I spose. I hope we will not move from here this winter. They keep up the story that this Brigade is going to N.Y. when the draft comes off but I don't see it. We have blankets enough to sleep warm but don't have butter & cheese enough. Oh, don't I wish I was at home this month to eat some of Mother's good butter and brown bread, biscuit, pies &c. &c. O <u>My</u> it's no use talking. Hard tack and pork with once in a while a loaf of soft bread & fresh beef, beans once a week. Well I'm in for it.

Good by for this time
Herbert

From Charles:

Brandy Station
January 12, 1864

We play only when we choose — the regiment have nothing scarcely for us to do. We practice every day, but mostly in one of the tents. It is certainly a pleasure to play in the Band — as much as to go to a good <u>sing</u>. When we go serenading it is usually voluntary on our part — go when and where we have a mind to — but all this takes only a small portion of our time. The rest has to be passed away in reading, writing or playing some kind of game.

I have made me a set of chess men to pass the time with when I can get any one to play with me. When I am done with one recreation I seek for something else. — Well, it is one day later and I shall soon be interrupted again by the call to practice — so will hasten to tell you of our last night's adventure. We took it into our heads to serenade John Minor Botts. So Herbert went and got permission and also got an officer, Captain Frost of Company A to

Members of the Botts family gather on their front porch where the band of the 10th Vermont performed many serenades during their stay outside of Culpeper, Virginia (Library of Congress).

go with us. (there is the bugle call — must go) — (got through — had a good time — practiced in one of the tents). About 8 P. M. we started and after a march of a mile or so we found ourselves before the elegant house of the renowned J. M. Botts! We opened our "brass batteries" and soon a man appeared with a bunch of grey whiskers on his chin and a pleasant eye and countenance — rather good looking for an old man.

We were invited up on the piazza, ascending 5 or 6 steps we found ourselves upon a large piazza, as much as 20 feet high. We amused and pleased him with our best prepared pieces and such others as he called for, which consisted of old National Airs. Such as drank liquor had what they wanted. He told us a story about an experience of his in St. Petersburg, Russia six years before. A lady of a party of several who, when something was said about the song "Yankee Doodle," wanted to know what was meant by "Doodle." Mr Botts answered, "My dear madam, what would a Yankee be good for without a Doodle"? — I didn't think the joke had much point!...

Guess I'll finish this page with a big KISS and turn over a new leaf.

Recruits are coming in every day—fifty came in last night—our Company is full again and others are nearly full. We hear the President has called for a million men to serve 90 days—I can hardly believe it. Strange stories float around camp—that we are going to New York—to Harper's Ferry and another that we got Texas.—

Herbert remained focused on the band, training his players (he received a new band recruit in February) and arranging music. By the end of January both brothers claimed that the band could play upwards of fifty pieces. The stylistic diversity of the literature performed was as impressive as the number of pieces learned. At various times Herbert and Charles referred to playing operatic excerpts, dance music, popular songs, marches, and the obligatory "patriotic airs." Herbert appears to have been comfortable with this variety of musical styles, and such confidence would explain the recognized quality of his band. The regiment was fortunate to have a musician of Herbert's talent and dedication. Charles, on the other hand, gamely worked on his performance skills, eventually gaining enough confidence to see himself as a valuable member of the band. Herbert also seems to have established a sense of pride and comradeship within the band, something not always found in other bands.[6]

From Herbert:

Camp near Brandy Station Va
Jan 17th 1864

Dear folks at home.

Recd your letter dated the 13th this evening. The mail carrier handed it to me just as we got through playing retreat at sunset. Was glad to get it too for you (Mother) are the only correspondent I have that writes every week or more every week. Neither Em, nor A.M. nor Ruth nor Jere nor any body pretend to write oftener than once a month except Jere. He writes once in two weeks & sometimes Em writes quite often. Charles gets lots of letters from his wife and most every one seems to get more letters than I do. But I hear from my dear old home nearly every week & that is worth every thing. I'm <u>awful</u> <u>glad</u> that you are going to send a <u>box</u>. Every body's getting a box from home now a days. Winter is the time for a soldier to enjoy him self if he don't have to move and has something good to eat. We get tired of Uncle Sams rations of hard tack & pork and long for a good meal of home <u>food</u> such as brown bread doughnuts pie pudding &c. &c. I want quite a quantity of stuff <u>and chg it to me.</u> viz. considerable butter & cheese, dried apple, and a few green ones, a big loaf of your <u>good</u> brown bread, a few mince <u>pies</u> just to see if I have forgotten how they taste & some of those things that I could always smell a mile from the house. <u>Doughnuts!</u> <u>Sausage</u>, sage or savory, to cook our fresh beef with. A little saleratus, Maple sugar, a bunch of white envelopes and a chain of writing paper like this. If Em is there let her send me any thing she likes in the <u>nutt</u> line. Im a great lover of nutts but haint had any for a year & a half now. If Ruth sends anything perhaps she will send a stuffed turkey or something of the kind. Send us just what you are amind to besides what I have mentioned.... O I want to go home so this winter, but <u>cant</u>. Aint it too bad? I am quite well contented though I have so much music to <u>play</u> with. We play 48 pieces now, have 50 in less than a week. Our old band never played over 45. Well I must close as it is around mail time. Shall look for the box inside of two weeks.

As ever yours
Herbert

From Charles, the same day:

Camp near Culpepper
January 17, 1864

Darling Ellie — I wish I could help you this winter so cold. I do not guess but I know that I am having by far the easiest time this winter. No work or hardships to endure and I guess my living is about as good as yours. I wish you could have had some of the soup we had to throw away because it became sour — we made too much and it was real good. We also have a good plate of beans waiting to be eaten — a good loaf of soft bread apiece. Our pork is good — much better than we had last winter. Our fresh beef, too, is tender and nice. We have a good frying pan to cook in now. We have tea — all we want — we sleep warm and in fact lack nothing but my little family to make life perfect. Last night we serenaded our beloved General who has just retuned. There were two ladies in his tent (I think his wife and sister) and a little boy about 8 years old who came over this morning to borrow Puffer's drum.

They are building a meeting house — wonderful! We now have 48 pieces we play. We can now play most anything they can bring us right off. The nearest we ever came to breaking down was one time on the march. Just at dusk while we were playing on a piece we knew but little, Herbert stubbed his toe which broke up the air of the piece and by the time he got going again he stepped into a mud hole — the rest of us couldn't see the notes and had to "make up" our parts, it took a while before Herbert got back on his job — but we soon picked up again and all went well.

<u>Thursday, January 21, 1864</u> — All quiet in the Army of the Potomac. No news of importance. We are doing some pretty good playing lately. Last night we went to General Morris's (by request) and played for the ladies, who gave us $5.00, which we shall expend for new music. We then went about a mile

and a half to serenade Captain Chase, Brigade Commissary. Had a first rate time — they treated us with a frosted cake, 2 feet long and one and a half wide — to finish up he presented us with $10.00 — pretty good for one night. Tonight we are to play at General Haus's for a party. It is plain that our Band is the favorite in the Division....

Mr. Bryant called to see us a few days ago — he is to put up a grave stone on Osman's grave when he goes through Washington on his way home.

An extended stay at winter quarters allowed for a variety of entertainments that kept the musicians extremely busy. Concerts for the soldiers were a common occurrence, and there was a grand ball that proved to be the talk of the camp: "A spacious hall, ninety-six by thirty-six feet, covered with tarpaulins and tent flies, had been erected by details of men from Carr's Division, and profusely decorated with evergreens and flags. Three bands were in attendance, and the whole scene was brilliantly illuminated."[7] At least one band from the George brothers' brigade, "the old '87th Silver Cornet Band,'" was involved with the festivities and "discoursed music rarely equalled and seldom excelled."[8] Another soldier described the pleasure provided by the musicians but did not pass up the opportunity for a humorous jab at his superiors: "The 1st New Jersey Brigade Band, and 87th Pennsylvania were engaged, and the music was excellent.... The leading generals of the Potomac army were present, the most prominent among them being Meade, Warren, Hancock, French and others. They enjoyed themselves very well, but the most of them were better at fighting than at dancing."[9]

While the soldiers were delighted with the music from the bands, they also enjoyed performing music themselves. Charles Richardson of the 2nd Vermont witnessed a performance by "two violins two guitars two flageolettes and a banjo," and an abundance of liquor ensured "a right merry time nearly all night."[10] Some of the local residences gave the opportunity for impromptu performances, with varied results, according to Lieutenant William Burroughs of the 14th New Jersey: "They have a very fine piano in it, and as Captain Alstrom is Provost Martial now, and stationed with us, it comes very opportune and we make the country around hideous with our howls."[11] The troops modified local structures and even constructed buildings to host their performances. According to another member of the 14th New Jersey: "Perhaps I have spoken of a concert saloon we have in this neighborhood. It has been largely attended all along. Now it is going to be converted to a church for our regiment and the 151st N.Y."[12] Some soldiers of a more religious bent complained when officers used the chapels for parties and dances.[13] Regardless of the venue such activities were invaluable to the troops, as noted by surgeon Rutherford of the 10th Vermont: "If it was not for thes amusements I do not know what we should do it would be so very dull. We can't read nor write all the time, and playing cards is all played out, and we shall have hardships enough by and by—to warrent our enjoy ourselves reasonably while we can."[14]

From Herbert:

Camp near Brandy Station Va
Jan 28 1864

Dear father and mother

I recd the box you sent me yesterday all O.K. Everything was in good order & I thank you ever so many times. You did not get my letters telling some things that I wanted but you sent most every thing I asked for excepting the brown bread and one of my tent mates got a box the same day with 3 big loaves of brown bread & I have all I want as long as it lasts. I shall not hurt myself eating for I have been in the army long enough to know how to eat & not hurt my self. Half the deaths in the army are caused by the men eating too much Pork &c. It is very warm now, we sweat awfully while practising. It is as warm as June in Vt and as pleasant every way. The mud has dried up and it really looks like summer. I presume while we are uncomfortably warm you are uncomfortably cold in VT but we shall have some cold weather, cold rains before April. What good health I have had since we left Seneca Md haven't I? I haven't seen a sick day, not what you might call sick since November 1862, I am enjoying better health than I have before since I was 14. Just as tough & fat. My weight is 135, I'm getting quite a name too as leader of the 10th Vt Band. We are called on to play Division HdQr's quite often. We play 50 pieces now & I expect 15 more from Dodsworth N.Y. soon. The old Col thinks we play pretty well now, & he partly apologized to me for calling us cowards too, says we obeyed orders, & thats the same thing as apologizing. I have just been getting up a temperence pledge in our band, I drew it up as follows. "We the undersigned members of the 10th Vt Band do promise that we will not drink any whiskey while doing duty as a band as long as we remain in the service of the U.S. Any member that shall willfully break his promise shall forfeit $1.00 to the Band for a vote of two thirds of its members. I have got most all the names of the members on to day, got two that always drink when we go serenading & have it offered us. Hope they will keep their pledge of course I signed it first but it won't help me any, I'm such an old drinker that I shall break it. Ha, ha, ha. Well its so warm I will close. Father you have not written yet. As ever your affection
Herbert

P.S. We play for a funeral this PM, one of the Cols died with chronic diarrhea, was wounded at the battle of Locust Grove too. Name is Bullard. The measles are in the regt. The mail has come & I got a letter from mother. Glad she is going to Concord. Hope the colts will break <u>good</u>. What do you do for a horse to drive now? Father while mother is at Concord please write me a letter. <u>Do</u>. I saw Mr. Bryant to day, he goes away next week. He is going to get a stone put up at Osman's grave in Washington. I send you my <u>revolver</u>. Colts five shooter all loaded, take care of it till I come. I sent my old bugle too by him. No more now.

Herbert

Along with musical performances, soldiers on both sides of the line managed to manufacture other forms of entertainment, including various games and even large-scale snowball battles.[15] One of the most popular pastimes for the men was the relatively new game of baseball, and soldiers of all backgrounds enjoyed the sport, according to Edward Bushnell of Company E: "There has been a matched game of bass-ball between the Commissioned and Non-commissioned officers of the regiment The contest not decided to-day."[16] Some enterprising members of the VI Corps, 3rd Division, put on minstrel shows, apparently of high enough quality that they could charge admission.[17] Camp at Brandy Station was not all fun, unfortunately. There were still the dreaded drills and reviews, and of course the bands were on hand to provide music for most of these activities. At brigade reviews the bands of the 10th Vermont, 87th Pennsylvania, and 151st New York took turns playing, giving other band members some rare time off.[18] Still, the resulting schedule was demanding to say the least. In the month of January alone the band of the 10th Vermont performed 3 concerts for the troops, 5 serenades for officers, 4 concerts for civilians, and one funeral.[19] With appearances at division headquarters, as well as playing for dress parades and inspections, the result was a special performance almost every day, in addition to rehearsal once or twice a day. Despite their numerous playing commitments, musicians were not exempt from other more unpleasant duties. At one point the drum corps of the 87th Pennsylvania was sent out to gather stones to help pave the streets in camp.[20]

Not all of the activities of the 10th Vermont were harmless fun. Soldiers were largely dependent on civilian sutlers for a variety of supplies and luxuries not provided by the government. Though grateful for the amenities these merchants offered, there was no small amount of resentment at the exorbitant prices some charged. Believing themselves to have been fleeced by one such merchant, the Vermonters retaliated by upsetting a sutler's tent late one night and making off with both money and goods.[21]

After relaxing for over two months, the brigade was again called to duty the first week of February. Members of the regiment were sent on a brief and unpleasant demonstration along the Rapidan, marching along the banks in the rain for two nights and a day, fighting knee-deep mud but no Rebels. Captain McManus of

the 151st New York summed up the regiment's attitude toward their latest assign-
ment: "What has been accomplished by this grand movement of the Army I cannot
learn, and wholly unable to conjecture."[22]
   From Charles:

Camp near Culpepper
February 5, 1864

We have a new recruit in the Band — a Mr. Wells — 44 years old and has a
son in Company D. We have the use of the meeting house to practice in —
it is a building 18 × 32 made of split and hewn logs for walls and floor.
   The ancient historical feat of Napoleon "marching 50,000 men straight
up a hill and then marched them down again" has been eclipsed by our march
to the Rapidan and back again. Saturday morning about 4 o'clock we were
surprised by the beat of drums — at 7 o'clock we were all ready to move, but
got no orders till about 5 P.M. when we had orders to march immediately —
leaving one well man in each Company to guard the tents. Our orders were
to leave our horns — all the Band, but Herbert and Dick were ordered to go
with the Hospital Corps. Everything indicated a fight. A drizzling rain made
it slippery and muddy. Dark overtook us at Culpepper — then came the hardest
of marches, but I will skip over a description of that march — dark, mud,
stones, stumps and brush etc, but it was about the hardest march we ever had!
We arrived at Poney Mountain and camped in a piece of pine woods about
9 o'clock. Herbert, Dick and I camped out in the wet and slept pretty well.
We heard firing all day Saturday — Sunday found everything quiet — everyone
drying blankets. The next morning about 8 o'clock we were on the move
towards the Rapidan. We finally reached where the fighting was — the first
Corps did the fighting. A rebel cavalry force had crossed the river — our troops
drove them back gaining a decided victory. They followed them back over
the river — fording and carrying their arms and cartridges over their heads.
They took 1300 prisoners — after which we all came back to camp, and the
Band (all who had brought their instruments) played several pieces. All were
lively and cheerful, enjoying the mud first rate. Once we heard shooting in
the distance, but it was of no consequence. Later we heard noise going on in
one of the other regiments and in gong over saw the fun — about a dozen men
were holding a blanket and tossing men up in the air. With a one, two, three!
The victim would go 12 or 15 feet into the air. Anything for sport!
   Last night at the sound of the bugle everyone knew where he was going
and every one gave a shout — but such a march! Mud from 4 to 16 inches
deep. We marched all the 13 miles without a stop and in the darkness — there
were a good many stragglers I can tell you!

After returning to camp at Brandy Station the 10th Vermont once again enjoyed a calm interval, now playing host to a number of dignitaries from Vermont, including recently elected Governor John Gregory Smith, cousin of Union general William F. "Baldy" Smith. The Reverend Charles Parker of Waterbury, Vermont, visited the regiment at the end of February and commented on the passionate participation by many of the soldiers in prayer meetings and services.[23] Perhaps it was this resurgence of religious activity that led Herbert to propose a temperance pledge for his band. If the band members were drinking too much it had little effect on their music, as the band was recognized for performing well; on February 25 the bands of the 10th Vermont and the 151st New York were chosen to play for division review, an occasion of which the George brothers were justifiably proud.

Two letters from Charles:

Camp near Brandy Station
February 12, 1864

Dear Ellie — I haven't written for several days I know, but we have been busy cleaning up since our muddy march.

The Band gets along pretty well now — Herbert has the blues pretty hard now. Today we went out to practice without the 1st E Flat Bass and the 2nd couldn't keep the time which made Herbert a little out of sorts. — The drum Corps is just beating out tattoo — I think I shall miss the drums when this cruel war is over! I guess we are the only temporate Band in the Army of the Potomac — pretty good for us, eh?

It is not quite so cold today, but we have had it very cold — water would freeze within 2 or 3 feet of the fire. I must tell you about the time we had serenading Thursday night. We had just got our suppers out of the way and commenced the cold evening by our various means of entertainment — some reading, some playing backgammon, cards or chess, some telling stories etc. when an order to go to General French's disturbed our quietness. Herbert tried to beg off, but it was no go. We were soon on the road rubbing our ears and thrashing our hands in the cold. We passed through Bandy Station which has been altered greatly since I saw it last. Large storehouses have been built and piles and piles of army stores. We finally found his quarters about 3 miles from us — there we found the 106th New York Band with whom we changed off—first one playing and then the other. We played in the house — the officer who had charge of us was so drunk he didn't know anything. Our style of music seemed to take better than that of the 106th — they were dismissed some time before we were. It was so cold we couldn't play out doors without our instruments freezing up.

February 23, 1864
11:00 P.M.

Dearest Ellie — What do you suppose set me to writing to you at this time of day? About 9:00 o'clock some had gone to bed — Herbert was writing — when along came Captain Frost to have us give them some music. We rounded up some violins and we all went down to the meeting house where were assembled 6 ladies and both the Colonel and the Major and 6 or 8 other officers. They finally decided to excuse all of us except Herbert and Dick who played their horns with the violins. They had a bully good time — the floor was somewhat rough but it only made the jump the smarter! We stayed a while and came back — so not feeling very sleepy I thought I might as well write a little.

We were paid off yesterday — I received $26.00. Today I had my picture taken — it is for Jere. I had a letter from Ruth with a picture of her children. Dick has just come in playing the clown.

I am arrested for not appearing at rehearsal today — the court-martial to come off tonight!

Yesterday we had Division review — two bands united. Tomorrow there is to be a Corps review — that is a big thing — I wish you could see it. There is nothing so magnificent in war as a Corps Army Review. Our two bands have been practicing together today. Colonel Jewett has refused to give us up for a Brigade Band — but did it in a gentlemanly way, satisfactory to all.

Tonight Herbert and I got to fooling and he pulled out a bunch of my whiskers. I will send to Nellie to tickle her nose with.

From Herbert:

Camp near Brandy Station Va
Feby 27th 1864

Dear folks at home

I have time to write just a line or two this PM, have been pretty busy for some time blowing and writing music. We had a Div review day before yesterday and I had command of all the musicians in our Brigade about 50 of them. I consolidated my band & the 151st N.Y. band and made a big band & made big music. I lead them both of course and then I had to see to the drummers & fifers, give them their instructions for the ruffles of honor to Maj Genl French who reviewed us. Every thing went off well. All were satisfied with the music. There is to be a Corps review in a few days & I shall have the same command again. It was to take place to day but the 6th Corps and our 1st Div have gone on a reconnoisance in force over the Rapidan. They passed here about 9 o'clock this A.M. I saw Jim George and he wanted me to tell you to tell his folks that he had gone out on a 4 days reconnoisance and they would not hear from him till he got back to camp again. It is very fine weather now. Gov Smith was here to day and we played for his dinner. There are some 10 or 12 ladies in camp now, and they had a dance last night. I played the cornet with the violins for them & Col Henry gave us all a dollar apiece, feel pretty tired & sleepy to day. I suppose Lieut Charley Bailey is at home now, wish I could go home for 15 days. <u>Can't</u>

Well good day all
From Herbert

The month of March saw a great many changes in the Federal armies, not the least of which was the appointment of Ulysses S. Grant as lieutenant general and commander of all Union forces. One band was given the honor of performing for Grant's arrival at Brandy Station, yet this proved to be a dubious honor as the assignment entailed standing and playing in the rain for some time. After many soggy hours the men were dispersed without a glimpse of their new commander. Later it was learned that Grant had already passed.[24] *The unpleasant weather was not an uncommon occurrence as there were too many days of snow, rain, and ice. On a positive note Herbert was finally granted a furlough and returned to Vermont from March 14 through 28. While home he missed a grand review of the entire army, the likes of which few of the soldiers had seen before, according to Edwin Hall of Company G: "All the Infantry, Cavalry, Artillery, Train wagons, and Ambulances that belonged to the Corps were out in full uniforms and presented an imposing spectacle. Such a one as only those that belong to the army can appreciate."*[25]

Charles wrote to Herbert of the antics of the band in his absence:

I have been out bumming with the <u>Yorkers</u> all day, and have just got into camp. Just imagine what a splendid Serenading party our fragments and the yorkers would make and you can imagine what a <u>nice</u> time we had playing at Corps Head Quarters. In the first place we had a small <u>affair</u> to attend to at <u>corps</u> <u>review</u>. Perhaps you would like to know how it was managed. To begin with it is the coldest day we have had since we serenaded Gen. French. "Father" carried his fife and went with the drum corps. Mc. carried an E flat one of the yorkers, I carried "Father's," and the rest that had horns carried them. Garvin and Puffer carried their drums. Clark, Barker, and Kent went empty handed with the drum corps. Sexton excused by surgeon & Delos stayed for guard. We had a bitter cold time of it I tell you: any amount of fun and play. All good natured, <u>not a bit of a quarrel</u>. The review was in front of John Minor's house or between there and the railroad, in the usual way. We were reviewed by Gen. French with his long string of guards, women, children, darkeys and all. We played <u>No.</u> <u>ten</u> while passing in review, and just as we took our position in the rear of the brigade to go home, orders were given to report at Corps Head Quarters, I think there was a mistake somewhere. I think the Gen expected the 10th Vt instead of the Yorkers, they called for some of our pieces, but didn't hear 'em muchly. We played till most sunset. Played <u>Yankee</u> <u>Doodle</u> <u>three</u> **<u>times</u>** **<u>double</u>** **<u>quick</u>**. A few <u>National</u> <u>aires</u>, a few <u>marches</u>, &c. Had a good supper and got back sound. That is the out lines of the days work. Yesterday we had a General inspection. Dick was <u>on</u> <u>it</u> some. I guess he feels some bad about his furlough and some lonesome because the <u>leader</u> is gone. I tell you it is lonesome without you. We miss you very much. I had the <u>Night</u> <u>Mare</u> and <u>Stud</u> <u>horse</u> last night. They have just played the last beat of tattoo. Nathan and father abed, my fingers are cold, and — Well I will wait awhile and think what to write. I have got only three letters to send you.[26]

Following the appointment of Grant the Army of the Potomac was again reorganized, and the 10th Vermont found itself in the 1st Brigade (Morris), 3rd Division (Ricketts), VI Corps (Sedgwick). This was the last time the regiment would suffer reorganization and the 10th Vermont would remain under this command structure for the duration of the war. This was fortunate as their division and corps commanders were solid professionals whose leadership helped the VI Corps to be recognized as one of the finest units in the Union Army.

As part of the new assignment the men of the 10th Vermont found themselves in the same corps as the original Vermont Brigade (2nd—6th Vermont Infantry Regiments), and Herbert and Charles had the chance to meet up with friends and relations. Morris' brigade was also expanded to include the 87th Pennsylvania

Wartime portrait of Maj. Gen. James B. Ricketts, commander of the 3rd Division, VI Corps (U.S. Army Military History Institute).

and the 106th New York, a unit one Vermonter was to refer to as "our favorite fighting companion as a regiment."[27] *There was a fair amount of resentment at the reorganization, though the 10th Vermont was pleased to be fighting under the Greek Cross, well-known emblem of the prestigious VI Corps. Of more concern to the Vermonters was the required change of base that followed their new assignment. The men were forced to leave their comfortable huts in exchange for dirty and run-down accommodations that they spitefully referred to as "Camp Miserable."*[28] *After hosting the armies of both the North and South the region was stripped bare. Roswell Hunt of Company D tried to describe the troubled landscape to a friend: "this is not much like Austin farme here fore thare is not a fence to be sene in the regen & thare is graves all over the ground & a bout every hous is burnt & it is seldom that thare is citzen in the cuntry for thare is in the army."*[29] *Despite the paucity of the new surroundings, the band members had reason to celebrate. During his furlough Herbert had secured new instruments and on April 6 they shared their good fortune in an evening concert for the troops.*[30] *According to Lemuel Abbott of Barre, Vermont, such performances were greatly appreciated as the music "relieves the monotony of dull camp life."*[31] *Abbott also noted that the regiment took great pride in their band: "are proud of our band, it being one of best regimental bands in the army."*[32]

From Charles:

Brandy Station
March 28, 1864

Dear Ellie — Herbert is back and we have our new horns. Mine is so much better than the old one that I love to play it.

Well, I can write some news — We are transferred to the 6th Corps — the whole Division — we now belong to the First Brigade — 3rd Division, 6th Corps. Our Brigade is still commanded by our <u>good</u> General Morris. But it is enlarged by the addition of 2 regiments from the 3rd Brigade — the 87th Pennsylvania and 106th New York — they both have Bands — the 87th is the best Band in the Division and there is few better in the whole army. Guess we shall have to be in the shade now, but then we can be second best in the Brigade and also in the Division.

The women are all ordered out of the Army — they will leave tomorrow I suppose.

<u>Saturday morning</u> — Well, I have lots to say so guess I'll begin where Herbert got back — Everybody was glad to see him and it was late before I had a chance to find out anything about home ... and anyway he fell asleep with his head on my portfolio. Our quiet enjoyment was of short duration — we received marching orders. We had heard rumors that we were to change

camps but hardly believed it, but that morning at 9:00 o'clock we were on the march with everything packed — went about 3 miles into the 3rd Maine's quarters and were feeling pretty good over our good luck for they were better than our old quarters, but all of a sudden it was discovered that there had been a mistake made — so we next went to one that was too small to accommodate such a regiment as ours — we then went to another camp which was plenty large enough for us and good tents. The Band got first rate tents, but just as we began to get settled an orderly came with orders to blow the assembly — we had to move <u>again</u> — this time about 1/2 mile only where we took possession of an old camp of the 40th New York, where we are now. This camp is not near so good as our old one — the streets are narrow and dirty and the tents are low. It appears that the 40th New York was a Dutch regiment. Nathan's brother is brigade wagon master so we get some favors that others do not. Today he brought up a load of boxes, tables etc. and I am now writing this on our old table which makes it seem like home. We are within 2 miles of Culpepper and about one mile from the railroad to the west of it....

The extended break did wonders for the men of the regiment and morale was high: "But the Tenth Vermont leads the army in such a way and is the pride of general officers from army headquarters down," observed Lemuel Abbott; "it is just the same in drill, parade, forced marching, fighting or any place it is put. The men have great esprit de corps, *and strive not to be outdone by any other regiment in anything."* [33] *The regiment must have impressed at least some of their commanding officers; at the corps review of April 16 they were given the honorary position in front and at the right of line.* [34] *The band of the 10th Vermont must have also continued to impress as it was repeatedly chosen for prestigious performances.*

Two letters from Charles:

Camp Mud
April 11, 1864

My dear Ellie — It has rained and rained and being camped in this muddy place is terrible. 120 men are cutting stockade timber — we are going to move on to the hill — from the preparations one would think we were going to stay our time out right here — but I can't see staying here very long....

We got our blankets wet again and slept under them wet. You would be afraid to do such a thing, wouldn't you? I have slept many times with my clothes wet and all my blankets wet.... We are getting to be about as indifferent to these discomforts as aborigines! General Grant is making a general overhauling of the "Army of the Potomac" — most every day we get some new orders — a few days ago he ordered no more regimental pioneers.

<u>Tuesday evening</u> — Yesterday we had Brigade drill — I had to "tag" the Colonel around as a bugler. When we have brigade drill, the four Bands are ordered to be in one place — they take turns playing — one band strikes up as soon as another stops. Herbert's new horn is the best in the Army of the Potomac — the best I ever heard — so loud and clear....

We did not get any mail for several days on account of the rain washing the tracks and bridges. Tonight I got a letter from mother — she spoke highly of you Ellie and thinks Nellie just as well governed as sister Ruth's children. I think that is a pretty good compliment for you for every one that knows Ruth knows that few excel her in management of children. I think if you are acknowledged by my mother to be as good as Ruth — you'll do. I love you greatly.

My candle is short having only the wick left — I must stop before I am left in the dark. It is a soap candle stick — a piece of bar soap cut square with a hole in it.

Camp near Brandy Station
April 19, 1864

Yesterday we had a Corps review by General Grant. He was mounted upon a splendid horse and the most beautiful and splendid saddle I ever saw. He very politely raised his hat as our General passed.

We acted as the Brigade Band, notwithstanding the 87th are in the Brigade. Herbert was very much surprised to be chosen in preference to them. I think they were a little jealous. We were wanted last night, both to serenade Division General Ricketts and General Morris, but we can play at only one place at a time — so we didn't accept.

Yesterday some artillery and some pontoon bridges passed on the way to the front. This morning the ambulances came around and carried away all the sick — everything looks like an advance pretty soon. I don't want you to feel so out of sorts with "Uncle Sam" — he is a good old "Uncle" after all. No doubt it does seem as if we weren't being treated very well — It is out of the question now to be given a furlough — none are given now.

Most of the Companies have moved into their new quarters, but no one expects to stay in them long. What does your father say about the presidential campaign? Does he favor Copperheadism or Unionism? Copperheadism is at a great discount here. I never heard a soldier say anything about them but what they expressed real disgust — they would shoot one quicker than they would a rebel. They'll have nothing to do with anyone in sympathy with the South.

On April 25 Colonel Jewett, the original commander of the 10th Vermont, was forced to resign due to his deteriorating health. Most of the soldiers and officers gathered to see him off and the band performed in his honor. Lieutenant Colonel Henry replaced Jewett, and Captain Dillingham, recently returned from four months in Libby Prison, was promoted to major.[35] By April the sutlers were ordered to leave camp, and the soldiers knew this to be a sign that the Army of the Potomac was preparing to move.[36] Company drills became more frequent and anxiety grew with the approach of combat. The days of concerts, games, and carefree camaraderie had come to an end as the soldiers knew they would soon return to the horrors of the battlefield.

From Herbert:

> Camp 10th VT Infty near Culpepper Va
> May 3rd 1864
> 8:30 P.M.

Dear folks at home

We march tomorrow morning at 4 o'clock. Reveille is to be sounded at 3 o'clock — <u>pretty</u> <u>early</u>. We shall probably go over the Rapidan. Now "<u>hurrah</u>" for the rebs. We are all O.K. hope the next time you hear from me I shall be a good deal farther South

Don't worry about us
In haste from
Herbert

P.S. this photograph is a very intimate friend of mine of the same rank that I am — (commissary Sergt) Just got your last letter. Sorry Em has got a sore thumb. A [fellow] is a bad thing. Em about my having so many lady correspondence as I told Mrs Bean I had. I meant realitives and all — Ha, ha, was it wrong? I did not like her style and wanted to discontinue the correspondence <u>& did</u>. I don't care for any lady now. Out of the family & Howe girls!!!!!! I'm free and shall remain so —
Herbert

With Grant in control the Army of the Potomac pursued serious preparations. The aggressive general was eager to shift his forces south towards Richmond and draw the Confederates out for a decisive battle. Plans were drawn up with Meade (still commander of the Army of the Potomac), supplies were gathered, and the troops looked to a major offensive. Bonfires were banned and the bands and drum corps were ordered not to play.[37] Preparations came to fruition on May 4 when the army broke camp early in the morning and crossed the Rapidan into the tangled region known as the Wilderness. The VI Corps was wakened at 3:00 A.M.

and within an hour had fallen in behind the II and V Corps as they crossed the river. The immense Army of the Potomac moved almost lethargically and by the end of the day was stretched along a fifteen-mile length of narrow roads from Todd's Tavern back to the river. Ricketts' division, holding the last position in the VI Corps, spent a quiet evening near the Rapidan, curious as to what the next day might bring. Charles and Herbert took advantage of the pause in the march to strike up the band for the troops' entertainment.

Lee's army of 65,000 had witnessed Meade's preparations and the initial river crossings, then moved quickly to stifle any move Grant might attempt towards Richmond. Ever the gambler, Lee chose to throw his smaller army against the Union line while it was immersed in the dense terrain. Meade, with close to 120,000 men, was forced to

Wartime portrait of Colonel William W. Henry, second commander of the 10th Vermont Volunteer Infantry (Roger D. Hunt Collection at the U.S. Army Military History Institute).

fight Lee here. For most of the day on May 5 it was the left flank of the Union Army that suffered the hardest combat. Many times it looked as if the Confederates would break through, but fierce resistance by Hancock's II Corps and some timely reinforcements prevented a Southern victory. Here some musicians were able to use their skills in support of the combat. General George Custer's cavalry brigade was supporting Hancock's flank on the Union left. Upon encountering elements of Longstreet's corps, Custer ordered his band to play "Yankee Doodle" and sent his troops into combat.[38] Other musicians were called in to support the fighting without their instruments. General Hancock ordered drummer boys to carry the wounded out and to carry ammunition back in on the stretchers.[39] The George brothers did not suffer the risks of their fellow musicians; since their unit was held in reserve, Herbert decided it was time to get a haircut! Obviously the young men from Vermont had become somewhat inured to the sounds and sights of battle. It was not until mid–afternoon that Ricketts was ordered to join the battle, so

Herbert, Charles, and the band were ordered back to the hospital as the wounded began to pour in. Here they were to stay all night assisting the surgeons. From the leisurely months spent at Brandy Station and the calming music of the bands, soldiers in blue and gray where now forced to hear music of another kind: "Now and then the monotony of the muskets was broken by a few discharges of artillery, which seemed to come in as a double bass in this concert of death."[40]

Charles was detailed to help move the wounded to Fredericksburg where he would spend a physically and emotionally draining week struggling to keep men alive. And here again musicians did what they could to help. As one ambulance train moved to the rear, a band from an artillery regiment played "When the Swallows Homeward Fly" as solace to their suffering comrades.[41]

As evening approached Morris' brigade was detached and sent in support of the V Corps' line. There was heavy shelling and the regiment experienced a number of casualties. It was an extremely unnerving experience for the men from Vermont. Oscar Waite of the 10th Vermont provided a vivid description of the fighting:

> All of this time we could do nothing but lie there, watching the tops and branches drop from the sapling pines in front as though snipped by invisible shears, and listening to the sounds of the terrible conflict on either hand. Every little while, above the splattering skirmish fire, we could hear the lusty cheers of Yankees on a charge; then would come the roll of musketry, as though a mile of barrels filled with bunches of fire-crackers were all touched off together. Next, perhaps, would be heard the hair-raising 'Y-e-ep, Y-e-e-p, Y-e-e-p,' of rebels trying a counter charge, followed by more musketry and more yelling. Mixed in with this, as though beating time, would be the almost regular boom of the few cannons which could be used along the roadsides.[42]

Later that evening Ricketts' division was reunited and joined the rest of the VI Corps on the right end of the Union line. Plans were drawn up for a massive attack across the entire line the following day.

Early the next morning Morris' brigade was again placed in reserve, this time behind Warren's V Corps in the center of the Union right flank about a mile in front of Wilderness Tavern. Shelling was heavy and the George brothers' brigade lost three killed and nineteen wounded.[43] The 10th Vermont was still kept from the front lines, though at one point they were moved forward to fill a gap that had formed between the V and VI Corps.[44] Frustration mounted for the Green Mountain boys as they were forced to stand and watch the fighting that surrounded them without responding in kind. As the day wore down Meade's army was to face near disaster, and it was then that the 10th Vermont would get their chance to fight.

Confederate general John B. Gordon had scouted the Union right and discovered that Sedgwick had failed to cover this flank. A plan was submitted and, after hours of delay, eventually approved.[45] At the onset of evening elements of

Ewell's II Corps under Gordon launched a series of strikes against the extreme right of the Union flank, forcing General Seymour's men (2nd Brigade, 3rd Division of Sedgwick's VI Corps) and elements of General Alexander Shaler's brigade (4th Brigade, 1st Division) to a broken retreat; Seymour and Shaler were both captured. Morris' brigade was ordered to bolster the crumbling flank, and the 10th Vermont, 14th New Jersey, and 106th New York charged the area where the enemy was approaching.[46] It was a bold move and the men threw themselves into the assault, passing retreating men and screaming "the war cry as we had never given it before or did give it again afterwards."[47] Edward Bushnell of Company E marked the inspiration such shouting gave to the men. The 106th New York began the chorus by giving the 10th Vermont a cheer, and then all the men gave a "deafening shout, the utterance of which proved to be the turning point of the contest, as all firing ceased as by instinct."[48] They recrossed the ground lost by Seymour's brigade, forcing Gordon's troops to a halt. Seymour's men were able to reform and the Union line was restored. Despite such frenzied combat the 10th Vermont lost only twelve men killed or wounded.[49] Their comrades in the 1st Vermont Brigade were not so fortunate; when the day's fighting came to a close, they could claim only half of the brigade fit for duty.[50]

For the men of the 10th Vermont the Wilderness was a coming of age. Their participation in a major engagement had made a difference; the Confederate assault was slowed, the Union troops were able to entrench, and night brought a halt to the fighting. The regiment had helped to forestall a breakdown of the right flank and saved Grant's army from possible defeat.[51] For once the regiment received recognition for their efforts. When passing the 10th Vermont later that evening, General Sedgwick was heard to tell General Meade: "We are safe enough with that regiment!"[52]

From Herbert:

Camp in the field over the Rapidan
State of Virginia
May 4th 1864

My dear mother —

I am going to commence a letter to you and write in it till I get a chance to send it. We had Reveille this morning at 3 o'clock and marched at 4. The whole army moved at the same time. We have marched about 20 miles to day crossing the Rapidan at Germania Ford and are now encamped a few miles this side for the night. We are not so near the enemy but what <u>music</u> is allowed and <u>my</u> <u>band</u> was the first one to "<u>strike up</u>." As soon as the other bands heard us they all commenced playing and we made some <u>noise</u>. It is now <u>sunset</u> we have had orders to stay here for the night and Charles has made up a bed for him and I and as we are <u>very</u> tired we are all going to bed. It was <u>very</u> <u>hot</u> and <u>very</u> <u>dusty</u> marching to day and all the boys feet are <u>sore</u>. <u>blistered</u>. Mine are all OK but my legs are tired and my <u>Knap</u> <u>Sack</u> <u>aches</u>! (shoulders) Good night all —

May 5th Thursday — Reveille this morning at 5 o'clock. After breakfast (tack & coffee) we started to find our <u>front</u> and the enemy. We halted before noon in line of battle within <u>sight</u> of the rebels. As we lay there in the woods — (By the way the country is all woods here where we fight) cannonading commenced along the line and we could hear musketry down on the left, it was uncomfortably warm and while the fighting was going I had my hair cut short — close to my head. One of the band boys had some shears and I sat down on an old stump while he <u>sheared</u> <u>me</u>. A little past noon Gen'l Burnside relieved us with a Brigade of the 9th corps and we went along to join our Div down towards the left where they were <u>fighting</u>. We came up with them about 3 o'clock and by that time the firing became very <u>hot</u>, mostly musketry on both sides. The trees were so thick they could not get artillery to play good at all. I had orders to retreat with my band to Div hospital for service as nurses and stretcher bearers which is some two miles to the rear of the line of battle so back we came to this place and here we are still. The other bands <u>fell</u> <u>out</u> and remain side the road some where in the rear so that we are the only band and the only nurses here yet. The wounded are coming in fast, the musket firing is terrible and our loss is very heavy. we went to work putting up tents for the wounded and bringing water &c. &c. It is now dark and still the <u>firing</u>. Our hospital is running over with poor fellows shot on the field, brought in by ambulances. Officers & men together <u>several</u> <u>hundred</u> of them.... The band boys were all on duty attending to the wants of the wounded & I am acting corporal of the <u>guard</u>! Charlie & McClure are both assisting the Surgeons in amputating. The Surgeon in Chief compliments them very highly for doing so much good. They are both good nurses. Several of the men have died since they came in here. Only 3 or 4 killed from our regt yet. Well I must close for tonight.

May 6th Friday — Some of the other musicians in our Brigade came in last night <u>late</u> and relieved our boys this morning who were pretty near <u>played</u> <u>out</u>. Indeed I do not know what the wounded would do if it were not for the <u>musicians</u>. Firing commenced early this morning and continued all day mostly musketry and our brave boys poured into the hospital by scores, wounded, many of them pretty bad....

May 7th Saturday — were on down near Chancelorsville but routed out last night and marched slowly with the ambulance train down here. The line of battle is changed and we are now in the rear a few miles, the line running

about East & West. Up to the present time 3 PM there has been less firing
than upon either of the other two days. Cant hear from our Brig, don't know
where they are. Some artillery firing to day. I saw a Brigade of Colored troops
to day under Burnside. They looked <u>bully</u> and they fight well. Saw some
officers among them that used to belong to this regt as privates & Sergts &c.
The niggers fight tip top. Our band boys are at work in the hospital today —
a lot of wounded have just arrived from the front. Dont hear of any killed
from the 10th Vt . It is awful hot and sultry.... We have lost 15 or 20 thousand
men in killed wounded & missing — probably not more than 15,000 — <u>It's</u>
<u>"tuff."</u> Charlie goes to Fredericksburg to day with the wounded as nurse. I
send this by him hoping he will get a chance to send it to you.

In haste
Herbert

*The armies disengaged and immediately began repositioning with Richmond
as the fulcrum. Grant launched a series of movements to the left in an attempt to
flank Lee's army and cut off the Army of Northern Virginia from the Confederate
capital. On May 7 the men of the 10th Vermont found themselves on the Chancellorsville Turnpike heading towards Fredericksburg, a difficult march lasting
about fifteen hours.[53] The severity of the march was made all the more unpleasant
as the men crossed over the battlefields surrounding Chancellorsville and saw many
grim reminders of the carnage from previous fighting. Charles, Herbert, and the
other musicians continued to move with the ambulance train, assisting the surgeons
wherever they chose to set up. Those working in the hospitals were now seeing a
level of butchery unlike anything they had experienced before; the young Charles
Gotwalt of the 87th Pennsylvania captured the gruesome scene: "Every few
moments someone came out of the hospital tent carrying an arm or leg and threw
it on a huge pile — over eight feet high, which continued to grow, this pile of limbs
to be buried later."[54] There were skirmishes throughout the march and units of
Morris' brigade encountered the enemy briefly. By May 8 the VI Corps had passed
through Chancellorsville to the east, then turned south to find the Confederates
well entrenched on Laurel Hill near Spotsylvania Court House. The V Corps had
already engaged the enemy, and by 3:30 P.M. Sedgwick's VI Corps had joined the
assault. Fighting was fierce at times, and at least one band — of the 140th New
York Infantry — played for their regiment as they charged into battle.[55] Such attacks
were futile against the superior Rebel positions. Enemy artillery battered the Union
forces and a withdrawal was ordered. Though Ricketts' division did not participate
in the primary assaults on Laurel Hill, the 10th Vermont again suffered at the
hands of their counterparts, losing sixteen men to stray gunfire and artillery.[56]
     May 9 the Vermonters were placed in support of the 1st New York Artillery*

somewhat between the V and VI Corps; eventually the New Yorkers were replaced by a battery from the 1st Massachusetts Light Artillery. Then tragedy struck the Federal forces: Charles and Herbert's brigade commander, General Morris, was shot in the leg, and corps commander General Sedgwick was killed, shot by a Rebel sharpshooter while standing in front of the 14th New Jersey.[57] One member of the 87th Pennsylvania remembered the general's final words as he chided a soldier concerned by the enemy fire: "Oh, they couldn't hit an elephant at this distance."[58] Colonel Truex of the 14th New Jersey would eventually be placed in command of the 1st Brigade in place of Morris, and Major General Horatio G. Wright of the 1st Division was placed in charge of the VI Corps. Wright soon received minor wounds himself, though he quickly recovered.

May 10 the men of the 10th Vermont saw no combat. Attempts were made at various points along the Confederate salient, and elements of the VI Corps under Colonel Emory Upton managed to force a breach at one point, but the Rebel placements proved too strong. The 10th Vermont took a turn on the front line and engaged in serious skirmishing at a location the soldiers named the "slaughter pens"; at one point the entire brigade charged the lines and managed to capture rifle pits, though neither army chose to follow up the attack.[59] Skirmishing was difficult enough that the 10th Vermont eventually found themselves out of ammunition, and Company A of the 151st New York was forced to come to their assistance. Other members of the 151st were heavily engaged as well, though the hungry soldiers managed to bring back some stray sheep after being forced from their position.[60] Shelling was heavy on both sides, and even noncombatants such as musicians suffered from the barrage. According to a member of the Stonewall Brigade: "The ambulance corps, the bands and musicians, with the pioneers, all had pits to get into, as at times the shells would fairly rain over us."[61] As was often the case when the blue and the gray found themselves in such close proximity, bands from each side inadvertently entertained the soldiers on both sides of the line. At one spot a Confederate band played "Nearer My God to Thee" and "The Bonnie Blue Flag," and a Union band responded with "The Star Spangled Banner."[62] On May 11 both armies paused for a day to restore themselves mentally and physically. The weather was particularly miserable with a steady rain pouring down on the weary soldiers.

Then on May 12 Hancock launched a major assault on the Confederate salient. Around 6:30 A.M. the VI Corps was sent to the western side of the Confederate entrenchments to support Hancock's attack, with Ricketts' division being the last called into battle at 11:00 A.M. The brigade, temporarily under the command of Colonel Schall of the 87th Pennsylvania, formed into battle lines and the skirmishers were immediately engaged.[63] As on previous days the terrain was difficult to cross and the men were immediately slashed by heavy fire while the

Confederates remained relatively secure behind their fortifications. Despite Hancock's success at the tip of the salient, the Rebel lines on the flank proved too difficult to take, and the assault sputtered to a halt. Though held in reserve for most of the day's fighting, the 3rd Division was still under a constant bombardment of artillery and musket fire, losing about 156 dead and wounded.[64] The men of the 10th Vermont could not help but be overwhelmed by the slaughter they witnessed around Spotsylvania. As Sergeant Edward Bushnell of Company E recorded: "I had often before read and heard of men being heaped up, and of blood laying in pools, but never before had witnessed a sight that came anything near such an expression."[65] Grant contemplated another assault, this time with the VI Corps in the lead, but fortunately for the George

A bust view of Major General Horatio Gates Wright, who assumed command of the VI Corps following the death of General Sedgwick (U.S. Army Military History Institute).

brothers the plan was aborted and darkness fell to the sound of sporadic firing.
    From Charles:

Fredericksburg
May 11, 1864

My darling Ellie — I know you are anxious to hear from me, but this is the first chance I have had to write. I have had to work some this last week, I tell you! The battle commenced last Thursday — we went to the Division Hospital just at dark. After marching all day and being tired out, I sat up taking care of the wounded all night, all the next day. Friday night, and I still kept on. I don't know how I stood it so well — but felt tough and took hold in earnest. The Surgeon complimented me upon my doing so well.

Well, I have got no sleep yet — have worked a week as hard as I could with not more than 2 hours sleep in 24 hours. Childs sent me off to bed several times, but I couldn't see any one suffer for want of help. I was on my own hook — had no orders from anyone — worked where I could do the most good. Considerable of the time I assisted the surgeons in dressing the difficult wounds. The wounded were packed up and started for Washington last Saturday. I was detailed by Surgeon Childs to go with them as nurse and I expected he recommended me to Dr. Bryant, for an arriving at Fredericksburg and getting the wounded unloaded he put me in charge of a hospital of 22 badly wounded men and I never had my abilities so greatly taxed as I did that night!

Monday — We got them out about 3:00 P.M. I had 3 or 4 men detailed to assist me but they made a mistake and got to the wrong place — finally I found myself with only two men — one a boy and the other a wooden man. I commenced dressing their wounds but only dressed about half a dozen before dark — all the tools I had was our drinking cups, canteens, bandages and lint. All the men were suffering with fatigue, pain and hunger, having had nothing to eat for nearly 24 hours. Such a trying time I never saw — one man died that night and another the next morning — the first was wounded in the abdomen and the other an amputated leg above the knee. At dark my perplexities had only commenced. There was no supper and the chief cook said they could not have any, but Dr. Bryant ordered him to cook it. When I came to get it I found the same mistake occurred as when the nurses failed to show up. The other hospital got it all. It was about 9:00 o'clock — and I had been promising them, the boys, their supper — but they got only a hard-tack and a drink of water apiece and no candle at that! I laughed and trained with them and they made a jolly (?) supper out of it. I sat up all night, tired as I was and got the good will from all the boys.

In the morning I commenced dressing wounds — some had been there 3 or 4 days, could you only pity me then? — responsible for the treatment of those poor fellows and nothing to do with. The doctor did not come till yesterday morning and then was so hurried he could do but little. I have but one man now who is mortally wounded, but I gues the most of them are ugly wounds and very painful. We are in a deserted house — the news from the front is good.

From Herbert:

1864
Camp near Spottsylvannia C. H. Battlefield of the 8th days fight.
(At Division Hospital)
May 13th Friday

Dear Folks at home —

I'm all O.K. yet. Our Band plays at Div Hospital all the time and acts as nurses. Charles went to Wash as nurses with the first lot of wounded & has not returned yet. The 4th lot of wounded start to day for Wash & I send this by Cap'n Steel Co K 10th Vt who is wounded. Yesterday was the hardest days fight we have had yet. Terrible. I think 50,000 will not cover our loss in killed wounded & missing in this campaign — Our regt has not lost very heavy yet Azro is O.K. too & Charlie Bayley — Please send word to all the folks that I am well in good spirits. It rains hard today. I have no time to write more.

Love to all
From Herbert

P.S. We have captured Gen'l Johnson & 5000 men. A lot of cannon too and a report says we have captured Mosby & 180 of his gang. The rebs are falling bad today

The next day Grant probed gingerly to learn the location and strength of Lee's new position, giving the 10th Vermont and the other regiments of their brigade a well-deserved break. That evening the VI Corps was ordered to swing completely around the Union Army, cross the Ni River, and take up position on the Union left flank. An attack was scheduled for 4:00 A.M. May 14, but delays derailed Grant's plans. Upon taking their position along the Massaponax Church Road the men of the VI Corps witnessed fighting on Myer's Hill overlooking the Confederate position. At 6:30 P.M. the 3rd Division was sent to the retake the hill, crossing the Ni River again and gamely forming into battle lines, only to find that the out-numbered Rebels had chosen to withdraw. Here the brigade was to spend the evening. Perhaps without even knowing it the men from Vermont were experienced veterans and took their new encounters with a remarkable degree of calmness. Consider Tabor Parcher's description of the day's events: "to the left & thare is whare the Johnneys lay thick from 1 to 6 deepe 5000 on a very small peace of ground. lay thare in line a little while & then mooved back toward the right built brestworks & then lay down went to sleep. slept well but once the Rebs charged our skirmish line but were all repulsed & it was quiet again. went to sleep again."[66]

The 10th Vermont and the rest of the brigade were lucky to get two relatively quiet days in camp. Despite the intensity of the preceding combat or the maneuvering Grant was planning, there was still a demand for music by the Union commanders. As a member of the 87th Pennsylvania noted: "In the afternoon of the 16th the band played at brigade headquarters, and in the evening at division headquarters. On the following day, the band entertained the regiment for an hour or two with fine music."[67] Musicians in gray also took the opportunity to entertain their troops, and the sounds of bands and singing drifted over to the Union lines.[68] Bands were also called on to function in a tactical role. According to Vermonter Oscar Waite:

That night, as usual there, at seven o'clock the big guns commenced booming, the fifes were all squealing, the bands were making what noise they conveniently could with the snare drums; and it seems that Grant, under cover of the racket, was moving off all of our trains, together with everything on wheels that would make a noise on the

road. Having heard the same kind of a pow-wow every night for a week, the rebels
— although on the sharp lookout— didn't suspect anything until toward morning.[69]

The men received an added boost when the mail finally caught up with
them, and lucky soldiers spent the day reading letters from home.
From Charles:

Fredericksburg
May 17, 1864

Again I have a few minutes to write a little to you, Ellie dear. I am still here
nursing the wounded and no prospect of getting away. One man died today —
John Polen, Company B, 120th Ohio. It is not quite as hard now as it was a
few days ago, then are getting along pretty well — there are two more, however,
that will die before long — one wounded in the bowels and the other in the
knee. There is a woman by the name of Mrs. Husband who cooks and fixes
up good things for the boys. The Sanitary furnishes her with supplies. We
also get things from them such as shirts, drawers, pillows, cushions and all
such things. One fellow had a pair of drawers with a letter in them. They
were made by a girl in Maine and she wanted an answer back to show some
of the Copperhead neighbors who do not believe we get anything by the sanitary commission. He is going to answer it. He was seriously wounded in the
thigh and will probably lose that leg.

Night before last I saved the life of Sergeant Gragg. An artery broke out
in his wound — they called for me and wanted me to go for the doctor, but
I knew it couldn't wait — I put one of my knuckles over the artery in the thigh
and was fortunate enough to find it immediately, though it was the first time
I ever tried it. I held it until we got help then put a bandage around the thigh
and a roll of bandages where my finger was — drew it tighter and I had it all
stopped. He would have bled to death in 5 minutes if I had not stopped it
right then!

The doctor looked at it — felt it all over — tried the pulse and never
moved the bandages — I had got it just right. They took him away the next
day and I have not seen him since.

<u>Saturday evening</u> — Night before last I got an order from Surgeon Childs
to report to my regiment — so I started on my journey. I came onto the Band
unexpectedly after going about 12 miles. Herbert was the means of getting
me back for which I am very thankful, for I could not stand it there at the
hospital much longer. That night we went on to the regiment which was at
or near Spottsylvania Court House behind breastworks and at the extreme
front. We played Yankee Doodle to them in sight and hearing of rebel pickets
up in a tree.

Saturday night just as we were moving out of our works preparatory to moving towards Ginneys Station the rebs pitched into us. The way our Brigade double-quicked to the inside of the breastworks wasn't slow! Our cannon belched away as saucy as they could. I have not learned whether they had many killed or not — we lost none! We left there about 9 o'clock on a very hard marc it being very warm — every body complained. Kent found a mare and colt hid in the woods — he took it along, colt and all and the boys packed on their knapsacks on the mare....

On the evening of May 17 Herbert and the rest of the regiment were ordered back across the Ni River near their previous position on the right of the Union Army, this time on the northern tip of the salient. The movement was predictably slow and Ricketts' division did not arrive in position until about 5:00 the following morning. By the time the men from Vermont were placed in line of battle the Union attack had fallen apart and the brigade found itself under intense and bewildering fire. Works were thrown up and the men were forced to hold in their trenches, waiting to see how Grant would handle their next move. They would not wait long, for Grant was already preparing his latest advance. When evening fell the VI Corps was shifting back to their location of May 15, between Myer's Hill and the Massaponax Church Road, now occupying the middle of the new Union line. Here Charles was able to rejoin the regiment and assume his duties with the other musicians. The soldiers were able to spend a day out of harm's way, relaxing and enjoying the music of the bands, though the 87th Pennsylvania was detached for rear-guard duty and experienced some brisk fighting.[70] The last few days had been harrowing for the men from Vermont. Kept from the worst of the bloody assaults in front of the Confederate lines, the men still found themselves under constant fire, losing a total of twenty-four killed or wounded. In this they were extremely fortunate, having some of the lightest regimental casualties for the battle.[71] For most of the battle of Spotsylvania Herbert had been busy at the division hospital. Here the musicians not only tended to the wounded but performed on their instruments as well. Their efforts were greatly appreciated by doctors and patients alike.[72] Herbert also continued to use the band's music in support of his regiment, even when the troops were near the front lines. Such moments of comfort were invaluable, for the men from Vermont would soon find themselves embroiled in fierce combat once again.

From Herbert:

Camp in an orchard near Spottsylvania Court House Va.

May 20th 1864

Dear Sister Emma

I'm alive and well yet. The rebel bullets do not harm me in the least as yet. Charlie is still at Fredericksburg as nurse. I expect him back every day now. We came into this apple orchard last night and expect to stay here all day to day. The man that lives here is a rebel congress man he says he will furnish <u>land</u> to bury Yankees on if the rebel army will only kill them. Gen'l Grant has put a guard on him and is going to burn this house down to night. One house was burned (so report says) this four noon a short distance from here. The <u>owner</u> killed one of our Colonels a few days ago & then hung himself. Any of the citizens around here would shoot any of us if they were not guarded — The rebs tried to capture one of our wagon trains yesterday but couldn't come it We took 350 of them prisoners but they <u>killed</u> several of our officers and captured all the teamsters. We had a pretty smart fight yesterday, not much to day. Its pretty warm and I shall not write much. The mail comes in now occasionally. I send you Cap'n Dodges photograph & Serg. Tom Hogles. Capn Steel is wounded and promised to send me his photograph when he goes to Washington. I have got nearly a dozen coming to me as soon as they can get them. Please write often. The teams are hitching up & guess we shall move soon now —

Good day
From Herbert

P.S. Charlie has just arrived from Fred — all O.K. He says Fred is full of our wounded a good many die of their wounds.

CHAPTER 5

May to July 1864

North Anna River; Cold Harbor; Petersburg, Virginia; and Monocacy, Maryland

The men of the 10th Vermont were given little time to relax after the bloodshed at Spotsylvania as Grant chose to send the Army of the Potomac on a movement designed to unseat the Army of Northern Virginia. By May 21 Wright's corps was following the rest of the army southeast in a race to flank Lee's army. The bands performed on the march, pleasing the soldiers but not the civilians. As George Prowell, historian of the 87th Pennsylvania explained: "As the army passed through this country of Confederate adherents, the blinds of the windows in the houses were usually closed, and scarcely a person was to be seen. But behind those blinds, scornful and revengeful eyes watched the 'Yanks' as they marched to the music of the Union."[1] Ricketts' division joined Burnside's IX Corps for the march, though before moving very far the sound of fighting drew them back to the other divisions of the VI Corps acting as rear guard. By the time they rejoined their fellow divisions the fighting was over, so they turned once again and followed after the IX Corps, catching them at dark near the Po River. The next day Grant ordered the entire VI Corps to push on to Guinea Station in an effort to concentrate his forces. The men were hungry and grumpy, having been up and marching for almost thirty hours straight while leaving their supply wagons somewhere behind. By 5:00 P.M. they occupied some old works at Madison's Ordinary, and many of the men fell asleep without even eating.

The next morning the troops were again on the march, moving in behind the V Corps on Telegraph Road heading to the North Anna River. About noon the tardy supply wagons caught up with the hungry troops, so Wright called a brief halt to allow the men to eat. Eventually the VI Corps arrived at the banks of the North Anna and quickly crossed at Jericho Mills to support Warren's V Corps that had already encountered leading elements of Lee's armies. They crossed around 6:00 A.M. on May 24, and Truex's brigade fortified positions on the right flank of the Union position. Despite the proximity of the enemy, many members of the regiment (including Herbert and Charles George) found time for a quick swim in the river. Pouring rain in the afternoon swelled the North Anna, stranding a number of wounded soldiers near Quarles's Mill. Brave musicians from the 56th Massachusetts offered to ferry the injured over the turbulent waters, first carrying men over on their backs, then building rafts to float the seriously wounded.[2] The following day the VI Corps moved farther east to scout the end of Lee's line, eventually becoming the right flank of the Union position. Skirmishers were sent forward to find weaknesses in the Rebel defenses and Ricketts' division was held in reserve.

    Once again Grant found Lee's position too secure, enough so that after one day's fighting he looked for a way to slip past the Army of Northern Virginia. This time the VI Corps would lead the movement, and on the evening of May 26 Wright's corps crossed back over Jericho Mills. The 10th Vermont was the last regiment placed on picket duty, remaining there until late in the evening to help mask the rest of the army's move across the North Anna. Bands were called upon to help the deception by performing as if all was normal in the Union camps; the band of the Vermont Brigade even exchanged pieces with a Confederate band across the lines.[3] The rain continued to pester the troops and the rivers were flowing high. By mid–morning the next day the George brothers and their comrades were given a break after marching all night but were soon ordered back on their feet, finally reaching the Pamunkey River near Hanover Court House in the evening. The following morning the VI Corps crossed the river at Nelson's Bridge and set up defensive lines stretching along Crump's Creek from the Pamunkey on their right to Warren's V Corps and the center of the Union lines. The 10th Vermont and the rest of their brigade were placed on the extreme left of the VI Corps line at the home of Dr. Pollard, a beautiful estate that made a favorable impression on Herbert and Charles. In spite of being in hearing distance of the cavalry battle at Haw's Shop, Ricketts' division never received orders to advance, so the men enjoyed a rare break from the incessant marching. Music aided the relaxation, according to one soldier: "Success to our arms, a beautiful spring day, lovely scenery, unusually good music by the band at headquarters, and a happy heart make this a red-letter day."[4]

    On May 29 the 1st Division was sent out on reconnaissance towards Hanover Court House. Confederate troops were eventually encountered, though the 10th Vermont saw no action. May 30 the VI Corps shifted down to form an angle with the V Corps and buttress the Union right flank along Totopotomoy Creek. Although they set out at 5:00 A.M., confusing roads, failed shortcuts, and swampy terrain meant that Ricketts' men did not get into position until almost 5:00 that evening. Line of battle was formed, skirmishers were set in front, but no attack was ordered. The following morning it appeared that the enemy had pulled back, leaving only skirmishers to delay the Federal army.[5] *Two divisions of the VI Corps pushed forward and soon found the Rebels in a well-entrenched position on the far side of the Totopotomy. The 10th Vermont was to find no combat here, for Grant was wearying of attacking Lee's fortifications, and General Phil Sheridan and his cavalry corps had experienced serious fighting near the crossroads of Old Cold Harbor and were in need of help. The 10th Vermont and the rest of the VI Corps were about to find themselves at the front of one of the war's bloodiest battles.*

From Charles:

Monday, May 30, 1864

Dearest Ellie — There was not much fighting yesterday — this morning we were routed early to move — went about 4 miles and found ourselves near the Court House. Stayed there an hour or two then moved 4 or 5 miles down the rail road. A citizen says we are 11 miles from Richmond and 4 miles from Mechanicksville. Our Brigade is now in the front lines with skirmishers ahead — we are behind with the rest of the regiment, but can hear the musketry go pop-pop. No wounded have come in yet. Our rations ran out tonight, but the supply train is coming in soon. Supplies are hauled all the way from Bell Plaines. I hope the mail may come with the supplies. You no doubt will look in vain for a letter for some time, for there will be no mail go out from here now because there is no transportation.

<u>Near Gains Mills Wednesday noon</u> — Yesterday we advanced a mile or two. The regiment was not in action but 12 or 14 got killed or wounded. I went to the regiment and brought back a wounded man. When I came away they had established a Brigade Hospital half a mile to the rear, but the wounded were carried to the Division Hospital. About 3:00 o'clock this morning we were routed out — General Grant is great for flank movements. This time the 6the Corps left the 2nd in position and took a circle to the left about 15 miles and hauled up at Gaines Mills or as near as we can get at present. This morning a division of our cavalry drove a division of rebel infantry out of their works at this place. The rebs charged upon them with <u>our</u> colors flying but it did not work. Our sharp shooters fired so fast they couldn't get a chance to fire back at all — besides we had 27 pieces of artillery opened upon them — the trees are all marked up. I picked up some beans the rebs spilled — am cooking them now. Our regiment is throwing up breastworks here.

<u>At Division Hospital about 4 P.M.</u> — Yesterday an attack was made by the 6th Corps and a detachment from the 18th and 10th Corps under General

Smith — also parts of General Butlers forces. Such an artillery fight I never heard — shells came whizzing by us at the rear at a fearful rate. About 6 o'clock our regiment charged over the breastworks and took more prisoners than we had men — they were glad to surrender!

During the evening of May 31 the VI Corps cautiously withdrew from its position and began the fifteen-mile march to relieve the sorely pressed troopers and perhaps break the Rebel line. In an attempt to cover this move, many bands were moved close to the front and ordered to play, thereby masking the noise of the army as it redeployed.[6] It was nearly 10:00 A.M. the following day when the VI Corps arrived outside of Cold Harbor, the exhausted men having marched for almost twelve hours straight. Upon their approach to the front, the Vermonters were shocked to see the carnage left from the previous fighting. Sheridan's forces were certainly grateful to see reinforcements arriving, and General Custer's band saluted the VI Corps.[7] Within two hours of arriving the VI Corps was deployed for an attack. Facing them across hastily constructed works were Kershaw's and Hoke's divisions of Anderson's I Corps. Under fire for most of the day, Truex's brigade was finally ordered to advance at 6:30 P.M.: the 14th New Jersey was placed in front, then the 151st New York, 87th Pennsylvania and 10th Vermont, with the 106th New York in the rear as close reserve.[8] Fortune favored Ricketts' division as a Confederate brigade under Hagwood had been taken from the front and shifted to the Rebel right, leaving a ravine unprotected.

This assault on the Confederate lines so late in the afternoon achieved no small measure of surprise. Truex's brigade led the division into battle through tough terrain that included woods, ravines, and swamp. The difficult ground worked against the Confederates as well as their artillery was unable to provide adequate covering fire, resulting in a dangerous gap between the divisions of Kershaw and Hoke.[9] The men of Truex's brigade were momentarily separated from the 1st Division on their right, but gamely continued forward into the ravine soon to be known as Bloody Run. Upon reaching the leading elements of the enemy the 14th New Jersey fired a round then dropped to the ground to allow the other regiments to move past. Finally the order "double quick march" came, and the 10th Vermont and their comrades broke through the enemy earthworks. "We moved up and took up our positions," William White explained, "which was changed a little however about 6 O.C. Shortly after we commenced moving forward and in the course of 20 minutes we were advancing in a brilliant Charge, through a [mess] of Standing & fallen trees, swamps &c. through a heavy shower of leaden & from hail, and a dense sheet of fire on we went."[10]

The brigade plowed through the pickets, faced left, then hammered into the 8th North Carolina. With momentum on their side the brigade continued forward

A rare photograph of a Union field hospital after the battle of Savage Station in June 1862. This was the ghastly environment in which Herbert and Charles spent much of their time (Library of Congress).

and fell upon the next regiment. The Vermonters and their fellow regiments captured officers and men of the 51st North Carolina, then fortified the position and withstood repeated attacks by the Confederates.[11] By now the regiments were jumbled together, and order was necessary if they were to hold their recent gains. Confederate reinforcements eventually pushed the brigade out of the recently captured position, and Truex's brigade built hasty works as close as fifty yards from the Rebel line. Ricketts' division was able to claim a total of 500 prisoners from the action. As the leading brigade of the VI Corps, the 1st Brigade suffered serious losses: approximately 344 killed, wounded, or missing.[12] Due to its position on the field, and the temporary exposure of their flank, the 10th Vermont alone lost eighty-one men killed or wounded. Truex's brigade lost more than any other Union unit on this day, and the 10th Vermont and 14th New Jersey were the most depleted regiments. Among those lost were Lieutenants Ezra Stetson and Charles G. Newton, both friends of Herbert and Charles. Two regimental commanders, Henry (10th Vermont) and Truex (1st Brigade, 14th New Jersey), were wounded and Colonel Townsend of the 106th New York was killed. Once again the musicians were in peril while fulfilling their medical duties, and many combatants noticed the danger facing those attempting to remove the wounded.[13] *Charles and Herbert spent most of their time at division hospital where the surgeons and patients suffered repeatedly from enemy shells. Amid this ferocious combat Truex's brigade had accomplished what few Union units had managed in almost a month of continuous fighting— they had passed Rebel fortifications and forced a lodgment within the enemy lines. It was an inspired performance by the men from Vermont and the rest of their brigade. Meade made particular note to congratulate Wright and his men for their achievements.*[14]

The next day was full of violent skirmishing as the rest of the Army of the Potomac arrived and began deploying. Unfortunately the troops had left their position on the Pamunkey so quickly that their supplies had yet to catch up with them, so the men had little food for two days.[15] Grant finally ordered a full frontal assault on June 3, and the 10th Vermont joined its brigade in the center of the right flank. This time the 10th Vermont led the attack, with the 151st New York close behind. Troops on either side of the brigade advanced only a short way, and suddenly the men of the 10th Vermont found themselves under vicious enfilading fire from both sides. The men pressed on and the VI Corps managed to overrun Confederate rifle pits but could advance no farther. Three Virginia regiments (19th, 28th, and 56th) had been placed in the gap through which the brigade had attacked two days before, so there was little hope for another successful advance. The fighting swayed back and forth, and at one point the VI Corps was pushed back, but Ricketts' division refused to retreat, even when raking fire began to shred their lines.[16] Colonel Schall, commanding the brigade in place of the wounded General Truex, was shot in the arm and replaced by Lieutenant Colonel Hall of the 14th New Jersey. The exposed position and intensity of the fighting took its toll on the Vermonters, resulting in sixty-two casualties that included three captains.

Subsequent assaults on the Confederate front were called off, though the troops were in seemingly perpetual combat up to June 12. This included the repulse of an enemy counter-attack by the Vermonters on June 9. Band members had their hands full tending to the wounded; there were astonishing number of casualties pouring in, and the musicians were hard pressed to keep up.[17] The number of casualties was such that members of the drum corps were ordered back to division hospital along with the band members to help with the overwhelming amount of wounded. In some of the bloodiest combat of the entire war the Yankees had failed to divest Lee's army, and the 10th Vermont had lost significantly. Between June 1 and 3 the regiment suffered a total of 180 killed, wounded, or missing; these were the some of the worst losses the regiment would ever see.

From Herbert:

On the field near Hannover Court House Va

18 miles from <u>Richmond</u>.
May 29th 1864

Dear folks at home.

We make out to be all right yet, but kinder <u>tired</u> and would like a few weeks rest. I have copied from my pocket diary what we have done &c every day since the Campaign commenced and sent two batches off by mail to you. If you have recd them you have a correct account of what I have been through where we have been & which no doubt will be interesting to you. I have forgotten where I left off coppying from my book but think it was Monday May 16th. I will commence with Monday & coppy up to to day anyhow —

May 16th All quiet to day — scarcely any firing — Reenforcements from Washington are coming in fast, mostly heavy artilery regts. We got a mail to day. I recd a dozen photographs from Concord — Tuesday 17th Still no firing. Our troops are building breast works. Very hot, uncomfortably warm Wednesday 18th There has been some pretty hard fighting to day. Our troops having rested feel like going in again.... Friday 20th We are with our regt this evening. It has been pretty quiet to day and we played several pieces at the hospital this afternoon. Charlie returned from Fredricksburg and just before sun set we came up here to our regt to play. The boys were very glad to see us, they cheered us and sung out "bully for the band now we will have some music." We have been playing both here to the boys and at Brigade Hd Qrs. Our Brig lays behind breastworks in sight of the "Johnies" up in a tree <u>spying us</u>. We are going to stay with our regt now till another gen'l engagement

Saturday 21st — This morning I went down to the left of our lines to see a company of Burnsides Indians they are dressed like our soldiers but their color is Indian all over. We played this four noon for Col Henry at a little house near our regt. All our troops changed position this PM we followed our regt. just at dark the rebs made a charge on our works but were repulsed with heavy loss our Brig double quicked up from reserve but were not needed. Mr reb fell back. It has been very hot to day. (Sunday 22nd).... I saw a curiosity this evening. A lady went away from here with colored attendants to hold up her dress as she went through the grass!!! Our soldiers burn a good many houses on this campaign, usually burn them when they find them <u>deserted</u>. We also confiscate all the <u>pigs</u> chickens cows oxen horses tobacco &c. &c.... Tuesday 24th This evening finds us about 20 rods in the of our Brigade line of battle — We have crossed the river — Started about 6 o'clock this morning and reached the river after marching about two miles crossed on a pontoon bridge, and halted to rest till most night when we advanced a mile or so and formed a line of battle, some skirmishing going on and some heavy cannonading.

"We musicians" were ordered back where we are now by our Brig commander we do not aprehend much fighting however to night. While we lay resting back near the North Anna river to day Charlie & I went in swimming & washed our shirts which made us feel much better....

Saturday 28th — This evening finds us about 2 miles from Hanover C. H. on the South side of the Pamunkey — in line of battle behind breastworks which our corps built since we came here — We started out about 6 oclock this morning found the river after marching about 3 1/2 miles. Crossed on a pontoon bridge. Where our Brigade is resting now at is about two miles from the Pamunkey. Our Band is at Brigade hospital a few rods in the rear of our regt. We are on Dr Pollocks premises, a very fine residence indeed I got some strawberries in the garden to day but the safety guard drove me away. There is a fish pond near the house — Mr Kent, one of our band boys confiscated an old mare & colt to day & we put our blankets on her & led her along. She makes a fine pack horse — I went in swimming in the Pawmunkey to day had a nice time in the water. Charlie went in too....

Sunday 29th — All quiet to day — troops moving into position but no firing — Our Brigade has remained in their works all day — We played for our regt this morning and this afternoon. Played 3 pieces at Brigade Hd. Qrs. this evening — The rebs have fell back. Dr Pollock took the oath of alllegiance to our Govt to day. He was a member of the rebel Congress

Monday 30th — To night we are present or accounted for at Oak Forrest, 3½ miles from Mechanicsville — and near the <u>Chikahomony swamp</u> — We marched at day light this morning and arrived here about 4 oclock this P.M. We have found the rebs and our skirmishers are quite busy just now — Some cannonading too. All the musicians were ordered to the rear and our Div is at the front — We are about 12 miles from Richmond....

Wednesday June 1st — Tonight we are in the woods down at Cold Harbor dodging the <u>shells</u>. Genl Grant made a flank movement last night. We marched all night & till morning today, when we got into position here at Cold Harbor, 8 miles from Richmond and near the Chickahominy — there has been a terrible fight this P.M. We opened upon the rebs with our whole Corps at 5 o'clock this P.M. & such a roar of artilery & musketry. We came near getting hit with shell — Our hospital got shelled out twice. Our troops <u>Advanced</u> took the rebel works — <u>Boregards</u> and chase them men like sheep — Our brave and beloved Col Henry had his fore finger shot off .... It was an awful bloody fight for 3 hours. Our Brig took more than their number in prisoners. Our regt took 4 or 5 hundred — several hundred — nearly a thousand rebs gave them selves up, run for our lines & sung out "how are you Yankees we are glad to see you" — We are going to Washington now & we know you are going to

Richmond They wont fight at all hardly We had a good many wounded in our Corps — The 18th Corps from Butlers commanded by Smith is here. They fought bully — We are in for it whole <u>hog</u> or none —

Thursday June 2nd
10 o'clock a.m.

The mail is going out to day — I must send this. We Band boys are all at division hospital taking care of the wounded. Charlie is here O.K. Have not heard from Charlie Bayley — Azro is O.K. yet — Col Townsend of the 106th N.Y. our Brigade was killed last night. We are taking the best care of the wounded that we can — Mother will you please send word to Jere — Ruth & A.M. that we are all right as yet. I have no time to write to them now Please write often now, Our base of supplies is at White House Landing — now — We are within 7 or 8 miles of Richmond

Love to all
From Herbert

From Charles:

Division Hospital Cold Harbor
June 8, 1864

Ellie darling — do you know it has been 2 long years since we have seen each other? We little thought when we parted that it would be so long — we then thought that 9 months would see the end of the war, but more than twice nine have passed and still we are at war and no end in sight. Almost every day some remnant of some regiment passes by on their way home. I almost begrudge them their happiness — and yet, why should I? They have endured 3 long years of separation from their homes while I have less than 2 years. The regiments are very small when they go home — one went by yesterday with only 51 men. I suppose in a short time the 2nd Vermont will be out then the 3rd and sometime it will be the 10th, but there will be but few men to go back that came with me. We have lost 200 since crossing the Rapidan River.

There is a rumor of moving tonight, but it is just rumor. At this hospital there are roll calls and details for nurses and other duties here. There are about 150 musicians and nurses at this hospital. My appetite is good — want to eat all the time — am lousy and dirty as usual!

I enjoy myself more here — I mean in the band — than anywhere else in the army. The band is my home and I get homesick for it when away from it. It is so with all the members. We are all satisfied to stay here where we are a little shy of bullets. At present it is dangerous at the front — the men have to keep their heads down or the sharp-shooters pick them off. Occasionally there is a cessation of hostilities to bury the dead — then the men from both sides mingle together, shake hands and exchange papers — for the time being every thing is friendly — then the next hour perhaps, they will be shooting at one another....

Herbert and two or three other boys are lettering boards to put up at the graves. There are about 20 buried from this division here. — a little music from the front now — should think they were mortars by the sound....

The men of the 10th Vermont now found themselves in nervous proximity to their Southern counterparts, and amid the sniper fire managed to chat with the Rebels and exchange goods.[18] *Finally on June 10 the brigade was removed from the entrenchments and set up a short way back, though picket and skirmish duty brought them close enough that the Vermonters could "hear the rebs talk and sing quite plain in our immediate front."*[19] *According to Horace Hanks of the 30th New York, bands participated in the exchange across the lines: "I was pleased last night just at dark to hear a Rebble Band playing in front of us they played a few tunes such as Dixy and then played Hail Columbia and our men gave them three cheers. Our Band a few days ago played the Start Spangled Banner and the Rebble Band gave their groans. They played Dixy our band groaned so they keep it up every little while."*[20] *The next day the brigade was finally withdrawn from the front. The intense fighting and heavy casualties had taken their toll on all of the troops, and the men were eager for what relief and recuperation could be found. Truex's brigade reported a total of 533 losses for the two weeks of fighting around Cold Harbor, with the 10th Vermont taking the most casualties of any regiment.*[21] *As of June 6 the 10th Vermont reported only twelve officers and 352 enlisted men fit for duty, leading Major Chandler to note: "The regiment is now so much reduced in officers that its efficiency is seriously impaired."*[22] *Here, as always, the band musicians played their part, as one observer recorded: "The luxurious vegetation, the scent of the flowers, the fireflies' glimmer, with the sweet strains of the Jersey band, made a welcome contrast to our late surroundings."*[23]

From Herbert:

> Under a cherry tree at Cold Spring Hill
> (or Spring Hill) near the Appomattox River Va
> June 19th 1864

Dear Mother and all the rest of the folks at home —

I still live! We make out to be down here between Petersburg and Richmond about one mile from Point of Rocks and in sight of Petersburg which is about 3 or 4 miles distant. I propose to coppy from my diary as I have done before and will commence where I left off—10 oclock AM. At <u>Cold Harbor</u> Friday June 3rd.... We sent off a lot of wounded to the White House All the musicians acting as nurses here were formed into shifts of 9 hours each this evening and I have charge of the 10th relief which comes off duty at 12 oclock to night — Saturday June 4th some fighting going on today. More wounded went to the White house Sexton my Bass drummer went with them as nurse — We have buried about 26 men in all at the hospital that died of their wounds — Got a mail this afternoon Sunday 5th — Not much firing Mr. Munsell my old Eb cornet got back to day also Capt Dillingham of CoB 10th Vt who was taken prisoner at the battle of Locust Grove last fall — we were very glad to see them both. I was doubly glad to see Munsell. We had a meeting here this afternoon. I attended — Monday 6th There was some heavy firing in the night last night but were handsomely repulsed — their loss was heavy ours very light.... Lt - Col Henry's commission as <u>Col</u> came to night and the 10th Vt are very glad to see him wear Eagles on his shoulders instead of the silver leaf. Now the 10th has got one of the <u>best</u> <u>Col's</u> <u>in</u> <u>the</u> <u>world</u>....

Wednesday June 8th — All the sick & wounded went to the White House to day pretty quiet. We expect that Gen'l Grant is up to some plan that we little dream of — we fixed up some head boards to the graves of our comrades buried here today — I made up one — E. C. Clement Co. A 10th VT died June 2nd 1864 — a few wounded came in today shot by sharp shooters and nearly all mortally wounded — We have had a few wounded rebs here — some died & some sent to White house — Played some this PM.... Sunday 12th — Got up with the head ache this morning. We struck tents at 9 oclock and moved out at 3 this PM. Came about 5 miles towards White House Landing when we parked the teams and came up here by the fence where I now write and shall stay all night my head aches yet —

Monday June 13th — Halt! finds us on the south side of the Chickahomminy to night at 6 oclock — very tired and foot sore..... This is the big flank movement Genl Grant has been planning — My head does not ache to night but my legs do — I am awful tired and dirty. Can write my name with my finger in the dirt on my face. Tuesday 14th — We are only two miles from the James River to night — I rested well last night started out at 6 oclock this morning, marched slowly to this place arrived here about one oclock this P.M. All the rest of the Bands have gone to their regts. Dr. Childs wont let us go. Says he cant spare us....

Wednesday 15th — We are down on the river this evening or very near it. We struck tents to day at 10 this A.M. marched here slowly at about two miles our hospital has pitched tents in the front yard of Rebel Major Dauthats house.... We played some this evening — Charlie & I washed in the James to day — Thursday 16th — 6 oclock P.M. — we have remained here quietly all day — waiting to get a chance to go over on the pontoon and probably we shall cross to night — I went to the river to wash again to day but the tide was out so could not very well on account of the muddy shore....

Friday 17th — Well tonight finds the ambulance train within 4 miles of Petersburg — Crossed the pontoons at 9 oclock last night (103 boats long) and marched all night long — and till two oclock this P.M. without halting at all scarcely — We are all completely tired out having marched about 20 hours without us slinging knapsacks only a few minutes for grub this morning.... I got into a wagon & rode about a mile last night about twelve oclock and it was the first bit of a ride I have had on a campaign since we joined the Army of the Potomac — I have never been so hard up on a march as I am to night ache all over especially my head —

Saturday 18th — Under a cherry tree at Spring hill on or near the Appomattox river about 3 miles from Petersburg. We started out at 10 oclock this morning and arrived here a little past noon. I got rested in a little ways last night but not half way through. Head aches yet and dont feel very smart. Went and washed in the Appomattox and felt some better....

Sunday 19th — We have moved about 5 miles I recon- I have had orders to report to the regt in the morning with my whole band. Am very glad of it too.

Monday 20th — Here we are at the regt at last but not able to play for my head aches too hard and the 10th Vt Band never played a piece without me yet. When Charlie & I got up this morning the ambulance train had moved about half a mile the rest of the boys following them but we got together at 9 oclock and joined our regt in going a mile and a half. The rebs were throwing shell among us about that time but I believe no one in our brig was killed. There has been heavy firing all day. We are in the woods for the night, and all the bands a playing but <u>mine</u> and I am waiting patiently for my head to stop aching. I took some salt this P.M. and Dr Clarck says I shall be all right in the morning. I have eaten nothing for two days....

Tuesday 21st at One oclock P.M. — I <u>do</u> feel better this afternoon and have to day the salts done me good — my head has stopped aching and pulse gone down — feel as though I should be all right again in a little while. Dont feel able to play & wont till I do. I am going to send this away to you now the mail will go out to day — Charlie is writing to Nellie — Col Henry has joined his regt too. I can see him from where I now sit on my knapsack. I will write a little to Em and send with this. I must close. As ever Herbert

Since Grant had taken command the Army of the Potomac had experienced a new phase in its existence. The continual pattern of move and attack revealed

aggressiveness seldom exhibited in previous commanders. Though heartened by this forceful attitude, the army had also paid dearly, suffering over 50,000 casualties since the beginning of the Overland Campaign.[24] *Grant's repeated movement by the left flank had certainly hurt Lee's army and proved that he intended to see it through to the end. Yet Grant had remained unable to generate the victory he needed to bring the war to a close. So after the bloodbath of Cold Harbor Grant evolved a new strategy. Richmond had been the strategic goal for the Northern armies since McClellan's Peninsula Campaign. Grant realized that a quick move to the south, bypassing Lee's army and seizing Petersburg, could allow him to cut off both the Confederate capital and Lee's Army of Northern Virginia. With this goal in mind Grant ordered one of the most successful movements of the entire war.*

On June 12 General "Baldy" Smith led his XIII Corps east to White House Landing where they boarded transports and quickly circled the peninsula, arriving at Bermuda Hundred just north of Petersburg with the intention of forcing Beauregard's force out of the area and seizing the city. Warren's V Corps moved south just past White Oak Swamp, covering the movement of the other corps while also leading Lee to believe that Grant was attempting another short flanking movement. The II and IX Corps withdrew from their lines at Cold Harbor and swung south for a crossing of the James River. The VI Corps held its position opposite the Rebel lines and was the last unit to withdraw. Lee was completely surprised by this movement, at first missing the departure of the Union troops, then placing the bulk of his army in front of New Market in the mistaken belief that this was where Grant would focus his next attack. The move was well planned and executed to near perfection. Unfortunately those troops to first arrive at Petersburg failed to take advantage of their superior numbers and advanced cautiously, waiting for the support of the other corps. This delay not only allowed Confederate general Beauregard to strengthen his position but also allowed Lee to quickly move troops down to help defend Petersburg.

On June 12 the 10th Vermont, now reduced to a third of its original number, was recalled from the front at Cold Harbor and sent south. Here Charles, Herbert, and the rest of the band were again called upon to use their music as part of a tactical maneuver. According to a member of the 106th New York: "So as to cover the noise which we necessarily made the bands were directed to strike up a lively air. This did not excite the suspicion of the enemy as the bands always perform at dark."[25] *No doubt the exhausting events of the previous month had taken their toll on Herbert, for he grew increasingly sick and unable to lead the band. The brigade crossed the Chickahominy at Jones' Bridge on the evening of the June 13, arriving at Wilcox Landing on the James River two days later. The VI Corps set up defensive works and protected the crossing of the rest of the army, and bands were employed to energize the troops as they crossed.*[26] *The Army of the Potomac boarded transports on June 16 and moved west to Bermuda Hundred, there to join General Butler's Army of the James currently besieging Beauregard's troops outside of Petersburg. They arrived at midnight, immediately formed ranks and marched to the front lines. Upon arrival the men of the VI Corps were promptly ordered to attack.[27] An unbelieving General Wright challenged Butler's orders and the attack was soon called off. The men bivouacked where they were and remained encamped the next day, suffering the whole time from enemy shelling. Vermonter Henry Burnham observed: "In the afternoon the rebs commenced shelling us a little and they got pretty good range of us too. The shells burst right over us and the peices came down pretty thick. There was six or eight wounded in the Regt none very serious."[28] Though given a momentary respite from fighting, there would be no rest for the 10th Vermont; orders soon arrived sending the men south as part of Grant's attempt to close the trap on Lee. Blooded veterans now — one indignant member of the brigade described Butler's untried troops as "fat and in fine condition"— the men from Vermont packed their gear and wearily but willingly set out for their next assignment.[29]*

From Charles:

Spring Hill
Saturday, June 18, 1864
Appomatox River

We left the James River about 6 o'clock — crossed on pontoon bridges — the 1st and 3rd Division crossed on transports and landed at City Point, but we had to foot it because we were with the Ambulance train. We marched all night and till 3 P.M. We marched to within 7 or 8 miles of Petersburg. Now we are on ground that Butler has had 3 battles on — fought mostly by his negroes. The ground for a mile about here is strewn with fragments of shell and full of holes torn up by them. Firing was heard very heavy towards Petersburg, to the left. A great deal of fighting has been going on today — do not know the results.

<u>Sunday</u> — 10 A.M. — Another Sunday, Ellie, and I have just been around looking at curiosities and other things of interest. I saw Petersburg, a rebel fort, and saw the men around it. Saw the course of the river 5 or 6 miles each way; saw the trees 18 inches though cut down by shells; saw holes 6 feet square dug by shells; saw where they drink from a spring made by one shell; saw and lifted a 100 pound shell that did not burst — went in swimming and came back to camp.

By June 18 Herbert was racked by illness, barely eating and unable to play. Though rest was greatly needed, duty required that he stay with the ambulance train while it followed the army in its maneuvers around Petersburg. Charles remained in good spirits, dividing his time between helping with the wounded and chumming with the regiment. Eventually Grant chose to attack the supply lines heading into Petersburg in the hope of breaking Lee's stronghold. He saw that the Weldon Railroad that linked the city to North Carolina was within striking distance, so the II and VI Corps, with cavalry under General Wilson's command, were ordered to seize and disrupt these vital tracks. The VI Corps set out on June 22. The plan had been for both Union corps to move west, with the VI Corps swinging north like a gate to seal off the enemy.[30] *The unfriendly landscape and miscommunication between commanders led to a gap forming between the corps, and Wilcox and Mahone of Hill's corps were there to take advantage.*

Musicians from the bands and drum corps were ordered half a mile to the rear to construct a brigade hospital; a line of battle was formed and the 10th Vermont moved forward with the rest of their brigade. The dense terrain continued to cause difficulties, as yet another hole appeared between the 3rd Division and their support on the left. The men of Truex's brigade suddenly found themselves exposed in the flank and rear, yet they managed to hold their lines and eventually repel the attackers. There was continuous skirmishing, sometimes heavy, and the blue and gray lines advanced and pulled back numerous times. The fighting was so difficult that one soldier claimed: "We have seen as hard times as we saw in the Wilderness."[31] *Unable to dislodge Hill's troops, the VI Corps began to fortify, establishing the end of the Union left flank surrounding the city of Petersburg. On June 23 there was another advance by the 3rd Division, VI Corps, and eventually the Federals seized and began to destroy the Weldon railroad. A fierce counterattack forced much of the VI Corps back to their previous position where they would remain for six days. The 10th Vermont was not engaged in the worst of this fighting, though their comrades in the 87th Pennsylvania and 14th New Jersey lost 123 men killed, wounded and captured in the ferocious skirmishing.*

Some enterprising soldiers took advantage of a break in the fighting to entertain each other with music of their own. The headquarters of the 3rd Division was in a local home, and some soldiers took liberties there: "A splendid piano was left in the house, and as several of the men could play, dancing and singing were kept up in a rude style for several hours."[32] *June 29 the 3rd Division was again sent forward to the Weldon Railroad, destroying more track as well as a depot near Rheims Station, then quickly returning to their camp on the Jerusalem Plank Road on July 2. The Confederates again struck back hard, and fellow Vermonters in the 11th Vermont Infantry were to suffer Southern vengeance; this regiment was separated in the withdrawal and surrounded, losing an astonishing twenty-four officers and 373 men taken prisoner.*[33]

From Charles:

Camp in the dirt.
July 1, 1864

My sweet Ellie — Now wouldn't you like to take a "bird's eye view" of our camp half way between Reams Station and where we were before and see the 3rd Division in a corn field — the dust completely covering them up — see the poor fellows spread down their rubbers to sit on and eat on — see them now, how systematically they manage their cooking to keep their vituals out of the dirt. Now they have just drawn their rations — see the little squads of men in little circles — there sits the Commissary in the center of the group dealing out the rations of sugar — goes the round with 2 or 3 spoons full, each man holding out his cup, can or bag, or whatever he happens to carry it in. One man draws for 4, another for himself, another for 2 etc, but they all stay there with their cups after they have drawn, hoping there may be some extra which will be given out until all is gone. Next the coffee. Here comes the dried apples — a handful for each one and about as many beans, then comes the hard tacks and meat. But what is all that growling about? Oh my! They have a piece of meat a dog wouldn't touch — then comes the whiskey — no grumbling about that. Each one gets a cup full — some do not drink so give or trade it away. I swapped mine for a spoonful of sugar. Now the dusty group is all through drawing and are scattered to their shades, which consist of fly tents stuck up on sticks. Now they are arranging their haversacks, but if you

The band of the 1st Connecticut Heavy Artillery entertained their fellows in the trenches around Petersburg before moving to more comfortable surroundings near Richmond (Library of Congress).

look closely you will see that each one fixes it differently. One carries his hard tack in his haversack, another in his knapsack — one puts his sugar in a bag, his meat in a cup, another, his meat in a bag and his sugar in a cup. One has a variety of cans, cups and bags, another, nothing and crams every thing all in together. Well, they have things fixed up now and are ready to go to cooking. See their little tin cups — you wouldn't know what they were by the looks, they are so black — these little cups that were bright tin. Now these little tin cups are sitting in a row on the fire — look into them — some have coffee, some apples, some beans, some meat. Well, now look over yonder in the field — what are all those men going after? Just see the canteens by their sides — they are after water but do they find it? Yes, there is a ditch running near by but the water in it is getting rather <u>soapy</u> — the banks are lined with men bathing — some stark naked, others washing their feet, their hands and face etc. but <u>never mind it will do for coffee!</u> — but some do not think so and go a mile further to a well. About 100 men are crowding around it fighting to get to it, but as only 2 or 3 can be served at once they will have to wait several minutes, they can't wait so head for the spring a little farther on, but it is beyond the picket line and no one can reach the spring so there is nothing to do but go back to the ditch and fill up with water and make their coffee. Such of the war! Nellie might be interested in this....

Herbert has been reading your letter. He says, "gracious Peter, I should like to have them come down here and walk 10 rods by the artillery and then talk about <u>dust</u>!"

For now there seemed no end in sight for the siege around Petersburg, and spirits were failing on both sides of the trenches. On July 4 the bands were called upon to boost morale, this time in celebration of Independence Day: "At the dawn of day all the bands belonging to the 6th Corps were placed in line in full view of the different brigades," recalled George Prowell of the 87th Pennsylvania. "They played in turn the different National airs. The music was a fitting accompaniment to the deep-toned reverberations of nearly a hundred guns, engaged in a fierce artillery duel with the enemy's heavy guns behind the defenses of Petersburg."[34] Here, as throughout the war, the music performed by the bands proved to be of immeasurable value to the morale of the soldiers. In his diary Lemuel Abbott noted: "It's quite comfortable this evening; the bands are all playing, and seem determined to help us pass the time as pleasantly as possible in spite of our uncomfortable surroundings. But if we are uncomfortable what condition must the enemy be in. It's a poor soldier who never thinks of such things."[35] According to Abner Small of Maine, soldiers in both blue and gray enjoyed the performances: "Often we saw the rebels crowding up to their works and listening to 'The Battle Hymn of the Republic' or 'America.'"[36] *Herbert and Charles George decided to celebrate the holiday with a special meal, spending the rather impressive sum of $3.25 on a variety of foods from a sutler.*

From Herbert:

> Camp 10th Vt.
> 6 miles below Petersburg Va.
> July 4th 1864

Dear father and mother

I rather imagine that you are feeling a little concerned about your boy Hebert but he makes out to be "all right" — It has been some time since I have written to any of correspondence. The fact is I have not had a drum to write or anything else for the last few weeks. The 6th Corps has been around here and there tearing up rail road for the rebels and doing many other things to help put down this rebellion. We have been away down to Reams Station to destroy the Weldon and Petersburg track. Got back day before yesterday. If I should tell you all about the dirt and dust you would not wonder that I have not written before. We have now got a pretty good [place] in the woods to stay for a few days and our Regt waggons have come up and I had got my valise. The <u>dirty</u> <u>raged</u> clothes come off my back in a hurry, and clean ones from my valise soon found their way on to my weary lean body. A clean shirt, socks, pants and over coat or jacket make me feel about 1000 percent better. and it is the first time in two months (for it is just two months to day since we left Brandy Station) that I have felt like myself. I said "weary lean body." I am not so lean as I am weary. I have lost only about 10 lbs of flesh on this campaign. I weigh some where between 120 and 125 lbs now. I am <u>well</u> and tough yet, got over my sick spell right off after taking the pills and salts. It was the first physic my little body had seen for about 10 months. Haven't I stood the hardship of this war this far pretty well, better than you had any idea I would. I have marched every march the regt has made since I enlisted and never have been obliged to fall out yet. I rode about a mile in an army waggon the night we crossed the James river but it was not because I couldn't walk — Div Hospital Steward told me to get into the waggon and it would be all right. As I was some tired I done so but rode only about a mile. I have been very agreeably disappointed in the strength of my constitution. I can stand a pretty hard <u>thumping</u>. Charles is tough but he is out of <u>Kilter</u> oftener than I am. I am very thankfull for my good health and shall hope to be blessed with the same good health as long as I remain in the army. Well! to day is the "4th of July" and Richmond is taken and held by _____ "the rebels"!!! and so is Petersburg. If I should express my opinion I should say that they will hold both places for some time to come yet. They aint agoing to be whipped so easy! Notwithstanding I think that Gen'l Grant is doing as well as any man can and will no doubt accomplish his <u>aim</u> in time but how long is the time to be, that's what I would like to know. Let him work and let the people wait and hope and pray. When the time does come there will be a big time among the soldiers I recon — I think I can stand it as long as the most of them but this has been and "allfired" hard old campaign and if you dont believe it. Just come down and spend a few weeks in the hot sun & dust. Talk about "warm weather" in Vermont . <u>Hump</u> March 10 or 15 miles under a Virginia sun and through Virginia <u>dust</u> and then talk about <u>hot</u> <u>weather</u>. The sun hot enough to cook eggs and dust so thick that you cant see a man 6 feet ahead of you in the road. <u>Bah</u>!!...

Since leaving their camp at Brandy Station, the men of the 10th Vermont had participated in some of the bloodiest fighting of the entire war. The 1st Brigade had lost over 800 men and officers; true veterans now, the soldiers from Vermont, New York, New Jersey and Pennsylvania remained committed to the cause and were anxious to play a part in bringing the war to a close. Their wish was granted. New orders arrived on July 6, and the 10th Vermont along with the entire 3rd Division was detached from the VI Corps for a special assignment. Little could the men predict that they would soon be called upon to participate in one of the most important campaigns of their enlistments.

Since April 1864 the Confederacy had operated a detached force under Major General John C. Breckinridge throughout the Shenandoah Valley. By threatening Union fortifications and supply lines President Davis and General Lee hoped to create enough of a disturbance to distract Lincoln and the Army of the Potomac from the operations around Richmond and Petersburg. This plan was largely successful, as those in command of the Union forces (General Franz Sigel followed by General David Hunter) not only failed to contain the Rebel forces but were themselves defeated in a series of battles. By the middle of the summer Lee had sent General Jubal Early north with elements of Ewell's corps to expand these operations and eventually make a move on the capital of the Union; many of these troops were tested veterans and considered some of the best fighting men of the south. In Grant's words, "The situation of Washington was precarious."[37]

July 6, 1864, Charles and Herbert joined the rest of the 3rd Division in a move north, there to join General Lew Wallace in his campaign against General Early. The 1st and 2nd Divisions did not join them immediately, but would eventually be moved to the capital to help fortify the perimeter defenses. From City Point north of Petersburg the men from Vermont boarded the transport Daniel Webster *for a trip down the James River then up the coast, arriving in Baltimore*

*the next day. To alleviate some of the boredom of the trip, bands aboard the trans-
ports performed for the troops. As one member of the George brothers' brigade
noted: "We have our Brigade Band on board which discourses some very sweet
music. Some of the boys are dancing a cotillion on the upper deck now."*[38] *Upon
arriving in Baltimore the men were kept stranded on the dock for hours by bureau-
cratic mix-ups; finally trains were boarded, and by the next morning the brigade
had passed through Monocacy Junction, Maryland. Colonel Henry and the men
of the 10th Vermont were the first to arrive on the scene, and following a brief
meeting between Henry and Wallace the Vermonters ate a hurried breakfast and
began deploying alongside Brigadier General Erastus B. Tyler's troops. Wallace
thought it advisable that the regiment demonstrate in such a way as to make their
numbers appear greater, and though exhausted from traveling and a lack of sleep,
Herbert, Charles, and the band aided the deception by playing as they marched
through Frederick.*[39]

From Herbert:

> On Board the transport "Daniel Webster."
> in the dock at Baltimore Md
> July 7th/64

Dear folks at home.

Quite a change in the program. We left camp below Petersburg yesterday
morning at 4 oclock for City Point then took the boat for Baltimore only our
Div came of the 6th corps. We are going on the cars to or near Frederick City
Md from here. The rebs are in force near Frederick and we are going to fight
him. We are now waiting to land. All the boats are not in yet. We have had
a good ride on Salt water and have enjoyed it much. Our march to City Point
was awful the sun was hot enough to roast a fellow and the dust so thick that
one could not <u>see</u> hardly two feet from him. It made us all sick. Then we had
to wait standing in the sun 12 oclock M. till 3 or half past 3 PM at the dock
for the troops ahead of us to load and I came very near being sun struck. Was
sick with head ache all last evening Better to day. Two of my band boys 1st
E♭ & 1st B♭ tenor players were made sick coming to City Pt and are both
going to have a fever they will be left here in the hospital. That makes my
band rather small now 3 out. We passed Fortress Monroe at 12 oclock last
night. Point look out at 15 minutes past 6 this AM. Annapolis at 15 minutes
to One this PM. and arrived here at 4. It is now 15 minutes past 6 — To day
is the first day we have been entirely out of hearing of artillery or musketry
since the campaign commenced <u>Seems Odd</u> —!! Well I must close. Will write
you as soon as I can — We read in the Baltimore papers that there are 30,000
rebs within seven miles of Frederick City. Sergt has 7,000 men on Md. Heights

Guess we shall have to <u>fight</u>. No more.
From Herbert

By the time the 10th Vermont arrived at Frederick City at least 16,000 Confederate infantry and cavalry were about ten miles to the west at Middleton. Wallace had perhaps 5,800 men with whom to hold the enemy, though many of these were untried garrison troops and 100-days men. Despite the odds, Wallace chose to stand and delay Early's force for as long as possible, at least until sufficient forces could be sent to bolster the defenses around Washington and Baltimore.[40] With new troops on hand, Wallace began to deploy; as Ricketts' men were seasoned veterans, they were put on the center and left covering the Georgetown Pike, the direct route to Washington. General Tyler and his green troops were placed to the north to guard the National Road to Baltimore. Wallace had originally placed his forces well forward of the river, hoping to keep the enemy away from the invaluable bridges. When it became apparent that he was vastly outnumbered and in danger of being flanked, he quietly pulled the troops back to Monocacy Junction to shorten his interior line. The secretive move worked almost too well, as Colonel Truex and has staff were nearly trapped behind enemy lines as they enjoyed their dinner at a local residence.[41] Wallace set the majority of his defense on the east bank of the Monocacy River; seventy-five men of the 10th Vermont, under the command of Lieutenant George E. Davis, and men from the 9th New York Heavy Artillery, were not so fortunate. This small group was stationed on the opposite bank to defend the strategically critical covered bridge. The men were ordered to hold as long as possible.[42] A fatigued Herbert and Charles George were now to face battle after one of the most brutal movements during their service: twenty-four hours on a transport, six and one-half hours by train, and about six hours forced march. Even worse, it was a sultry, humid day with temperatures in the nineties.

The morning of July 9 skirmishers from the 10th Vermont encountered leading elements of Early's army. At 9:00 the Confederate artillery opened, and the attack began in earnest along the river. Vastly outnumbered, Lieutenant Davis' small band of men managed to hold back General Ramseur's probes for hours, repelling assaults and suffering withering fire. It was after noon before the enemy finally forced the weary Vermonters back, pressing them over the railroad tracks as the covered bridge was set on fire by Wallace's orders.[43] Lieutenant Davis would be granted the Medal of Honor for his stubborn defiance in the face of such overwhelming odds, the first such award to be granted to a member of the 10th Vermont Infantry.

Confederate batteries quickly found their range and poured fire into the Union ranks. Unfortunately the 3rd Division was outgunned by artillery as well *as musketry. Wallace chose to split his limited artillery, leaving three pieces with Ricketts and sending three north to support Tyler's troops.*[44] *At 8:30 A.M. a force of dismounted cavalry under General McCausland forded the Monocacy downstream and attacked the VI Corps from the south. Early hoped to surprise Wallace, but his troops were spotted crossing the river.*[45] *At 10:30 McCausland's line was reformed and a full attack was launched at Ricketts' division. As they had done at Payne's Farm, the men of Ricketts' division now faced some of the best veterans of the Confederate Army. But the 10th Vermont and their brigade were stocked with battle-hardened soldiers as well, and they calmly deployed to meet this threat head on, with the bulk of the 10th Vermont holding position on the extreme left of the flank. The Confederates approached confidently but were surprised to be met by a devastating volley from the VI Corps veterans.*

Resistance by Ricketts' division was so stubborn that General John B. Gordon was forced to throw his entire division against their line. Beginning around 2:00 P.M. General Clement's brigade of Georgians and two brigades from Louisiana under Zebulon York pushed forward, yet Truex managed a series of counter-strikes after reforming his line behind the Washington Turnpike. The 14th New Jersey and 87th Pennsylvania stormed a local house to drive out Rebel sharpshooters, and shortly thereafter the 151st and 106th New York regiments were ordered to charge, successfully scattering the Confederate lines and capturing prisoners. The fierceness of such resistance confounded Gordon and his men; the Rebel high command had made the mistake of believing they were facing only untried militia.[46] *For much of the day both Generals Gordon and Ramseur continued to send their men in close formation in echelon, only to be mowed down by the steady fire of Ricketts' men.*

George E. Davis, 10th Vermont, was awarded the Medal of Honor for his courageous performance at the Battle of Monocacy (Massachusetts Commandery Military Order of the Loyal Legion and the U.S. Army Military History Institute).

The 1st Brigade repulsed attack after attack, managing to hold against superior forces for almost eight hours. Wallace himself declared that "the splendid behaviour of Ricketts and his men inspired me with confidence."[47] *Here the men of the 10th Vermont*

A photograph from 1893 showing the field over which the 10th Vermont fought during the Battle of Monocacy (National Archives through the Vermont Historical Society).

faced some of the toughest combat of their careers. As Henry Burnham described: "The rebs had three or four lines of battle and we had only one in the afternoon we had some hard fighting, neither side had any entrenchments and we were in plain sight of each other and all we had to do was to stand and shoot at them as fast as we could."[48]

At 3:30 a third general assault was launched, and though Ricketts' men seemed close to holding, they began to run out of ammunition. At the same time Gordon had also managed to shift cannon and send enfilading fire against Truex's brigade. The men on the Union left flank had repulsed three full attacks by Gordon's troops before the situation became hopeless. Seeing another line of battle forming convinced Wallace of the need for retreat, knowing as he did that ammunition was running low and there was now no hope for reinforcements.[49] Ricketts, however, was unwilling to disengage, and waited for written orders before complying. By now men on both sides of the line had experienced some of the toughest combat of their careers. As General Gordon recalled: "To and fro the battle swayed across the little stream, the dead and wounded of both sides mingling their blood in its waters; and when the struggle was ended a crimsoned current ran toward the river. Nearly one half of my men and large numbers of the Federals fell there."[50]

At 4:00 P.M. the VI Corps began a retreat back to Frederick, and again the experience of the troops was revealed. Every regiment managed a fighting retreat; men of the 14th New Jersey and 87th Pennsylvania even mustered a brief counter-charge, driving the Rebels back before withdrawing once again.[51] Still, the collapse of the entire line lead to disorganization, and the retreat threatened to become a rout. Due to Ricketts' delay, parts of the 10th Vermont were separated from the rest of the brigade and forced to escape on their own under heavy enemy fire. In the frenzy of the escape both color bearers for the regiment fell, and Corporal Alexander Scott of Company D grabbed both flags — "woefully tattered and torn" — and carried them to safety, thereby earning the second Medal of Honor granted to a member of the 10th Vermont in a single day.[52] Many of the Vermonters sought creative means to keep from being captured. Private Henry Burnham of Company G and some of his comrades found a handcart, placed it on the railroad tracks, and pushed themselves to safety.[53] Despite such obstacles, most of the soldiers even-tually managed to escape, rejoining the other members of their division in New Market. One member of Herbert's band was not so fortunate: William Garvin, bass, was captured and sent to prison in Richmond.

Though forced to withdraw, the efforts of the 3rd Division under Ricketts and Wallace successfully delayed Early's advance for an entire day, thereby allowing other Union troops to form a more significant defense against Early's campaign against Washington.[54] For their gallant stand these men would eventually receive numerous commendations. Public opinion, however, was quick to judge the general and the troops under him for the loss. General Wallace was initially censured by Halleck and others in Washington for what appeared to be a failure.[55] This mis-perception was eventually rectified, and the defenders of Monocacy received a hero's welcome marching through the capital a few days later. Yet an enormous price was paid for such heroism. The night following the battle the division reported 106 killed, 506 wounded, and 511 missing or captured. As was often the case with such intense fighting, those in secondary positions, including musicians acting as stretcher-bearers and orderlies, were killed along with those engaged on the front line.[56] The 14th New Jersey lost 140 of 350 men, almost half of their force; Lieutenant Colonel Hall was seriously wounded and never returned to the war. All told Ricketts lost about one-quarter of the men he took into battle that day. The Confederates lost upwards of 1,000 men, mostly from Gordon's division.

The battered remains of Wallace's command retreated to New Market, bivouacked for the evening, then moved on to Ellicott's Mills the following morn-ing. Here the local civilians offered their own music as well as food to help the weary troops.[57] While the remainder of the division waited at Ellicott's Mills, members of the 10th Vermont were sent closer towards Baltimore to guard the junction of the Washington and Baltimore rail lines. Members of the band man-aged to climb on top of a railroad car for much of the trip. The evening of July ll what remained of the Vermonters gathered at the Relay House: eighty-one men at one count, though many who had become separated eventually rejoined the regiment. The 10th Vermont officially reported a total of fifty-six killed or wounded, while the men from Pennsylvania lost seventy-four. As Early's forces had moved on towards the capital, the 10th Vermont saw no action for a few days, then on July 14 moved to Washington to rejoin their division. The following day the band led the regiment in a parade down Pennsylvania Avenue.[58] Here the 1st and 2nd Divisions had met Early's forces at Fort Stevens, easily repulsing the Confederates from their well-fortified position. Having defeated Wallace at Monocacy, Early believed the road to Washington was open, "but, to the surprise of his troops, they saw the well-known banners of the Sixth Corps, and found that Washington, instead of being weakly defended, was now guarded by veterans of the Army of the Potomac."[59] Early wisely withdrew his army and set out for the Shenandoah Valley. Once in Washington the exhausted men of Ricketts' division were no doubt hoping for some time in camp to rebuild their battered ranks. Unfortunately the other two divisions of the corps were rested and eager for battle. Instead of heading south to rejoin the Army of the Potomac, or even setting camp in the vicinity of Washington, the heroes of Monocacy were ordered west in pursuit of Early.

From Charles:

Relay House, Maryland
July 11, 1864

Darling — since I last wrote we have done some of the hardest fighting and marching on record. I can hardly believe that men can endure so much even when I see it with my own eyes. Take our 3rd Division and see what it has done!!! — When we left Petersburg they were all worn out with fatigue — marched through that awful dust, which is the worst thing man can do. It was so crowded on the boat that they got very little sleep that night — next night slept till 2 A.M. when we took the cars for Frederick city — arrived there about 11 A.M. — marched through the city — stopped long enough to eat breakfast then marched back again — had dinner then through again — took supper then at dark marched through it again and on down the turn pike about 3 miles, crossed the Monocacy down to the rail road bridge. This march was very hard it being in the night and the roads bad — besides we were out of rations. We were routed out early Saturday morning — attempted to draw rations, but had to give it up. The rebs were coming — we got into line of battle and drew rations as quick as we could, then commenced fighting about 8:00 A.M. and fought like tigers, five times our number — were overpowered and forced to retreat.

We marched all night and till 4 o'clock the next day, making about 40

miles in 24 hours and then after being about worn out at that! Some came
on cars but the most of us were on foot. Then we took the cars for this place
(Relay House). We are doing picket duty under command of Colonel Henry.
Since I commenced this we were routed out (100 days men) by the long roll
call. The rebels are reported close — Commencing back to Friday morning —
we did not get together on the cars, but the most of us band boys got on top
of them. I laid down and had a good sleep. Everywhere along the road we were
greeted with cheers, waving of flags and handkerchiefs. It made my heart choke
to see their respect fort the flag and the veterans of the Army of the Potomac.
The people in the city were very hospitable — nearly every door had a pail of
water for us. I will pass over the march to Monacacy and commence there.

Herbert did not come in with the rest. While we were drawing rations
Saturday morning the rebs were throwing shells among us. One man was
wounded. After they took their final position we sought ours, but never found
it till we got here. We scattered in 2 or 3 directions. I went to a store — saw
a grist mill and got behind it — had just got there when some wounded came
in — one from my Company. I helped dress their wounds, while doing so the
shells came howling by close to us. When helping the boys into the ambulance
several bullets struck close by — we took shelter near the canal, when a shell
struck within 6 feet of us. We went for the Division Hospital, but never found
it for the reason there wasn't any! We followed the rail road and under the
protection of a little hill we found the ambulances and the wounded, which
served for a hospital for the time being.

Herbert was not very well and I thought I would stick to him — about
noon our boys made a charge and drove the rebs but it soon became evident
we were outnumbered. About 3:00 P.M. I heard the rebs making a charge and
as there was no shells or bullets lying in our direction I went on to the hill to
watch the battle, and I saw what but few ever get a chance to see — a battle
where both sides can be seen. The rebs were charging down the hill upon our
men — I knew it was our Brigade. They had 3 lines of battle where we had
only one. Their lines overreached ours on both ends — in fact we were assailed
on 3 sides — pretty soon the wounded began to come in — the fields were dot-
ted all over with bodies, but not so thick on our side as theirs. Our unerring
rifles told heavily upon them. We drove them back once, but then they charged
our left and drove it a little, but they were stubborn about retreating a few
rods, which they were forced to do, but then they again took a stand and
charged our center. We had to give way but slowly! On our right we had a
battery, but they had 5 times as many men — finally they turned their batteries
on our retreating column — and I left! We all went on the retreat. I went to
the next hill and stopped to see the progress of the battle and to help the

wounded along. I was helping one wounded man, whom I almost had to carry, but the rebel cavalry came in so close it meant loss of life or capture and I had to leave him. I had to run like everything as it was! I came up to the rear of the straggling column — we all took it slowly until danger of sunstroke was past. I overtook Herbert 6 or 8 mile from Monocacy and stuck with him. If I hadn't he never would have got up. I carried his trunk and led him by the hand part of the way — he gave out about 20 miles further (about half way here). We stopped and lay down till morning. We both took a drink of whiskey. (for the first time).

I routed him out at the first appearance of daylight — we had slept nearly four hours. We felt some rested and pushed on — resting occasionally. Came up with the Division about 8:00 A.M. in camp — they had been there only about 15 minutes.

Herbert threw away his knapsack and all but his rubber blanket — I took his shirt and feetings. We made our breakfast of coffee (made with cold water and strained through a towel) and hard tacks. The column started soon after we came up. Herbert soon gave out — I helped him along — he kept falling back — finally I got him a ride behind another rider just before he staggered and fell. The rest helped him along so that he got within 6 or 7 miles of our next stop. We managed to get into Ellicot's Mills along with the rest — I don't know quite how we did it. I am just as tough as a man can be — I guess I could have gone on to Baltimore, 10 miles further.

From Herbert:

Relay House Md.
July 14th 1864

Dear folks at home

Just a word — I am all tired out & cant seem to get rested any although we have been here doing nothing for 3 days. We went up to Frederick & fought the rebs — got whipped & had to retreat 40 miles in a hurry. Such a hard march I never had. I'll tell you all about it when I feel like it. I came near falling out & being taken prisoner. My first Bass player was taken prisoner & the other one is sick. Two others sick & I'm about sick so the Band is played out for a day or two. Our regt is pretty small now. Only about 200 muskets and guess it will fall short of that. We are now ordered to move somewhere but can't tell anything about were.

Write often
in haste,
J. Herbert

Having experienced some of the worst that the war had to offer, Herbert and Charles were no longer the "band-box boys" first encamped around the Potomac. Now they were blooded veterans of one of the Union's most respected corps, and it showed. William De Forest of the 12th Connecticut, recently brought east after being stationed in Louisiana, was startled by what he saw: "The Sixth Corps, one of the best in the Army of the Potomac, is lying near us. They seem to be badly demoralized by the severe service and the disastrous battles of the campaigns in Virginia. Their guns are dirty; their camps are disorderly clutters of shelter tents; worst of all, the men are disrespectful to their officers."[60] The aftermath of Monocacy proved to be one of the most difficult times the regiment had experienced. The weather was extremely hot, making the long marches excruciating, and the men's spirits plunged to their lowest point. The losses from Monocacy had greatly weakened Truex's brigade and the 10th Vermont in particular. As one Vermonter noted: "Co H are neither all killed nor taken prisoners but there is only about 25 left in the company for duty and there is but two or three companies in the regiment that are any larger and some of them are considerably smaller."[61] The brigade was to lose their commander as well. In preparation for the move General Truex wanted to put his horses on board a troop train. Division commander General Ricketts refused his request, even though Ricketts' horses were on the same train. An argument ensued, and Truex was dismissed for insubordination and disobedience.[62] Colonel William Emerson of the 151st New York assumed command of the 1st Brigade.

The tired troops left Washington on July 15, 1864, passing through Leesburg and eventually catching the rest of the VI Corps two days later. General Wright was now in command of the largest force of his career: his own VI Corps, Emery's XIX Corps, and Crook's Army of West Virginia

10th Vermont Infantry Monument at the Monocacy Battlefield (private collection).

with elements of the IX Corps, totaling 25,000. The following day Wright's army passed through Snicker's Gap and met Early's troops across the Shenandoah River on the evening of the July 18. Crook and his men attempted an advance, but the Union forces were readily stopped and forced to pull back. Darkness closed in with armies holding on each side of the river.

From Charles:

Shenandoah Valley
"Snicker's Gap" Virginia.
<u>July 19, 1864</u>

Ellie, my dear — I hardly feel like writing today, but guess I had better. Since I wrote last we have been continually on the move with no time to write. I had hoped to be able to write some news of some great victory, but everything seems either bad or not so good as I would wish. Some of the men seem to be getting discouraged — long hard marches — sore feet — hot weather — and the accomplishment of so little is having its bad effect. Yesterday we had a fight over here. Hunter's men fought and got driven back. They say they have done nothing but fight and retreat for the last month. Their supplies got cut off and they went without eating — except beef and what they could pick up along the way for the last week. They were worse off than we are and have had a harder time of it.

We crossed the mountains yesterday. As soon as we could we took up our position on the right just in time to see the fight. We could see it all being on a hill this side of the river and the combatants on the other side. Our artillery opened up on them from here and did great execution, but we did not have men enough and were driven back — but I do not think our losses were heavy.

I sent you my last letter from Relay House. We left there Thursday — took cars for Washington — stayed there one night — marched from there though Georgetown, D.C. — camped for the night at Oxfords Cross Roads. (18 mile march). Next day we pushed on to Leesburg — forded the river one mile below Edwards Ferry — passed our old camping ground at Camp Grover and Seneca. When we reached our destination Sunday night near Goose Creek, near Leesburg, not more than 20 men came in from our regiment. Other regiments had still less. They all straggled out. Herbert and I came in with them, but Herbert is pretty well played out from marching. He gets so mad sometimes he will almost talk "Copperheadism." I have not yet been too tired — they cannot tucker me out marching. Today the rebels are moving towards Harper's Ferry.

Our Band has only 11 members now — 4 in the hospital and one captured.

After a day of rest Wright's troops pushed over the river, as Early had already withdrawn. A brief reconnaissance failed to reveal Early's army and Wright was ordered to return to Washington with the VI and IX Corps, leaving Crook to deal with Early. The Vermonters believed their time in the Valley was over and that a return to Petersburg was imminent. For the first time there were misgivings among the regiment, and Herbert in particular experienced his lowest point in the war. Since the battle of Monocacy and the pursuit of Early the brigade had covered over 170 miles on their aching feet.[63] Though bitter about their experience at Monocacy and frustrated by the seemingly useless march to the Valley, the men from Vermont remained proud and did not hesitate to show it, according to Lemuel Abbott: "We marched through Leesburg with stars and stripes waving and bands playing national airs, something unusual for us to do without it's a large place."[64] By July 23 they were outside Washington where much needed supplies were distributed. The troops welcomed the arrival of their long-overdue pay, rested and rebuilt their strength, and moods quickly improved. It seemed as if the worst might be over, and the men of the 10th Vermont prepared to rejoin the Army of the Potomac.

From Herbert:

> Camp near Tanleytown
> 3 miles from Georgetown DC
> July 24th/64

Dear folks at home —

Well here we are again near Washington after traveling about 175 miles for <u>nothing</u> it seems to me — We have marched from Washington to Edwards Ferry & from there we forded the Potomac & marched through the country over past Leesburg & through Snickers Gap — crossed (<u>forded</u>) the Shenandoah river & valley up to or near Berryville then turned about after resting three or four hours and marched back through the river & Gap to Leesburg & down to chain bridge passing Camp [Griffen] crossed Chain bridge & came over here arrived here last night at 4 o'clock — All this marching we done in one week and just before this we had the 40 mile retreat from Frederick City to Baltimore and if we aint just about all <u>played</u> <u>out</u> I'll give up. I am completely worn out and so are all the soldiers in our corps.... If they march us much more I shall have to fall out & go to a hospital to get rested — I wore my boots all out on the last march & had to travel in my <u>stocking</u> <u>feet</u> one day (<u>on the</u> <u>stones</u>). I picked up two or three old stockings & put on my feet to save my own stockings. A man in the 87th Penn Band took pity on me & gave me a pair of shoes that he had with him that he didnt wear so I was all [hunk] then I saw a good many soldiers barefoot & in their stocking feet on the road. <u>rather rough</u>!! The prospects are not very bright for soldiers & a good many are dispondent & faithless. If they want to save the <u>spirits of the Soldier</u>s they must not use them so hard. Grant is wearing his army all out. He had better give them rest soon or they will all play out. Our Brig of 5 regts has only 840 men in it Officers & all for duty — thats the way the army is used up. What are we coming to? Are we going to conquer the rebs or not? <u>I</u> doubt it <u>this year</u> but we will in time of course — <u>We must.</u> When my time is out they will command <u>me</u> no longer. <u>Whiskey</u> <u>rules</u> <u>this</u> <u>army</u>. I dont like whiskey for a commander. If I should tell you one half what I know you would not wonder that the solders have lost their patriotism.... If they march me to death <u>twice</u> <u>more</u> I shall come down on the Gov't like a "<u>Bee</u> <u>on</u> <u>a</u> <u>posy</u>" <u>Ahem</u>! When I get my Blue clothes off I shall just be right on my "mess." I'll have good vituals & <u>whiskey</u> wont command me — Well I must close dont show this letter to any body they will think I am a <u>Copper head</u>! I have told nothing but the truth but I am no <u>copper head</u>. Charlie is OK & I shall be with a few days rest. Write often

From Herbert

P.S. 12 o'clock noon. Mail has come & I got a letter from Jere. He was at home having a good time just as I was 4 months ago. Let him have it — 13 months longer & if I live I'll be there too & I'll <u>stay</u> too....

CHAPTER 6

August to November 1864
Shenandoah Valley Campaign

Despite their previous setbacks, General Jubal Early's Army of the Valley was by no means defeated and it continued to threaten Union stability in the Shenandoah Valley. In an effort to silence this threat once and for all, the 10th Vermont and the rest of the VI Corps headed west once again on July 26. It was a solemn moment as the 10th Vermont passed Frederick and the battlefield at Monocacy. Bodies of dead comrades were found and burial details were formed. Ricketts' division spent a brief time in the area, visiting comrades who had been left in hospitals and homes while receiving care from the locals. On July 29 the entire corps moved to Harpers Ferry to link with other Union forces, and the following day they set out for Frederick once more, though this time the march was impeded by poor organization and crowded roads. The weather was dangerously hot, so much so that many experienced and hardened men of the George brothers' brigade fell out during the march. Eventually they made it back to Frederick, enjoying a five-day stay in an area they knew well. Their visit coincided with an appearance by Lieutenant General Grant, there to discuss regional strategies with his commanders. On August 5 the regiment moved back to Monocacy Junction, kindling more difficult memories of the arduous clash just a month before. Orders came down telling the Vermonters that they were again to report to Harpers Ferry. The VI Corps arrived at the new headquarters on August 7 with the bands of the brigade playing "John Brown's Body" and the men singing along.[1]
From Herbert:

Camp near Hyattsvile Md.
July 27th 1864

Dear folks at home!

I have just rec'd a letter from mother with a silk handkerchief & $1.00

all right. Got the linen one day before yesterday — We have been paid off 4 months pay & I expressed $75.00 to Jere yesterday kept $11.00 had to buy some things at Washington so have not got much money left. I had to get a rubber coat as I had no rubber blanket. (It was stolen from me you remember.) Paid 6.50 for the coat. We staid in or near Georgetown only two days & half and didnt get half rested when we started off up this way. We left Georgetown yesterday noon & arrived here this P.M. at 4 oclock. No it was between 2 & 3. It is about 35 miles from here to Georgetown. We came 17 miles yesterday & 18 to day. Tired & no appetite I am so near worn out that I have lost my appetite but I am as <u>gritty</u> as a <u>bear</u> and <u>wont</u> give out anyhow. They can march me to <u>death</u> but my constitution is so strong that I do not get sick. But it <u>seems</u> as though they were trying to wear my life out this summer <u>Hang</u> em let them <u>go</u> <u>it</u> I am going to <u>live</u> some how if possible — Only 13 months longer.... Charlie is well — The mail goes out immediately. Write often —

From

Herbert

P.S. If you want any money send to Jere for some of mine

From Charles:

<u>Harpers Ferry</u>
<u>July 30, 1864</u>

Ellie dear — here we are again at Harper's Ferry —

We were some surprised by seeing General Grant and lady at Monocacy — every car cheered him. I suppose he has left General Meade in charge of the siege of Petersburg. Grant is not much larger than I am.

Another week has passed and I am still among the living and in good health. We have been having another hard march. We left Washington Tuesday and arrived here yesterday noon, it being about 70 miles. Now 70 miles may not seem so big to read of but I tell you 70 miles in 4 days by a set of worn out men is a hard task! I do get so tired at times I think of the easy chair at home. My feet ached at times pretty bad but have not got sore. A day or so of real rest would make me all right again. Herbert needs rest — weighs 115 pounds — he will fail up if he does not get some rest — then down goes the Band and I take a gun! I have a little self interest in carrying part of his load. I do most all his cooking and don't let him carry in water. I shall keep him along as long as I can. We do not play in the Band much now. Yesterday we had only 8 mouthpieces. Ellie, you will have to excuse me for not writing more — I have not had time to write much on this march — every meal has been eaten in a hurry, many time while on the march — and our sleep did not average even 4 or 5 hours.

I see that the papers are silent about the movement of the 6th Corps, but you may know we are looking after the raiders! that is our business just now! I don't know just how many hundred miles we can travel, but one thing is certain, the 6th Corps has had the hardest time of any Corps in the field. This Brigade of five regiments is not so large as our 10th Vermont was when we crossed the Rapidan.

> The mail will go out soon so I will close, my dear.
> "Thinking of thee, and the comforts of home,
> Of the pleasures I've lost, while soldiering I roam!"

From Herbert:

> Camp near Buckettstown Md
> near the rail road between Point Rocks
> and Monocacy Junction
> Aug 5th/64

Dear folks at home.

In the dirt and hot sun with a fly tent for a shack I seat myself on my knap sack with a drum for a table to answer a letter I got from home lately with a lot of questions in it. I wrote to you while we were resting for a day up near Frederick. We moved out the next morning and came down here. All of our Corps is here we are on the Monocacy river have been here since day before yesterday noon. Had orders to be ready to move at daylight this morning and packed up every thing but we still remain here & it is half past two PM. It is so hot that it would be impossible to move troops they would all be sunstruck.... I hope the 6th Corps will stay here and do picket duty on the Potomac and I sincerely hope that we have got through with the hardest marching for this year. I begin to feel like a new man now with only 3 days rest. Now for the answers to your questions. Our Brigade is formed with the 10th VT. 87th Penn. 106th N.Y. & 151st N.Y. and the 14th N.J. Our 2nd Brigade has the following regts in it. The 126th 110th & 122nd Ohio regts 67 Penn. 138th Penn. and 9th N.Y. Heavy Artillery. Thats all of our Div.... Yes I think good bread would do more towards keeping up the spirits of the soldiers then poor whiskey (or good either). We buy bread of the citizens here in Md. a great deal. I have paid out considerable money lately for <u>good</u> <u>bread</u> and I am getting up a big appetite on it too. We steal apples and make sauce to eat with it. We got a few lbs of flour day before yesterday and I make some good flour gravy to eat on our bread too.... Col Emerson of the 151st N.Y. commands the Brigade now. Genl Morris has not returned. He is in N.Y.

City now. Lt. Col. Chandler is a very disagreeable man drunk all the time. He is sick now in some Gen'l Hospital—Col Henry <u>is</u> with us & <u>Bully</u> <u>for</u> <u>him</u>. His finger has got well that was shot off at Cold Harbor. We haven't got a Captain with us now that was with us when the campaign commenced. Guess thats about all the questions. (No one more). Yes most certainly I feel thankful that I have been spared for two years amid so many dangers and if I live to see Sept 1865 I should be still more thankful—The Baggage wagon came back and the officers baggage didn't so guess we should not move to day—None of my sick band boys have returned yet.... I must tell you that Charlie & I have not had a tent up nor have we slept under cover since we left Petersburg till yesterday. A month today 3 days that we didn't pitch our tent. Slept right out doors all the time & got rained on only once then we lay still & got wet. Well I must close. Love to all

 From Herbert

Wright's VI Corps was now officially detached to the newly formed Army of the Shenandoah under the command of General Phil Sheridan. Grant had decided that a more unified command was necessary to end the Confederate operations in

Photograph from 1864 showing General Phil Sheridan (center, standing) with his generals: Henry E. Davies, David McMurtrie Gregg, Wesley Merritt, Alfred Torbert, and James H. Wilson (Library of Congress).

northwestern Virginia. On August 7 the previously scattered sections — the Middle Department, Department of Washington, Department of the Susquehanna, and Department of West Virginia — were consolidated to form the Middle Military Division under Sheridan.² Colonel Emerson remained in command of the 1st Brigade following the dismissal of Truex, though the 10th Vermont had a change of commanders. Colonel Henry was continuously ill, and Major Dillingham took temporary command of the regiment while Henry recuperated. The ferocity of combat over the last few months had taken its toll on the commanders of other regiments as well: Major Vredenberg now commanded the 14th New Jersey, Captain Robertson was in charge of the 106th New York, and Colonel Fay commanded the 151st New York in place of Emerson. Colonel Shall still led the 87th Pennsylvania.

By August 10 Sheridan's army was on the move towards Winchester where Early and his army were reported to be operating. It was a trying march as the extreme heat again caused many soldiers to fall by the side. On August 11 the enemy was sighted on the opposite bank of Cedar Creek, leading to some mild skirmishing. Two days later the VI Corps was sent out on reconnaissance in force, eventually finding Early well entrenched at Fisher's Hill. The Federals withdrew back across the creek.

From Charles:

Strasburg, Virginia.
August 13, 1864

We are on another campaign and of all the others this is the hottest — it is all we can do to stand the heat! And it has been dry so long that water is very, very scarce! We received marching orders Wednesday A.M., having had a rest of 2 or 3 days, during which time a force was concentrating for a <u>raid on the johnnies</u>. We were on the road at 5:00 A.M. — every road was occupied by troops or trains for miles. We march most of the time through fields and woods. Passed through Charlestown, (the place where John Brown was hung) about 9:00 A.M. (At Harper's Ferry I saw the building in which he was captured.)

We played through Charlestown and were complimented by General Rickets. Charlestown shows the ravages of war very much — it has been occupied by both sides many times. Marks of cannon balls were seen on the houses.

Shells were seen in the roads and buildings were fitted for forts by having little shooting holes knocked out. We marched till 3:00 P.M. before we had our dinner. About every man had a hand in plundering. Herbert was much played out that night — was sick when we started — threw up his dinner. Next morning he got a pass for the ambulance where he has been ever since. Thursday we were wagon train guard and marched very slow. I got a bunch of honey and a quarter of mutton for my plunder that day. The honey I took second handed and the mutton was dropped by a cavalry man — he never stopped to pick it up so a couple of us boys did. We get all the apples ad green corn we want — a field of 10 or 15 acres of corn will be harvested in 2 hours.

(Friday) we came on again — marched on the pike most all the way — passed through Newtown and Middletown, Virginia. Last night we came up to the johnnies — there was considerable skirmishing going on with Hunter's Corps in the advance. This morning we advanced to within a mile and a half of Strasburg. We are in sight of the johnnies but can't get to them very easy — they have a strong position. Our Generals did not consider it advisable to attack them — last night we moved back about 2 miles....

Reports came in claiming that reinforcements were augmenting Early's army, so Sheridan chose to avoid a full engagement and began to withdraw.[3] Early pursued and pestered the Yankees north to Charlestown; a defensive camp was prepared by August 18, and the 10th Vermont and other regiments were resupplied. For three days the men saw no action and were grateful for the break even though it poured rain. As the soldiers passed south through Charlestown, they recalled the trial and execution of the abolitionist John Brown. Edwin Haynes, the regimental historian, was to recall:

As they marched through these streets, it seemed as if every soul was touched with the memory of the old hero, and ten thousand voices broke forth into singing- "John Brown's body lies mouldering in the ground." A dozen bands played the air to which these words were set; and what with the music, the singing, and the measured tread of thirty thousand men, with their very muscles, as well as their vocal organs, in time and tune, afforded a spectacle that time cannot erase from the memory of the participant or the beholder. Surely, his soul is "marching on," was the unavoidable impression created by this spontaneous tribute to his memory. This was one of the real Battle Hymns of the Republic, and its ringing chorus had a mysterious inspiration, that ever brought rest and quickened pace to weary feet, and awakened fresh zeal in desponding hearts.[4]

Even as the proximity of the enemy limited the chance for organized music, Sergeant Edward Bushnell received a musical gift from home, a copy of the song "Brave Boys are They."[5] Evening sings remained a delight for enlisted men and officers alike, and after years of campfire concerts the appearance of new material was probably greeted with relish. Certainly the men were grateful for anything uplifting. The past few months had been grueling and the defeat at Monocacy weighed heavily on their minds. John Louiselle of Company F dolefully admitted: "I don't know how it will turn out we appear to be getting the worst of it about these days. But the old saying is its always darkest before day we may prosper better after a bit."[6]

On the morning of August 21 the Confederates pushed through the skirmish line of the Federals, quickly overrunning the outer perimeters. Resistance lines were formed, the 3rd Division was ordered into battle, and the Confederate advance was halted. That evening Sheridan's army withdrew even further to Hall-town, and there was no major combat aside from brief sorties by the Confederates. Early was unable to provoke or dislodge the Army of the Shenandoah, so he with-drew back towards Bunker Hill. On August 28 Sheridan began pushing forward in response; various units of the Federal army attacked the Rebel positions, so the Southern troops pulled back on all fronts, eventually settling on the far side of Opequon Creek. At one point Ricketts' brigade was called upon to support General Merritt, who was attempting to hold the Smithview Bridge. The brigade charged, repelled the graycoats, and held the bridge.[7] By now both armies had returned to their approximate positions from the beginning of the month, with the VI Corps placed east of Winchester near Berryville.

For two weeks Sheridan remained stationary, consolidating his forces and preparing for a major offensive. This break was well received by the 10th Vermont; fatigue was taking its toll on the men, having marched 700 miles since their arrival in Baltimore. Unfortunately the weather did not cooperate, and it seemed to rain more often than not. Lemuel Abbott noticed how the musicians of the band once again stepped in to support the troops with music: "Time hangs heavily and were it not for the bands I should be almost homesick."[8] Fortunately for Her-bert the 87th Pennsylvania's term of enlistment was ending soon, and he was given some of their music for his own use. By this point in the war both band musicians and their audiences were grateful for any new music, as years of playing the same arrangements could make the music sound "decidedly worn out" according to one bandsman.[9] It must have been a frustrating time for the young bandleader, how-ever, as many of his musicians were sick, and one of his band members had been captured at the Battle of Monocacy. It may be that the shrinking number of players led some to question the status of the band, as Herbert expressed concern that his group might be dismantled. Yet not all news was bad news for the George brothers. Herbert and Charles learned they were receiving special reinforcements of their own, when on September 2 their brother Jeremiah enlisted for one year as a musi-cian with Company G.

From Herbert:

Camp 10th Vt
Halltown Va
Aug 24th 1864

Dear sister Em —
     I have time for a few lines this morning and will hurry off a letter to you I am well now and am fatting up. After our 50 miles raid up to Strausburg

& back I feel tip top but have been so busy that I couldnt write to you. The 87th Penn Vols are going home in a few days now (time is over) and I have been getting a lot of music of their band to play after they go home and it takes time to copy it off you know — My bass drummer has lost his book and I have got to send for the parts at home to coppy them off again. I want you to send them to me by mail. The music is in my red trunk and come on cards and the rest on sheets. Now of the card music I want you to send me the Bass drum parts to the following pieces. "Viva La America" "Wood up Quick Step" "Elfin Waltzes" "Glory Halelujiah" "Sontag Polka" "On to the field of Glory" and "Anvil Chorus" — These seven cards do up in a wrapper and send by mail paper postage 2 cts. mark on it <u>music</u>. Of the sheet music tear off the side that has the drum parts to the following piece — Mocking Bird Quick Step. Blarney Medley. Brightest Eyes Q. S. Dirge By Ringold & one by Dodworth. Cicilien Vespers Quick Step. Cavatina from Lucia. Marksmens polka. "Ernani" or Introduction to Ernani. March du Sacre. Violet Medley. Grand Terzetto De La Duches from Lucretia Borgia. Grand March from Bellisario. We are growing Old Quick Step. Vailance Polka. Song of the Spring Waltz. and Gig Medley. All of these pieces you understand are on sheets and the drum parts are on one leaf and some other part on the other. Tear off the side that has the drums on and roll them up like a newspaper and send by mail, mark on it "<u>Sheet</u> <u>music</u>" so the P. M. can see it. pay paper postage Please send this music along now immy and you will oblige me very much. My sick musicians do not get well very just none of the 5 that are absent are able to return yet. Some I guess will go into the Invalid Corps and I shall have to learn some new players. <u>Sorry</u>. I haven't time to tell you about our 100 mile march up to Strausburg and back in the hot sun but will some time. I was sick 3 days & went with the ambulance train, didnt ride any though but they carried all my things for me so I managed to get along. It was so hot some days that men <u>died</u> from sun stroke on the road.... Well I must close — Will write again soon. By the way did you ever receive Munsells photograph? My 2nd Eb players I mean? I sent it home a long time ago & never heard from it. I now send you Sargt Stickneys. He is acting Sergt Major now. Please let me know if you receive these pictures

Write soon
From
Herbert

From Charles:

<u>Camp near Hamiltown, Virginia.</u>
<u>August 27, 1864</u>

Ellie dearest — the prospects now certainly look fair. Grant and Sherman are both progressing well in their sieges, while Mobile is in a fair way to be captured — every week shows an advantage gained. I have always looked upon Mobile as the most important palace we could get — it is a good base for supplies for an army. My faith never was stronger than it is now!

A word about <u>our</u> position. It seems that Sheridan followed up the rebs to Strasburg and found them too strongly posted to attack and had to fall back on account of supplies. At Charlestown the whole army went into camp with the expectation of staying quite a while, but the johnnies attacked us there and it being a good camping ground only, we had to fall back to fighting ground. We are about 3 miles from Harper's Ferry — our line of battle is several miles long being on elevated ground. To the front is nearly a half mile, which the enemy would be exposed to our fire if the attack.

The whole line is protected with breastworks with the artillery at the rate of 30 pieces to the mile. It so happens that our regiment occupies the extreme right of the line with nothing but cavalry on our flank. As the Band is on the right of the regiment we hold the right end of the line.... Herbert got a letter from Jere last night — he has enlisted as bugler in the 61st Massachusetts. Herbert has just written him to get transferred to this regiment if he can — we need him in the Band. We have only 12 members in our Band. Herbert, 1st E Flat; Munsel, 2nd; McClure, 1st B Flat; myself 2nd; Ebeneezer Johnston Foster, alias "Little Drummer, alias "Nellie" alias "Sis" plays the 1st Alto; Kent, 1st Baritone; Goldsmith, B Flat Bass, Dick, Bass Tuba; Sexton has taken the snare drum; Watson, the cymbals and Stuart the Bass drum. Nate Hamilton, William Clark and Dan Backer are in the hospital in Vermont. Garvin, a prisoner. Wells has been in the ranks carrying a musket since the 1st of July till last Wednesday. We had to take him back for the want of better. Forster, or "sis" is a good player and the best little fellow you ever saw. He is only 16 years old now — has curly red hair — a handsome boy. Dick drinks hard sometimes — Here we got to practice now — so good bye for now — I love you.

<u>Monday morning</u>
<u>August 29, 1864</u>

Darling Ellie — we are gain on the march. We passed though Charlestown ad played "Old John Brown" which was very appropriate seeing that was where he was hung. We are having fine times eating green corn — it is right in its prime!

Amid the threat of a major engagement, as well as the frustration of undesirable camps and inadequate food, the band members continued to be concerned when the rumor resurfaced that the band's existence was in doubt. Charles believed that General Wright had ordered the breakup of the bands and the return of the musicians to the ranks. Charles and Herbert had grown accustomed to their role as musicians and remained confident that the quality of their ensemble would prevent the band of the 10th Vermont from being dissolved. On a brighter note, Charles and Herbert looked forward to the approaching reunion of the three surviving George brothers.

Two letters from Charles:

<u>Sunday Morning</u>
[September 4, 1864]

We are under marching orders now — the rebs are shelling us and we shall move pretty soon. We went into a new camp Friday night. It was in the woods and a very pretty place. We had orders to put up summer quarters — had boards all ready to make bunks of and expected to have a good time; before 10 o'clock that night an order came to be ready to march at 4 o'clock the next morning. The whole army moved on difficult roads towards Berryville, arriving at Clifton Farm about 2:00 P.M. The 19th Corps had found and engaged the enemy — have hared since that they wiped them out. This morning firing commenced on the left — shouldn't wonder if we had a battle today. I can hear the rattle of musketry now and I can hear a band too. <u>Tuesday</u> — We advanced to Berryville last Saturday — not much fighting. Have been building breastworks. We are getting indignant at the way we are used as a Band. Herbert just got a letter from Jere — he is coming to this regiment. There is an order out breaking up Regimental Bands and having Brigade Bands — our chances are more than good to get into one — there will be 24 men and will take about all of us. Herbert will probably lead.

<u>Camp near Berryville.</u>
<u>September 9, 1864</u>

My dearest Ellie — (Friday) — Quite an excitement is being evident among the bands. General Wright has issued and order for all detailed musicians to take up muskets. Colonel Emmerson is trying to get a Brigade Band out of them. Neither the regiments nor the bands will submit. The leader of the 106th is 2nd Lieut. in one of their Companies. He has the offer of Band Master and is going and is going to take it. He has to be <u>mustered out</u> before he can be mustered in. He is going to be mustered out and then <u>go home</u> and <u>not</u> be mustered in. "Bully for him"! Herbert was just up to see the Major. It is pretty certain that the Bands will be broken up. Guess I can take a gun as well as anybody — "Bully for me"! I had just as lief be in the ranks as here as far as the danger is concerned. We have to keep with the regiment during battle. Herbert has just got back — the thing is "<u>did.</u>" I shall report to my company this afternoon.

(<u>Sunday noon</u>) Band not broken up yet. The Major had orders to send us to our Companies but they are trying to keep the band in tact. We played last night (per order) at Brigade Headquarters — also at regimental and dress parade. (Sunday evening) — All quiet in the Shenandoah Valley. The regiment is filling up fast. Battles got back — he was wounded at Cold Harbor. I shall tent with him if I go back to the Company. The officers are trying hard to keep up the Band!

While Charles and Herbert worked to keep their band together, Jere had finally made the decision to join his brothers in the war. He returned to Newbury, Vermont, enlisting there to make sure he could join his brothers' regiment. He spent time with his family and practiced on cornet and fife, intending to join the band when he reached the front. While his initial experiences with army life might not have been as glorious as he had envisioned, Jere accepted his new surroundings with cautious optimism.

Two diary entries from Jere:

Newbury VT.
September 8th

Have spent the past three days very pleasantly at home visiting. Fixing and getting fixed. Tuesday, I went with Father, out to Town Meeting and voted for State Officers. J. Gregory Smith, for Governor. Wm. R. Shedd, representative for Newbury.

Yesterday went with Father partridge hunting, — more hunting than partridges.

To-day Albert arrived from Lancaster, about sick with a cold. My cold is better. Mother has relined my blouse, put pockets in it and it is all O.K. She has also made my thick shirt with which I am much pleased. Also a night-cap and swathe.... I have got one-quarter ounce of quinine to carry for medicine and other little things. I feel well prepared for my dangerous journey and life for a year. I am bound to go armed and equipped for war so far as knowledge will direct and money buy.

To-morrow I leave home for the war. Hitherto my life has been spent in New England in common avocations, not without sufferings and disappointments but always surrounded by friends and the comforts of life. Now I give up these and go to the field to endure the hardships of war. A great change in my life, but I hope to be able to come a stronger and wiser man. I shall love the adventure, hate the rebels, and fight for the "flag of our Union."

Conscript Camp,
Fairhaven, Conn.
September 11th

Friday Morning I left home for the war, feeling as well, tough and smart as I ever felt, in the best of spirits. I was so confident of returning in a year that I felt not the pang of parting with parents and Sister as might have been supposed. My heart was touched when Father bid me "good bye" for I noticed that as he added "May the Lord bless you and be with you" his voice trembled and he turned silently away. I knew that He realized that he was parting with a son, whom I know he loves, with only a war chance of ever seeing him again. I was indeed deeply moved as I answered in the same terms. It seems as though I never loved him better than I have during my two visits this summer. He seems to overflow with goodness. Not that he is any more so than Mother, for she was always so. I notice it more in him because he was <u>not</u> so when I visited home last summer.

I had a jolly good parting with Emma and Mother at the depot, and my last salute was "hurrah" with a wave of both hands and a laugh.

Arrived safe at Windsor and was mustered into the U.S. service between the hours of two and three P.M.

Rations of cold beef, bread and coffee were served in a cellar under the hotel, after which we in a company of about seventy-five repaired to the dancing hall in the [?] building where quartered for the night. On the floor wrapped in our blankets we tried to sleep, but the boys were so noisy all night—that a few little snatches of slumber, was all I could get. Albert being about sick anyway, looked pretty hard in the morning but comes out all right to-day.

About three o-clock yesterday P.M. 105 of us soldiers left Windsor for this place where we arrived about eleven. The country and river scenery, as we follow down the Connecticut, is very fine, especially between Brattleboro and Springfield. I was surprised to see so much tobacco growing and drying. At Springfield I first felt the bitterness of a slave, the inferiority of a private soldier and the power of military authority, <u>because</u> I have been accustomed to my own liberty and equality with everybody. The train made quite a long stop, and stepping from the platform of the car, walking leisurely away, not thinking of going out of sight. When I had proceeded about half the length of one car I heard a man running behind me, and as I turned round was seized and roughly handled by the man who was in charge of us. The forcible argument which he used with his strong arm and the toe of his boot to get me back into the car, was entirely unnecessary, as I needed only to be <u>told</u> to <u>obey</u>. Calling it all right, I silently took my seat, wondering if this was the beginning of "red tape" what would be the end....

In spite of the almost constant yelling and singing of the boys in the car I slept most all the way in Albert's arms, who slept some. Shouldering our knapsacks, haversacks and canteens, we marched three-quarters of a mile to this place, whistling to keep step by, in the absence of a fife and drum....

Some have been playing ball, others playing cards and gambling. Two young fellows were just at it close by me, with fifty cents a game at stake. I begin to see something of camp life, which is wicked enough to make a civil man sick.

On September 17, 1864, Grant met with Sheridan to discuss operations in the Valley. After seeing Sheridan's plans for ousting Early's Army of the Valley, Grant encouraged immediate implementation and thereafter left the Valley Campaign in Sheridan's competent hands. For once the Union forces were in possession of superior intelligence, including relative strength and deployment, so confidence was high for a successful operation.[10] The next day Sheridan mustered his army; supplies and rations were distributed and the camp was dismantled, though it was not until early the next morning that the troops began to move out. General Wright came near to upsetting the Union approach when he tied up the narrow roads with his supply train (despite Sheridan's orders to avoid this at all costs).[11] Finally the Army of the Shenandoah, now numbering over 42,000, crossed Opequon Creek. At the front of the Union formation was Emerson's brigade, placed to the right of the 2nd Division and to the left of Keifer's brigade, with the 151st New York set forward as skirmishers. Under extremely heavy artillery fire the Federal troops advanced over difficult ground, with the 10th Vermont (now numbering 350 effectives) and 14th New Jersey leading the way for much of the time.[12] By 10:00 A.M. they had dislodged the enemy pickets and formed into a line of battle. Stillness came over the field as both sides paused to evaluate the situation and prepare for the inevitable battle.

Just before noon a signal gun sounded, triggering a general advance by the Federals. The results were disastrous. The 3rd Division found itself facing Ramseur's and Rodes' troops on higher ground and with a deadly range of fire, so it was forced to hold in place. Eventually the entire VI Corps, following the lead of the Old Vermont Brigade, charged the Confederate positions. Any success they achieved was soon lost as the 3rd Division found itself dangerously unprotected. Emory's XIX Corps was positioned to the right of the VI Corps, and as each corps advanced a gap formed between the two. Keifer's brigade, holding the right end of the 3rd Division, suddenly found itself to be the end of the line with their right flank exposed. The troops of the Vermont Brigade to the left of the 3rd Division continued to advance despite the lack of support and found themselves caught in a ravine and under heavy fire. Confronted by entrenched enemy troops across an

Alfred Waud's sketch titled "Sept. 19th 10:30 A.M. Rickett's [sic] advance against Rhodes [sic] division in the woods" (Library of Congress).

open field and their right flank in doubt, the men of Emerson's brigade crouched down to avoid the overwhelming fire and await support; some elements of the division broke and fled to the rear. One Confederate artilleryman claimed that his batteries fired four times the number of shells that they had in any previous battle.[13] Seizing this advantage, Battle's brigade of Confederate general Robert Rodes' division charged into the gap. Colonel Keifer saw the gap and attempted to fill it with his brigade, though he had too few men to withstand the Rebel onslaught. Both of Ricketts' brigades were forced to withdraw quickly and with little order. Fortunately reinforcements from the VI Corps' 1st Division arrived soon thereafter, including the brigades of Russell and Upton, and the line was stabilized.[14] Ricketts and Getty threw their divisions forward once again, and the rest of the Union troops followed. Though repulsed at first, the Yankees persevered and managed to push back Ramseur and Rodes' lines in a few locations. Early's troops responded with attacks of their own so that soon the lines were intertwined and heavy skirmishing reigned for nearly 3 hours.

The brutal fighting had been especially hard on the Vermonters. Major Dillingham, popular commander of the 10th Vermont for barely a month, lost a leg from solid shot and died within a few hours. Captain Lucius T. Hunt of Company H took command of the regiment.[15] The battlefield was still for awhile as the Confederate forces believed they had successfully repelled Sheridan's army and concluded the day's fighting. Sheridan had other plans, and shortly after 4:00 P.M. he attacked again, this time sending Crook's VIII Corps and the majority of the Union cavalry to flank the Confederates from the north. A renewed assault by the VI and XIX Corps, including Emerson's brigade, now proved too much for the defenders. The gray lines crumbled and a rout through Winchester ensued, ending the Battle of Opequan Creek (or 3rd Winchester). The Army of the Valley was shattered, losing thousands to casualties and as prisoners, including the irreplaceable General Robert E. Rodes.[16]

Though successful at day's end, the VI Corps paid dearly for their victory, losing 1685 in the ferocious fighting.[17] The 10th Vermont suffered heavy losses as well: sixty-five killed or wounded, including Lieutenant Hill, Lieutenant Abbott, and Captain Davis. Ricketts' division suffered the highest casualties of the VI Corps.[18] However, Rickett's men now felt a measure of revenge for their defeat at Monocacy, and the soldiers took pride in the performance of their regiments, brigades, divisions and corps. Their actions here and throughout the Valley Campaign certainly impressed General Sheridan, who was later heard to say, "Give me the Sixth Corps and I will charge anywhere."[19]

The following morning the Federal troops pursued Early's army through Middletown, catching them just past Strasburg. The Army of the Shenandoah went into camp for the night while Early fortified his position on Fischer's Hill. Sheridan carefully deployed his troops, lulling his opponent into believing that he was entrenching. On September 21 Federal units advanced at key points along the line, driving in pickets and securing higher ground. The following day Sheridan launched a surprise attack on a number of fronts. At 11:00 A.M. Ricketts' 3rd Division, occupying the right side of the Federal line, pushed forward and began to flank Early's army, securing the west slope of Flint's Hill. This assault worked to distract Early's attention as Crook and his units snuck down from the north and attacked the enemy lines from the rear.[20] Keifer's 2nd Brigade took the lead, followed by Emerson, and after almost an hour of brisk fighting began to force the Confederates back. The appearance of Crook's units forced Ramseur, the Confederate commander on the flank, to redeploy in an attempt to meet the new threat, and the VI Corps seized the opportunity and smashed once again into the enemy lines.[21] Again the Rebels were caught off guard; the Federals swept through their opponents and quickly drove them from their placements. An excited Henry Burnham proclaimed: "We done something that never has been done there before, and that was to flank them out of there. When we drove them out of their breas works they scattered just like sheep."[22] Ricketts' division overran and secured a number of enemy works, including six artillery pieces, forcing the Rebels into a

Guards standing over Confederate prisoners captured at the battle of Fisher's Hill, Virginia (Library of Congress).

broken retreat. The men from Vermont could also claim to have captured fifty-eight prisoners.[23] *Here as always the musicians found themselves in dangerous situations. Henry J. Babbitt, a musician with Company D, 151st New York, was taken prisoner during the battle.*[24]

From Charles:

Camp near Strasburg
September 21, 1864

All well, my dearest!—great battle fought and a great victory. We have had one of the hardest battles of the war—our loss must be as much as 1500. I feel thankful my flesh and blood are still uninjured. As soon as the battle began and the wounded came in we went to the Hospital—we had some narrow escapes though from shells. Our Brigade was in the heat of the battle and lost heavily. Company G and H suffered the most.... There are only 16 left out of 26. Major Dillingham was killed—had his leg taken off by a shell. Company H had 4 killed and 7 wounded. The regiment had 10 killed and 49 wounded....

We left camp Monday at 2:00 A.M. and marched fast till we came to the johnnies. Then came the fighting. The roar of artillery and musketry was terrible! Once a portion of our men fell back a short distance, but the rebs gave way at last, then we gave it to them! Prisoners by the thousand were taken.

(Tuesday) — This morning our troops followed them to Strasburg, where we are now. We keep taking prisoners — but they are in their old stronghold. I think we shall get them out though. The band boys came on yesterday afternoon. Today cheer after cheer is heard as they have the congratulations message from the President and General Grant. The rebels have lost very heavily. WE are in our old position here. I think the 8th Corps is on a flanking movement. 900 fresh cavalry came in yesterday. I saw about 3000 rebs in one pile at Winchester. — Our wounded are all in Winchester now. — The rebel wounded are there too — the ones they did not take away with them. Our hospital during the battle was 4 miles from Winchester.

My health is good — so is Herbert's. Jere has not arrived yet. — our artillery has just gone out on the run! — so long for now, your Charlie.

The battle at Fischer's Hill was a decisive victory for the 10th Vermont, Rickett's division, and the entire Army of the Shenandoah.[25] *The VI Corps joined the XIX Corps in immediate pursuit, chasing the Confederates for three days through Mt. Jackson and New Market to Harrisonburg, where Early turned to the mountains for escape. Countless Southern troops were captured, including some unfortunate musicians in gray, according to Elisha Hunt Rhodes of Rhode Island: "Two of these men [prisoners] had brass instruments, having belonged to a Rebel band, but the others were soldiers. I made them retain the instruments and marched them into Winchester and delivered them to the Provost Marshall. The Corporal rode upon them as they were sitting under a tree."*[26]

Jere had not yet arrived; in fact, he was still in Washington waiting for transportation to take him to the Shenandoah Valley to join the 10th Vermont. He and some friends took advantage of the time to view the sights in the nation's capital.

From Jere:

Soldiers Rest
Washington, D.C.
Monday Sept 26th, 4 P.M.

Coming events do not always cast their shadows before, as yesterday when I left off writing, I had no idea of the adventures I have since had. Perceiving that we were not likely to start from Washington till to-day, Albert, H. L. Farnham and I started out to see something more of the place. Taking a Georgetown car we rode to the President's house, where we made quite a lengthy visit. Visited the park in front of the White House in which is the equestrian statue of Gen. Jackson. A very nice thing. We then went into the back grounds on the other side which looked very much like Gen. Butlers at Lowell. The summer house built of glass is as large as most all farm houses. On returning to the front we found Mr. Lincolns body guard of cavalrymen in attendance and were told that he would soon come our for a ride. Of course we all felt delighted with the prospects of seeing the President. We were not disappointed. He came out and looked like a man. Dressed in black with a tall hat. Telling the coachman to wait a bit he walked off leisurely but direct in the direction of the war department. His gait, was not at all elegant, but dignified. When he returned there was quite a crowd collected in front for the same purpose that we were. He returned our salute but looked annoyed, as though he didn't like to have a crowd there to see him every time he appeared out of his house. He looks careworn but resembles his picture very much. The door of his carriage being open, we had the audacity to enter and sit in his private buggy. Took some sprigs of cedar and some pebbles from his garden....

Had a good nights sleep in spite of the noise. Early in the morning we three boys started out again. Traveled around a while hunting and sight seeing. Tried to go to the Soldiers Home to visit Osman's grave but found we had no time for fear the squad would leave before our return. Had a good breakfast at the same place where we supped last night, after which Farnham returned direct to camp, while Al and I went to visit the Smithsonian Institute. This was another great treat.... Having used up all the time we dared to there, we hurried home, but judge our feelings of surprise and consternation when as we were passing a squad of armed soldiers, we were ordered to halt and show our passes. Having none to show they lodged us in the guard-house. Wasn't this a pretty fix? Al Kimball and Jere George in the guard-house! Well there we were in a small square room of brick with grated doors and windows, with perhaps a dozen others, imprisoned for various causes to be fed on bread and water until released. I looked at Al, he looked at me and we both laughed, but I felt a blush of shame in face. We did not cry, sulk nor swear,—took it cool, conversed with the other fellow prisoners, resolved to "take things as they came" and hope for the best.

Jere and his companion were soon released and eventually returned to their camp. Unfortunately it would be at least three weeks before Jere was able to join his brothers.

There was no such sightseeing for Herbert and Charles. On September 29 the VI Corps moved as far south as Mount Crawford, chasing Rebels and destroying enemy property, then returned to Harrisonburg to resupply. Here Colonel Henry, previously on sick leave, rejoined the regiment. There was a moment of sad farewells as the 87th Pennsylvania prepared to head home, their enlistment having expired. Approximately 200 Pennsylvania men remained to finish their service and were placed in a battalion under Ricketts.[27] Having routed the Army of the Valley, Sheridan turned his attention to the second half of Grant's strategy for the valley—the seizure and destruction of enemy crops and supplies.[28] Beginning on October 6 the Army of the Shenandoah turned north, arriving at Strasburg two days later, where the band of the 10th Vermont was given special quarters in a hotel. From here they marched to Front Royal and Millwood, eventually arriving at Middletown.

From Herbert:

Camp 10th Vt near Harrisonburg Va
Oct 2nd 1864

Dear Sister

I will write a line again as the mail goes out again to day or starts but will not reach you in two weeks perhaps — you see the mail comes in and goes out with the supply train and it takes a <u>week</u> for that to come from Harpers Ferry here or from here to H. F. We are over one hundred miles from our base of supplies and shut out from the <u>world</u> most in this Valley between the Blue Ridge and the Alleghaney mountains. We have been up the valley farther still, up to Mt Crawford, 15 miles this side of Staunton but did not stay only one night. We got a lot of apples and peaches &c. live tip top up here, but I suppose that we shall have to <u>foot</u> it back to Winchester before winter. The supply train came in this morning & brought a mail. I got a letter from home dated Sept 22nd — Col Henry came back with the train, he is looking finely and we are glad to see him — My Band <u>still</u> <u>lives</u> and we played to him and the regt <u>cheered</u> him <u>lustily.</u> Tell mother that if the band does break up I do not <u>fife</u> for Co. G. She must have forgotten that I am Principal musician of the regt and dont belong to any Co. I fife for one Co. as much as another. Co. G. has nothing to do with me — Jere is fifer there now or will be, he has not arrived yet. The weather is fine. Charley is well & I believe I am — I dont think my band will be broken up at all. I know well enough that it wont — I am a 11 months man now, shall soon be 9 — time flies I have no postage stamp so cant pay this letter Everything is lovely and the goose hangs high as ever your brother
Herbert

Both concerned and offended by this destruction (a time those in the Valley called "The Burning"), Early gathered his scattered forces and pursued Sheridan, but he could do little more than annoy the Army of the Shenandoah. As the valley seemed to be under Federal control, the VI Corps was ordered to return to Petersburg, setting out for Washington on October 10. A frost greeted the men when they awoke, adding to their eagerness to head back south.[29] New orders were received before they could get very far, dragging the corps back to their previous location with all haste. Early had succeeded in reforming his army and the two forces were once again in dangerous proximity. General Wright had intercepted a message from Longstreet to Early claiming that when he arrived "we will crush Sheridan."[30]

From Charles:

Strasburg
October 9, 1864

My dearest Ellie: I am again where I can have a chance of sending out a letter. We broke camp at Harrisburg last Thursday. At an early hour the whole army was on the move. We expected to go only to New Market that day and kept looking for dinner before we got there, but we kept on, went through it and clear to Mount Jackson before we got our dinner — (25 miles). Got there about 4:00 P.M. — stayed over night and next day came to Woodstock. Our regiment did provost duty that night in the city. The Band had a whole hotel to ourselves — but nary a landlord nor a bed. Yesterday we came to this place, where we met the trains — drew rations and got our mail.

We have made the valley from here to Staunton a complete desolation — nearly every barn for two miles each way is burned and a great many houses and other buildings. Thursday and Friday were warm — I never sweat more on a march than on these days. Yesterday was cooler and today is very cold. I have got on drawers and undershirt. Last night and this morning there was considerable cannonading on our rear, which shows that Early is still alive. But the whole of Lee's army could not drive Sheridan from this place if he chooses to stay. Whether he chooses to stay or not remains to be seen. I would not be surprised to see Petersburg soon. The news is cheering — what we get, but it is a week old when we get it.

I received your next to the last letter last night. The other is due next mail. I don't like to have you call yourself a "War Widow" — you are still my darling Ellie! my precious wife. There's something lonely about "widow" that makes me feel sad. Do not let your anxiety make you unhappy or make you grow poor. Let the hops of the future make you happy all the time. All your hopes will by the aid of God be realized — only wait for the appointed time — your soldier boy will come home again when the war is over. I have dreamed of you a great deal lately. One night I kissed you just as long as I wanted to and then went to sleep.

You ask me if I have gotten weaned from a bed — I have not. I always think of a good bed at home with you when I lie down to sleep. Last night I had a miserable bed — couldn't fit myself into it — too many bunches in it.

Jere has not got along yet. Colonel Henry, Lieutl Colonel Chandler and Captain Saulsbury are back again. Kiss and hug Nellie for me. Love to you. Charlie.

From Herbert:

Camp near Front Royal Va
Oct 12th 1864

Dear folks at home

I must drop a line home — The 6th Corps is all here near Front Royal and the men are at work repairing the Manassas rail road to Strasburg the 8th and 19th Corps are at Fishers Hill — We had quite a long march up the Shenandoah to Harrisonburg & Mt Crawford and back but I stood it bully We are now in the Luray Valley I suppose — The supply train came up to day with 5 days rations but Jere didn't come. He is at Bolivan Heights. Some think that we shall winter here in these parts somewhere — We are called on to play at Brig Hd Qts to night & must go immy. Shall be blowing in 15 minutes from now — C is well. Have not heard from home in a long time Did you get Puffers picture? My Band is O.K. & will not be broken up — Col Henry has got back to us —

No more now
In haste
J. H. George
Send some stamps

By October 14 the VI Corps was in position near Middletown on Cedar Creek, in the second rank of the Union formation in a reserve position. Complacency had settled on the Union troops as they believed that their opponents were demoralized and of little threat. Sheridan himself had retired to Winchester, placing Wright in command of the army. Ricketts took temporary command of the VI Corps, and Colonel Keifer of the 2nd Brigade was placed in charge of the 3rd Division. The 10th Vermont was certainly due a respite; after their return to the Winchester area they could claim only seventeen officers and 260 men fit for duty.[31] Casualties had drastically thinned the command staff of Herbert and Charles' brigade as well. Colonel Henry of the 10th Vermont was the only colonel remaining in command of a regiment. The other units were led by captains: Janeway (14th

*New Jersey), Briggs (106th New York), Wiles (151st New York), Ruhl (remaining
battalion of the 87th Pennsylvania). Bands were given leave to perform and musicians of the 1st Connecticut Cavalry in Custer's division were one of the ensembles
to put on an impromptu concert.*[32]

   *It was at Middletown that Jere was finally able to catch up with his brothers.
After passing through Harpers Ferry the recruits had spent days trying to find
their regiments, and the men's inexperience at marching and life in the field made
the journey all the more difficult. Whatever hardships Jere had incurred were
quickly overlooked as the George brothers were reunited once again.*

   From Jere:

Camp of the 10th VT., with 6th Corps
Cedar Creek, near Middleton, VA
Monday Morning, October 17th '64

Glory Hallelujah! Thank God I am at last with my brothers and find
them and friends well.

   Saturday night I wet with Albert again to stay in the Union man's house.
Albert was very sick for a few hours with a pain in his stomach but was relieved
late in the evening. In the morning I went out and noticed that at camp they
were unusually busy and noisy. Thinking they might be drawing rations or
preparing to march we hastened our steps in that direction.

   We found them preparing to march and drawing half day's rations. I had
time to fry a little bacon and make some coffee for breakfast and dinner. Left
camp at half-past seven. Albert was not able to go and as we marched away
I saw him seated on the ground with a lot of sick who were to be taken to
the hospital. We came over the same road that we had traveled last Wednesday
as guard for a supply train. The prospect was that we should reach the 6th
Corps before night yet I dared not believe it. I put my load on a train and
felt light and happy. We rested often and the march was an easy one. We
halted for dinner at two o-clock, two miles back. Arrived here at half-past
four but it took till dark to dispose of us. We had to go to Division headquarters then to Brigade Headquarters, then Regimental and Company Head
quarters. I had looked in vain for Herbert and Charles and had begun to
think that they didn't think much about my coming until I had been standing
at Regimental Head quarters quite a long time and a few rods from their tent
I saw Herbert coming. Had been around among different crowds and companies looking in vain for me. I should hardly have recognized Charles nor
he me. They are both tough and fat as ever. I find everything all right for me
to play in the band, though it is not yet decided what I shall play. I found a
long letter from Ann Maria and from Mother and three from Abbie, though

the first and most important one which was sent to Newbury, has not come, also one from Brother Frost of Athena Lodge Boston. I was tired and hungry last night and Charles made me some tea during the evening. Went to bed between Herbert and Charles where I was quiet warm, but was feverish, pulse quite fast and a pain in my left side such as I had when at home last July. This morning the pain is worse, but feel well otherwise. I find everything just as lovely and pleasant as I expected. For the coming year I rather to be with Herbert and Charles than any body else. We all love each other as we love ourselves and are a happy family in one tent....

While the George brothers were celebrating their reunion, there was less congenial activity across the lines. The Confederates took advantage of their unsuspecting opponents to launch a rapid and vastly successful attack early in the morning of October 19. The weather did not help the Yankees as a heavy fog obscured the field. Skirmishers were quickly overrun, the Union front left was flanked, and soon all the front lines of the Union were in confused retreat. Both the VIII and XIX Corps were overrun and broke for the rear. Confederate general Kershaw's division poured into the Union center, while General Gordon's II Corps, including the divisions of Pegram and Ramseur, deluged the Federal left flank, causing chaos to erupt through the Army of the Shenandoah. The VI Corps, hearing the sounds of battle, formed lines and prepared to engage. Wright initially ordered Ricketts to bring his divisions to the front, then reversed that order and told Ricketts to prepare to form a defensive position and repulse the enemy.[33] The 2nd Division, under the command of General George W. Getty, formed a horseshoe in the center of the crumbling Union line and managed to fend off three separate attacks before falling back to join the rest of the corps.[34] The quick work of this division in forming a line of battle, and the brave stand amid charging Rebels and fleeing Yankees, would prove to be the salvation of the Union forces.

The George brothers and their division were as surprised as any, and for some units it was only the wounded, command staff, and band members in camp when the Rebels hit the lines.[35] Emerson's brigade was placed at a right angle to the division, forming two lines of battle facing south on a ridge north of the valley of Meadow Ridge.[36] By about 8:00 A.M. General Ricketts had managed to place his three divisions in line, though increased artillery fire required them to pull back to the next crest. While forced to withdraw at each renewed assault, every move backwards allowed the three divisions of the VI Corps to pull closer together and ultimately merge into a solid, immoveable line.[37] The 10th Vermont reformed with their comrades and began to pour fire into the Rebels. Anxious to recapture three pieces that Captain McKnight's 5th U.S. Battery had lost in the retreat, Colonel Henry ordered the 10th Vermont forward. Sergeant William Mahoney, color bearer of the regiment, was the first man to reach the battery where he mounted a cannon and waved the colors. Despite such bravery there were not enough troops to support the Vermonters in their newly gained ground, and after fifteen minutes the men were driven back. The assault was successful in that the regiment managed to regain the lost guns, dragging two of them by hand back to safety.[38] *Colonel Henry was to receive the Medal of Honor for his regiment's performance at this time.*

General Ricketts was seriously wounded during the morning's fighting and was replaced by General Getty, commander of the 2nd Division.[39] *Colonel Henry was overcome by his poor health and forced to retire from the field; he was replaced by Captain Henry Dewey of Company A. Captain John Salsbury of the 10th Vermont would eventually take command of the 87th Pennsylvania due the loss of any more senior officers. General Wright himself took a wound in the head but continued to lead the army. Despite such losses to the rank and staff the VI Corps refused to break. Confederate forces put continuous pressure on the Ricketts' flank, forcing the VI Corps to withdraw even further. The men of the VI Corps were determined, however, and only pulled back only when ordered. After withdrawing about a mile the men were able to form a line at a crossroad about 9:00 A.M. Even Confederate general Gordon was forced to admire their performance: "Only the Sixth Corps of Sheridan's entire force held its ground. It was on the right rear and had been held in reserve. It stood like a granite breakwater, built to beat back the oncoming flood."*[40]

There was a lull in the fighting after 10:00 A.M., the Confederates believing they had gained a significant victory over their Union counterparts. The 3rd Division was able to establish a line near the Valley Pike and even managed to build quick breastworks. It was now that Sheridan reappeared on the battlefield, having finished his legendary ride from Winchester. The Army of the Shenandoah was quickly reformed, orders were distributed, and a counterattack was launched. The VI Corps formed a single line on the Union left, supported by cavalry under General Merritt, there to hold the enemy while the remainder of the army pushed through on the right. One straggler took heart upon seeing the VI Corps formed in line of battle: "The bloody Sixth is going in. They'll stop these blasted cusses. They say that, by Jesus, they'll hold 'em."[41] *As the Confederates began another advance, they were surprised to meet stiff resistance and were driven back. The Union cavalry was sent on a flanking maneuver and the Rebel offensive began to unravel. By 4:00 Sheridan gave the order for a general advance. Initially the move faltered, as the two brigades in the 3rd Division overlapped, dangerously exposing a flank. The troops pulled back, reorganized, and set out once again towards the sound of firing. The 10th Vermont and the rest of the 3rd Division, by now in the center of the Union Army, drove forward through woods and across an open field, successfully driving the Confederate troops back to a stone fence. Momentum was with Emerson's brigade and a charge was made on the fence, breaking the gray line and forcing a broken retreat. Here the brave Sergeant Mahoney, the color bearer who had led the advance to recover McKnight's cannon, was killed.*[42]

As with Winchester and Fisher's Hill the battle became a rout, and the Army of the Valley poured back over the creek and fled south. Austin Fenn of Company H, 10th Vermont, blithely summed up the day's struggles: "In short they whipped us in the Morning but was whipped all to pieces themselves at night."[43] *A jubilant Union Army settled into the camps they had been forced to abandon so hastily in the morning. The Federals were now able to celebrate a major victory, and bands were called upon to work overtime. According to Colonel Charles Wainwright: "General Crawford has sent out a circular authorizing the bands of the corps to play until one A.M. in honor of the victory. I should not suppose that the musicians would be over-thankful to him for the permission: but they are still at it (midnight), while the men, by their frequent cheers, seem determined to make a night of it."*[44]

The Battle of Cedar Creek was one of the proudest moments for soldiers from Vermont. With the rest of the army crumbling around them, the stubborn resistance of the VI Corps allowed Sheridan to reform his army and turn a potential disaster into a major victory. As one member of the 10th Vermont proudly claimed: "It was fitting that the Sixth Corps should have been allowed so largely to have so brilliantly rung down the curtain on the great Civil War stage in this section."[45] *While elated by their latest victory, the men of the 10th Vermont were stunned by their losses: sixteen killed, sixty-five wounded, and four captured, over one-third of the troops they took into battle that day.*[46] *Even a recently recruited band member and fifer for Company H, Chauncey Corbin, was wounded. The brigade as a whole lost 270 men. As with every major battle the losses would no doubt have been much worse had it not been for those assigned to look after the wounded, as Colonel Keifer of the 2nd Brigade was to note: "To an efficient medical corps, however, belongs the chief credit for the good work done in caring for the unfortunate."*[47] *Fortunately both Charles and Herbert survived unscathed once again; for Jere, it was a harsh welcome to the war.*

From Charles:

October 20, 1864
3rd Division Hospital
Newport, Virginia

My very dear loved ones: I hasten to inform you of the glad tidings that I am <u>well</u> and <u>unharmed</u> — as also my brothers Herbert and Jere and the rest of the Band. But I cannot say so for the rest of the regiment. 88 of them are numbered among the killed or wounded....

We were awakened yesterday morning very early by musketry on the right — pretty soon it commenced on our left in good earnest! We got up as quick as possible and were none too soon! The Brigade marched toward the firing, while we went the other way. In less than ten minutes our camp ground which we had just left was a battle field and the Johnnies drove and followed us this side of Middletown, where the tide of battle turned. From prisoners we learned that the rebs had marched all night around the base of the mountain and came up on the 8the Corps by surprise, who then left all their things and ran. That left the 19th Corps to fight the Johnnies. Owing to such rapidity of movement <u>they</u> had to fall back. Then the old 6th Corps went at them! and the rebs found themselves against a snag then — the 6th held them for a while but were obliged to fall back on account of position. General Sheridan was at Harper's Ferry and was going to make a flying trip to Washington before coming back to the army. On his way back from Washington he spent a night at Winchester. He learned about the attack and about faced. He passed us Band boys about half past nine, his horse in a dripping sweat. Such a picture of earnestness and determination I never saw as he showed as he came in sight of the battle field, chasing past the 8th Corps straggling back to Winchester. The roads were full of men coming back to the rear in retreat. <u>What a scene for a painter</u>! The boys commenced cheering him — throwing their hats on the air. Sheridan took off his old hat and swung it and yelled — "Turn around boys! Follow me! Wee will give them such a whipping as they never had before!" And he was as good as his word. As he rode along the line cheer after cheer went up for the little man on the black horse that had brought him so swiftly to the line of battle. As he continued to swing his <u>old hat</u> at us he called to us and told us we were all right!.

An hour and a half prepared them for a charge. The rebs were driven in great confusion over the river and all their artillery captured, which amounted to 43 pieces besides all <u>they</u> captured from <u>us</u> the day before. We also captured all their ambulance train loaded with wounded. The latter are here at our hospital. We also captured over 2000 prisoners — our cavalry is driving the rest of the Johnnies back today. Our troops are on their old camp ground as Sheridan promised we would be that night! This is a larger victory than the other. "<u>Bully for Sheridan</u>"! ... Jere came Sunday night just after I mailed your letter. He stood it well and he looks tough and well. Herbert is ailing a little but he will come around right soon.

We are doing duty at the hospital now. They will not let us go to our regiment. I will write again as soon as I can but I fear I will be very busy for a while. So long for now, my dear.

From Herbert:

Old Camp near Middletown Va.
Oct. 22nd 1864

My dear sister

I will just write a line to day as the mail goes out this noon — We are back again the same old camp that we had before the fight of the 19th. The rebs didn't get any thing from me except my new rubber coat that I bought in Georgetown $8.00 out only. I let a fellow take it to carry that drove the Brigade Surgeon wagon and he lost all of his things and my coat too. Now I am <u>rubberless</u>!! Guess I will have to draw another rubber and then it will be three times and out. I guess that we shall stay here a spell now. Its cold enough to go into winter qrs — It was awful cold last night and I sat up from 2 oclock this morning till daylight by the fire and the wind blow so that I like to have frozen one side while I warmed the other. We are expecting to get some over coats very soon now & I have got a chance to get one & not pay for it so guess I shall not send for mine at home but may be I shall, cant tell yet — It rained last night before 12 oclock and we didn't have any tent up so we laid still under the blanket & got wet. The water ran under us & wet us pretty bad. Jere did not complain any. He stands it well — Albert has not come yet dont know how he is — I got your letter written a part to me & part to Jere — Tell mother that Dan Fuller is reported <u>dead</u> — Co. G lost 4 killed & 7 wounded in the battle of the 19th — Our regt lost 86 in killed wounded & missing — 6 missing and I think 13 killed Little Sis in my Band had a brother killed he was a Sergt in Co. B — Tell mother I would like a pair of stockings sent by mail as soon as convenient. I never have heard from my money that I sent home. There was $50.00 of my own & 50.00 of Charlies. The bills are on compound interest & are as good as a bank mother must keep it for me. How are you all getting along. Must close Love to all
Herbert

Various elements of Sheridan's army set up camps around Winchester, with bands helping to celebrate the triumph. The 10th Vermont stayed some time near Middletown, then moved back towards Winchester on November 9 and settled near Kernstown. Despite the overwhelming victory under their belts, the troops were ordered to fortify positions while rumors circulated that they would be sent to Harpers Ferry to guard the railroads there. The recent campaign had been a particularly taxing period for the men from Vermont and the VI Corps as a whole. The corps, now even more deserving of their nickname "the bloody Sixth," had lost a total of almost 5,000 men, a frightening proportion of the almost 13,000 they had in September.

The regiment was finally able to recuperate after months of long marches and heavy fighting. The soldiers held a presidential election (the George boys voted for "Old Abe"), were reviewed by their commanders, and celebrated Thanksgiving on November 24. The weather refused to cooperate, however, and the men put up with rain, snow, and generally cold weather.[48] *This did not keep the band members of the 10th Vermont from a bit of adventure. A small system of caves was located nearby the camp, and various members of the band, including Jere, spent some time spelunking.*[49] *The only military action was a brief skirmish on November 12 when Rebels attacked their pickets, but after a short and severe fight the Confederates withdrew. Many men were fortunate to receive long-overdue furloughs for visits home. Charles George was one of those lucky few, spending some time in Newbury visiting with family. Herbert and Jere were kept busy with the band, as both brothers were now copying and arranging new pieces for the band. Jere arranged "Angels My Darling Will Rock Thee to Sleep" which the band immediately began rehearsing; he also arranged a piece to celebrate Herbert's birthday on October 28.*

Certainly the men were due a break. Casualties had slimmed the ranks of the regiments in the George brothers' brigade; the 151st New York was down to only five companies and forced to reorganize into a battalion under the command of recently promoted Lieutenant Colonel Charles Bogardus.[50] *George Burnell of Company C, 10th Vermont, noted that casualties were so high that Sam Greer,*

The 2nd Rhode Island Infantry, a member of the VI Corps during operations in the Shenandoah Valley, shown with their band at the head of the column from early in the war (Library of Congress).

who had started as company cook, had been promoted to 1st Lieutenant and placed in charge of the company.[51] *The weary men from Vermont envisioned a calm period in the valley, relaxing and rebuilding the regiment now that the threat to Washington had been removed. Hopes for a quiet time in winter quarters were soon dashed; new orders were received and the men of the 10th Vermont found themselves on the march once again.*

Two letters from Herbert:

> Camp 10th Vt Infty
> Nov 13th/64
> 5 miles from Winchester Va

Dear folks at home —

Spose you'd think we are all dead if we dont write so I'll write a line — When there is nothing going on I dont care to write as there is nothing to write about. We have moved from Middletown to this place — about 4 or 5 miles above Winchester — came here the 9th inst and the troops are building breast works & forts so that I guess we shall go into winter quarters. We are building log huts already and every looks as though we should remain all winter. Hope we shall. Jere & Charlie are well — I rec'd the bundle with socks & shirt — also the piece of music from Em & the stamps you sent a spell a go. Colonel Chandler says it is the Adjts Genls business of the U.S.A. to send the muster & pay roll to the 2nd Auditor &c & that it will be sent in time — We had a little fight here yesterday & to day & Genl Custer captured 150 prisoners & two canons from the rebs & all their ammunition train — Bully for Custer — We three boys voted for <u>Old Abe</u> this election. Band prospers finally Jere has arranged several pieces for us — We built a splendid shanty back at M — & moved the next day after it was completed — we built it of boards — built one here yesterday & didnt like it so. Tore it down again — we are living on the ground now but have a good stone fire place — shall build another log house by & by — All three of us have got over coats now furnished us for nothing so I shall not want mine at home unless I happen to loose this one — Dont want anything sent out by Express — live well enough on "Sams" rations. Al Kimball was not expected to live the last I heard from him — sick with fever at Winchester. Heard from him 4 days ago — Azro is here — <u>well</u> . I have no more to write — Tell Em I'll see about the album after we are paid off again. This photograph is a very particular friend of mine. A cornet player in the 87 Pa regt — now a <u>citizen</u> he served his 3 years —

Good day — in haste

From Herbert

Camp of the 10th Vt Infantry near
Winchester Va Nov 29th 1864

Dear folks at home

    I wrote a letter to Charles over a week ago and was quite anxious that he should receive it before he started on his return to the regt but the mail has not left the regt since I wrote it nor has there been any mail in for over a week and now it is too late to mail one to Charles as it will not get to New-bury before the 4th of next month probably for it will not leave here till day after tomorrow, so I will not send it but write another one to all of you.... Jere and I have enjoyed ourselves hugely here alone — we agree so nicely. When we get out of the army we shall have to go into some kind of business together because we like each other so well. I suppose it is because we are so near alike — He does not want to go into a tailors shop to work again so guess we shall have to go into <u>music</u> in some shape or other. Perhaps we may go <u>west</u>. Speaking of "west" makes me think — [Grimal] Hill has gone into a store in Prairie Du Chien Wis. as clerk or "<u>boy</u>" I think he would make a good mer-chant. Jere plays Charleses part now while C is away, he makes it go nicely. We have got pretty well fixed up for winter but dont know whether we will remain long or not. Some think that we shall move back onto the Rail Road — We are going to loose our <u>best</u> <u>friend.</u> <u>Col Henry</u> he is going to resign his commission on account of poor health. His health is very poor. Too bad I am awful sorry — and our next best officer — Capt Hunt the ranking Capn in the regt is going to resign on account of <u>his</u> <u>health</u>. He was wounded at Cold Harbor and is not well at all — Probably never will be very stout again. This will leave Lt Col Chandler in command of the regt. <u>Sorry for that too</u> — But — only 9 months longer thank fortune. It is quite warm to day — very pleasant I have a slight cold that I caught a spell ago — feel pretty well. So you are going to sell the colts? Well I dont care much if you get a good price for them — Put my money in a good place is all I want — use what you want of it — I havent had a letter from home or from any body for over a month what do you think of that. I want a letter awfully please write some body — No more now

From Herbert

CHAPTER 7

December 1864 to April 1865:
Petersburg, Virginia

After three grueling months in the Shenandoah Valley the 10th Vermont was allowed only a few weeks of rest before being summoned to duty once again. On December 3, 1864, the men of the VI Corps caught trains for Washington by way of Harpers Ferry, and from there they boarded transports to City Point outside of Petersburg where they arrived two days later. The 3rd Division and their comrades were once again placed south of the city in the region around the Weldon Railroad. Though called out once to form for battle the regiment saw no action, and soon they were moved to Fort Dushane along the Weldon railroad, where they remained for three cold and wet weeks. The veterans of the 10th Vermont were struck by the infernal appearance of the area surrounding Petersburg. Months of siege had left the ground trampled, and little if any wood could be found for miles around. Camps were constructed from whatever could be scrounged, yet such efforts were to no avail as the men were ordered up to the siege lines surrounding the city. Here they would remain for the next three months.

From Charles:

Fort Duchin.
On the Weldon Rail Road.
December 21, 1864

My own precious wife: I have been waiting and looking for a letter for a long time — at least it seems a long time. Your last one was so full of love that I pine for another — that is the way of this world I guess — the more we have the more we want. I shall never forget that big tree in Concord, where we said good bye. Jere says that is a famous tree — famous for being well known. It is at least well known to us. I turned around to see you after I had gone a piece, but did not see you. After I went to the depot I had to come back almost to the tree to get an order for transportation.

It has been raining for over 12 hours — commenced in the night. We moved into our new tent yesterday. I tell you it seems good to have a dry place to sleep and to get up this morning well and rested. We have a good fireplace — draws well, throws out the heat real good. It has a crane and hooks. Yesterday we cooked beans in it and today some condensed vegetables. We have a bunk wide enough for three, and are going to have a table and cupboard. But alas!! We expect to move tomorrow. General Seymore wants us back in the Brigade. The officers and men are very indignant that he should wait till we had built our quarters before he moved us. It is very muddy here now and I expect it will get wetter — it continues to rain.

The news from Sherman is of the most encouraging character. The hopes are that the rebellion will play out pretty soon. Deserters say they are done fighting! It is just a month ago that I was in Vermont. The months continue to wear away. The time will soon come when I can again clasp you in my arms and to think that we are never to be again separated through life.

I received a small paper — The Youth's Companion — by mail — don't know if we should take it for Nellie or not. What do you think? What does Nellie study and how does she get along? I would like to have her take writing lessons....

It was a comparatively quiet period for the regiment, now under the command of the recently promoted Lieutenant Colonel George B. Damon.[1] Colonel Henry's continued poor health, complicated by his injury at the Battle of Cold Harbor, finally forced him to step down as leader of the 10th Vermont. This was but one of the many changes in the command staff. Ricketts' wound had proven too much for the brave but battered general, so General Truman Seymour now took command of the division.[2] Colonel Emerson was released from active duty and returned home, and General

Lt. Col. George B. Damon, final commander of the 10th Vermont Infantry, was from Newbury, Vermont, hometown of the George brothers (Roger D. Hunt Collection at the U.S. Army Military History Institute).

Truex returned to command the 1st Brigade. An awkward moment arose for the men from Vermont when one of their commanding officers came under censure. In his official report of the Battle of Cedar Creek, Colonel Keifer, then in command of the 3rd Division, accused Lieutenant Colonel Charles G. Chandler of cowardice and leaving the battle for the rear of the army. This was not the first time his actions had been questioned, and Chandler was dismissed from the service by General Order 28, December 24, 1864.[3] This must have come as somewhat of a relief to the George brothers and the rest of the Vermonters, as Chandler had done little to endear himself to the members of the regiment.[4] The band suffered a loss as well when Dan Barker, one of the two remaining bass players, was discharged on account of sickness. He would not live to see the end of the war.

From Charles:

<u>Camp near (before) Petersburg.</u>
<u>December 28, 1864</u>

My ever dear Ellie: <u>First</u> in my heart's affections and foremost in all my thoughts. I feel happy to tell you that I am now in good quarters. We have been floundering around in the mud for nearly a month and during that time we have built three houses and I tell you it is no small job to build here. Timber is more than a mile distant, and the mud is a great incumbrance. You remember that I told you in my last letter that we were expecting to move. The regiment did to this place (about a mile) last Friday, but the Band waited till Monday. When we moved we came with the whole tent — taking it down, chimney and all, loading it into the wagon. It made just a load. I should have said that all the tents are drawn over in wagons. It took 4 days. When we got here we found it pretty muddy, for it had rained all night the night before. We have been three whole days on building, and have worked hard, too, but we have the best tent we ever had. Our fireplace and chimney is good as the old one. Our bunk is wide enough for all three and is made of hewed timber — logs split and then hewed. Then we have a table, upon which I am writing, and which I hewed out of a pine log two feet in diameter. I hewed it down to 12 inches — but it was too wide and we split off six inches and made a shelf just over the table. It is 8 feet long. Under the table is another shelf for meat. Then we have a movable seat so we can sit up to the table <u>to eat</u>. Then we have a stationary seat six feet long, and the bunk also can serve as a seat. Another thing we have is a <u>good floor</u>! Herbert and I have been all day hewing and laying it. We had to carry it half a mile on our backs — but we shall never be sorry. It does seem good to have a floor to step onto. The first night we slept in this tent we had no fireplace and of course no fire. The end of the tent was wide open yet and the rain had made all ground very muddy —

so it was very muddy in the tent — so muddy that to stand in one position long we would go in over our shoes. We worked hard <u>all day</u> — <u>ate no dinner</u> and had our supper to get after dark. Herbert's face was pretty long — guess Jere and I felt some blue, but didn't say much about it....

Since December 25 the troops had enjoyed a secure camp near Warren Station. Bands took advantage of the relative calm to entertain the troops, as a member of the 106th New York observed: "Behind us within sight our camps stretch away to the right and left. they are now full of the music of hundreds of brass bands which we can hear as far to the right and left as the ear can reach I can distinctly hear the band of the 106th playing their favorite pieces."[5] When not playing, musicians such as Nelson Stowe of the 14th Connecticut cleaned their instruments, arranged music, or simply had fun. Others were less fortunate. William Patton and his fellow drummers and fifers found themselves assigned to building huts, policing the camp, and even rounding up stragglers after a brief skirmish between pickets.[6]

The 10th Vermont was at the front line on intermittent picket duty for months, and the cold, rainy weather — coupled with the proximity of the enemy — created a stressful situation. Timothy Messer, Company H, described the circumstances: "We have to go from two to three miles to where we do picket duty altho

Soldiers at rest after drill, Petersburg, Virginia, 1864. The soldiers are seated reading letters and papers and playing cards (National Archives and Records Administration).

our camp is almost within gun shot of the rebs line but we go farther to the left & the first division picket here. We have a fire on picket but are not allowed to go to sleep in the night."[7] There were exchanges with enemy pickets and countless deserters flocked to the Union camps.[8] Still, the men from Vermont retained the positive attitude that had sustained them through the past three bloody years. As Lieutenant William White said: "We have got winter quarters built here and are having very good times now. I don't know how long we shall stay. I was on picket last night I could see the Johnies once in a while but they did not trouble us."[9]
From Jere:

Before Petersburg 1865

For a wonder we have remained in this camp <u>two weeks</u> and continue to occupy the same house we did January 1st, though rumors of another move have been quite prevelent for a few days.... My 1st B^b tenor horn came last Saturday, January 6th it has been a long time coming, all the time in the hands of the Express Co. A little curious that I should have been an enlisted musician more than four months before I got an instrument to play on. I commence immediately to play with the band, having learned to finger some on Charlie's Bb cornet. I have arranged "Come Where My Love Lies Dreaming" as a serenade and it goes good. It is perhaps worthy of remark that the first time the band played it in public, was the first time I played with my new horn. There are several different arrangements of this song played by different bands in this corps, but Dr. Clarke, our surgeon who is something of a musical critic, said before he knew it originated in our band that it was the best arrangement he ever heard, this I consider quite a compliment. Last Friday I went over to the First Division to witness a tragical act where I didn't have to pay anything extra for a reserved seat on the "Parquettee."

The stage was several acres of ground surrounded by an audience consisting of the whole division, formed in a square with an opening on sone side. The most prominent actor was a deserter who was shot and he did not suddenly come to life again to appear before the curtain and make a low bow in answer to cheers for the beautiful manner in which he died, as they do in Boston theaters. No, he died as natural as I ever saw Booth or Forrest, but remained dead. It was rainy and muddy and we had to wait quite a long time before the prisoner appeared. Had we been obliged to stand so long in the mud on duty we should have called it rough indeed. At length we heard a band in the distance playing a Dirge march. The band was preceeded by mounted officers and followed by six men carrying an unpainted coffin, then the guard, between the front and rear guard was an ambulance containing the driver, chaplain and prisoner. The guard in full dress uniform with white gloves. They marched with reverse arms. The regiments were all "open water" with the front rank facing the rear, thus leaving a space wide enough for a carriage to pass between. When the procession one end of the opening they entered this road and passed around the whole square that all might see. The bands playing solemn dirges all the while. When they came around to the opening again and half way across they halted at the place of the execution where a grave had been dug. The prisoner was I should judge about 35 years of age with whiskers and mustache, tall and slim. The story was that he had enlisted as a Volunteer in the union army, receiving a large bounty, then deserted to Canada and was captured on a blocade runner at Wilmington by General Butler. I shall never forget the look of dispair, of gloomy sadness, of utter hopelessness that was pictured on his pale face and fallen countenance as he silently took his seat on his coffin which lay across his open grave. It was sickening and I turned to leave, but remembering that he deserved it and that I had gone there through the mud on purpose, I resolved to watch operations to the last. The guard, twelve in number was stationed ten paces in front, in two ranks and I noticed they looked very sad for they had a solemn duty to perform. They had been detailed to <u>shoot a man</u> by proper military authority and must do it. That their feelings may suffer less only five guns out of six has a ball in it the other a blank cartridge, these are prepared and given them in this condition so that no man may know which one has the blank cartridge with powder but no balls. Each man may well say then that "perhaps it was me that fired the blank." The sentence was read, a prayer offered by the chaplain, then the prisoners hands and feet were tied, his hat taken off and a handkerchief tied over his eyes. Immediately after this the provost martial gave three commands, each in one word. "Ready!" "aim"; "fire." At the first six rifles were taken from the shoulder and cocked. At the second six deadly weapons were pointed at the heart and at the third five bullets entered the breast of the deserter and he fell back expiring without a groan or a move with his feet over the box scarcely out of their tracks. There was such a crowd of spectators that during the prayer I was forced back out of sight and being small and short did not again see him until just after he was shot, then when I looked there lay the rebel a lifeless, yet quivering mass of flesh. The first fire was affectual or mortal had it been otherwise the second rank would have been ordered forward for the same duty. The time occupied in reading the sentence, prayer and other arrangements was about ten minutes. When a man is taken sick he has hopes for recovery but when his sentence has been read and he sits on his coffin by his open grave that is to be his narrow house forever, with the official guard in front he has <u>no</u> hope. All is lost. The glittering world is nothing to him now. No one to appeal to. No earthly friend to help him, he must die. What then were that man's thoughts as he sat there so still? We shall never know for he spoke not. Such is the fate of the deserter. Hanging and shooting deserters is quite frequent in this vicinity but this case is the only one I have witnessed.

Two letters from Charles:

<u>Camp near Petersburg. January 21, 1865</u>

Lovely Ellie: Today has been the roughest of the winter, not so very cold, but very uncomfortable. In the night it commenced raining, the ground had frozen a little and the rain which fell froze and formed a crust over everything. This morning our tents were covered with ice and the door frozen in. All day it continued to rain, never slacking for a moment and just cold enough to prevent the ice from melting — and still not cold enough to snow. We found it comfortable enough as long as the wood lasted, but 3:00 o'clock this afternoon found us fireless. Didn't I have a sweet time going half a mile after wood? Tonight, all is forgotten — we now have a bright blazing fire made from a pitch pine stump and we are as cozy and comfy as you please. I expect a letter tonight — <u>a letter</u>! how much I think of the little thing when it comes. It seems to say "I received my instructions and tokens of love from they darling Ellie in the good old State of Vermont, and have come with speed to covey them to you." I break the seal, and behold the words so lately made by my dear one....

Deserters continue to come in every day. I heard a sad story the other day from one of our returned prisoners. His name was John Betters, Company H, 10th Vermont. He was a nurse at Division Hospital. I was well acquainted with him, and so was every one in the regiment and recollect well the time he was reported as missing. He with 7 others crossed the picket line near this place about the 26th of June for apples, supposing our cavalry videttes were still on guard beyond them. They went unarmed, but were surprised by two rebel cavalry men, who with revolvers drawn, ordered them to surrender. <u>They surrendered</u> — were taken to Petersburg, remained there a while and then to Libby, to Danville, Andersonville, and Savannah. In the various prisons they were robbed of their clothing and every thing else. He had a gold ring which he saved by putting it under his tongue. Others saved some little things by secreting them in various places, as under their arms and even in their posterior.... Oh Ellie, I hope I shall never be taken prisoner!

Herbert had a short letter from W. Garvins — he is a prisoner in Danville, Georgia. Jere is very busy again arranging music. We play 5 or 6 of his pieces now.

My feet are cold — I must go and warm them! Leroy drops in on us every little while — cracks a few jokes, tells a story or two, or a conundrum — gets all to laughing and out he goes. Herbert is blowing Tattoo.

Camp 10th Vermont Volunteers.
February 4, 1865

Dear Ellie: I have just been taking a walk with Mac. It is a beautiful day, warm and calm. We walked to division Hospital. The hospitals were all cleared out preparatory to active campaigning. I will tell you more about that by and by. The hospital will accommodate about 40 — good bunks, fireplace etc. The other tents were neatly arranged — streets, walkways etc. neatly made and swept clean. From there we turned to the left seeing many pretty camps, a signal tower that is nearly complete — 40 feet square at the bottom and 140 feet high. The whole rebel camp can be seen — also the city of Petersburg. About half a mile farther we came to a fort. Stepping up on the works I saw another line of works less than a mile in with men at work on them as thick as bees — also a large camp. I asked a bystander what troops they were (thinking they might be our picket line), but he answered, "those are the Johnnies." I thought at first he was trying to bluff me but found he was in earnest. As I conversed I found we were on the extreme left of our line — the camp in front were rebs! The heft of their army lay there. General Lee's Headquarters were pointed out in full view. Their forts all in plain sight. They were all hard at work on them — and our men on ours. Either could stave the other camp all to pieces! I could see both sides of the picket lines only a few rods apart — the men conversed together freely — get their wood between lines and exchanged newspapers daily. When I stood there our officer of the day rode along the picket line entirely unmolested. I learned it had always been that way in that place. A little farther to the right was a thick clump of pines which neither side would allow the other to cut. Their line being on one side and ours on the other, only a few rods apart. At this place their deserters usually came in. The way they get in is that there is two picket posts stationed near together — one to watch the other, and sometimes one post will agree to fire high and let the other through to the other side....

    Since I commenced this letter I have practiced once, played for Dress Parade, and for the 87th Pennsylvania. You know that we have had no snare drummer since Puffer left us. Well, the 87th snare drummer re-enlisted, so we exchange. He plays in our band and we in turn go and play for his regiment. He is young, steady, good looking and a fine fellow. His father is a volunteer in the rebel army. They lived in Baltimore — two of his sisters are Sesesh, but his mother and one sister are strong Unionists. Tonight we play at Division Headquarters. It is so warm today we need no fire in our tents.

Received a letter from Addie Nourse in answer to mine. Will send it to you next time.

From you loving husband.

From Herbert:

> Camp of the 10th Vt Vol Infantry
> Before Petersburg Va
> Feby 6th/65

Dear sister Emma

I sent out a letter home last night but forgot one thing — I want you to look over my <u>Band</u> <u>Music</u> and pick out the two following pieces & send <u>all</u> the parts to me by mail — "Cavatina and Chorus from Il Trovatore" (if it is there) and the "Grand Terzetto "De, la Duchels" from Lucretia Borgia. I am afraid the Cavatina and Chorus is not there — There is a Cavatina from "Lucia" but I dont want that if only the "Grand Terzetto &c" is to be found. send all the parts — <u>please</u> — and as soon as possible and oblige —

Munsell is afraid he cant get up as smart letter as you so he hesitates about writing to you — We have not moved yet — Our forces have captured the <u>South</u> <u>Side</u> R. R. and took a lot of prisoners & wagon mules &c — The 5th Corps done the fighting. The Rebellion is going down — every day — The constitution is to be changed — & Slavery done away with entirely — The band will soon be <u>free.</u> The Confederacy is nearly "gone up" as the saying is — The Union arms are successful every where — If "alls well" I'll soon be home — Six months & a "few" at the longest.

Good day

From Herbert

From Jere:

> Army of the Potomac
> Feb. 8th 1865

We did not move and know not the cause of the order. Saturday night another order came to move next morning and we packed many of our things but did not move that time.... This forenoon Charles and I went about two miles to the left following the breast-works. Saw George Peach at the Third VT., it was very interesting to see the city of soldiers.

Camp after camp we pass as though it was a City. The line of works forts and abattis all interested me to see how artfull and formidable was their construction. From one point we could plainly see the rebel camp. On our way back we passed through our 2nd Corps, where we witnessed another new and to us novel scene. "How are stocks"? Stocks up, stocks down. We hear much about stocks. Some men put their money in stocks, and others their necks. The latter I have seen in operations in Vermont, but never till to-day did I see men with their feet in stocks. I have read of the stocks as a punishment and seen pictures of it long ago, but to-day had the privelege of seeing it in operation. For some offence three soldiers were being cruelly punished in this way. There were places for their arms also but they were at liberty and they kept swinging and thrashing them to keep them warm. Two huge pieces of timber pinioned their feet with holes only large enough for the ankle above the foot. I was informed that it was a common way of punishing offenders in that Regt. Shortly after our return to camp the band went to Div. Hospital to play to the funeral of William Merritt, of Co. G. from Bradford. This is my first attendance to a Military funeral. After remarks at the grave by the Chaplain, three volleys of musketry were discharged after which we played "Rest Spirit Rest." The Chaplain was from another Regt. The 10th Vt. has none. There are rumors again to-night of another move. As the line has been extended a gap is left and some troops must fill it. We shall not probably go more than one mile. I have been busy writing and arranging music. Our books are getting pretty well filled with music "Arranged by J. N. George" I like it very much. Think I could be content to do nothing else but write and arrange music. President Lincoln has met the rebel Vice President at Fortress Monroe and both have returned. Their object was to make peace. What they accomplished we know not yet.

A band serenading outside the headquarters of General George L. Hartsuff in Petersburg (Library of Congress).

The holidays came and went with the bands doing what they could to bolster the men's spirits. Officers as well as enlisted men took advantage of the lull in fighting, according to one enlisted man: "A 'time' was had at Brigade Hd.-Qrs. last night in which the tripping of the 'light fantastic toe' was a very prominent feature."[10] The band of the 10th Vermont returned to full strength when two recuperating band members returned to the ranks. Ever the concerned bandleader, Herbert again sent home for music, looking for new pieces to liven up his busy performance schedule. Other bandleaders met with their counterparts from different regiments to exchange pieces.[11] Jere was likewise kept busy, both playing in the band and arranging music. Charles helped copy parts and faithfully practiced his instrument, apparently with positive results. All the musicians of the brigade were kept active, as Abiel LaForge of the 106th New York noted: "The officers of the 14th NJ gave an entertainment in the Brigade court room this evening. had a very fine time dancing and singing our band officiated; It is the only string band in the brigade, so has plenty of demands."[12] The band of the 10th Vermont performed at many such social events, including playing pieces in between scenes performed at a local theater.[13]

From Charles:

February 16, 1865

I have been laboring today, Ellie, for <u>Major Damon</u>, building him a tent. If it were not for that old affair between us I should like him. (I still remember when he prodded me with his bayonet to make me march in the deep mud). He is pleasant and agreeable and well liked in the regiment. He asks especially for Kent and me because we are natural mechanics. The ground is frozen 12 inches deep — has now thawed 6 inches — and such muddy walking I never saw — tonight we are having a thunder shower. Wouldn't you like to hear thunder and the deep-toned cannons from Dutch Gap with about 40 bass drums all pounding away at the same time? — yes and bands playing on two sides and drum Corps rattling all around, besides numerous strains of vocal music — and I might have said, a sprinkling of picket firing. I've heard all these this evening — it is now after 9:00 o'clock — I commenced writing this letter this morning, and then was called out to work.

Tonight the other boys occupied the table — I sat back and read the last newspaper — by that time the last candle was burned out, so "Charlie" had to cut some pork and fry it out for the grease and make a "slut" — (a slut is a greasy rag in a dish and lighted for light). Now I have the first chance at the light — it is often midnight before we "retire." All four sleep in one bunk.

Jere sticks to his arranging music. I think I am improving fast — they all appear to miss me more than they do Mac. I play some solos that he can't play. I wish I had the B Flat instead of the 2nd. I am copying some of the E flat into a book to send home. They will be pretty to play or to keep for the songs. We now have 114 pieces — there are a great many really pretty airs. I have improved a great deal in the execution of my instrument....

Our regiment has to do picket duty at Fort Fisher. The pickets are friendly — both sides get their wood in the same place and have a good sociable time all day — trade knives, exchange papers or anything else. The 6th Corps line is over 4 miles long — it extends east to the line which runs north and south, or within three miles of Petersburg. The 9th Corps joins our right — our left extends to Fort Fisher — then the 2nd corps and then the 5th. A kiss — Good night my dear.

From Herbert:

> Camp of the 10th Regt Vt. Vol Infantry
> Before Petersburg Va
> March 4th/65

Dear Father

Please accept this picture as a present from your three "soldiers." We had it taken to day — in honor of "Old Abe" He takes the chair to day for 4 years longer — When you look at this picture you can think that it was taken in front of Petersburg which we were in the Army of the Potomac — Don't you think we all look remarkably healthy and fat. Spose you wont like to believe it but I am the heaviest of the three — Yes sir, its a fact, we were all weighed to day and Charlie raised only 132 lbs. Jere weighed 138 and I made out to bring up 140 — Never was so heavy before By the way — dont you make fun of my mustache in the picture for I have just commenced to raise one — if you look sharp you will see a dark streak on my upper lip. Jere has got quite a set of whiskers he had them colored before sitting for the picture — J. says it must be my mustache that made me weigh the most. Ha, Ha. Well — only five months and a few now and if "all is well" we will present our selves in person to you all — dont you let Em feel bad because I played such a nice game on her! did I just do it though? My Bass player that was captured at Frederick City Md last July (9th) has been exchanged and will soon be with us probably. That will make three of my players back that I lost last summer — Dan Barker, my other Bass player that was sick has since died. He is the one that gave me the watch last winter. That makes two of the original members of my band gone. Osman and Barker. I hope that they belong to a better band than mine now. — Azro is here in my tent now — he is tough and black. We've been having some hard rains lately — it has rained some every day for a week or so — pleasant this P.M. Guess I have written enough — We think the <u>Rebelion</u> is fast playing out down here — don't think it can last much long. Now father, wont you answer this letter <u>your self</u>? Please do — This from your soldier boy.

Love to all

Herbert

From Jere:

March 7th 1865

It has been a very pleasant day warm and quite dry ground. This A.M. I visited the picket line where I found myself in close proximity with the rebs — live rebels, within speaking distance but they were very quiet. With a glass I saw very plainly their tents, camps, works, soldiers drilling, etc., I could also see the steeples of churches in [Petersburg]. It was interesting and will not soon be forgotten.

Our band was called to Brigade Head Quarters a few evenings since where we saw some sport. They invited us into a good tent which had a good floor used as a court room. A lot of Officers were there and they were in for a good time. They sang, smoked, danced and drank whiskey till a very late hour. We came home at twelve. They danced quite well.

Whiskey has been freely used among the officers this winter. They often get together and spend the greater part of the night in a drunken carousal to the disgust of a decent private. Officers in our own Regt. are as bad as any. He that was Captain of my company when I came out is now Lieut. Col. Geo. R. Damon commanding the Regt. I am sorry to see such a handsome promising young man making a fool of himself by drinking.

From Charles:

<u>Rainey weather</u>
<u>March 8, 1865</u>

Ellie darling: <u>More mud</u>! tonight we are going to play for the 50th New York Engineer Corps. They have some of the oddest and most tasty buildings I ever saw — they would give credit to our pretty New England village. The general outside finish is pine, with the bark on — all sorts of beading and imitation molding are finished with pine the same way. They have a theatre which will accommodate about 1000 persons. The great arch doorway with its large posts all covered with small pines. They now are putting on a steeple 30 feet high. We play tonight in the theatre between scenes. General Meade is going to be there. Foster got back last night. I will send his photo — what do you think of it? Will send Munsel's too. And I will send my receipt for the money I send to mother for you. You will see by it that if the money does not arrive safely the company are holders for only 30 days. You had better ascertain if it has arrived. Whew! How it rains! Another great victory for Sheridan. A few more victories and we will see them suing for peace.

The prolonged stalemate allowed for continued theatrical and musical enter-tainments, though not all activities at this time were lighthearted. The lack of fighting meant plenty of time for drills and rituals, leading musicians like Charles Putnam of the Old Vermont Brigade to complain of "playing almost incessantly."[14] *On occasion the ranks would form to witness an execution, a sobering experience for all the troops and one of the more difficult tasks for regimental musicians. Per-haps the impending combat added an underlying measure of familial stress, for a schism appeared between the George brothers, the first and only time this would occur during the war. Fortunately it would not last long.*

From Jere:

March 12th

Still we occupy our quarters watching the departure of Winter and enjoy-ing ourselves as well as we can....

Yesterday a deserter and bounty jumper was shot in our division. Being on duty with the band we were obliged to remain where stationed which was so far off that I could see only the general movements. He followed his coffin around the square on foot. As he passed us I had a fair view of his face. He carried a sort of a "dare devil" expression which made my sympathy for him much less than for the one I saw a few weeks ago. He was young under twenty I should judge. An Englishman. The story was that he had jumped thirteen bounties and deserted to the rebels. A Catholic Priest attended him. After they halted at the grave the culprit kneeled before the coffin first removing his cap, placed it on the coffin while the priest donned a robe and said service. I suppose I could hear nothing. He remained on his knees about five minutes then rose and from force of habit quietly put on his hat and was putting his hands in his pockets, when probably by request he took off his cap again. For a long time the priest stood before him talking I suppose. The prisoner knelt again. As all things have an end, so did the priest's endeavor to save the soul of the doomed man. He was then seated on his coffin and his hands tied behind him, his eyes blinded by a white cloth then left to be shot. At the same instant that the smoke issued from the guns, we saw him fall back before the report of the rifles reached our ears. We were marched by where lay the dead deserter with his face nearly white as this paper.

We were called on one evening last week to go and play for "a nigger performance." In the engineer corps near here where they have tools to work with, they have splendid quarters most as good as a cottage house at home, shingled roof, glass windows, etc. They have built a large hall in the shape of the 6th Corps badge which will contain an audience nearly as large as any New England Church. The hall is for entertainments. A few soldiers who think they have the talent black their faces and play minstrels. They have got Morris Bros. on the brain. The stage was pretty well lighted with candles with new tin plates to reflect the foot lights. Our band served as an orchestra to play between acts. Our station was in front of the stage. There was a reserves enclosure especially for the officers. Before the performance commenced Gen. Meades appearance was hailed with three hearty cheers from the audience followed by "Hail to the Chief" from the band. I had a good view of the commander of the Army of the Potomac. He is very good looking. Heavy whiskers, very black, probably colored. During the performance which followed, several local complimentary jokes were cracked at his expense always followed by laughing and cheers. As a critic to the performance, I should say that it lacked life, animation all through. The singing, violin and tambourine were very dull and lifeless. The bone and banjo playing was good. Clog dancing good for a soldier. Jokes and dialogues rather poor. On the whole it was a fair entertainment for soldiers in the field to get up. The architecture of the building is very beautiful. It has a steeple and spire running very high. Angles and triangles, curves, circles and all sorts of architecture may be seen there, equal to any cathedral in Boston.

From Herbert:

> Camp of the 10th Regt Vols from Vt.
> before Petersburg
> March 16th 1865

My dear Sister Em —

As it is almost certain that we are to march very soon some where . I think I had better send home what photographs I have haven't so I wont have to tote them around. I sent you another one of Will Clark and one of my "wife" (Sis) I have got his photo at last but it does not look as well as he does. The hair is natural but his eyes are not as bright as they really are. His skin is as fair and smooth as any girls and he is just as pretty as one too. I mean to try and get another photo better than this some time but I guess you will think this one is pretty. How is it? Please dont [spoil it kissing] him!!! I have got two more but have concluded not to send them. They are <u>Ladies</u>. will keep them to look at. One is a Pa. correspondent. She wrote me two letters & sent her photo and I wrote her only one and did not send her more. Didn't like her style. The other is one that I had had ever since I was home a year ago.... There is a terrible wind to day. Our tent shakes so that I can hardly write. My Bass player that I told you about that was taken prisoner at Frederick City Md. and was exchanged a while ago is dead. His name was Wm. Garvin. he died at Annappolis a few days after he was exchanged. Poor fellow he was starved to death in prison. Confouned the rebel Barbarians. They are inhuman. Well I must close — Will Clark does not read your letters nor hear them read. He is my Chum though. Charlie and Jere mess together and Will and I. — I do not mess with C. and J. at all — scarcely — I was so lonesome before Will came that I didn't know what to do with my self — C. & J. played chefs all the time most and I had to seek company out round or else tent alone for when they get at a game of chefs they dont know anything else till the game is up — now I can mate with Will and enjoy myself — Please dont mention this to them in your letters for it might cause hard feelings & I dont want that. Well I must close — write often

Much Love
From Herbert

It wasn't until March 25 that the 10th Vermont was to see combat again. Following a failed attempt by Lee's forces to break out of the siege at Fort Steadmen, General Meade seized the opportunity to test the weakened defenses on other fronts. The 10th Vermont was on picket duty about 300 yards from the enemy pickets at Forts Fisher and Welch, waiting to be relieved, when firing was heard nearby and orders came to prepare for an advance. Wright took advantage of the situation north of him to press the enemy on his front. The pickets now found themselves on the first line of battle with 230 men of the 10th Vermont and 160 men of the 14th New Jersey, all under the command of Lieutenant Colonel Damon. At 3:00 in the afternoon the 1st Brigade advanced towards the forts, but excessive fire from the enemy artillery forced Damon's men back.[15] More men and artillery were brought up and General Seymour ordered another attack at 4:00. This time the Federals broke through the enemy trenches following the charge of the 10th Vermont and the 14th New Jersey. The Vermonters seized numerous rifle pits, managing to capture 160 prisoners while losing only two killed and four wounded for their efforts.[16] Thanks to Wright's prompt and aggressive assault the VI Corps now held a position within one-half mile of the enemy lines.
From Charles:

<u>The Brave 10th.</u>
<u>March 24, 1865</u>

Still in camp, my ever loving and loved wife, and we are still counting off the days in the old camp. There has been no news or movement in this part of the army since my last letter. Nothing but the same routine of camp life. Our daily guard mountings, drills and picket details constitute about all our variety of life. Our amusements are very limited — games of ball, jumping and a few other bodily exercises, — playing chess and checkers are also in favor with the men. Jere and I had a present from Leroy — a set of chess men — cost $1.20....

Jere and I still intend to go West. I think we shall go to Minnesota. I will now adjourn till after your letter — "Paper kiss."

Sunday

Since writing the above, we have had a great battle and a great many lives lost on both sides! The position is much the same as it was before, only we hold their picket line. We captured somewhere from three to five thousand prisoners, which with their thinned ranks is a great loss to them. From what I can pick up of facts, I set our loss at four thousand and theirs at six thousand. You will see when it comes out in your newspaper. The attack was made by the rebels in a very treacherous way. Friday night deserters came in in squads till they amounted to about 500, and as is the custom, they were taken into one of the forts to deposit their muskets. After they were inside they showed their characters by capturing the fort and turning their guns on our men. At the same time an assaulting column came to their assistance. The result was that they captured a lot of our men, and got most to General Meade's Head-quarters before they were arrested. They were soon overpowered and large numbers captured and slaughtered — the fort captured them back again and quiet was restored. This was near Petersburg and on our right. But Grant did not see fit to let the matter rest there, but attached their right (our left). Our regiment was on picket at the beginning of the attack — near Fort Fisher. They alone captured about 600 prisoners. Our loss was very small — we captured their picket line which has formidable breastworks, and held it. The 2nd Corps made a charge farther on the left.— the result, I have not yet heard, but the roar of musketry was as loud as I ever heard. The firing died away at dark, and has not resumed again this morning. General Sherman arrived at City Point yesterday with his force all safe. He will be a great help to the army on the left.

From Jere:

MOVE! CAMPAIGN!

We left our comfortable Winter quarters yesterday morning and are now on our Summer Campaign in the field. Since the fight on Saturday last, active operations have been going on in the army, preparatory for the approaching struggle.... Yesterday morning at half past eight when we had no idea of moving we were startled by the bugle call to "strike tents" from Brigade Head-quarters.

Once more we packed and at 11 A.M. took our house, bed, furniture and provisions on our backs and bid good bye to winter quarters. As we came this way we notice that many camps had recently been vacated. It seemed that the 25th, 24th, 2nd and 5th corps had gone with General Sheridan to the left. We now occupy breastworks which were vacated by the 2nd corps. We are in plain sight of the Johnnies and our demonstrations here are to deceive them, make them think we have come to stay, and that our numbers are greater than they are. Our bands were kept playing in the afternoon and evening, drum corps practicing, etc, etc., We find pretty good quarters here but not so good as the tents we left. This tent has no floor, no door, no seats, no table, and a poor chimney. It has two bunks one above the other, the top one being about four feet from the ground. This elevated bed Charles and I took possession of about eight oclock last night. About 11 or 12 o-clock Charlie had the night mare. (No uncommon thing for him) and as usual I began to punch and shake him, but no ordinary shaking would bring him out of it. In my intense desire to shake him out of the might mare I forgot that he was on the front side of an elevated bed only wide enough for two to lie on, and when I gave him an extra nudge, off he went to the ground meeting "terra firma" on his hands and knees and terribly frightening the occupants of the lower bunk (Bill Clarke and Herbert.) He took all the blankets with him and I found myself all of a sudden in a very lonely condition without covering or bed fellow. Both had taken "French leave." The fall did him no injury and it is needless to say the fall brought him out of the night mare. It was a comical affair and we laughed long and well....

From Herbert:

Camp of the 10th Vt
in the field before Petersburgh Va.
April 1st 1865

Dear folks at home

We've been right on our campaign for the last few days — we broke up winter quarters last Wednesday and have been maneuvering about in front of the Enemy ever since. To day I split my index finger on my right hand open with my table knife and have got so many rags on it that I cant hardly write at all — causalities of to day — H. George wounded slightly in hand — We boys are all well and enjoy our selves first rate. Hope the war will soon cease Johnson's rebs are hard up sure — I send home Capt Davis's photograph and Lt Fosters — take care of em — I want you to send me one pkg of envelopes and about two quires of writing paper this size — by mail <u>immediately</u> — and I really need a pair of Socks — Got any? If you have please send me a pair as soon as convenient and I cant get any postage stamps here either guess had better send a dozen & then I guess I'll send home a <u>small</u> <u>bill</u> in this letter for safe keeping it will be safer there than here want it? Therefore Enclosed please find $20.00 in compound interest. Please tell Ann Maria that I have written to her <u>twice</u> since she says she has heard from me — I'll write again but you say she is going to be at home soon now so she will hear from us Emma. I got your letter which was written <u>to</u> <u>me</u> only — All O.K. I'm mum. Got to go and play for Capt Damon

Love to all

J. Herbert George

Both Lee and Grant saw that the operations around Petersburg were coming to an end. For many days rumors had been circulating that a major offensive was in the works, and the men began to anticipate an assault on the Petersburg lines. Wright believed his corps could crack through the enemy's lines, brazenly telling Grant: "The corps will go in solid, and I am sure will make the fur fly."[17] *At midnight of April 1 the VI Corps was placed in a giant wedge facing Wilcox and Heth of A. P. Hill's Corps; the 2nd Division formed the point with the 3rd Division on the left wing and the 1st Division on the right.*[18] *Tension ran high as each soldier sensed the importance of the impending assault, though Vermonters like Timothy Messer handled it like the veterans they were: "We have been through the usual amount of packing up by day & by night, shifting positions, being in readyness to march at a moments warning &c &c & there has been a considerable Canonading & musketry on the left of us."*[19]

It was a bitterly cold evening. Many of the men stomped their feet to keep warm, drawing fire from the enemy pickets and risking any attempt at secrecy. After hours of waiting, the signal gun sounded at 4:00 A.M., and the regiment immediately charged forward. The boldness of the move was a surprise to the Confederate high command and the bluecoats found the defenses unprepared for the size and speed of the assault.[20] *The Federals quickly passed through the enemy's pickets. Lines of battle were reformed, and the men pushed on to the next set of works. Though successfully clearing the redoubts, intense cannon fire forced them to pull back briefly. Despite intense musket fire and shelling from field artillery, the brigade managed to breach the defenses, passing over abatis and mounting the parapets. After fierce hand-to-hand fighting, the Federals successfully overpowered the Rebels and the 10th Vermont led the way into the final line of defenses, there earning the honor of being the first Union regiment to place their colors on the Confederate works.*[21] *Corporal Ira F. Varney, Co. K, was the color bearer for the assault, leading his fellow Vermonters in the final taking of the wall. The soldiers were again reformed and directed against the next fort, which likewise fell. By*

Confederate earthworks outside of Petersburg, Virginia (courtesy Vermont Historical Society).

this point the men from Vermont and New Jersey had moved so quickly that they had outpaced the rest of the Federal forces. Suddenly they found themselves facing a substantial counterattack. The troops held for almost twenty minutes until almost surrounded, when the men were forced to fall back to the safety of the recently captured works. The remainder of the brigade, as well as elements of the 2nd Brigade, joined the 10th Vermont and 14th New Jersey, and the men in blue advanced rapidly again, eventually linking up with the rest of the 3rd Division. The third and final fort was successfully taken, despite heavy fire from both rifle and cannon.

Intent on taking advantage of their success, the troops of the VI Corps swung to the left and rapidly drove to Hatcher's Run, capturing countless prisoners and over twenty guns. Upon learning that the II and V Corps were approaching Hatcher's Run, Wright turned back and continued the move on Petersburg, halting only two miles southeast of the city. Fatigued by their efforts the corps halted in front of Longstreet's position, preferring to allow the Confederates to retreat unmolested. The following morning the 3rd Division joined the rest of the army entering the recently evacuated city to the sounds of "Yankee Doodle" and other patriotic pieces.[22] At least one musician celebrated the recent victory with a unique salute: "After a hurried breakfast which we were almost too happy to eat, came the 'Pack up' call, to which the bugler added a perfect imitation of a long drawn out triumphant crow of a rooster. Someone wondered how he could do it on a bugle, and soon found out that he didn't, he had a trombone."[23]

From Jere:

> In a large field on the South Side R.R.
> 15 Miles West of Petersburg, Va.
> Friday Morning 8 o-clock
> April 4th 1865

The 6th corps has halted for a rest and I take the first opportunity to record the events of yesterday — the most interesting and important of the war. Richmond has fallen, Richmond is ours. Richmond and Petersburg have been captured at last. Victory! Victory! Glorious Day! I thank God that I have lived to see the fall of Richmond. Yesterday those two obstinate rebel Cities were surrendered to our forces. They having been evacuated the night before by rebel troops Jeff Davis & Co. When I have learned the particulars I can record them. Glory enough for this time writing that Richmond was taken yesterday third of April, Emma's Birthday (17). I will no return to the time of my last writing which was Sunday afternoon at the hospital. That night our band was detailed as nurses only three or four at a time. It came my turn at half past ten and I stayed two hours and a half. I found plenty to do to attend to the wants of the suffering brave. No scene of woe, of human suffering is worse for humanity to look upon than the hospital of wounded soldiers on the eve of battle. Hundreds of these brave men are brought to one place and laid down side by side, there to wait till they can be attended to by the surgeons. Each in his pain patiently or impatiently waits his turn to an arm or leg cut off or a flesh wound dressed as the case may be. It is bad enough to go through a hospital a few days after or any time after the wounds are all dressed, the blood washed off and they look neat and clean, but on the eve of battle we see blood, blood and ghastly wounds of every description, bloody clothes, bloody heads, bloody bodies, blood everywhere. Aye the best blood of all nations too. Some bear their misfortunes with fortitude bowing meekly to fate, while others take it hard and bitter. Many in their extreme pain groan at every breath while others are quiet. Who can picture the scene or imagine the sounds of the distressing groans of pain if they have not been there? They are grateful for favors. When I slowly walk along the long lines of our brave boys giving a drink of water from my canteen or changing the position of a disabled foot, arm or head that it may rest easier. They almost invariably reward me with "thank you sir." My place of work during the night was in the great church of the Engineer's previously described in this diary as an opera house. It was filled with wounded besides the whole Division hospital and long rows of tents on the ground. 48 of our Regiment were wounded and four killed. One of the wounded was a mate of my boyhood Edwin Tuthill. He received a ball in his left foot and right leg, which as he expressed it took away all of his underpinning. He has been in every battle with the Regiment except one and always escaped unharmed until this time.... We entered Petersburg about noon and the first white man we saw was President Lincoln on horseback accompanied by naval and military officers with cavalry guard. He returned our salute with his right hand as we passed and I shall ever forget the happy, gratified, satisfied smile that lit up his countenance, making his homely face so radiant with joy and smiles that it was indeed pleasant to look upon. The City had been in our possession but a few hours and he was already taking a triumphant survey over the conquered remains of the City which had to come under his rule. We saw but few white people but many negroes who were as jubilant and happy as it was possible for them to be. Such was the scarcity of food that many children — some white begged of us to give them a hardtack. "Hurrah for the old flag — Give me hardtack" has been a by-word in the band ever since....

From Charles:

<u>Monday morning.</u>
<u>April 3, 1865</u>

Ellie dear — the band boys are all well, which I suppose will be your greatest anxiety to learn and you will be glad to know it. But the rest of the regiment I cannot say so of. They have lost heavily, but not so heavy as at Winchester or Cedar Creek. But they have won themselves a name that will last <u>long</u>. I will take up the history of this army since I last wrote, and write as long as I can. The operations on the left were were mainly as I wrote in my last letter and were of such a character as to call Lee's whole available force that way. So Thursday night everything was in readiness for a charge of the 6t and 9th Corps. They were to start at 12 midnight and <u>pounce</u> upon the unsuspecting rebels, destroy their works and cut Lee's army in two. Everything was in readiness at that hour, knapsacks packed and left in the streets with a guard. But the order was countermanded....

<u>Saturday</u>

After we had gone to bed it began to be whispered that a charge was to be made in the morning. At 10:00 o'clock P.M. there commenced the most fearful cannonading the history of the world could ever afford. The whole line from City Point to Hatcher's Run was engaged. I cannot describe it! It is beyond description! The rebels did not reply opposite our Corps but guess they did at the 9th. At 12:00 they quieted down and the troops were silently taken out of their camps. This time they were told they were going to repel a charge from the rebels, and expected one. Of course this was to prevent a repetition of the occurrence of the previous night. Most of the boys expected what was coming. At 4:00 o'clock on Sunday morning a signal gun was fired from Fort Fisher, and the column started. They had been lying in line of battle three hours on the skirmish line. None but they know how they dreaded it. They knew fearful battles they might have to go through and the raking fire of artillery. The shrewdness of Grant was right in his conjecture that their line was weak — their men were nearly ten feet apart. The whole Corps was massed in one place and walked straight to their works and then captured them. They then wheeled to the left and assaulted the first fort and captured it, and the next and the next. Then the 25th Corps filled in their place and they about faced and captured the forts on the right of where they broke through and traveled towards Petersburg. Various reports are current concerning that famous city, but I cannot learn the truth. I know I saw it in flames this morning and heard some explosions. After they broke the line several of us went over into the reel camp and have got some trophies. I've got a tin plate, a case knife and a good wool blanket, which I intend to carry home....

CHAPTER 8

April to June 1865

Sailor's Creek; Appomattox Court House; Danville, Virginia; and Burlington, Vermont

At Petersburg the men of the 10th Vermont had fought valiantly in what was probably their longest and most successful charge of the war. The price for their success was surprisingly light: three killed, four wounded, and four captured. There was no time to enjoy the victory, however, as the Union troops were immediately dispatched in pursuit of Lee's retreating army. The VI Corps was sent west to join Sheridan in blocking Lee's retreat south and to cut off access to desperately needed supplies.[1] Sheridan had requested the men he had fought with in the Shenandoah Valley Campaign, and Grant concurred. For almost sixteen consecutive hours the men marched through arduous terrain, eager to catch the retreating Army of Northern Virginia. Wright's VI Corps led one wing of the pursuit and on April 6 found itself in heated combat. Lee's army had been slowed at Deatonsville, which allowed advance elements of Sheridan's cavalry and the 3rd Division to catch Ewell's corps at Sailor's Creek. Separated from Longstreet in front and Gordon in the rear, Ewell was caught in a deadly situation. The Confederates were forced to stand and fight, if nothing else to delay the Union forces and allow Lee time to reorganize.[2] Seymour threw his division at Ewell and a vicious brawl erupted. So committed were the troops that the musicians contributed their part to the fight, according to one witness: "The bands were brought to the front; and as we were now lying across the path of the rebels, the air was made musical with Hail Columbia and kindred National airs. It was a saucy act, but it was inspiriting to the Union troops."[3] Not everyone was impressed with the appearance of musicians during the battle. As General Keifer noted:

> *Sheridan was accompanied by a large mounted brass band that commenced playing Hail to the Chief, or some other then unwelcome music. This drew the fire from the*

battery with increased fury on the whole party.... Being in immediate charge of the forces there, I invited the Generals to get out of the way, but as they did not retire I ordered a charge upon the "noisy band," and thus caused the whole party to retire to a place of greater safety.[4]

The 1st and 2nd Brigades fell on Confederate general G. W. C. Lee's left flank, crossing the shallow but wide creek and storming straight into enemy fire. The charging soldiers were greatly surprised to be met by a thunderous volley of coordinated musket fire, though the advancing blue lines held.[5] *The 10th Vermont was placed behind its fellow regiments and as a result suffered no casualties. There was a desperate element to the fighting now, as both sides sensed that the end of the war was in sight. Simon Cummins of the 14th New Jersey tersely summed up the final charge: "We the 6 corps advanced in 3 lines of battle and they fell back in their breast works. Then we charged on them and fought like tigers for an hour then what was not killed and captured surrendered."*[6] *So complete was the victory that almost 8,000 men, including General Ewell and his staff (including six generals) were forced to surrender. Though soon to be overshadowed by the events at Appomattox Court House, the Battle of Sailor's Creek was both critical to Lee's defeat and a terrible conflict in its own right. Sheridan described it as "one of the severest conflicts of the war, for the enemy fought with desperation to escape capture, and we, bent on his destruction, were no less eager and determined."*[7] *Once the battlefield was secured the 10th Vermont again set out after the remainder of Lee's army. On April 8 the VI Corps crossed the Appomattox River, swung north and then west to cut off any chance of a Confederate retreat in that direction, and finally contained the Army of Northern Virginia at Appomattox Court House.*

From Jere:

> On the march near Burkville, Va
> Friday 9:45 A.M.
> April 7th

While we are halted to rest a few minutes I will commence my record of yesterdays operations. Another hard fight and glorious victory for the 6th corps.... The contest was so long that I began to fear lest we had got into a larger nest than we could handle. But the 6th corps knows nothing of retreat. It was never beaten in battle and never will be. It fights only to conquer....

Our band fell out just before the first charge and we were consequently very near the fight, though woods and hills prevented our seeing it. We did not consider it prudent to venture on the other side of the hill while the battle raged. The hottest of the fight was about 5 o-clock. During its progress we cooked our supper but I had no appetite. The fight was so severe and long (about one hour and a half) that I was for once somewhat agitated, not exactly

excited, I knew our regiment was there and I knew by the durance of the
charge that the enemy was strong in number. After they surrendered, of course
the firing ceased and we (the band) went on. When we got to that awful mudhole the 2nd Div. was just passing through. It was then after but a clear full
moon gave us light. There was no other way to cross so in we plunged with
the crowd. The mud was thin as gruel and thick as pudding. We waded only
because we <u>must</u>. Our veterans say it was the worst place they ever went
through. Here we lost Charlie and did not find him till the next morning.
When safe across I rolled up my pants and drawers, threw away my socks and
stuck my bare feet into my shoes to go on to the Regiment if possible. It was
something unusual for this Band to go on and join the Regiment so soon after
a fight, leaving the wounded and work at the hospital for others, but it was
decided to do so this time. We had not got more than half way over the battlefield when we were halted by the corps surgeon who ordered us to stop
there and bring in the wounded from the field. Obliged to obey him we laid
down our instruments. We went off in squads of four, searching though the
fields and woods for the living among the dead. Goldsmith, Kent, Mack, and
I went one way, keeping a few rods apart. The ground was thickly strewn
with dead and wounded rebels but we found only a few of our men. This was
the roughest job I ever undertook. It was night with a bright moon. The
ground I trod on was but an hour before the fierce struggle of life and death.
It was a field of death, and there I wandered on from one prostrate form to
another searching for life among the many dead. We were in too much hast
to hunt for booty on the dead rebels, though Goldsmith took a gold watch
from one. When I came to a man lying on the ground I would touch his face
to see if dead or alive. Sometime alive but oftener dead. Some who were stuck
with our shell were terribly mangled. Seeing so much of this in the moonlight
in the woods with the fatigue and excitement of the day had some effect on
my nerves and by the time I had helped carry in one man I felt sick with no
desire to go out again. When we had brought in what Union men we could
find, we started again toward our Regiment about ten o-clock. We passed by
a long ditch by the roadside in which the Jonnies had taken refuge from our
merciless shell. It was about six feet wide and nearly as deep which made it
a very good place to get into but a very hard place to get out of and the unfortunate rebels were consequently shot by our men as they advanced. If they
tried to get out they were shot and if they refused to surrender they were likewise shot. And there they lay dead, one piled upon another. It was indeed a
sad sight....

We reached the regiment just before they started on the march again.
Found Charlie all right he having gone directly on from the mudhole and

joined the regiment in the evening. We continue our chase to-day, after the remnant of Lee's forces. They cannot be far away.

From Charles:

Farmville, Virginia
[c. April 8, 1865]

Dearest Ellie — We arrived at the railroad near Amelia Court House Wednesday night about dark — stayed there over night in line of battle, which showed that we were near the enemy. The 5th Corps get there soon enough to support the cavalry who were holding the railroad. In the morning the Corps made a reconnaissance and found them gone — time they made for Lynchburg. We had marched 25 miles on Wednesday, but went to work with a good will, chasing the rebels again. Sheridan had captured 2000 or 4000 prisoners and 6 pieces of artillery and now was hunting them out again. We found them about noon. The cavalry was waiting for us — they could not drive the enemy alone. Our Division was on the lead — the roads had been very bad and we were pressed to our utmost! Not more than two-thirds had come in — before our brigade had half arrived the 2nd brigade started the charge. Ours followed in a few minutes — pretty soon the captured johnnies began to come back — our Division drove them more than a mile from the first charge. By this time the First Division came up and formed a line — the artillery came thundering along and pretty soon they began to "talk" — The rebs had a strong position but had no artillery to use. The two Divisions, 1st and 3rd, charged them nearly three miles — went through swamp where the mud was leg deep — but they went through, and up the hill — captured hosts of men and artillery.

Custer came in on their rear and captured everything in that part of the line. General Ewell and General Lee's son and General Kershaw were captured. We Band boys did not go to the hospital as there were very few that were wounded. This morning we started at 7:00 A. A. — did not march far before we struck the Lynchburg road just below Ferntown — there we came in contact with the 24th Corps works — they were now ahead of us in the chase. A few miles farther and we made halt. While halting there a division of cavalry came in with 30 rebel battle flags, all in one squad. We left there about noon, crossing a stream on a narrow bridge. Now we find ourselves here. The rebs are making a stand and preparations are being made to attack....

There is no movement this morning. The day is beautiful. Last night the air was very cold — we could not sleep much.

After tensely holding position on Lee's left flank, word was finally received that General Lee had surrendered. The reaction of the men was beyond words:

"Our division officers and we and all the banners assembled and a prayer was made by our chaplan and sung the doxoligy. The band plaid Hail Columbia & Yankey Dodal, All the men were wild with excitement and got as though they were crazy."[8] *Herbert George enthusiastically claimed that his was the first band to play, and their music inspired the other bands to perform as well. As part of the celebration General Seymour gave a brief speech, and Colonel Truex rode past his troops waving his hat to the cheering of the men. Since March 29 the 10th Vermont had taken a total of forty-eight casualties, not as high a number as some of their previous campaigns, but shockingly high when one considers that the total enlistment of the regiment on March 31 was only 475 fit for duty.*[9] *So any celebration at the surrender of the Army of Northern Virginia — and the beginning of the end of the war — could not help but be tempered by the painful absence of so many comrades.*

From Herbert:

April 10th 1865
Camp of the 10th Vt. Vol Infty

<u>On the field of Glory</u>

Where Gen'l Robt E. Lee Surrendered the confederate army to Gen'l Grant on the 9th day of April —1865

My dear home —

Long ere this letter reaches its destination you will hear the <u>joyful</u> news of the surrender of the Confederate army to Genl Grant — Oh such a <u>time</u> never was known as there was here yesterday — No one can ever imagine the scene — What would I have given if you <u>all</u> could have been present with us when the Surrender was made — Men cried and shouted for joy — guns were fired and Bands played the National airs — Cheers after cheers from thousands of soldiers rent the air — it seemed as though there would be no end to them. Try to picture to your selves — several hundred acres of land covered with troops, throwing their hats in the air and <u>yelling</u> with all their might. Batteres firing salutes — flags waving and Bands playing each one trying to out do the other in showing how <u>good</u> <u>they</u> <u>felt</u>. I cant <u>tell</u> <u>it</u> but I will tell you how our Division done — Genl Seymour comdg the Div had all the flags in each regt in the Div called together and him self & staff with Each Brigade commander with their Staffs in the center — <u>Bands</u> <u>included</u> and there they had it. Toasts and cheers and music — then music cheers and toasts &c. This was kept up till all got tired — It happened that My Band was the first to play — or perhaps I will say we get the start of the rest and <u>played</u> <u>first</u>. I commenced to play with only 5 of the band — the rest were off seeing what was to be seen and hearing what was to be heard — but they heard us <u>fifing up</u> & the other 9

came running up & caught up their instruments in a hurry — Hurrah for the
Union — Hail Columbia, Star Spangled Banner, Yankee Doodle, or any other
man. We Boys are all right yet. Had a hard march but got well paid for it.
We are now about 25 miles from Lynchburg and not far from 100 miles from
Petersburg — I was in Petersburg the 3rd of April Em's birth day — its a nice
place. Got some tobacco there for father — Tobacco is at a discount now —
dont cost any thing. The colored people all along the road all say as we pass
them "God Bless you." Tickled to death most. But they were all hungry. In
Petersburg the little white girls were out on the side walk saying "three cheers
for the union give me a hard tack. One was singing "O come come a way"
but all were "out of rations" — I picked up a boy about 10 years old up in Not-
away County the 5th inst and he is with me yet....

From Charles:

Monday Morning
April 10, 1865

HURRAH!!!! HURRAH!!! HURRAH!!!!
GENERAL LEE HAS SURRENDERED!!!

Peace is near at hand! —- Oh! my dear Ellie!! I cannot express to you the
emotions of my heart. Yesterday was the most eventful day of the war. A day
that will never be forgotten!!! Never were such demonstrations of joy exhibited
as there was from five to eight o'clock. I will explain to you first the situation
of the armies and try to tell you something about the enthusiasm of the 6th
Corps.

Friday's operations proved to be a severe blow to Lee. Sheridan had got
him in a tight place — captured several thousand prisoners and obliged him
to burn his wagon trains. We left Farmville about 9:00 A.M. Saturday — after
traveling a few miles we came upon the burned train — the roads were strewn
with the debris of camp equipage — kettles, secretary desks, papers, books
and everything belonging to Headquarter wagons were scattered over the road
for miles. About 600 wagons were burned. After marching about 4 miles we
began to hear cheering ahead. — Pretty soon it came to us — General Lee had
sent in proposals for a surrender and made terms of peace. Grant sent back
that he had no authority to make peace. He would accept nothing but an
unconditional surrender. That day the 2nd and 5th Corps got another haul
of prisoners and wagons. Sunday morning we heard firing at the front and
were hurried on.

The first news we heard was that Lee had sent a flag of truce again —
wishing to have an interview with Grant. Grant sent word again that he would

accept nothing but an unconditional surrender!—Lee sent word again that he would not surrender <u>then</u>. General Thomas had taken Lynchburg with only the 4th Corps and a division of cavalry attacking in the rear—and in the battle captured about 45,000 prisoners. Everything was then in readiness to attack on all sides—we had him surrounded and his army was so reduced that he could not whip either side. The 2nd corps were in readiness for a charge.—Our Corps was massed about two miles in their rear—Grant then sent word to Lee that he would give him till 5:00 P.M. to surrender. The story is soon told—Lee came to terms and Grant renewed his previous title of

<u>"Unconditional Surrender Grant"</u>

And Ellie, when the news reached or Corps, such a scene of excitement I never have witnessed. About half an hour later it was confirmed by Grant, Meade and Staff riding by. Cannons were immediately whirled into position and commenced firing—such a hollering I never heard. Cheer after cheer went up—hats thrown high into the air—men throwing their arms up and swinging their caps and every other type of demonstrations of joy were going on. I began to think the Band ought to play a part too—I found Herbert playing with only five members! Hail Columbia—the rest soon joined. As we played I looked at our division in front of us—there everything was in motion—the air was full of caps and hats—officers from General Seymore down to Lieuts. were on their horses "riding every which way"! Flags were waving—cheer after cheer from thousands of soldiers rent the air and it seemed as if there would be no end to the noise. Just try to imagine, if you can, seeing all this and hearing the yelling of the men—batteries firing blanks and bands playing (other bands took up the strains). It is almost impossible to describe joy these men were showing. For an attempt to describe it think of <u>bees</u> when they are swarming and imagine every one to be a man and you will get a faint idea....

Did I tell you that when we passed through Petersburg on April 3rd we saw President Lincoln? (I don't remember)—he was on horseback and was surrounded by a crowd of colored people shouting, "God bless Massa Lincoln." Everyone was cheering and at the same time asking for something to eat—"give me some hard-tack."

Today is rainy and cold—the mail goes out at 6:00 P.M. and it is now 5:00—I expect mail tonight. My dearest love to you always—your Charlie.

With the surrender of the Army of Northern Virginia the jubilant men of the 10th Vermont longed to return to their home state. The war was not over, though, as there was still concern about General Joseph E. Johnston and his army, then passing through North Carolina with General William T. Sherman close on

*their heels. So while the V Corps stayed to collect the flags and arms of Lee's troops,
the VI Corps was ordered southeast to Burkeville, Virginia, a primary junction
for the railroads. On April 12 the men passed through Farmville, and the next
day found themselves marching in a heavy rain. They passed near the battlefield
of Sailor's Creek and were shocked to find many of the dead unburied.[10] Stationed
briefly outside of Burkeville, the men were allowed to relax for the first time in
weeks. The Vermonters received a welcome ration of whiskey as well as coffee, and
the bands provided relaxing music, according to Simon Cummins of the 151st New
York: "The morning is warm and pleasant. The bands are playing & the boys are
sitting & laying around."[11] The men were pleased when their old division commander, General Ricketts, paid them a visit. Then the troops received the unbelievable news of President Lincoln's assassination. After using their music to uplift
the soldiers so many times, now Herbert, Charles, and Jere had to play in honor
of a nation's tragedy, "a mournful air which sounds very solom" according to
Private Cummins.[12]*

Two letters from Herbert:

Camp of the 10th Vt Infty
Near Burksville Station (or Junction) Va
Apl 14th 1865

Dear folks at home —

"You "uns" are wondering where "we "uns" are now aint you? We are all
here at Burksville in camp for a <u>rest</u>. The camps are all in order and the
baggage has come up — Recon we will remain here for the present. Say a week
or so. Every body has got sore feet and are pretty well tired out generally. I
suppose we chased the Johnnies about 100 miles from Petersburg before Lee
surrendered — Then we had to come back here after our supplies. Was three
days coming back to this place bad roads. muddy — Undoubtedly the war is
over now and soon some body will publish a song and call it Now this Cruel
war is over! I want to have it arranged for my Band as soon as it comes out!!
Aint I glad I belong to the Gallant 6th Corps? What a <u>name</u> the 6th & 2nd
Corps have got. "Bully for us" little Phil Sheridan says — "Give me the 6th
corps & I can go any where" Hurrah for Phil!! Mead says he shall remember
the 6th Corps. Hurrah for <u>Mead</u>! Grant says he can <u>trust</u> the 6th corps any
where. Hurrah for <u>Grant</u>. Lee says the 6th Corps always broke his lines when
they tried. Hurrah for _____ The 6th Corps — All the other corps fight well —
<u>splendid</u> but the 6th more splendid. The 3rd Div played a prominent part all
through the campaign. They were the first through the reb lines and were
right on their fight all the time. Our Div was the first to charge the enemy at
the Battle of Sailor Creek or some call it Burksville but it was on the creek

and our whole line charged right through the swamp & creek up to their waist. Our band worked till midnight picking up wounded on the field. Hosts of Johnnies <u>killed</u> there but not many of our own men. I wrote to you from the place where Lee surrendered, probably you have recd it <u>Big Time</u>.... Guess I will close up now Hope to see you all next September

Herbert

Camp of the 10th Vt.
Near Burksville Station
April 19th 1865

Dear sister Em —

Your letter of the 3rd inst just rec'd. It got lost and just found its way to its owner Mother letter of the 11th also recd — We are all well and enjoying our rest after our hard march. Some think that we shall remain here in this camp for several weeks and others think that we will march to City Point in a few days — Mother wants to know what I think about getting home to help father plant <u>corn</u> now? Why I think just as I always have — that I shall not be there!! Not what I would be delighted to help plant the corn but I shall have to plant it in Va. I still think that we will have to stay our time out. Charlie thinks that we will go home next month but I tell him "I cant see it." There is a **heap** of things to be seen to before any troops are discharged. Probably they will not send any troops that have less than six months to serve away down to <u>Texas</u>. But in my opinion <u>no</u> troops will be discharged inside of two or three months. We have only four months now to stay and then they will undoubtedly <u>discharge</u> us. To day is a day of <u>mourning.</u> President Lincolns funeral is to day and all the flags are at half mast. Religious services are being held in every regt. No unnecessary work to be done.... Oh! I forgot to tell you that I was in the City of <u>Petersburg</u> on your birth day. I <u>was</u> and saw a few pretty girls there too. And I saw our late President Lincoln there horse back with Admiral Porter. The first time I ever saw Mr Lincoln close to and had a <u>fair</u> view of his face. He looked better than his picture does. I believe there is nothing I want to <u>eat</u> so bad as I do some <u>maple sugar.</u> I would give anything almost for as much as I could eat of maple syrup & warm biscuit. "<u>O! My</u>" how my mouth waters for some. I believe that doughnuts would be in the shade if there was pleanty of biscuit & sugar at hand. Wont you please come & take <u>tea</u> with me this evening? <u>hard tack</u> and salt <u>hog</u> — <u>poor at that?</u> You can have it <u>raw</u> or fried just as you like. I take mine <u>raw</u>!! Oh! hum I must close my disconnected, black, homely letter and <u>stretch</u>. Pretty warm.

Good Bye for now
From Herbert

From Charles:

<u>Burkeville, Virginia.</u>
<u>April 19, 1865</u>

My own precious wife — I am thinking of you tonight — and have been doing the same all this long day. Thinking of the good times coming and looking for events to hasten my return home to you. Time is hanging heavily with us, although we are having an easy and pleasant time. The fact is we are looking for our discharge from the service very soon now — and how anxiously we wait for the papers to give us some insight to the future. Tonight there is a rumor that we will move in the morning. Today has been kept in mourning for the late President. We had a discourse from Reverend Perry from Hygate.

<u>April 21, 1865</u>

(Friday) — We have got the late details of the assassination of President Lincoln. What a tragedy!!! When I think of the cheerful, pleasant <u>and kind hearted face</u> I <u>met a few days ago in Petersburg</u> it seems too horrible to believe! I shall never forget the expression of his face as he returned our salutes....

Ellie, I have been thinking about going West — I hate to give up the idea — in going there I can see everything prosperous and to stay in Vermont I can see nothing, but the same series of <u>hard times</u> that has followed us ever since we were married. By going West I can see a pleasant homestead made from the wild, but fertile land — a homestead fashioned after my own ideas — beautiful gardens and pleasant shade trees and orchards. You may think I see through a magnifying glass, and I know the fertility of the soil and rapidity of growth in Vermont and I could stay in Vermont and be happy, but my chosen locality has always been in the broad western prairies. I do not want you to feel bad because I want to go, for I shall never go without your willing consent. I know too well the ties that bind you — it is your mother — and it would mean that I would be taking you away from her. I love her and do not wish to do that, which will cause her to grieve. I think that if we should emigrate and succeed well, your father would soon follow. He is too good a farmer to spend all his days among the rocks and hills of Vermont, when there is such a splendid country within reach. I did not intend to write a <u>sermon</u> when I commenced, but I see I have. They are just having "Tattoo" — how long before I shall be where I can go to bed without the <u>fife</u> and <u>drum</u> for summons!...

Today I have been roving around through the woods and fields. How good it seems to get off alone out of the noise. I had a good wash in a brook. Say! How would you like to sleep with me — I am neither dirty nor lousy and my breath is unadulterated with the perfume of tobacco or liquor. I am the same Charlie I was 32 months ago. I feel proud to go home (if I am permitted to do so) with no bad habits learned in camp. <u>Few can say so.</u> — Jere is among the few, too. He might stay here any number of months or years and come out the same Jere. I cannot say precisely the same of Herbert. He does not drink or gamble, and I don't think he will, but he gets <u>mad</u> pretty easy and swears pretty bad and sometimes he swears when he isn't mad. He has become a pretty good smoker, but that is not very bad — he is what one might call a fellow of good habits out <u>here</u>, but I should rather see him like Jere.

By April 23 the men were on the move again. The constant marching was having an impact on the soldiers; Jere was forced to fall out at one point leaving Charles to carry his instrument. Despite their fatigue the 10th Vermont marched proudly, members of one of the most distinguished units in the Union Army and victors of some of the hardest fighting the war had seen. There was a measure of scorn shown to those who had previously doubted the qualities of these men in combat, according to Sergeant Albert Harris of the 14th New Jersey: "We fully appreciate the bounteous praise the worthy editor of the Herald heaps upon the gallant sixth Corps. Mr. Bennett did not view things a year or two ago, in the same true light that he now does."[13] *The VI Corps was then ordered eighty miles*

Drawing of Danville, Virginia, showing the prisons used to hold captured Union soldiers (Library of Congress).

southwest to Danville, Virginia, arriving there on April 28. Herbert's band supplied patriotic music at various points throughout the march, bringing forth a cool response from those loyal to the Confederacy, according to Edwin Hall: "At one village I remember (I think it was a place called Mount Laurel, said to be the home of ex-governor Wise of Va.) as we passed through, all the bands played and the troops sang 'John Brown's Body Lies a Molding in the Grave' until the ex-governor went nearly crazy."[14]

Danville had been the temporary home of the Confederate government following the fall of Richmond and Petersburg, and as such was seen by some as a bastion of Southern sentiment. Major General Wright called all the musicians together and ordered them to lead the troops and play as they marched into town.[15] *It was a challenging experience for the members of the band of the 10th Vermont as they had to play non-stop from one end of town to another. This time their performance brought forth jubilant responses from among the ex-slaves: "They would jump and sing for joy as soon as the Brass band would strike up with some old National Air."*[16] *The 10th Vermont feared that yet another march was soon to follow when news was happily received of Johnston's surrender to Sherman near Durham, North Carolina. Now what the George brothers had hoped for so long seemed possible — that soon they would be returning to the Green Mountain State.*

From Charles:

6:00 P.M.
Danville, Virginia.
April 27, 1865

We have gone into camp one mile south of the city — we were pretty tired when we started, but a good wash and prospect of stopping to rest makes us feel much better. The march has been a long one — five days in succession and probably not far from 100 miles. The distance by railroad is 81 miles. We have come much farther, of course, by following the road. The weather has been cool and pleasant and the roads in good condition. We entered Danville this afternoon.

The city is about as large as Nashua, New Hampshire — located on the Dan River and on high ground — shade trees — pretty gardens and some very tasty houses. The old Vermont Brigade were doing good duty all along the street, they being the leading Brigade of the Corps today. The 10th Vermont Band played two pieces as they marched through the city. We could see the hospital building and all the line of fortifications around the city. There were two substantial bridges over the railroad that are in good condition. The rebs left last night, I understand. As far as our business down here is concerned, it is still a mystery. The mail has come regularly — I have seen a New York

Herald of the 22nd. While passing through Halifax, the home of Governor Wise, the man who hung John Brown, we played "John Brown's body"....

April 28, 1865

My darling — mail is going out directly, and I guess I will send my letter on sooner this time. I slept well last night — better than usual. My sleep is generally rather broken and I am troubled considerably with night mares — I will surely be glad when I am done soldiering — four months more at the most — probably three will terminate it — perhaps two, and maybe, just maybe only one!

We are within two miles of North Carolina. There is no reliable news yet from Johnston's army.

Ever your loving husband, Charlie.

From Jere:

Danville, Va. Friday Eve. Apr. 28

News! Glorious news again has come to cheer us. Johnston has surrendered! This came official this afternoon, which was the cause of another joyous time among us. No more marching after him, but we may have to march somewhere. News also came last night in official dispatch that J. Wilkes Booth the murderer of President Lincoln has been killed in an attempt to capture him. "Sic semper tyrannis" the Virginian motto which the bold assassin used as he crossed the theatrical stage for the last time after he had fired the fatal shot may now well be said of him "So be it with tyrants." I saw him at the Boston Museum as a star actor, about a year ago in the play, of "Richard III." In his last fight with "Richard" he was of course overpowered. I shall never forget the fury of his eye and his bloody face a he appeared in the closing scene. "When he fell to rise no more with "Richards" sword apparently thrust through his body, he groaned, struggled and as the curtain fell feigned death as natural as though it was a real murder. That blood was paint, and that fight and death a mockery, a "make believe." But now it is real. He has acted his last tragedy. The red which stains his face is his own life's blood and he dies this time not to live again. The two closing scenes are nearly alike to look upon, but far different in this last from that on the stage. There he comes to life in a moment to die over and over again, but now like the doomed deserter whom I saw shot. He returns to life no more. He was a fine looking young man and a splendid actor. Indeed none but a skillful actor could have executed the awful deed and get out as he did.

We are anxious to get the particulars of his capture and death a tragic affair in the extreme also of Johnston's surrender....

From Herbert:

> Camp of the 10th Regt Vt Vols
> Danville Va.
> April 29th/65

My dear sister Em —

Guess I will write a letter this P.M. and finish tomorrow. We have got our tents up on <u>stilts</u> and bunk in all right for a [XXX] day or two. Perhaps we shall stay here a month and perhaps not longer than tomorrow. We dont know anything about what is to be done with us. Old Joe has surrendered and so I dont think that we will have to go any farther south. A week ago to night we went to bed at Burksville little thinking that in the morning we should start on such a long march as we did. They put us over the road in quick time I tell you. We marched out 20 miles a day for five days about 120 miles the way we came to Danville. By rail it is about 85. I suppose we came here to cut off Joe Johnsons retreat and it seems that he surrendered soon after we started & as soon as he found out that we were enrout for Danville. It is only about two miles and a half from the N. C. line. We are about a mile and a half north of the City. We played through the town two pieces. Awful hard work all tired out and if we didnt sweat I'll give up — My mouth was so dry that I had to take a swallow of water from my canteen every half minute! I stood the march all the way pretty well didnt fall out and kept at the head of the regt in my place all the way. My feet got pretty hard up and the cords under my left knee were awful lame but I wouldnt fall out. I have marched <u>every</u> <u>march</u> <u>that</u> <u>the</u> <u>regt</u> <u>has</u> <u>yet</u> and have been able to keep up every time excepting the skedaddle from Monocacy to Baltimore 40 miles last July. I was too sick & too much worn out then to march with the column. I have never been absent from the regt <u>sick</u> never have been <u>punished</u> for anything, and have never had a cross word spoken to me by an officer since Col Jewett went home. I hope to be able to keep with the regt until I go home. Jere kept up with us every day but one and then he was only an hour & a half behind when we camped for the night....

From Herbert

The VI Corps stayed at Danville for over two weeks, cheerful at the prospect of a break from marching. The musicians were treated to a unique social excursion when Colonel Damon secured passes for the entire band and took them into North Carolina to perform for civilians. Soldiers of the 106th New York attempted their own entertainment one evening, but to mixed results:

> *My men were singing and dancing a "walk arround" to-night and making consider-able noise the Col. sent down word to have it stoped. I went out and calling them to*

attention, informed them of the fact that the Col. was a great lover of good music, but make a distinction — not flattering to himself between "music" and "noise," that he classed the present performance as "noise" and therefore I was under the painful necesity of directing them to cease.[17]

Here the men would learn of the honor bestowed on them by Major General Meade in a speech published in the Corps' newspaper, The Sixth Corps. *Referring to the final assault on Petersburg, Meade claimed "that in my opinion, the decisive movement of this campaign, which resulted in the capture of the Army of Northern Virginia, was the gallant and successive charge of the Sixth Corps, on the morning of the 2nd of April."*[18] It was no doubt uplifting for the men to finally receive such recognition for their sacrifice and bravery in the final operations of the war.

The prisons of Danville held poignant surprise for the George brothers. Inside one prison cell they found Herbert's name carved on a wall by the former bass player of the 10th Vermont's band, William Garvin, who had been captured at the Battle of Monocacy.

From Charles:

Danville, Virginia
May 3, 1865

The sun is about two hours high. Our suppers are eaten and we are in high glee over the prospect of going on a "bum." Tonight Colonel Damon called Herbert to his tent and inquired if he would like to take his band over the line into North Carolina <u>with him</u>. He wanted to visit there and would like to take his Band. Of course it suits us first rate....

May 4, 1865

Ellie, our "bum" last night consisted of a 4 mile ride out and back. The only reception we had (or treat) was a drink of water — we were not invited into the house and it was so cold we suffered came home <u>hungry</u>. The man was a Union man too. Such is <u>Southern Chivalry or Hospitality</u>! Tonight it is proposed to go about 10 miles and get better treatment — or condemn North Carolina chivalry. At the house where we went were two rebel deserters — <u>they</u> thought if it hadn't been for Davis, Lee would have surrendered two years ago, and if Stephens could have had the reins in his hands he would have done the same. They said our cavalry came near capturing the train that Davis was on when he left Danville for Greensboro, North Carolina. They wounded the engineer in three places; Davis had his gold with him on this train.

The 6th Corps paper printed at Danville today gives the order from Secretary Stanton about reducing the army. There seems now to be very little doubt but what we shall be discharged this month. What do you think of that!!—Dare you hope? I do! I believe troops are now being paid off and discharged as fast as it can be done. It may be some time before our turn comes, but Ellie dearest, I am looking forward to the happy time with you with the greatest of pleasure!

From Herbert:

Camp of the 10th Regt Vt Vols
Danville Va
May 6th 1865

My dear Sister Em.

I have written once or twice since I heard from you but I think I will write a short letter this PM. It is very warm, altogether too warm for comfort but notwithstanding the heat &c I have been away to our Div Hosptl to play for a funeral. We are encamped in the woods where we get the benefit of a hard wood shade but the sweat will roll off from us still. We had a grand excursion down into North Carolina the other evening. Col. Damon got horses and mounted our <u>whole band</u> and took us down 4 or 5 miles into N.C. to play to some young ladies. We had a splendid time. No one went with us but Major Brown of Div Staff. Col. had to get a pass from Gen. Wright to get through the picket line. He done it to please us he said for we wanted to go into the state of N. C. and could not go without he got a special pass to take us out. The most of us were armed with revolvers. I had a big one about a foot long stuck on my belt. We were out pretty much all night. I enjoyed myself hugely—as did all the boys. The Col. wants to go again and go about 10 miles to another place. Talks of going to night. Hope he will. I have been into the prison where my bass player Wm Garvin was confined that was captured at Monocacy July 9th. I found his name written on the brick wall in one corner several times in his well known hand writing and I found <u>my</u> name written there with his in his hand writing. One place the following was written "Wm. W. Garvin 1st Tuba player 10th Vt Band J. H. George Leader captured July 9th 1864 at Frederick City Md. Long is the lane that has no end." Poor fellow he was starved to death there and died at Annappolis after he had been exchanged. Oh such a horrid place to confine men in! I broke off a piece of the window sash of the window that he had to lookout of and sent it by mail to his wife in St. Albans. Charlie and Jere have gone down to visit the prisons today. We expect to go to Washington in a few weeks now and perhaps a few days and perhaps be discharged by the first or middle of June. Guess we will be home by the 4th of July. There is no <u>way</u> now. How funny it seems — <u>This</u>

cruel war is over. The Stars & Stripes are triumphant and now float proudly over every state capitol. I have lost my boy so it's all right mother. He fell out on the march from Burkeville here & has probably gone home. Let him go. But he was <u>smart</u> anyhow. Oh dear its so hot I can't write any more....
Bro Herbert George

Two entries from Jere:

Danville
Friday, May 12th

Still in camp, all signs of moving towards home having failed. News now is not so exciting as it has been during the past month. I manage to keep busy with reading, writing and music. Am perfectly healthy and well contented. My lame hip has got well and I am resigned now to stay all summer if it must be. Monday night we were called on to go to the City and play for some of our Brigade Officers and the people of the house where they were visiting. It was a pleasant moonlight night and all went well, except that we were not invited into the splendid mansion before which we seranaded. There are four or five members of this band who love whiskey very much and never refuse when it is offered. It is the usual custom in the army when a Band is invited out by officers to treat with whiskey. On this occasion the one who came out to thank us said it could not be had that night, but told us to bring two canteens to his quarters next morning. Accordingly Sexton went over and got it. The consequence was four drunk and one fight before night. Sex made a [furious] assault on Charlie without provocation, striking him on the head while he was quietly frying meat at the fire. Charlie jumped over the fire clinched and they had three or four rounds of a general rough and tumble knockdown only the knocking blows and kick were mostly given by Sex who had his full strength after the full clinch. The excitement sobered him just enough to make him strong and desperate. Charlie heroically defended himself but was afraid of hurting his drunken adversary by which leniency he got the most bruises. Sex is very quick motion and made free use of his fists and boots doing his best to annihilate Charlies face and eyes, and taking out a handful of whiskers from his chin. Charlie being the strongest at length held him fast to the ground till he begged and gave his word to be peaceable when he was released. Both had bloody faces but no serious injury to either, except the name of being engaged in a drunken fight. Nearly everyone blamed Charlie for not choking the insolent drunken savage before letting him up, but he was neither excited nor angry and acted with deliberate judgement. It was well that he did not but very few would have been so merciful. I was writing and quietly kept my seat and interested witness of the whole. Next day when

Sex was sober he humbly apologized, they had a long talk and now Charlie George and D. B. Sexton are good friends. Every few days do we see some disgraceful effect of whiskey. Oh that everybody hated intemperance as I do. How can men with common sense make fools of themselves in such a low, vulgar, disgraceful way?

Tuesday Morning
May 16th

A move in prospect, though still in camp we have but a half hour longer to remain. Orders came yesterday and all are now ready to "sling knapsacks" and start towards <u>home</u>, though it may be long before we get there. I had a fine time yesterday, ad last evening at the house where we went to seranade in North Carolina. They wanted their piano tuned so Col. Damon took Herbert and I down there on horseback to do the job yesterday. It was my first attempt at piano tuning but was successful in getting it into pretty good order. They gave us dinner which was a novelty for us. We were in a real house, sat in a real chair up to a real table with a white cloth on it and earthen plates and dishes. Only think of it a soldier of the field eating on an earthen plate and such other nice or rather civilized accommodations, besides all this we sat at the same table with Lieut. col. Damon, the commander of our Regt. We had bacon and corn meal dumplings, hoecakes and a thin cake of the same material, this with molasses went well. I testified my relish for the dinner by working well while at the table. Things seemed so good and civilized that for a few minutes I almost forgot that I was a soldier. After the piano was tuned Herbert and I sang a lot of songs which I enjoyed so much as I played and sung that again I forgot that I was a soldier. After this we had the greatest treat of all. We were turned loose into a bed of ripe strawberries in the garden where we filled ourselves with the delicious fruit in a little while, again did I forget that I was a solder living so long on hardtack. Thus did I pick and eat a meal of strawberries in North Carolina upon the 15th day of May 1865, and thus did I enjoy "Southern Hospitality" so oft spoken of in times past. We were each presented with a boquet of flowers and after a very pleasant sociable time we returned at sunset and it was a beautiful sunset and I enjoyed the ride very much. I am getting to be quite a horseman. On our return to camp we heard the greatest news that has ever reached us by telegraph, the capture of Jeff Davis, the murderous bloody old traitor, the tyrant rebel chief caught at last and he must die. For four long years have we been after this chief of murderers now he is ours. We wait a few days to see him hung to a "Sour Apple Tree." In evening we had another good time. Some of our line officers took us over to seranade at a house just out of the city where they were visiting.

Finally the men moved to the Richmond area on May 17. Celebrations continued as the troops were called together and paraded through Richmond, though by now the men were growing anxious to return home. As the soldiers in gray were no longer the enemy, Jere turned his attention to the "gray backs" (lice) that seemed intent on making him miserable. Other troops visited the sights of Richmond, including Libby Prison.

From Charles:

Manchester, Virginia.
May 17, 1865

Homeward Bound!!! Darling Ellie. Yesterday morning we broke camp at 4:00 A.M. Our brigade took the lead of the Corps and consequently were the first to take the cars. Our regiment being in the rear of the brigade had to take the second train, which left at 3:00 P.M.—part of the 2nd brigade came on that train. The 2nd Division will follow as fast as the cars can take care of them. It took us 24 hours to come through. We had gone into camp in an oak grove about a mile from the city. Richmond is in plain sight and steamboats can be seen passing on the James River. We shall probably stay here till the Corps all get here. The first Division being on the Petersburg road will come the other way. We will all probably be in by Friday night—we do not know whether we shall go to Alexandria by transport, by rail or foot. Do not look for us inside of three weeks.

From Herbert:

Richmond Va
May 19th 1865
11 oclock AM

My dear sister Emma

I'm bound to write you a letter from Richmond. Here I am on the Capital Park about six rods from the rebel Capitol—Jere is with me and we have just been over the Capitol. It is an old building and not larger than Newbury Seminary, homely and old fashion. Not much like the Capitol of the U.S. at Washington.... Our regt is encamped at Manchester opposite this place. We have been "On to Richmond" a long time, but have just this day entered it— It seems funny that I am writing in Richmond. I hope soon to write in Newbury Vt and think if I live I will by the middle of July. I do not think that this city is as pleasantly located as a good many others that I have seen—The west side is all burned down and look deserted. There is considerable business going on but nothing compared with N.Y. or Boston. There is some statuary here that is very good—Washington on horseback and below him is Jefferson,

Mason, & Henry — set upon marble. The capitol is on high ground. I should think about 6 feet above the river. We intend to visit Libby prison before we return to camp it is on our way from here — Charlie will come over here tomorrow probably and write his letter to Mr Peach as he promised to do so some day — Jere is writing to Abbie now — We expect to start for Alexandria the first of next week on foot and we shall march through city — it is about 130 or 140 miles to Alexandria and weshall have a hard march but one thing will change — It will be the <u>last</u> <u>one</u>. when we go Washington it will be to go home & not on foot either The 9th Vt. is in the the 24th Corps and are encamped about a mile & a half from our regt and we went with our instruments & seranaded them last night. Had a splendid time. They treated us on ice cream & doughnuts and Lemonade — a <u>gay</u> time we had. Got home about 11 P.M. They thought the 10th Vt <u>Band</u> was one of the best in the army! The day before we left Danville Jere & I went down into N.C. a few miles to tune a piano. Had a fine time had. We tuned the piano in good shape and the young lady gave a boquett of flowers I have got it yet will bring it home with me. I am going to try and give a concert in Newbury when we go home if the boys will stick together I will — if not I <u>cant</u>. I have nothing in particular to write so I might as well close. I wanted to write from <u>Richmond</u> thats all so good day — Keep this letter —

As ever your brother
Herbert

Two entries from Jere:

Camp Stuck in the Mud
May 28th
Sunday P.M.

We did not march though it has been a fair day, probably on account of bad roads ahead for the waggons and a part of the train not coming up from the rear through the mud. It has been rather a dull day for me having no letters to write and nothing to read except my testament. Charlie's eyes are sore and I do all the cooking. We expect to continue our march to-morrow morning at five o-clock. I was somewhat annoyed last night by a squad of "grey backs" which took the liberty of using the surface of my body for a parade ground without asking my permission. Occasionally one seemed to be quietly walking his lonely beat, while others acted as though they had got their parole and were roaming at will all over the territory and especially my country seat (?) I have been "skirmishing" to-day and put a whole Brigade to flight with great slaughter. I murder all I can find every day but cannot annihilate them till I get where I can have hot water and a change of clothes. Since we were in winter quarters in February I have kept myself quite free from these horrible aggravating and blood thirsty lice. The unavoidable scourge of all armies and all soldiers. Until quite recently scarcely a man in the band kept free from them so long as I did.

5th Days March —16 miles
Tuesday Night
May 30th

Started from Fredericksburg at half past seven and got into camp here at half past three. A hot day and many fell out but I have not yet heard of any deaths to-day. I am tough as an ox, feet some sore but not very tired. Appetite good, drinking three qts. of coffee every day on the march and "lap my chops" for more. It so happens that the 10th and 11th Vt. Regt, camp to-night side by side. The 11th is in the Vt. Brigade; 2nd Division. The 10th and 11th bands are brought together for the first time. One of them just said he didn't know before that the 10th had a band. It was a singular coincidence that the two bands happened to pitch close together in these pine woods, neither being aware at first who the other party was. When we started this morning we passed though the City of Fredericksburg and across the Rappahannock River on pontoon bridge then over the heights. The city is almost in ruin, scarcely a house or church seems to have escaped Burnsides shot and sell. Many buildings were burnt and many destroyed. It was interesting to see the relics and effects of shot and shell in a City. Hundreds of cannon ball holes in the walls and roofs of buildings all over the city are now to be seen. Some nice houses which were shot though are now occupied as before. Burnside's troops also charged through the City doing much damage. Their bullets which must have rattled like hail left their marks in all directions. One tall marble monument in a burying-ground bore the marks of seven lead balls. The brick wall which enclosed the cemetery had several aperatures made by cannon balls. The 6th corps was engaged in this severe but unsuccessful fight and came near being captured saving themselves only by retreating back across the river. It was however only a part of the present 6th corps. The 10th Vt., and several other fighting regiments did not then belong to the 6th corps. It must be gratifying to those who were in it to return now and see the place where they fought. I am glad that I have had the priveledge of seeing this famous battle ground and half ruined city. Our mail that we looked for did not come neither did we have a chance to send letters.

The grand review of the Army of the Potomac down Pennsylvania Avenue was scheduled for May 23, followed the next day by Sherman's western troops. Unfortunately the 10th Vermont and their comrades could not make it to the

capital in time. Unable to secure space on either a train or transport for his corps,
General Wright ordered the troops to begin their return home on foot. The general
set a grueling pace though the weather slowed the men considerably. On May 29
the men were horrified as they passed the devastation at Fredericksburg. They
finally arrived at Bailey's Crossroads outside Washington on June 1, grateful that
the strenuous march was over. As one soldier described it: "And I can safely say
without any fear of contradiction that we literally ran all the way from Danville
to Arlington Heights, just across the Potomac from Washington."[19] *On June 7 the*
men were reviewed by the governor of Vermont and other state officials, then joined
the VI Corps for its review down Pennsylvania Avenue the following day.
    From Charles:

Washington D. C.
June 18, 1865

Prospect is real good!! There is reason to believe that we shall start for
Vermont sometime this week! But it is generally known and expected that we
shall stay at Burlington a week or so. I believe I should like to have you come
out, but cannot tell yet whether it would be best. I shall write again Thursday,
when I hope to tell you just where and when we shall be at Burlington. In
the meantime you can be deciding whether you want to come. I shall write
from New York, too.

The papers will all be done by Tuesday night, and it is thought that we
shall leave Thursday. I think you had better direct your next letter to Burlington, Vermont, Company G, 10th Vermont. I am now writing in Lincoln Hospital on Puffers table. Herbert, Jere and I got passes to come to the city. We
left camp at 9:00 o'clock this morning — crossed the aqueduct bridge to
Georgetown — took street cars from there to the head of 14th Street, Washington.
In the cars we fell in with several Newbury men — one was Burnham — his
father used to be in company with Tim Morse. We passed Carver Hospital,
where Osman died, and from there to the soldier's burying ground. We found
no difficulty in locating Osman's grave, although there were over 6000 buried
there. A man is hired for gardener and to set out trees. The ground is neatly
laid out and small trees are growing all over — set out in order.

Jere made arrangements for some flowers to be planted there by Osman's
grave. The gravestone is medium size and is a pretty one. Near the burying
ground is the Soldier's Home — a home for disabled soldiers from the regular
army. It is a very costly building and very pretty — there are about 100 in it
now, and some have been there for 15 years. The President's summer residence
joins it — such a pretty flower garden you never saw! I would write more, but
Jere is waiting for me to go to meeting — Good by, Your Charlie.

The men from Vermont began to say their farewells to comrades as the 14th New Jersey mustered out and headed for home June 20. The original enlistees of the 10th Vermont were mustered out of Federal service on June 22. One hundred and fifty men who had enlisted later were transferred to the 5th Vermont. There was a great deal of sadness mixed with joy as the men who had fought together for so many years were parting, probably never to see one another again. The departures were celebrated in style: "We had a grand illumination through out our Brigade last night as there was 2 regts a going home we gave them a good cheering (the 10 Vermont Vols & the 106th N. Y. Vols) and they marched around with a candle in each of their bayonets. It did look splendid."[20] And with the end of the fighting came the end of the music that had inspired the soldiers for so many years. Edwin C. Hall of Company G admitted what the end of the war sounded like to him: "But I hope there are better times coming when I will be free to go and come without the sound of the bugle."[21]

The men of the 10th Vermont started home on June 23, passing through New York City where they visited the home of their former commander, Major General Ricketts. The next morning they departed for Vermont, arriving in Burlington early on the morning of June 27.

From Herbert:

Burlington
June 27
4 o'clock A.M.

Dear mother

The 10th arrived here safely this morning at 2 oclock — Had a grand reception for the boys. It was rainy & <u>dark</u> but the ladies cheer out & as we came into the town hall where we now are they sang <u>Union</u> <u>songs</u> to us & showered hundreds of boquetts on our heads as we passed in to <u>eat</u> — Oh I tell you I felt — all over. Almost cried. I was so happy — Our Band played home again "sweet home" "Happy are we to night boys" "When Johnny comes marching home." "Tramp tramp or the prisoners hope" and some others. Our music was highly appreciated I can tell you. We had to play so much all the way from Washington here that my legs are <u>awful</u> sore, but I dont care I'm <u>home</u> almost. We started from Camp last Friday morning, have been ever since on the road — Feel pretty <u>tired</u>. C. & J. are all right. There is to be a grand celebration at Rutland the 4th and the commitee of the affair have requested the 10th Vt Band to come & play for them — We played things there on our way up & they thought that we have the best Band in the State & want us very much. Now it is doubtful if we get paid off & discharged by the 4th & if we do <u>not</u> I think we shall accept the invitation and I want one,

two, or <u>all</u> of you to come there too. I will pay the fare of one or <u>all</u> if you can be there. They are going to have a <u>big</u> time. I want an answer <u>immy</u>. Try & come some if you so to hear my <u>band play</u>. I am very tired but shall not go to sleep this mng it is just light enough now to see good — I have got a large nice boquett that a lady gave me this morning — dont you wish you could smell of it? Saw Col Henry this mng too. Col Damon did not come home with the regt he was transferred to the 5th Vt. Brevett Maj Salsbury took us here — I intend to telegraph for my pants this morning but if I dont please send them to me by express here immy. If I telegraph I cant pay for the dispatch as I am out of of money. I want the pants any way <u>immy</u>. I will close love to all in haste
From Herbert

From Charles:

<u>Burlington, Vermont.</u>
<u>June 27th</u>

Ellie darling! — we arrived here this morning at 2 o'clock. All well and very happy! I would not have begrudged $25.00 if you had been here at the reception. I am sorry I did not write for you to come — we were greeted all the way with great enthusiasm, but Burlington beat them all! How our hearts swelled with joy as we entered the reception room all decorated with flowers and tables richly laden with everything good to eat. A choir of a hundred ladies singing, "Rally 'Round the Flag Boys." The ladies were in the gallery and threw bouquets to us till every man had one. I cannot half describe the scene nor one tenth of the feeling. We have played all the way home till our lips are sore. Everyone appreciated our band playing very much — and well they may!

I want you to come on here — there is going to be a great celebration at Rutland, Vermont and the Band is invited to play. I should like very much to have you and Nellie to be there. <u>I think it will pay</u>. I'm afraid there is a prospect, too, of our not being paid under a week. Hope that is not so.

Come Thursday — if you come I will meet you at the depot — come by the way of White River Junction. I will write again tomorrow. Take the cars at Bradford and inquire at the telegraph office — I may send a telegram for you.

We will be seeing each other very soon, my own darling. My love, Charlie.

The homecoming at Burlington was all that the returning troops could have hoped for. Despite the early hour the men were greeted by numerous citizens as well as their former colonel, William Henry, who had been relieved due to his

injuries. Ever proud of his band, Herbert led his ensemble in numerous perform-
ances for the enthralled civilians and was promptly invited to give a concert in
Rutland. Edwin M. Haynes, regimental chaplain, noted that it was in Burlington
that the regimental band of the 10th Vermont performed its last piece, "Home
Again."[22] *On July 3 the remaining members of the 10th Vermont were finally dis-*
charged from the regiment—thirteen officers and 451 soldiers, from 1,016 when
the regiment was mustered in August of 1863.[23] *Charles, Herbert, and Jere George*
were finally going home.

Yet as joyous as their return was, the absence of brother Osman remained a
painful reminder of the life-changing ordeal they had just survived. On their way
home the three brothers had stopped to pay their last respects at Osman's grave.
As Jere described in his entry of 18 June 1865:

Our passes to visit the city [Washington, D. C.] came this morning so
Charlie, Herbert and I started about nine o-clock. Without delay we came
direct to this place which visit is the main object of our pass. Here is the grave
of our much loved Brother Osman, who was a patriotic and good soldier but
his constitution was not equal to his tasks. He suffered much and long, but
death at length relieved him and he now fills a soldier's grave and I trust his
soul is with Jesus among the redeemed in Heaven where all is happy. Although
he is so happy there we would feign have kept him here have had him endure
the world's trials that he might be with us. It is well God knows best. We
three remaining Brothers who visit near him since his death and for a few
weeks before his death. He died among strangers and by them was buried in
this beautiful spot. Mr. Bryant has caused a marble stone to be erected at the
head of the grave on which we find the following inscription:

> OSMAN C. B. GEORGE
> 10TH VT VOLS
> DIED DEC. 2 1863
> AGED 23 YEARS
> A CHRISTIAN PATRIOT

Also a foot stone with his initials O. C. B. G. A cedar bush or tree is growing
about three feet from the foot stone and as it grows taller will shade the grave
in the forenoon. The wood headboard at the grave next to him on his left
hand bears the following inscription.

> NO. 6961 D. W. BERRY, JR.
> 6 N. C. CO. C. DIED NOV. 11, 1863
> — REBEL —

Thus does our Brother lay side by side with a rebel soldier. The same thoughts
are suggested which I wrote at Danville. In death they rest in peace. The
thought of going home soon is pleasant to us but to know that we must leave

Osman here, dead in this grave, that he cannot go home with us, that he will <u>never</u> go home, never be with us again — it is sad. There will be a vacant chair and we shall miss him. Sadly do we go from this spot. We leave him in his long home, in his quiet sleep of death. His home is in Heaven and may we all meet him there. Were it expedient we would like to leave a writing on the grave or head stone something like the following.

> The war is over, the rebellion is crushed, peace is restored and we are now going home, but our Brother returns not with us, he rests here with his six thousand comrades. "We shall meet but we shall miss him. There will be one vacant chair." Signed by three remaining brothers, Charles H. George, Jere N. George, J. Herbert George.

Charlie thinks it would be too conspicuous so we will not do it. The best we can do for Mother is to carry home some little pebble from the grave and some white clover leaves and cedar branches. It is useless to plant flower shrubs now as they would soon die without attention.

The bonds of brotherhood that had strengthened during the war remained firm throughout the rest of the George brothers' lives. Music continued to be a special means of expression and connection for Charles, Jere, and Herbert; at a gathering after the war (perhaps in celebration of Herbert's anniversary) the family celebrated with a musical concert that drew on the impressive talents of the entire family:

<u>Part First</u>
1. New Jerusalem (Full Chorus)
2. Glee, "Alpine Echo" (Double Quartette)
3. Harmonica Solo (J. H. George)
4. Song, "Waiting" (Miss Nellie E. George)
5. Duett, "The Swallows' Farewell" (Mr. & Mrs. J. N. George)
6. Trio, "Memory" (Mrs. J. N. Miss Nellie E. & Mr. J. H. George)
7. Song Sacred (Mrs. Emma George Farnsworth)
8. A Lullaby "Sweet and Low" (Double Quartette)
<u>Part Second</u>
9. Poem, Original (Rev. Geo. N. Bryant)
10. Song, "Tell me Mary" (J. H. George)
11. Male Quartette, "Lovely Night" (C. H., J. N. and J. H. George, C. H. Clifford)
12. Song, "Swiss Song" (Mrs. J. N. George)
13. Duett, "Flow gently Deva" (J. N. and J. H. George)
14. Cornet Solo, "Silver Stream" (J. H. George)
15. Good Night (Bon Soir) (Full Chorus)[24]

Charles George returned to Vermont to be with his beloved Ellie and Nellie, and "true to his love for the beauties of nature and the 'soil,' became a farmer" in the family's home town of Newbury, Vermont.[25] *Yet the west continued to call to Charles, so he opted to move to North Dakota 1882 on the government's homestead offer to veterans. By the following year his family had joined him. Charles was remarkably successful at this time, eventually turning a grant of 480 acres into a steading of 3000, the whole estate becoming known as Georgetown. As his health began to fail Charles sold his land and moved, first to St. Thomas, North Dakota, then to a small fruit farm near River Falls, Wisconsin. He worked there until a stroke in 1906 forced him to retire permanently. Charles then rented his farm and moved into the town of River Falls, where he died in 1914.*[26]

Jeremiah George returned to Boston following the war and married Olivia E. Glazier in 1869. Their one surviving son, Frank, was born in 1870. Jere worked a variety of jobs, including tailor, shoe-cutter and store clerk. Apparently Jere never matched his brothers' professional success; the security both Charles and Herbert obtained remained elusive. He and Herbert visited Charles in North Dakota frequently, and Jere may have considered resettling there permanently. Unfortunately he died in 1887, at the age of 50. His loss was a serious blow to the family; the year after his death, one of the brothers (probably Charles) wrote a poem to his memory:

The 1890 reunion of the 10th Vermont Regiment in Boston (courtesy Vermont Historical Society).

In Memory of Brother Jere

Christmas morn! The "Gate's ajar."
And rings "A merry welcome" there.
It is the voice of legions clear,
Another angel joins us here.

Another left the mortal man;
"From dust to dust return again."
Rejoicing they and making "merry,"
Greeting they, the soul of Jere.

Why should we, in flesh so sore,
Mourn because he goes before?
Why should we expel a tear,
Because they welcome brother dear?

We are mortal, that is why
Poor earth bound beings have to cry
Memory brings the past to view
Shows the noble, good and true.

See! A boy in childish glee,
From care and tribulation free.
A youth who doeth nothing wrong,
But joins his voice in manly song.

A brother free from selfish acts,
A son in whom no reverence lacks,
A school-boy tramping through the snow
Playmate Jere! All love him so.

See! A man of tender years,
Battling midst the stormy ways,
Rising up the ladder Fame,
Falling back, to rise again.

Never designed to be dismayed,
Because his fortune wasn't made.
Rising early, working late.
Succeeding not, nor called it fate.

See him in his "coat of blue,"
A soldier boy, a soldier true.
Side by side brothers three
Played and sang in boyish glee.

Threw their hats so high in air,
At Appomattox, three brothers there.
See him when the war is oe'r
Proudly coming home once more.

Higher now the bugles soar,
Singing now the songs of gore,
See him hunting oe'r the land,
All in vain for future hand.

See him wed the girl of choice;
Blending well their songs of voice,
See him with his children three
Mingling in their childish glee.

See him when the disease hard stricken
Sending Bertha home to heaven.
Battling with the poison still,
Conquering with an iron will.

Ever loving, always working,
Through the busy world kept plodding,
Growing old with cares and sorrows,
Gentle still, no trouble borrows.

Gone! Yes gone to rest we say,
Gone! Till we shall pass away,
Gone! Till Resurrection day,
Gone! To greet us if we may.

J. Herbert George returned home after being discharged from the Army of *the Potomac. After staying in Newbury, Vermont, for a brief while, he moved to* *Boston and apprenticed in a piano factory. He met Mary Abbie Mason (1852–* *1930), and in September 1870 the couple was married and settled in Norwich,* *Connecticut. The Georges were to have four children, but tragically three of these* *infants would not live past the age of three. Only Herbert Mason George (b. 1876)* *survived to adulthood. Inspired by his experience with the band during the war,* *Herbert continued to pursue music as a career. He directed a church choir and* *organized concerts as well. He taught vocal music in the public school system and* *at the Norwich Y.M.C.A.; on his pension application he referred to himself as a* *"supervisor of music," and the caption under his photograph in the regimental* *history reads "Prof. J. Herbert George."* [27] *He also drew upon his experience in* *the piano factory to tune pianos. Proud of his involvement in the war, Herbert* *was commander of the Grand Army of the Potomac post in Norwich. He was also*

Company G, 10th Vermont, at the reunion of 1890. Herbert George is seated in the bottom row, fifth from the left (courtesy Vermont Historical Society).

commander of the Columbian Commandery of the Knights Templar in Norwich and active in the Sons of the American Revolution and the local Masonic Lodge. February 11, 1916, at the age of 72, he suffered a stroke and was forced to retire. Herbert and his wife moved to Minneapolis, Minnesota, to be closer to their son as well as Herbert's sister Ruth Clifford. It was here that he died on January 15, 1925.[28] His final years may have been difficult, as there are indications that his health declined severely. The stroke he suffered left him blinded in one eye, and vision in the other eye deteriorated with each year. He was partially paralyzed on the right side; his death certificate cited senility as the cause of death.[29]

The George brothers' experiences during the Civil War were similar in many ways to their fellow soldiers. They found it exhilarating and depressing, full of horror as well as glory. As musicians, however, they participated in a way distinct from most of their comrades, and their experiences were unique both in their responsibilities and their perceptions of the conflict surrounding them. Charles entered the war as a loving husband and as an older brother dedicated to protecting his siblings. The war tested but did not break his devotion; he remained amazingly positive throughout his enlistment and provided a solid foundation for those around him. It is not surprising that Charles was so successful following the surrender at Appomattox, for the war served to strengthen those traits that defined his character. Jere's proclivity towards contemplation deepened throughout the war. Of all the brothers he seemed to dwell on larger issues, yet any tendency he had towards poeticizing reality was grounded by the horrors he had witnessed. Like his older brother, Jere's outlook on life had been tempered by the end of the war. For Herbert the war was a time of maturation. Called upon to perform a dizzying array of musical tasks, Herbert thrived in the environment. Instead of collapsing under the pressures of his duties and the strife around him, Herbert grew as a person, contributing his best to the war effort and honing skills that would stay with him for the rest of his life.

Chapter Notes

Introduction

1. George T. Stevens, *Three Years in the Sixth Corps* (Albany: Gray, 1866), 390.

2. Walter Clark, *Histories of the Several Regiments and Battalions from North Carolina, in the Great War 1861–'65* (Raleigh: Uzzell, 1901), vol. 2, 399. Ironically Lee and Grant were opposed on this issue as well as on the field; Grant was apparently not fond of marching bands, and claimed: "I know only two tunes: one is 'Yankee Doodle,' and the other isn't." Horace Porter, *Campaigning with Grant* (Secaucus, NJ: Blue and Grey Press, 1984), 83.

3. "Songs written just before and during the Civil War mirrored events and emotions of the time with such precision and passion that if all other records of the war had been lost, it would be possible to reconstruct from these songs an accurate and vivid picture of that period — the military and political events, the heroes and villains, the civilian folk heroes, the patriotic fervor and pride of both sides, the tragedies and heartbreaks of civilians and soldiers alike." Charles Hamm, *Yesterdays: Popular Song in America* (New York: Norton, 1979), 253–254.

4. Robert H. Rhodes, ed., *All for the Union: The Civil War Diaries and Letters of Elisha Hunt Rhodes* (New York: Orion Books, 1991), 213.

5. Richard Crawford, *America's Musical Life: A History* (New York: Norton, 2001), 272–281; Margaret H. and Robert M. Hazen, *The Music Men: An Illustrated History of Brass Bands in America, 1800–1920* (Washington, D.C.: Smithsonian Institution Press, 1987), Chapter 4; Brian Smith, *Bandstands to Battlefields: Brass Band in 19th Century America* (Gansevoort, NY: Corner House, 2004); Richard K. Hansen, *The American Wind Band: A Cultural History* (Chicago: GIA, 2005), 11–54; Robert Garofalo and Mark Elrod, *A Pictorial History of Civil War Era Musical Instruments and Military Bands* (Charleston, WV: Pictorial Histories, 1985).

6. Charles E. Benton, *As Seen from the Ranks: A Boy in the Civil War* (New York: G.P. Putnam's Sons, 1902), 161–162.

7. S. Millet Thompson, *Thirteenth Regiment of New Hampshire Volunteer Infantry in the War of the Rebellion, 1861–1865: A Diary Covering Three Years and a Day* (Boston: Houghton, Mifflin, 1888), 104.

8. Quoted in Steven Cornelius, *Music of the Civil War Era* (Westport, CT: Greenwood Press, 2004), 192.

9. George R. Prowell, *History of the Eighty-Seventh Regiment, Pennsylvania Volunteers* (York, PA: Press of the York Daily, 1903), 72; Joseph W. Muffly, *The Story of Our Regiment: A History of the 148th Pennsylvania Vols* (Des Moines: Kenyon Print. & Mfg. Co., 1904), 354.

10. Published accounts by Civil War field musicians include William Bardeen, *A Little Fifer's War Diary* (Syracuse: Bardeen, 1920); Henry M. Kieffer, *The Recollections of a Drummer-Boy* (Boston: Ticknor, 1889); Augustus Meyers, *Ten Years in the Ranks, U.S. Army* (New York: Stirling Press, 1914); Delavan S. Miller, *Drum Taps in Dixie: Memories of a Drummer Boy, 1861–1865* (Watertown, NY: Hungerford-Holbrook, 1905); George T. Ulmer, *Adventures and Reminiscences of Volunteer, or a Drummer Boy from Maine* (n.p., 1892).

11. Kenneth E. Olson, *Music and Musket: Bands and Bandsmen of the American Civil War* (Westport, CT: Greenwood Press, 1981), 86–93. For example, cavalry regiments had calls for maintaining their mounts. The other soldiers certainly felt that the blowing of camp hours kept them occupied; one soldier claimed that "26 bugle calls to attend every day keeps us so [busy] we dont have much time

to ourselves." Quoted in Bell Irvin Wiley, *The Life of Billy Yank: The Common Soldier of the Union* (Indianapolis: Bobbs-Merrill, 1952), 45. See also Dwight A. Gardstrom, *A History of the Fourth Regimental Band and Musicians of the Fourth Minnesota Infantry Volunteers During the War of the Great Rebellion: 1861–1865* (Ph. D. dissertation, University of Minnesota, 1989), 35, 109–110.

12. Entry of 28 June 1862, Diary of Tommy Gordon, Special Collections and Archives, Utah State University, Logan, UT.

13. William Bircher, *A Drummer-Boy's Diary: Comprising Four Years of Service with the Second Regiment Minnesota Veteran Volunteers 1861–1865*, ed. N. L. Chester (St. Cloud, MN: North Star Press, 1995), 32. Such significant reductions in numbers were not the result of combat casualties alone; short enlistments, disease, and other factors combined to produce such attrition. Yet the dangers of combat were a reality for many field musicians. For examples of the daily lives of field musicians, see the Civil War diary of Sylvester Daniels, in Papers of Theophilus M. Magaw (HM 48002), The Huntington Library, San Marino, CA; Diary of Charles C. Perkins (CWTIColl), United States Army Military History Institute, Carlisle Barracks, PA [hereafter referred to as USAMHI].

14. U.S. Government War Department, *The War of the Rebellion: A Compilation of the Official Records of the Union and Confederate Armies* (Washington, D.C.: U.S. Government Printing Office, 1880–1901), ser. 3, vol. 1, pp. 152–153 [hereafter referred to as OR].

15. Olson, *Music and Musket*, 72; see the entire chapter ("The Organization of Bands") for a detailed discussion of band enlistments. There were even bands stationed as far west as Ft. Churchill, Nevada Territory, in 1861; *OR*, Ser. 1, Vol. 50, Pt. 1, 538.

16. *OR*, Ser. 3, Pt. 1, 803.

17. 5 December 1861, *OR*, Series 3, 1, 728. The cost of army bands had begun to strain the military's budget early in the war: for example, on 31 July 1861 the House and Senate authorized the Secretary of War to refund "such sums of money as may have been expended by the said volunteers in the employment of regimental or company bands during the period of their service under said proclamation..."; *OR*, Ser. 3, Pt. 1, 372.

18. General Order 91, 26 October 1861, *OR*, Ser. 3, Pt. 1, 597.

19. *OR*, Ser. 3, Pt. 2, 278.

20. Ibid., 336.

21. Alonzo H. Quint, *The Potomac and the Rapidan* (Boston: Crosby and Nichols, 1864), 96.

22. Olsen, *Music and Musket*, 78.

23. See *OR*, Ser. 1, Vol. 51, Pt. 1, 411.

24. A. F. Sperry, Gregory J. W. Urwin, and Cathy Kunzinger Urwin, *History of the 33d Iowa Infantry Volunteer Regiment, 1863–6* (Fayetteville: University of Arkansas Press, 1999), 122; James R. Middlebrook, letters of 23 June and 1 November 1864, in Middlebrook Family Papers, MS 73139, Connecticut Historical Society, Harford, CT; see also *OR*, Ser. 1, Vol. 39, Pt. 1, 793.

25. Charles E. Gotwalt, *Adventures of a Private in the American Civil War* (privately printed, n.d.) USAMHI, 4.

26. Soldiers offering their own money to secure a band is one of the most significant indications of the desire for music. This was true of all types of regiments, even those that might not have wealthy members; for example, see Keith P. Wilson, *Campfires of Freedom: The Camp Life of Black Soldiers During the Civil War* (Kent, OH: Kent State University Press, 2002) 171.

27. See Marshall Moore Brice, *The Stonewall Brigade Band* (Verona, VA: McClure, 1967); Harry H. Hall, *A Johnny Reb Band from Salem: The Pride of Tarheelia* (Raleigh: North Carolina Confederate Centennial Commission, 1963); Frank Rauscher, *Music on the March, 1862–65, with the Army of the Potomac: 114th Regt. P. V., Collis' Zouaves* (Philadelphia: Fell, 1892); Letter to father, 23 January 1864, in Warren Hapgood Freeman and Eugene Harrison Freeman, *Letters from Two Brothers Serving in the War for the Union to Their Family at Home in West Cambridge, Mass* (Cambridge: Houghton, 1871), 99.

28. Entries of 25 May and 5, 12, 16 June 1862, Henry Klag Diary, Virginia Historical Society, Richmond, VA.

29. Letter to wife, 15 October 1864, in James I. Robertson, Jr., ed., *The Civil War Letters of General Robert McAllister* (New Brunswick, NJ: Rutgers University Press, 1965), 520–521.

30. Entry of 14 August 1862, Ludolph Longhenry, *A Yankee Piper in Dixie: Civil War Diary of Ludolph Longhenry* (unpublished typescript), Karrmann Library, University of Wisconsin–Platteville. A colonel stationed at Fort Washington summoned the brass band of the "4th regt of Artillery" to come to his headquarters to play for his men's entertainment; letter to "Friend George," undated, George and Alvah Lawrence Papers, Fenton Historical Society, Jamestown, NY.

31. Entry of 17 September 1862, Ludolph Longhenry, *A Yankee Piper in Dixie: Civil War Diary of Ludolph Longhenry* (unpublished typescript), Karrmann Library, University of Wisconsin–Platteville.

32. This was true for the musicians of the 10th Vermont; see Almon Clarke, "In the Immediate

Rear: Experiences and Observations of a Field Surgeon," in Military Order of the Loyal Legion of the United States, *War Papers Read Before the Commandery of the State of Wisconsin. Military Order of the Loyal Legion of the United States*, vol. 2 (Milwaukee: Burdick, Armitage & Allen, 1896), 87–101. At one point Clarke claimed to have had a "hundred or more" musicians at his call (p. 95). In some cases bands remained in camp while their units moved out; see Brigadier General Curtis' orders of 28 December 1861 in *OR*, Ser. 1, 8, p. 473. See also Charles E. Benton, *As Seen from the Ranks; A Boy in the Civil War* (New York: G.P. Putnam's Sons, 1902), 161–162.

33. Allan Nevins, ed., *A Diary of Battle: The Personal Journals of Colonel Charles S. Wainwright, 1861–1865* (New York: Harcourt, Brace & World, 1962), 437.

34. James A. Davis, "Musical Reconnaissance and Deception in the American Civil War," *Journal of Military History*, 74/1 (January 2010): 79–105; and "Music and Gallantry in Combat During the American Civil War," *American Music*, 28.2 (Summer 2010): 141–172.

35. George Contant, *Path of Blood: The True Story of the 33rd New York Volunteers* (New York: Seeco, 1997), 142–144.

36. *Pittsfield Sun*, 3 March 1864: 2; Alfred S. Roe, *The Tenth Regiment, Massachusetts Volunteer Infantry, 1861–1864, A Western Massachusetts Regiment* (Springfield, MA: Tenth Regiment Veteran Association, 1909), 246–247.

37. Keith H. George, *George Genealogy* (Kingman, AZ: H and H, 1991); Frederic P. Wells, *History of Newbury, Vermont, from the Discovery of the Coös Country to Present Time* (St. Johnsbury, VT: Caledonian, 1902). Additional biographical information can be found in Edwin M. Haynes, *A History of the Tenth Regiment, Vt. Vols.*, 2d ed. (Rutland, VT: Tuttle), 438ff.

38. Augustus B. Easton, ed., *History of the Saint Croix Valley* (Chicago: H. C. Cooper, 1909), 604.

39. Pension file for Osman C. B. George, National Archives.

40. Pension file for Osman C. B. George, National Archives. One neighbor referred to James George as a "Drunkard and Spend Thrift."

41. Letter to Charles, 31 March 1862, in James Herbert George Collection.

42. Pension file for Osman C. B. George, National Archives.

43. Wells, *History of Newbury*, 555.

44. Howard Coffin, *Full Duty: Vermonters in the Civil War* (Woodstock, VT: Countryman Press, 1993), 15–16. See also McPherson, *Battle Cry of Freedom*, 604ff.

45. This was not true of all musicians, some of whom resented being placed under the command of surgeons and orderlies. Such was the case for members of the 11th New Hampshire band; see Charles L. Rundlett Papers, Accession 32581, Library of Virginia, Richmond, VA.

46. Entry of 2 April 1865, Jere George Diary. See James A. Davis, "'All Sounds of Life and Rage': Musical Imagery in the Writings of Civil War Soldiers," *Nineteenth Century Studies*, 21 (2007): 183–197.

Chapter 1

1. Albert Jewett was born in St. Albans in 1829, trained as a civil engineer, and after spending time in the west returned to Vermont to open a business in Swanton. With the outbreak of the Civil War he joined the 1st Vermont Infantry. At the end of his term of service he was reappointed to the 10th Vermont where he was to spend the rest of his military service. Following the war Jewett returned to Vermont, continuing with his previous business and involving himself in the development of regional railroads. Edwin M. Haynes, *A History of the Tenth Regiment, Vt. Vols.*, 2nd ed. (Rutland, VT: Tuttle), 71–76.

2. *OR*, Ser. 3, vol. 2, p. 178. *Report of the Adjutant & Inspector General of the State of Vermont, for the Year Ending November 1, 1862* (Montpelier: Walton's Steam Press Establishment, 1862), 73. Hereafter cited as VA & IGO.

3. Haynes, *Tenth Vermont*, 438.

4. The quality of weapons was poor enough to lead to some spirited discussions between the governor of Vermont and the secretary of war; see *OR*, Ser. 3, vol. 2, 386–387, 522; see also Colonel Jewett, letter to General Washburn, 11 September 1862, and letter to Governor Holbrook, 17 October 1862, in Records of the Adjutant and Inspector General, Microfilm F26066, Vermont State Archives and Records Administration, hereafter cited as VSARA, Middlesex, VT. See also George G. Benedict, *Vermont in the Civil War: A History of the Part Taken by the Vermont Soldiers and Sailors in the War for the Union, 1861–5*, 2 vols. (Burlington, VT: The Free Press Association, 1886–8), 12–15.

5. John A. Hicks, 10th Vermont Infantry, Letter of 3 September 1862, CWMiscColl, United States Army Military History Institute, hereafter cited as USAMHI.

6. Oscar Waite, "Three Years with the Tenth Vermont," unpublished manuscript, Vermont Historical Society, Montpelier, VT, hereafter cited as VHS, 19.

7. Willard M. Thayer, letter to his wife, 17 August 1862, in Esther M. Thayer Correspondence, VHS.

8. The basic service history of the 10th Vermont Infantry can be found in Benedict, *Vermont in the Civil War*, 276–341; Haynes, *Tenth Regiment*; VA & IGO.

9. Tabor Parcher, letter to wife Sarah, 11 September 1862, in Tabor H. Parcher, Manuscript Files, Bailey/Howe Library, University of Vermont, Montpelier, VT, hereafter cited as UVM.

10. Colonel Jewett, letter to General Washburn, 11 September 1862, in Records of the Adjutant and Inspector General, Microfilm F26066, VSARA, Middlesex, VT. The bustling atmosphere of the interim camps is described well in Robert Goldthwaite Carter, ed., *Four Brothers in Blue: A Story of the Great Civil War from Bull Run to Appomattox* (1913. Reprint, Norman: University of Oklahoma Press, 1999), 83ff.

11. For example, see Milo M. Quaife, ed., *From the Cannon's Mouth: The Civil War Letters of General Alpheus S. Williams* (Detroit: Wayne State University Press, 1959), 17ff.

12. It is interesting to note that Herbert also had little regard for the regimental chaplain, Edwin M. Haynes. Unfortunately for Herbert and Charles, Haynes was to become the regimental biographer, a fact that might explain why there is no reference to the brothers or the band in the first edition of the regimental history.

13. Willard M. Thayer, letter to his wife and children, 20 September 1862, in Esther M. Thayer Correspondence, VHS.

14. Waite, "Three Years with the Tenth Vermont," VHS, 31.

15. Waite, "Three Years with the Tenth Vermont," VHS, 32.

16. Sergeant Albert C. Harrison, Co. G, 14th New Jersey Infantry, quoted in Bernard A. Olsen, ed. *Upon the Tented Field* (Red Bank, NJ: Historic Projects, 1993), 154–155.

17. Dan Barker, letter to friend John, 25 October 1862, VHS.

18. W. W. Blackford, *War Years with Jeb Stuart* (Baton Rouge: Louisiana State University Press, 1993), 164–181.

19. *OR*, Ser. 1, Vol. 19, Pt. 2, 42–44, 52–54; Olsen, *Upon the Tented Field*, 53–4.

20. Benedict, *Vermont in the Civil War*, 281.

21. John Y. Foster, *New Jersey and the Rebellion: History of the Services of the Troops and People of New Jersey in Aid of the Union Cause* (Newark, NJ: Dennis, 1868), 357; J. Newton Terrill, *Campaign of the Fourteenth Regiment New Jersey Volunteers*, reprint of 2nd ed., 1864, in David G. Martin, ed. *The Monocacy Regiment: A Commemorative History of the Fourteenth New Jersey Infantry in the Civil War, 1862–1865* (Highstown, NJ: Longstreet House, 1987), 11.

22. VA & IGO, Annex B, 73–104.

23. Timothy B. Messer, *Civil War Letters of Timothy B. Messer, Tenth Vermont Volunteers*, E. Phelps, ed. (Greenfield, MA: Hall, 1986), 12. Some soldiers managed to find entertainment of a more intimate kind; see the rather graphic description provided by Private Tabor Parcher, Co. B, 10th Vt., in Marshall, *A War of the People*, 225–226.

24. Tabor Parcher, letter to wife Sarah, 19 November 1862, in Tabor H. Parcher, Manuscript Files, Bailey-Howe Library, UVM.

25. Philip Arsino, letter to mother, 24 November 1862, in Correspondence of Philip Arsino, VHS.

26. Terrill, *Campaign of the Fourteenth*, 12. Later, when the 14th New Jersey was presented with a regimental flag, they were required to hire a band for the ceremony.

27. Lieutenant William Burroughs Ross, Company B, 14th New Jersey; quoted in Olsen, *Upon the Tented Field*, 63, 74.

28. Benedict, *Vermont in the Civil War*, vol. 2, 283. This was probably Captain Elijah White's cavalry, a group of men from Montgomery County who were sympathetic to the Southern cause and led numerous raids into the area; Roger S. Cohen, Jr., "The Civil War in the Poolesville Area," *The Montgomery County Story* 5, no. 1 (November 1961): 9.

Chapter 2

1. Cohen, "The Civil War in the Poolesville Area," 1.

2. The regiment's Morning Report for 14 September 1862 has the drum major listed as deserted. Morning Reports, 10th Vermont Infantry, Microfilm F26066–26067, VSARA, Middlesex, VT.

3. Henry Burnham, letter to sister Lora, 26 April 1863, in Henry P. Burnham Papers, VHS.

4. August H. Crown, letter to friend George, 24 March 1863, in Records of the Vermont Civil War Centennial Commission, VSARA, Middlesex, VT, F2849.

5. Sheila M. Cumberworth and Daniel V. Byles, *An Enduring Love: The Civil War Diaries of Benjamin Franklin Pierce (14th New Hampshire Vol. Inf.)* (Gettysburg, PA: Thomas, 1995), 93–99.

6. William White, letter to Jacob Wead, 14 January 1863, in William White Correspondence, VHS.

7. "It snows like fury today and the wind blows like the oald harry and it seems like an ould Vt. storm. I guess we shall live through it." Messer, *Letters*, 12.

8. See Letter to "Friend George," 24 March 1863, Letter of Augustus H. Crown, Company D, 10th Vermont Infantry, VSARA, Middlesex, VT; Paul and Rita Gordon, *A Playground of the Civil War: Frederick County, Maryland* (Frederick, MD: Heritage Partnership, 1994), 135.

9. Caroline C. Lutz, *Letters of George E. Chamberlin, Who Fell in the Service of His Country Near Charlestown, VA* (Springfield, IL: Rokker, 1883), 254–263.

10. Cumberworth and Byles, *An Enduring Love*, 99–102.

11. Dr. Joseph Rutherford, letter to his wife, 10 April 1863, in Dr. Joseph Rutherford Papers, Bailey-Howe Library, UVM. Rutherford also mentions "sings" on April 15 and 28.

12. Henry Burnham, letter to sister Lora, 19 April 1863, in Henry P. Burnham Papers, VHS.

13. Dr. Joseph Rutherford, letter to his wife, 14 April 1863, in Dr. Joseph Rutherford Papers, Bailey-Howe Library, UVM. Troops stationed in secure locations with little or no chance of combat were much more able and inclined to enjoy music and dancing; for example, see Elmer Howell, Diary (1863), Manuscripts and Special Collections, New York State Library, Albany, NY.

14. Sween and Offut, *Montgomery County*, 76.

15. It is curious to note that Herbert and Charles received the same amount from the state — $237.06 — at the end of the war, so Herbert's promotion apparently did not increase his salary with the state. *Pay Roll of Vermont Volunteers for Extra State Pay*, Microfilm F26190, VSARA, Middlesex, VT.

16. Charles Gotwalt of the 87th Pennsylvania named the sum of $1,200 raised to purchase instruments for their new band. Gotwalt, *Adventures of a Private*, USAMHI, 4. If we were to assume that Herbert's band began with ten brass players, and the average cost of a new instrument ranged from $23 to $50, the total for the ensemble would have been at least over $300. This total is based on c. 1864 prices. See Robert Garofalo and Mark Elrod, *A Pictorial History of Civil War Era Musical Instruments and Military Bands* (Charleston, SC: Pictorial Histories, 1985), 25. For an interesting exchange concerning the formation of a regimental band, see Thomas Smith's letters to his wife, September–December 1863, Tompkins Family Papers (1800–1877), Section 24, Virginia Historical Society, Richmond, VA.

17. Henry Burnham, letter to sister Lora, 21 June 1863, in Henry P. Burnham Papers, VHS.

18. Henry Burnham, letter to sister Lora, 6 September 1863, in Henry P. Burnham Papers, VHS. In April of 1865 Herbert numbers his band at fifteen, then sixteen; sixteen is the accepted number for a brigade band as proscribed in General Order 91 of 1862. For more on the changing size of regimental bands, see Olson, *Music and Musket*, 50. Frank Rauscher notes that his band (114th Pennsylvania) often had one-third of its members on the sick list. Rauscher, *Music on the March*, 15.

19. Haynes, *Tenth Vermont*, 440.

20. Richard Moon had originally enlisted as a musician in the 2nd Vermont Infantry, and upon the completion of his term reenlisted with the 10th Vermont. He also played in the band of the 10th Vermont. VA & IGO lists 1 July 1863 as the date of his promotion.

21. The 10th Vermont, 87th Pennsylvania, 151st New York all claimed to have bands at some point; though there is some chance that members of one regiment would refer to another regiment's band as theirs, it seems these regiments had distinct ensembles. Even one of the last units to join the brigade, the 106th New York, claimed to have had a "string band." LaForge, diary entry for 20 March 1865, CWMiscColl, USAMHI. The 87th Pennsylvania formed a band in January 1863. Prowell, *87th Pennsylvania*, 56–57.

22. Dr. Joseph Rutherford, letter to his wife, 22 May 1863, in Dr. Joseph Rutherford Papers, Bailey-Howe Library, UVM.

23. Letter to friend, 28 May 1863, P.S. Scribner Papers, 1863, Pearce Civil War Collection, Navarro College, Corsicana, TX; George Crossett, letter to sisters Cornelia [?] and Lee [?], 20 June 1863, in Crossett Family Letters, VHS; Gordon, *A Playground of the Civil War*, 137.

Chapter 3

1. Lieutenant William Burroughs Ross, Co. B, 14th New Jersey Infantry, June 24, 1863; quoted in Olsen, *Upon the Tented Field*, 126.

2. William Hopkins Morris (1827–1900) was a graduate of West Point, Class of 1851. He served in garrison duty and spent some time out west, then resigned his commission and joined his father as assistant editor of the *New York Home Journal*. At the outbreak of war he was commissioned a captain and served as a staff officer through September 1862. He was then appointed colonel of the 6th New York Artillery and joined that unit in the defenses around Baltimore. Morris was promoted to brigadier general November 29, 1862.

3. Letter to wife, 30 June 1863, Dennis Tuttle Papers, Manuscript Division, Library of Congress, Washington, D.C. After losing their instruments at Gettysburg, the unfortunate drum corps of the 150th Pennsylvania went months without playing; Kieffer, *The Recollections of a Drummer-Boy*, 131.

4. Albert A. Nofi, *The Gettysburg Campaign: June–July 1863* (Conshohocken, PA: Combined Books, 1986), 54, 162–163.

5. Sergeant Albert C. Harrison, Co. G, 14th New Jersey Infantry, quoted in Olsen, *Upon the Tented Field*, 136.

6. Terrill, *Campaign of the Fourteenth*, 19.

7. Carter, *Four Brothers*, 330.

8. Helena A. Howell, *Chronicles of the One Hundred Fifty-First Regiment New York State Volunteer Infantry 1862–1865* (Albion, NY: Eddy, 1911), 39.

9. Howell, *Chronicles of the 151st New York*, 53.

10. Henry Burnham, letter to sister Emma, 29 June 1863, in Henry P. Burnham Papers, VHS.

11. Simon Cummins, *Give God the Glory: Memoirs of a Civil War Soldier* (Eagle River, MI: Jones, 1997), 34.

12. John D. Billings, *Hardtack & Coffee: The Unwritten Story of Army Life* (1887. Reprint, Lincoln: University of Nebraska Press, 1993), 246.

13. Charles George, letter to wife, 28 July 1863.

14. Haynes, *Tenth Regiment*, 41.

15. "While chasing Lee up the valley we had managed to keep so far ahead of our supply trains that for three days we were practically out of rations. Foragers on both sides had cleaned up everything along the line of march, and our regiment, at least, was actually suffering from hungry." Waite, "Three Years with the Tenth Vermont," VHS, 62.

16. *OR*, Ser. 1, Vol. 27, Pt. 1, 579–580.

17. Benedict, *Vermont in the Civil War*, Vol. 2, 287. Cornelious Tenure of the 6th New York Artillery noted the proximity of enemy pickets and snipers. He also mentioned the unpleasantness of the area: "the men Sufferes a goodelle for water witch is very scarce here." See Larry H. Whiteaker and W. Calvin Dickinson, eds., *Civil War Letters of the Tenure Family: Rockland County, N.Y., 1862–1865* (New York: Historical Society of Rockland County, 1990), 44.

18. William White, letter to Jacob Wead, 23 August 1863, in William White Correspondence, VHS.

19. Foster, *New Jersey and the Rebellion*, 358.

20. Messer, *Civil War Letters*, 21.

21. Henry Burnham, letter to sister Lora, 26 August 1863, in Henry P. Burnham Papers, VHS.

22. Tabor Parcher, letter to wife Sarah, 6 September 1863, in Tabor H. Parcher, Manuscript Files, Bailey-Howe Library, UVM.

23. Henry Burnham, letter to sister Lora, 6 September 1863, in Henry P. Burnham Papers, VHS.

24. Benedict, *Vermont in the Civil War*, Vol. 2, 287.

25. In many regiments it was the drum corps and not the band that performed for guard mounting. This seems to be the case for the 10th Vermont.

26. Willard M. Thayer, letter to his wife and children, 5 October 1863, in Esther M. Thayer Correspondence, VHS.

27. Entry of 27 September 1863, Diary of Thomas Francis Galwey, Manuscript Division, Library of Congress, Washington, D.C. Bandsmen in gray had also been called upon to help their comrades in arms; Confederate Generals Ewell and Early even used their bands to generate the impression that they had more troops in position than they really did. See William D. Henderson, *The Road to Bristoe Station: Campaigning with Lee and Meade, August 1–October 20, 1863* (Lynchburg, VA: Howard, 1987), 49.

28. Joseph Bradford Carr (1828–1895) was a native New Yorker. At the start of hostilities he was commissioned colonel of the 2nd New York and led that regiment all the way through the Peninsula Campaign. At Second Bull Run he was given a brigade and promoted to brigadier general. By 1863 he was commanding a division in the III Corps, and he continued to command various divisions in the field throughout the war.

29. Foster, *New Jersey and the Rebellion*, 359; Olsen, *Upon the Tented Field*, 173–174; Prowell, *87th Pennsylvania*, 95–96; Terrill, *Campaign of the Fourteenth*, 31, 35.

30. Philip Arsino, letter to mother, 16 October 1863, in Correspondence of Philip Arsino, VHS.

31. Martin F. Graham and George F. Skoch, *Mine Run: A Campaign of Lost Opportunities, October 21, 1863–May 1, 1864* (Lynchburg, VA: Howard, 1987), 8.

32. Letter to home, 18 November 1863.

33. Haynes, *Tenth Regiment*, 55–56.

34. Robert Knox Sneden, *Eye of the Storm: A Civil War Odyssey*, C. F. Bryan and N. D. Lankford,

eds. (New York: The Free Press, 2000), 145–146. Brother Charles notes: "Orders are, not to have any bugling or drum beating on this march." Charles George, "Dear Ellie...," 71.

35. Dennis Schank and Scott Schotz, *Baptism of Fire: the 151st New York Infantry at Mine Run* (Lockport, NY: n.p., 1999), 14–15; William Swinton, *Campaigns of the Army of the Potomac* (New York: Charles Scribner's Sons, 1882), 392.

36. Edward Ellis, *The Camp-Fires of General Lee: From the Peninsula to Appomattox Court-House* (Philadelphia: Harrison, 1886), 332; Prowell, *87th Pennsylvania*, 99. George Stevens, surgeon of the 77th New York, bluntly calls French's movements a "blunder," Stevens, *Three Years*, 293.

37. J. Warren Keifer, *Slavery and Four Years of War: A Political History of Slavery in the United States* (New York: G. P. Putnam's Sons, 1900), II, 61. The engagement in which the 10th Vermont fought has received many names over the years, including Locust Grove, Orange Grove, Robertson's Tavern, and Payne's Farm.

38. Terrill, *Campaign of the Fourteenth*, 42. In fact this probably was the first time that the 3rd Division was the first to engage the enemy; Peter Vredenburgh, "Letters of Major Peter Vredenburgh of the Battles and Marches of the Old Fourteenth Regiment New Jersey Vols.," in D. Martin, ed., *The Monocacy Regiment: A Commemorative History of the Fourteenth New Jersey Infantry in the Civil War, 1862–1865* (Highstown, NJ: Longstreet House, 1987), 144.

39. According to Keifer, he recommended that Morris push forward, and Morris declined. A Rebel assault forced Morris to pull back and re-form, and it was then that the successful attack was launched; see *Slavery and Four Years of War*, II, 62. A drawing of the troop placement by Surgeon Rutherford can be found in Marshall, *A War of the People*, 199.

40. Vredenburgh, *Letters*, 144.

41. Terrill, *Campaign of the Fourteenth*, 43; Foster, *New Jersey and the Rebellion*, 359.

42. Quoted in Marshall, *A War of the People*, 198. Rutherford promptly moves his hospital back some ways to General French's headquarters. Others commented on the heavy amount of firing; see Thomas W. Hyde, *Following the Greek Cross: or, Memories of the Sixth Army Corps* (Boston: Houghton, Mifflin, 1894), 175.

43. Hyde, *Greek Cross*, 175.

44. *Orleans American*, December 17, 1863, quoted in Paul Stephen Beaudry, *The Forgotten Regiment: History of the 151st New York Volunteer Soldiers and Sailors in the War for the Union, 1861–5* (Cleveland: InChem, 1995), 65.

45. Howell, *Chronicles of the 151st New York*, 287.

46. Vredenburgh, *Letters*, 145. The stand made by Morris' brigade is all the more impressive when considering the lack of support provided by other units, especially Smith's 3rd Brigade; Prowell, *87th Pennsylvania*, 100–101; Report of Brigadier General Joseph B. Carr, *OR*, Ser. 1, Vol. 29, Pt. 1, 777.

47. Schank, *Baptism of Fire*, 22–23.

48. *OR*, Ser. 1, Vol. 29, Pt. 1, 753–754.

49. *OR*, Ser. I, Vol. 29, Pt. 1, 779–780.

50. Lieutenant William Burroughs Ross, Co. B, 14th New Jersey Infantry, quoted in Olsen, *Upon the Tented Field*, 188; Report of Brigadier General Joseph B. Carr, *OR*, Ser. 1, Vol. 29, Pt. 1, 776–779. According to Wilbur Fisk, a fellow Vermonter: "The Tenth Vermont was in the fight, and there was a report that night that they broke and ran; other reports contradicted it. I have heard that they bore the test and held their groud like men, although a line ahead of them broke and skedaddled back right through their ranks; and for a Vermont regiment, this is decidedly the most rational story to believe." *Hard Marching Every Day: The Civil War Letters of Private Wilbur Fisk*, Emil and Ruth Rosenblatt, eds. (Lawrence: University Press of Kansas, 1992), 169.

51. John O. Casler, *Four Years in the Stonewall Brigade* (1906. Reprint, Dayton: Morningside Bookshop, 1971), 197–198.

52. Eric A. Campbell, ed., *"A Grand Terrible Dramma": From Gettysburg to Petersburg: The Civil War Letters of Charles Wellington Reed* (New York: Fordham University Press, 2000), 158–159; Terrill, *Campaign of the Fourteenth*, 45.

53. Schank, *Baptism of Fire*, 28–29; Vredenburgh, *Letters*, 146–147.

54. Entry of 20 December 1863, Diary of John L. Ryno, Interlaken Historical Society, Interlaken, NY.

Chapter 4

1. Benedict, *Vermont in the Civil War*, Vol. 2, 293. Musicians were equally susceptible to the illnesses that plagued each army; John L. Houck, fifer of the 140th New York, complained of a "pain in my side, and that "I play at dress parade and tattoo that is all but I know that hurts me very much for every time I play I play I have to spit blood." Letter to wife, 4 November 1863, John L. Houck Collection, Manuscripts and Special Collections, New York State Library, Albany, NY.

2. Edward Bushnell, diary entry for 2 February 1864, in Records of the Vermont Civil War Centennial Committee (microfilm F-2849), Vermont Public Records Division, Middlesex, VT; see also Lieutenant Marcus Stults, Co. H., 14th New Jersey Infantry, quoted in Olsen, *Upon the Tented Field*, 213. Soldiers from many regiments, including the 87th Pennsylvania, were encouraged to reenlist. Thomas Crowl, 87th Pennsylvania, 10 January 1864, USAMHI.

3. Lemuel Abbot's diary entry for January 5 makes a reference that implies that Herbert had received a furlough, though there is nothing else to support this: "Herbert George, the band master, has been in this evening relating his experiences during his leave in Vermont. It almost makes me homesick." Lemuel A. Abbott, *Personal Recollections and Civil War Diary* (Burlington, VT: Free Press, 1908), 4.

4. Abbott, *Diary*, 1–30.

5. Ibid., 1–2; see also Waite, "Three Years with the Tenth Vermont," VHS, 109. Another soldier noted that "Christmas was ushered in by all the bands in camp playing lively tunes at daylight." Prowell, *87th Pennsylvania*, 108. Many soldiers report social events in the period following the Mine Run Campaign; Ezra Simons of the 125th New York Volunteer Infantry, describes band concerts and balls for the officers and men; see Simons, *125th NY*, p. 188–189. As was noted earlier, Private Tabor Parcher, Co. B, 10th Vt., describes less wholesome forms of entertainment at Brandy Station in Marshall, *A War of the People*, 225–226.

6. Another VI Corps bandsman described the tension between their bandleader and the musicians as well as between various members of the band; see Artemas H. Skinner Papers, Manuscript Collections, Worcester Historical Museum, Worcester, MA. Henry Klag and members of the band of the 95th Pennsylvania sent a petition to Secretary of War Stanton and to a member of Congress to voice dissatisfaction with their leadership; entries of January and February 1862, Henry Klag diary, Virginia Historical Society, Richmond, VA.

7. Haynes, *Tenth Regiment*, Chapter 4. See also Hyde, *Greek Cross*, 179; Prowell, *87th Pennsylvania*, 109–110.

8. Letter from "Typo," 30 January 1864, in *Adams Sentinel*, 9 February 1864.

9. Terrill, *Campaign of the Fourteenth*, 51.

10. Entry of 19 April 1864, Diary of Charles H. Richardson, Manuscript Division, Library of Congress, Washington, D.C.

11. Lieutenant William Burroughs Ross, Co. B, 14th New Jersey Infantry, quoted in Olsen, *Upon the Tented Field*, 197.

12. Lieutenant Marcus Stults, Co. H., 14th New Jersey Infantry, quoted in Olsen, *Upon the Tented Field*, 231.

13. John Louiselle, letter to his wife, 9 March 1864, in Greene-Louiselle Family Papers, Bailey-Howe Library, UVM. Or as Henry Burnham notes, "I have heard that the Christian Commission dont think much of it either." Henry Burnham, letter to sister Emma, 6 March 1864, in Henry P. Burnham Papers, VHS.

14. Dr. Joseph Rutherford, letter to his wife, 10 March 1864, in Dr. Joseph Rutherford Papers, Bailey-Howe Library, UVM.

15. Casler, *Stonewall Brigade*, 202. Even the musicians were recruited to play for the troops in the mock battle.

16. Edward Bushnell, diary entry for 30 January 1864, in Records of the Vermont Civil War Centennial Committee (microfilm F-2849), Vermont Public Records Division, Middlesex, VT.

17. Terrill, *Campaign of the Fourteenth*, 54. Similar minstrel shows were put on in the Confederate camp as well. As one Rebel soldier noted, "I have never seen better since the war, as we had amongst us professional actors and musicians; and the theatre became a great place of resort to while away the dull winter nights." See Casler, *Stonewall Brigade*, 204–205.

18. Prowell, *87th Pennsylvania*, 114–116.

19. Abbott, *Diary*, 1–14; Letters of January, 1864, from Charles and Herbert George. For another busy schedule, see entries of January and February, 1863, Diary of John L. Ryno, Interlaken Historical Society, Interlaken, NY.

20. Prowell, *87th Pennsylvania*, 109.

21. Waite, "Three Years with the Tenth Vermont," VHS, 104–106.

22. Quoted in Beaudry, *Forgotten Regiment*, 81. See also the letter from Corporal Simon Lesage to Timothy Messer, 17 February 1864, Messer, *Letters*, 35.

23. George Hall of the 14th Georgia Volunteers described almost daily prayer meetings, as well as "sermons" and "preaching" in the evenings; see entries for August–March 1863–1864, in George Hall Papers, Manuscript Division, Library of Congress, Washington, D.C. See also Howard Coffin, *The Battered Stars: One State's Civil War Ordeal During Grant's Overland Campaign* (Woodstock, VT: Countryman Press, 2002), 5–8.

24. Shelby Foote, *The Civil War: A Narrative*, vol. 3, *Red River to Appomattox* (New York: Vintage Books, 1986), 9; Edward Bushnell, diary entry for 24 March 1864, in Records of the Vermont Civil War Centennial Committee (microfilm F-2849), Vermont Public Records Division, Middlesex, VT.

25. Edwin C. Hall, letter to his parents, 15 March 1864, in Edwin C. Hall Papers, VHS. A biography of Hall and a number of his letters can be found in Norbert Kuntz, "A Brookfield Soldier's Report: The Civil War Recollections of Edwin C. Hall," *Vermont History* 57, no. 4 (Fall 1989): 197–225.

26. 16 March 1864, in the James Herbert George Collection, Huntington Library.

27. Abbott, *Diary*, 76. After the reorganization, the 3rd Division consisted of only 2 brigades. The 2nd Brigade, led by General Seymour (soon replaced by Kiefer), included the 6th Maryland, and the 110th, 122nd, and 126th Ohio; Foster, *New Jersey and the Rebellion*, 361; Ulysses S. Grant, *Personal Memoirs*, C. Carr, ed. (New York: Modern Library, 1999), 516–518.

28. Howell, *Chronicles of the 151st New York*, 57.

29. Roswell Hunt, letter to Wealthy Field, 1 May 1864, in Civil War Letters to Wealthy Field, VHS.

30. Abbott, *Diary*, 33. In his letter of 25 April 1864 Charles described the band membership as follows: "We line up so — Front rank: Herbert, Dick and I; 2nd rank: Wells, Hamilton, Foster, Clark; 3rd rank: Calvin Dewey, Stuart, Sexton."

31. Abbott, *Diary*, 2.

32. Ibid., 9–10.

33. Ibid., 34.

34. Ibid., 37.

35. Benedict, *Vermont in the Civil War*, vol. 2, 296. William Henry, a native of Waterbury, Vermont, had been in the pharmaceutical business at the onset of the war. Originally a lieutenant with the 2nd Vermont, he was forced to resign due to pneumonia. After regaining his health he was commissioned major of the 10th Vermont and was to serve with the regiment until his health would again force him to resign. Henry returned to his business after leaving the army and also pursued a career in politics. He was elected to the state senate for numerous terms, and twice was mayor of Burlington (Haynes, *Tenth Regiment*, 348–52).

36. Edward A. Johnson, 151st New York, letter of 17 April 1864, CWMiscColl, USAMHI.

37. Haynes, *Tenth Regiment*, 95. However, another witness described the army's departure: "As the almost countless encampments were broken up [with] bands in all directions playing lively airs." Quoted in Ward, *Civil War*, 288. It seems probable that musicians were ordered to be silent while preparations were made in the hopes of gaining some element of surprise. Perhaps that order was rescinded as the army began to move, some band became anxious and played despite orders, or even the chaplain that claims bands were playing was merely attempting to enrich his description. See also Mark Nesbitt, *Through Blood & Fire: Selected Civil War Papers of Major General Joshua Chamberlain* (Mechanicsburg, PA: Stackpole Books, 1996), 120.

38. Robert G. Scott, *Into the Wilderness with the Army of the Potomac* (Bloomington, IN: Indiana University Press, 1985), 139–141.

39. Gordon C. Rhea, *The Battle of the Wilderness, May 5–6, 1864* (Baton Rouge: Louisiana State University Press, 1994), 230.

40. Stevens, *Three Years*, 307.

41. Clarke, "In the Immediate Rear," 94. See also Bardeen, *A Little Fifer's War Diary*, 114–125.

42. Waite, "Three Years with the Tenth Vermont," VHS, 122.

43. Report of Brigadier General William H. Morris, *OR*, Ser. 1, Vol. 36, Pt. 1, 722–24.

44. The fighting along the front was so intense that at one point Morris' brigade was the only unit left in reserve; Edward Steere, *The Wilderness Campaign* (1960. Reprint, Harrisburg, PA: Stackpole, 1987), 194, 257, 296.

45. John B. Gordon, *Reminiscences of the Civil War* (New York: Charles Scribner's Sons, 1903), 244–245. This was not the last time the 10th Vermont would encounter Gordon. In many of their future battles the men of Vermont would find themselves pitted against Gordon's veterans.

46. Report of General Morris, *OR*, Ser. 1, Vol. 36, Pt. 1, 723. Steere, *Wilderness Campaign*, 444–445; Rhea, *Battle of the Wilderness*, 423. According to Benedict, only the 10th Vermont and the 106th New York made the charge. Benedict, *Vermont in the Civil War*, vol. 2, 296.

47. Abbott, *Diary*, 46–47.

48. Edward Bushnell, diary entry for 5 May 1864, in Records of the Vermont Civil War Centennial Committee (microfilm F-2849), Vermont Public Records Division, Middlesex, VT.

49. Report of Brigadier General William H. Morris, *OR*, Ser. 1, Vol. 36, Pt. 1, 722–724. Likewise the 14th New Jersey suffered minimal casualties. Foster, *New Jersey and the Rebellion*, 361.

50. Some reports have the Old Vermont Brigade losing 1,000 men at the Battle of the Wilderness; ultimately this brigade would suffer some of the highest losses in the entire Union Army; Scott, *Into the Wilderness*, 77; see also Marshall, *A War of the People*, 221; Coffin, *The Battered Stars*, 99–122.

51. Grant, *Memoirs*, 532. Gordon was unaware that Sedgwick had any troops in reserve; he believed that it was only the onset of night that halted his victory; Gordon, *Reminiscences*, Chapter 18.

52. Abbott, *Diary*, 48.

53. Report of Brigadier General William H. Morris, *OR*, Ser. 1, Vol. 36, Pt. 1, 722–24.

54. Gotwalt, *Adventures of a Private*, 12. Simon Cummings also describes the staggering amount of wounded following the battle; see, *Give God the Glory*, 68ff.

55. Gordon C. Rhea, *The Battles for Spotsylvania Court House and the Road to Yellow Tavern: May 7–12, 1864* (Baton Rouge: Louisiana State University Press, 1997), 57.

56. Abbott, *Diary*, 50–51.

57. Martin T. McMahon, "The Death of General John Sedgwick," *Battles and Leaders of the Civil War* (Edison, NJ: Castle, 1990) 4:175; Prowell, *87th Pennsylvania*, 134; Lieutenant William Burroughs Ross, Co. B, 14th New Jersey Infantry, quoted in Olsen, *Upon the Tented Field*, 235.

58. Gotwalt, *Adventures of a Private*, 12.

59. Prowell, *87th Pennsylvania*, 136. This may be Spindle's field, at the foot of Laurel Hill; see Rhea, *Spotsylvania*, 285.

60. Beaudry, *Forgotten Regiment*, 108; Howell, *Chronicles of the 151st New York*, 72–73.

61. Casler, *Stonewall Brigade*, 210.

62. Rhea, *Spotsylvania*, 176–177.

63. Report of Colonel William Truex, *OR*, Ser. 1, Vol. 36, Pt. 1, 724–727.

64. Many reports note that the fire was so intense in the area around the VI Corps that countless trees were cut in half. Stevens, *Three Years*, 335.

65. Edward Bushnell, diary entry for 13 May 1864, in Records of the Vermont Civil War Centennial Committee (microfilm F-2849), Vermont Public Records Division, Middlesex, VT. See also Coffin, *The Battered Stars*, 179–182, for additional poignant descriptions of the horrors witnessed by Vermonters.

66. Tabor Parcher, diary entry for 13 May 1864, in Tabor H. Parcher, Manuscript Files, Bailey-Howe Library, UVM.

67. Prowell, *87th Pennsylvania*, 139.

68. Gordon C. Rhea, *To the North Anna River: Grant and Lee, May 13–25, 1864* (Baton Rouge: Louisiana State University Press, 2000), 114.

69. Waite, "Three Years with the Tenth Vermont," VHS, 175.

70. Rhea, *To the North Anna River*, 191; Prowell, *87th Pennsylvania*, 143.

71. Report of Brigadier General William H. Morris, *OR*, Ser. 1, Vol. 36, Pt. 1, 722 724.

72. Other musicians found themselves in harm's way while assisting the surgeons; nurses and musicians of the 5th Corps, 1st Division, were captured by Confederates though soon "recaptured"; Letter to wife, 17 May 1864, John L. Houck Papers, Manuscripts and Special Collections, New York State Library, Albany, NY. Throughout the war soldiers remarked on the benefits of band performances on the wounded in hospitals; for example, see David H. Donald, ed. *Gone for a Soldier: The Civil War Memoirs of Private Alfred Bellard* (Boston: Little, Brown, 1975), 230–231.

Chapter 5

1. Prowell, *87th Pennsylvania*, 144; Rhea, *To the North Anna River*, 222–223. Regiments without bands filled the air with singing.

2. Rhea, *To the North Anna River*, 349.

3. Entry of 26 May 1864, Civil War Diary and Journal of Charles B. Putnam, 1863–1865, VSARA, Middlesex, VT.

4. Quoted in Gordon C. Rhea, *Cold Harbor: Grant and Lee, May 26–June 3, 1864* (Baton Rouge: Louisiana State University Press, 2002), 90.

5. Report of Colonel William Truex, *OR*, Ser. 1, Vol. 36, Pt. 1, 724–727.

6. Ezra D. Simons, *A Regimental History: The One Hundred and Twenty-Fifth New York State Volunteers* (New York: Simmons, 1888), 125; Michael V. Sheridan, *Personal Memoirs of Philip Henry Sheridan* (New York: Appleton, 1904), Vol. 1, chapter 20.

7. Abbott, *Diary*, 69–70.

8. Prowell, *87th Pennsylvania*, 148–149.

9. Maury Klein, *Edward Porter Alexander* (Athens: University of Georgia Press, 1971), 118; Jennings Cropper Wise, *The Long Arm of Lee: or the History of the Artillery of the Army of Northern Virginia* (1915. Reprint, Lincoln, NE: University of Nebraska Press, 1991), 2: 817–818.

10. William White, letter to Jacob Wead, 9 June 1864, in William White Correspondence, VHS.

11. Coffin, *The Battered Stars*, 291–293; Marshall, *A War of the People*, 223; N. A. Ramsey, "Sixty First Regiment," in Walter Clark, *Histories of the Several Regiments and Battalions from North Carolina,*

in the Great War 1861–'65 (Raleigh: Uzzell, 1901) 3: 512. Even an earlier critic of Ricketts' division found its performance inspiring, though still managed to criticize: "The division of Ricketts, which Hancock called a 'weakly child,' suddenly blazed out, and charged with the bayonet; an example I hope it will follow up! The 'weary boys' at first broke and ran as usual." George R. Agassiz, ed., *Meade's Headquarters 1863–1865: Letters of Colonel Theodore Lyman from the Wilderness to Appomattox* (Boston: Massachusetts Historical Society, 1922), 138–139.

12. Foster claims that the 14th New Jersey lost 240 killed or wounded in only 2 hours; Foster, *New Jersey and the Rebellion*, 263

13. Stevens, *Three Years*, 349.

14. Report of Colonel William Truex, *OR*, Ser. 1, Vol. 36, Pt. 1, 724–727.

15. Cummins, *Give God the Glory*, 72.

16. Agassiz, *Letters*, 144; Grant, *Memoirs*, 584; Rhea, *Cold Harbor*, 343–345.

17. The principal musician of the 87th Pennsylvania commented on the intense duty in the hospitals; Prowell, *87th Pennsylvania*, 153.

18. Private Tabor Parcher, Co. B, 10th Vt., in Marshall, *A War of the People*, 235–37; Stevens, *Three Years*, 354.

19. Abbott, *Diary*, 80.

20. Letter to Mattie, 13 July 1864, Horace Tracy Hanks Papers, Manuscripts and Special Collections, New York State Library, Albany, NY.

21. Report of Colonel William Truex, *OR*, Ser. 1, Vol. 36, Pt. 1, 724–727; report of Brigadier General William H. Morris, *OR*, Ser. 1, Vol. 36, Pt. 1, 722–724.

22. Report of Major Charles G. Chandler, *OR*, Ser. 1, Vol. 36, Pt. 1, 727.

23. Hyde, *Greek Cross*, 214.

24. Vermont in particular had paid dearly, according to historian Howard Coffin: "it appears that the total loss of the state of Vermont in the Overland Campaign approaches 3,000 men. Thus, the little state of Vermont, with wartime population of about 315,000, saw nearly 1 in every 100 of its people become casualties of Ulysses Grant's drive from the Rapidan to Petersburg." Coffin, *The Battered Stars*, 352.

25. Abiel T. LaForge, 106th New York, diary entry for 14 June 1864; CWMiscColl, USAMHI.

26. One aide to Grant noted that "drums were beating the march, bands were playing stirring quicksteps"; quoted in Ward, *Civil War*, 305.

27. Prowell, *87th Pennsylvania*, 162–163.

28. Henry Burnham, letter to sister Lora, 19 June 1864, in Henry P. Burnham Papers, VHS.

29. Howell, *Chronicles of the 151st New York*, 76.

30. John Horn, *The Petersburg Campaign: June 1864–April 1865* (Conshohocken, PA: Combined Books, 1993), 78–79; Noah Andre Trudeau, *The Last Citadel: Petersburg, Virginia, June 1864–April 1865* (Boston: Little, Brown, 1991), 69.

31. Vredenburgh, *Letters*, 154.

32. Terrill, *Campaign of the Fourteenth*, 70.

33. Timothy B. Mudgett, *Make the Fur Fly: A History of a Union Volunteer Division in the American Civil War* (Shippensburg, PA: Burd Street Press, 1997), 87.

34. Prowell, *87th Pennsylvania*, 171. See also entry of 4 July 1864, diary of Walter Graham, VHS.

35. Abbott, *Diary*, 88–9.

36. Abner Ralph Small, *The Road to Richmond: The Civil War Memoirs of Major Abner R. Small of the Sixteenth Maine Volunteers* (Berkeley: University of California Press, 1939), 153.

37. Grant, *Memoirs*, 606. There was also a secondary plan to send a covert detachment to Point Lookout, Maryland, to rescue Confederate prisoners; see Jack E. Schairer, *Lee's Bold Plan for Point Lookout: The Rescue of Confederate Prisoners That Never Happened* (Jefferson, NC: McFarland, 2008).

38. Lieutenant William Burroughs Ross, Co. B, 14th New Jersey Infantry, quoted in Olsen, *Upon the Tented Field*, 252. See also Joseph Bilby, "9 July 1864: The 14th New Jersey Infantry at the Battle of Monocacy," in *The Monocacy Regiment: A Commemorative History of the Fourteenth New Jersey Infantry in the Civil War, 1862–1865*, David G. Martin, ed. (Highstown, NJ: Longstreet House, 1987), 169. The band of the 87th Pennsylvania played "Maryland, My Maryland" among other tunes; Prowell, *87th Pennsylvania*, 175.

39. Jim Leeke, ed., *Smoke, Sound and Fury: The Civil War Memoirs of Major-General Lew Wallace, U.S. Volunteers* (Portland, OR: Strawberry Hill Press, 1998), 239–240; Crawford, *Reminiscences of a Veteran*, 482.

40. Leeke, *Smoke, Sound & Fury*, 250–251. See also Marc Leepson, *Desperate Engagement: How a Little-Known Civil War Battle Saved Washington, D.C., and Changed American History* (New York: Thomas Dunne Books, 2007), Chapter 7.

41. B. Franklin Cooling, *Monocacy: The Battle That Saved Washington* (Shippensburg, PA: White

Mane, 2000), 81; see also Bilby, "Battle of Monocacy," 173–174; Foster, *New Jersey and the Rebellion*, 367.

42. Originally this detachment was placed under the command of Major Chandler of the 10th Vermont, but Chandler mysteriously left the field. This left Captain Charles J. Brown, 1st Maryland Infantry, Potomac Home Brigade, the ranking officer, but he gratefully relinquished command to Lieutenant Davis. Report of Major General Lew Wallace, *OR*, Ser. 1, Vol. 37, Pt. 1, 191–200; Cooling, *Monocacy*, 120.

43. Bilby, *Battle of Monocacy*, 177–179. It is said that in an act of chivalry the Confederate artillery stopped shelling until the Vermonters had crossed the rail bridge. However, many Vermonters were wounded while attempting the crossing; see Cooling, *Monocacy*, 156; Leepson, *Desperate Engagement*, 108–109.

44. *OR*, Ser. 1, Vol. 37, Pt. 1, 197. What artillery the Union forces did have was apparently quite successful, especially against Rebel artillery; Runge, *Four Years*, 86–87.

45. Gordon, *Reminiscences*, 309–310.

46. George E. Davis, "Washington in Peril," August 1884.

47. *OR*, Ser. 1, Vol. 37, Pt. 1, 197.

48. Private Henry P. Burnham, Co. G, 10th Vt., in Marshall, *A War of the People*, 246–247.

49. *OR*, Ser. 1, Vol. 37, Pt. 1, 205; Report of Colonel Emerson, *OR*, Ser. 1, Vol. 37, Pt. 1, 205–206.

50. Gordon, *Reminiscences*, 312. For the severity of the Confederate losses, see Cooling, *Monocacy*, 148–149.

51. Bilby, *Battle of Monocacy*, 180; Vredenburgh, *Letters*, 156; Prowell, *87th Pennsylvania*, 182.

52. Edwin Dillingham, letter to mother, 13 July 1864, Dillingham Family Papers, 1858–1958, MS 257, Woodson Research Center, Fondren Library, Rice University, Houston, TX.

53. Marshall, *A War of the People*, 247.

54. Grant, *Memoirs*, 606–7. Today there is a monument dedicated to the 10th Vermont at Monocacy National Battlefield.

55. Gloria B. Swift and Gail Stephens, "Honor Redeemed: Lew Wallace's Military Career and the Battle of Monocacy," *North & South* 4, vol. 2 (January 2001): 44–45.

56. Vredenburgh, *Letters*, 157.

57. Davis, "Washington in Peril."

58. Abbott, *Diary*, 122.

59. Porter, *Campaigning with Grant*, 239.

60. William De Forest, *A Volunteer's Adventures: A Union Captain's Record of the Civil War*, J. Croushore, ed. (Baton Rouge: Louisiana State University Press, 1974), 165.

61. Messer, *Letters*, 43.

62. Lieutenant William Burroughs Ross, Co. B, 14th New Jersey Infantry, quoted in Olsen, *Upon the Tented Field*, 259.

63. Thomas E. Pope, *The Weary Boys: Colonel J. Warren Kiefer and the 110th Ohio Volunteer Infantry* (Kent, OH: Kent State University Press, 2002), 76.

64. Abbott, *Diary*, 125.

Chapter 6

1. Howell, *Chronicles of the 151st New York*, 92.

2. It is interesting that soldiers from Vermont made up one-tenth of Sheridan's Army of the Shenandoah: 8 infantry regiments (including the First Vermont Brigade and the 10th and 11th Vermont), and one cavalry regiment.

3. Sheridan, *Memoirs*, vol. 1, 481–483.

4. Haynes, *Tenth Vermont*, 242–243. This episode made quite an impact on those present, and was noted by many commentators; see Stevens, *Three Years*, 390; Rhodes, *All for the Union*, 178.

5. Edward Bushnell, diary entry for 20 August 1864, in Records of the Vermont Civil War Centennial Committee (microfilm F-2849), VSARA, Middlesex, VT.

6. John Louiselle, letter to his wife, 19 August 1864, in Greene-Louiselle Family Papers, Bailey-Howe Library, UVM.

7. Sheridan, *Memoirs*, vol. 1, 496–497; George E. Pond, *The Shenandoah Valley in 1864* (New York: Charles Scribner's Sons, 1883), 141.

8. Abbott, *Diary*, 142.

9. Nathanial Shober Siewers Papers, Special Collections, UNC–Charlotte, Charlotte, NC. Later Siewers admitted: "For my part I am getting pretty tired of our old pieces." Letter of 12 June 1864. The band of the 1st New York Dragoons went through a frenzy of copying, arranging, and practicing;

see entries of January and February 1865, Walter H. Jackson Diary, Bentley Historical Library, University of Michigan, Ann Arbor, MI.

10. Roger U. Delauter and Brandon H. Beck, *Early's Valley Campaign: The 3rd Battle of Winchester* (Lynchburg, VA: Howard, 1997), 212–5.

11. Pond, *Shenandoah Valley*, 158.

12. Captain Lucius T. Hunt claims that the 10th Vermont totaled "267 muskets"; *OR*, Ser. 1, Vol. 43, Pt. 1, 243–244.

13. William H. Runge, ed., *Four Years in the Confederate Artillery: The Diary of Private Henry Robinson Berkeley* (Chapel Hill: University of North Carolina Press, 1961), 97.

14. Sheridan, *Memoirs*, vol. 2, 22–3; Mudgett, *Make the Fur Fly*, 99.

15. Report of Colonel Emerson, *OR*, Ser. 1, Vol. 43, Pt. 1, 231–2; Benedict, *Vermont in the Civil War*, Vol. 2, 320.

16. General Gordon gave a gloomy description of the chaotic state of the Confederate retreat in his *Reminiscences*, Chapter 23.

17. Pond, *Shenandoah Valley*, 168.

18. Jeffry D. Wert, *From Winchester to Cedar Creek: The Shenandoah Campaign of 1864* (Mechanicsburg, PA: Stackpole Books, 1997), 103–104. Many members of the VI Corps felt their role at Opequon Creek was largely ignored and that subsequent claims of breaking under enemy fire were unjustified; see Abbott, *Diary*, 150–209.

19. Abbott, *Diary*, 173.

20. Sheridan, *Memoirs*, vol. 2, 36–40; *OR*, Ser. 1, Vol. 43, Pt. 1, 232.

21. Keifer, *Slavery and Four Years of War*, vol. 2, 121. Pope, *The Weary Boys*, 81–82.

22. Henry Burnham, letter to sister Lora, 26 September 1864, in Henry P. Burnham Papers, VHS.

23. Report of Captain Lucius T. Hunt, *OR*, Ser. 1, Vol. 43, Pt. 1, 243–4. There was some disagreement as to what units could take credit for captured prisoners and artillery; see Wert, *From Winchester to Cedar Creek*, 124. Some claimed that the Rebels retreated in good order, falling back by alternate brigade; see Runge, *Four Years*, 101.

24. Howell, *Chronicles of the 151st New York*, 190.

25. Ricketts' division was clearly the most heavily engaged unit during the fight at Fisher's Hill and received numerous commendations; Sheridan, *Memoirs*, vol. 2, 36–40.

26. Rhodes, *All for the Union*, 187.

27. Prowell, *87th Pennsylvania*, 212.

28. Wert, *From Winchester to Cedar Creek*, 157–160.

29. Edward Bushnell, diary entry for 10 September 1864, in Records of the Vermont Civil War Centennial Committee (microfilm F-2849), VSARA, Middlesex, VT.

30. Sheridan, *Memoirs*, vol. 2, 59–60, 63.

31. Report of Lt. Colonel Charles G. Chandler, *OR*, Ser. 1, Vol. 43, Pt. 1, 244–6. Colonel Henry reported 17 officers and 280 men.

32. Gregory J. Urwin, *Custer Victorious: The Civil War Battles of General George Armstrong Custer* (London: Associated University Presses, 1983), 205. This is no surprise, as Custer surrounded himself with music at every chance. Custer followed in the shoes of his commander, General Sheridan, who was also fond of using bands for motivation.

33. Wert, *From Winchester to Cedar Creek*, 198.

34. Mudgett, *Make the Fur Fly*, 106–113.

35. Crawford, *Reminiscences of a Veteran*, 486.

36. Report of Lt. Colonel Charles G. Chandler, *OR*, Ser. 1, Vol. 43, Pt. 1, 244–246.

37. Keifer, *Slavery and Four Years of War*, vol. 2, 137–138.

38. Report of Colonel Emerson, *OR*, Ser. 1, Vol. 43, Pt. 1, 231–232; Report of Colonel William Henry, *OR*, Ser. 1, Vol. 51, Pt. 1, 283–284.

39. Ricketts took a bullet through the chest, a wound that disabled him for life.

40. Gordon, *Reminiscences*, 340. That same day Gordon remarks to General Early "That is the Sixth Corps, general. It will not go unless we drive it from the field." Gordon, *Reminiscences*, 341.

41. De Forest, *A Volunteer's Adventures*, 217.

42. Keifer, *Slavery and Four Years of War*, II, 147–150. By now it would seem that Chandler had left the field, and Captain Henry H. Dewey, Company A, led the 10th Vermont in their final charges.

43. Letter to wife, 20 October 1864, Austin Fenn Papers, 1864–1865, Pearce Civil War Collection, Navarro College, Corsicana, Texas.

44. Nevins, *Diary of Battle*, 473–474.

45. Abbott, *Diary*, 257. Captain Damon was to put forward three members of the 10th Vermont for the Medal of Honor for their performances in the Valley Campaign. See *OR*, Ser. 1, Vol. 42, Pt. 3, 1084. Veterans of the VI Corps remained adamant that it was their corps that held while the others

broke; Foster, *New Jersey and the Rebellion*, 374; Marshall, *A War of the People*, 261; Sheridan, *Memoirs*, vol. 2, 95; Stevens, *Three Years*, 421–422.

46. Report of Lt. Colonel Charles G. Chandler, *OR*, Ser. 1, Vol. 43, Pt. 1, 244–6. The Adjutant & Inspector General's report lists casualties as 14 killed, 66 wounded, and 5 missing for a total of 85.

47. Keifer, *Slavery and Four Years of War*, vol. 2, 153.

48. Cummins, *Give God the Glory*, 130–131.

49. Entry of 14 November 1864, Jere George Diary.

50. Beaudry, *Forgotten Regiment*, 185–6; Crawford, *Reminiscences of a Veteran*, 481.

51. George W. Burnell, "The Development of Our Army," *War Papers* (MOLLUS, WI, Vol. 2) (Milwaukee, WI: Burdick, Armitage & Allen, 1896), 75–76.

Chapter 7

1. George Damon was one of the most popular members of the 10th Vermont. He was born in Quebec, Canada, in 1835. His family moved to Vermont where he was educated and followed a career in law. At the time of his promotion letters or recommendation were secured from Seymour, Truex, and even Major General Wright; see Report of the Adjutant and Inspector General, VSARA, Middlesex, VT, F26066.

2. There were some, including Keifer, who were not pleased to see Seymour placed in command of the division; see Pope, *The Weary Boys*, 95. According to a member of the 14th New Jersey, the soldiers' lives were somewhat strained under the leadership of General Seymour, a strict disciplinarian; Abiel T. LaForge, 106th New York, diary entry for 27 December 1864; CWMiscColl, USAMHI; Terrill, *Campaign of the Fourteenth*, 103.

3. Report of Col. J. Warren Kiefer, *OR*, Ser. 1, Vol. 43, Pt. 1, 229: "It is painful to mention the bad conduct of Lieut. Col. Charles G. Chandler, Tenth Vermont, Maj. G. W. Voorhes, One hundred and twenty-sixth Ohio, and Gilbert H. Bargar, One hundred and twenty-second Ohio Volunteers. These officers shamefully deserted their comrades in arms, and went to the rear without authority or good cause." See also letter to Brigadier General Thomas, 7 January 1865, in Papers of Captain George Evans Davis, Rhode Island Historical Society, Providence, RI.

4. Edward Bushnell complained of Chandler's unnecessarily fastidious behavior during inspections; diary entry for 1 May 1864, in Records of the Vermont Civil War Centennial Committee (microfilm F-2849), VSARA, Middlesex, VT. Oscar Waite expressed his dissatisfaction with Chandler and went so far as to question his courage; Waite, "Three Years with the Tenth Vermont," VHS, 165. Colonel Henry sent a confidential letter to General Washburn in which he accused Chandler of causing "mischief" in the regiment, and predicted that Chandler would not be with the army very long; letter to General Washburn, 27 April 1864, in Report of the Adjutant and Inspector General, VSARA, Middlesex, VT, F26066.

5. Abiel T. LaForge, 106th New York, diary entry for 16 December 1864; CWMiscColl, USAMHI.

6. Entries of 21–26 December 1864, Nelson L. Stowe Diary, 1864, Connecticut Historical Society, Hartford, CT; entries of November and December 1864, in William H. Roberts, *Drums and Guns Around Petersburg* (Bowie, MD: Heritage Books, 1995).

7. Messer, *Letters*, 65.

8. Assistant Surgeon Joseph C. Rutherford, in Marshall, *A War of the People*, 288–290; Cummins, *Give God the Glory*, 143; Edward A. Johnson, 151st New York, letter of 14 February 1865; CWMiscColl, USAMHI.

9. William Whitehill, letter to his cousin, 3 January 1865, in William H. H. Whitehill, Manuscript Files, Bailey-Howe Library, UVM.

10. Edward Bushnell, diary entry for 17 February 1865, in Records of the Vermont Civil War Centennial Committee (microfilm F-2849), VSARA, Middlesex, VT; see also the entry of 20 March 1865: "A dance and a gay time at Brigade Head Quarters." See also Terrill, *Campaign of the Fourteenth*, 103–104.

11. "One of the boys from the 11 Pa. Mtd. Rifle Band came over and brought us a piece of music to exchange, a Potpourri, 'Yankee Notions.' It takes thirty five minutes to play it." The piece was copied by the next day. Diary entry of 4 January 1865, Henry J. Peck Correspondence, Manuscripts and Special Collections, New York State Library, Albany, NY.

12. Abiel T. LaForge, 106th New York, diary entry for 20 March 1865; CWMiscColl, USAMHI. See also the entry for 7 January 1865: "I was up to Hd. Qrs. this evening. they had the string band up there and some dancing and other fun was going on."

13. Charles George, "Dear Ellie...," 119.

14. Entry of 16 February 1865, Civil War Diary and Journal of Charles B. Putnam, 1863–1865, VSARA, Middlesex, VT.

15. Foster, *New Jersey and the Rebellion*, 376; Messer, *Letters*, 67. Reports vary as to the success of the first assault, though there is no doubt as to the success of the mission and the gallant role played by the 10th Vermont.

16. Report of Lt. Colonel Damon, *OR*, Ser. 1, Vol. 46, Pt. 1, 307–309; Terrill, *Campaign of the Fourteenth*, 114–115. See also Letter to wife, 20 March 1865, Austin Fenn Papers, 1864–1865, Pearce Civil War Collection, Navarro College, Corsicana, TX.

17. *OR*, Ser. 1, Vol. 46, Pt. 3, 423; Trudeau, *The Last Citadel*, 367.

18. Mudgett, *Make the Fur Fly*, 119ff. See also Horn, *The Petersburg Campaign*, 240–243.

19. Messer, *Letters*, 69.

20. Longstreet, *Manassas to Appomattox*, 604–605.

21. "I am happy to be able to state that the Tenth Vermont was the first regiment in the division to plant a stand of colors within the enemy's works,— that it bravely performed its entire duty throughout the day, and kept up so perfect an organization as to elicit the highest commendation of the brigade and division commanders." Lieutenant Damon, Report of Action, 20 April 1865, in Report of the Adjutant and Inspector General, VSARA, Middlesex, VT, F26066. Another Vermont soldier, Captain Charles Gould, 5th Vermont Infantry, was awarded a Medal of Honor for being the first Union soldier to enter the enemy works; Coffin, *Full Duty*, 338–339. Members of the 14th New Jersey and 87*th* Pennsylvania claimed the honor as well; Prowell, *87th Pennsylvania*, 221. General Truex, in his report to the Adjutant General, 6th Corps, 3rd Division, claims "The first colors inside the works were those of the 10th Vermont Vols followed immediately by those of the 106 N. Y. Vols. and 14th N. J. Vols." Report of the Adjutant and Inspector General, VSARA, Middlesex, VT, F26066.

22. Entry of 3 April 1864, in Roberts, *Drums and Guns*, p. 65; report of Brigadier General Seymour, *OR*, Ser. 1, Vol. 46, Pt. 1, 978–979; Trudeau, *The Last Citadel*, 376.

23. Waite, "Three Years with the Tenth Vermont," VHS, 253.

Chapter 8

1. Grant, *Memoirs*, 720.

2. Derek Smith, *Lee's Last Stand: Sailor's Creek, Virginia, 1865* (Shippensburg, PA: White Mane Books, 2002); Longstreet, *Manassas to Appomattox*, 613; Swinton, *Campaigns*, 611.

3. Simons *125th NY*, 284.

4. Keifer, *Slavery and Four Years of War*, vol. 2, 206.

5. Beaudry, *Forgotten Regiment*, 192–194. Keifer, *Slavery and Four Years of War*, vol. 2, 208–209.

6. Cummins, *Give God the Glory*, 157.

7. Sheridan, *Memoirs*, vol. 2, 180. Many participants viewed the action at Sailor's Creek to be one of the most heroic performances by both the Union and Confederate troops, e.g. Longstreet, *Manassas to Appomattox*, 613–615.

8. Cummins, *Give God the Glory*, 157–158. At another point Cummins says the bands play "Hail to the Chief & St. Pateracks Day in the Morning & Yankey Doodal" (158).

9. Report of Brigadier General Seymour, *OR*, Ser. 1, Vol. 46, Pt. 1, 979–980.

10. Beaudry, *Forgotten Regiment*, 203–204.

11. Cummins, *Give God the Glory*, 161.

12. Ibid., 164. See also letter from Lieutenant Artemas H. Wheeler to Captain Davis, 14 April 1865, Papers of Captain George Evan Davis, Rhode Island Historical Society, Providence, RI.

13. Sergeant Albert C. Harrison, Co. G, 14th New Jersey Infantry, quoted in Olsen, *Upon the Tented Field*, 310.

14. Edwin C. Hall, "Our Marches After the Surrender," unpublished manuscript, 218, in Edwin C. Hall Papers, VHS.

15. Beaudry, *Forgotten Regiment*, 203–204.

16. Sergeant Albert C. Harrison, Co. G, 14th New Jersey Infantry, quoted in Olsen, *Upon the Tented Field*, 314.

17. Abiel T. LaForge, 106th New York, diary entry for 5 May 1865; CWMiscColl, USAMHI.

18. *The Sixth Corps* 1, no. 2 (Friday, April 28, 1865).

19. Crawford, *Reminiscences of a Veteran*, 491.

20. Cummins, *Give God the Glory*, 182–3.

21. Edwin C. Hall, letter to his parents, 5 May 1865, in Edwin C. Hall Papers, VHS.

22. Haynes, *Tenth Vermont*, 440.

23. Fox lists the number of total losses for the regiment as 352; see William F. Fox, *Regimental Losses in the American Civil War* (Albany, NY: Albany, 1889).

24. Program included with Jere George's diary; in private possession.

25. "Dear Ellie," p. 134.

26. Augustus B. Easton, ed., *History of the Saint Croix Valley* (Chicago: Cooper, 1909), 604–605; City of St. Thomas Centennial, *A Century of St. Thomas Times* (St. Thomas, ND: s.n., 1980), 101–102.

27. Lowell Mason, considered the father of public school music in America, referred to himself as a "superintendent of music"; see Michael Broyles, *"Music of the Highest Class": Elitism and Populism in Antebellum Boston* (New Haven: Yale University Press, 1992), 62. Many musicians of the time used the self-appointed title professor; see Barbara Owen, "Edward Little White, Professor of Music," *American Musical Life in Context and Practice to 1865*, James R. Heintze, ed. (New York: Garland, 1994), 133–147.

28. George, *George Genealogy*; Wells, *History of Newbury*.

29. At least one descendent remembered Herbert fondly, though with a fair amount of embellishment as well: "But the outstanding figure in the musical background was J. Herbert George, the youngest brother of Grandpa. He was Supt. of all music in the city of Boston for 30 years. He was also head cornetist in the Boston Symphony orchestra. He led two Civil War bands, the Connecticut and Vermont regiments. He also played the taps at President Lincoln's funeral. He was considered about the best cornetist in the U.S. His nephew C. F. George was director of the Chicago Municipal Band for many years.... He played until 90, and then went blind as a result of vibrations they claim." Charles A. McLean, personal letter of December 1954. I am indebted to Judy McIntyre, great-great-granddaughter of Charles George, for sharing this passage with me.

Bibliography

Archival Material

Manuscripts in Private Possession
    Phillips, Elva B. " 'Dear Ellie...' Civil War Letters from Charles to his Wife Ellen,
        1862–1865." Typescript.
    Diary of Jeremiah George. Typescript.

Area Research Center, University of Wisconsin–River Falls.
    Eva George Ritchey, *My Life* (mimeographed copy).

Bailey-Howe Library, Special Collections, University of Vermont, Burlington.
    John Louiselle, Greene-Louiselle Family Papers.
    Tabor H. Parcher, Manuscript Files (includes letter by Ezra W. Contant).
    Dr. Joseph Rutherford Papers.
    William H. H. Whitehill, Manuscript Files.

Bentley Historical Library, University of Michigan, Ann Arbor, MI.
    Walter H. Jackson Papers (1852–1936).

Brookfield Historical Society, Brookfield, VT.
    Urial Abbott Clark, Jr., Civil War Diaries.

Connecticut Historical Society, Hartford.
    Nelson L. Stowe Diary, 1864, MS 78010.
    Middlebrook Family Papers, MS 73139.

Fenton Historical Society, Jamestown, NY.
    George and Alvah Lawrence Papers.

Huntington Library, San Marino, CA.
    James Herbert George Collection (mss. George correspondence).
    Civil War diary of Sylvester Daniels, in Papers of Theophilus M. Magaw (HM 48002).

Interlaken Historical Society, Interlaken, NY.
    Diary of John L. Ryno.

Karrmann Library, University of Wisconsin–Platteville.
    Longhenry, Ludolph. *A Yankee Piper in Dixie: Civil War Diary of Ludolph Longhenry,
        Platteville, Grant Co. Wis.* Unpublished typescript.

Library of Virginia, Richmond.
    Charles L. Rundlett Papers, Accession 32581.

Manuscripts and Special Collections, New York State Library, Albany.

Horace Tracy Hanks Papers.
John L. Houck Papers.
Elmer Howell, Diary (1863).
Henry J. Peck Correspondence.

Manuscript Division, Library of Congress, Washington, D.C.
Thomas Francis Galwey, Diary.
George Washington Hall, Papers.
Charles H. Richardson, Diaries.
Dennis Tuttle Papers.

Montgomery County Historical Society, Rockville, MD.
The Montgomery County Story.

National Archives and Records Administration, Washington, D.C.
Charles Harvey George, Pension Record.
James Herbert George, Military Service Record.
James Herbert George, Pension Record.
Osman C. B. George, Pension Record.

Pearce Civil War Collection, Navarro College, Corsicana, TX.
Austin Fenn Papers, 1864–1865.
P.S. Scribner Papers, 1863.

Rhode Island Historical Society, Providence.
Papers of Captain George Evans Davis.

Special Collections, University of North Carolina–Charlotte, Charlotte.
Nathanial Shober Siewers Papers.

Special Collections and Archives, Utah State University, Logan.
Diary of Tommy Gordon, bugler.

U.S. Army Military History Institute, Carlisle Barracks, PA.
Henry W. Bower, 87th Pennsylvania Infantry — CWMiscColl (letters, 1863–1864).
Thomas Crowl, 87th Pennsylvania Infantry — CWMiscColl (letters, 1862–1864).
Charles E. Gotwalt, *Adventures of a Private in the American Civil War* (privately printed, n.d.) (87th Pennsylvania Infantry).
John A. Hicks, 10th Vermont Infantry — CWMiscColl (Enlisted man's letter, Sep 3, 1862).
Edward A. Johnson, 151st New York Infantry — CWMiscColl (Enlisted man's letters, July 27, 1863 — February 15, 1865).
Abiel T. LaForge, 106th New York Infantry — CWMiscColl (letters and diaries).
George Miller, 87th Pennsylvania Infantry — Papers (letters, 1861–1865).
Charles C. Perkins, 1st Massachusetts — CWTIColl (diary).
Charles E. Skelly, 87th Pennsylvania Infantry — HCWRTColl (letters, 1861–1863).

Vermont Historical Society Library, Monteplier.
Philip Arsino Correspondence.
Dan Barker Letter.
Henry P. Burnham Papers.
Crossett Family Letters.
Walter Graham Papers.
Edwin C. Hall Papers.
Roswell Hunt, in Civil War Letters to Wealthy Field.
Esther M. Thayer Correspondence.
Oscar E. Waite, "Three Years with the Tenth Vermont," unpublished manuscript.
William White Correspondence.

Vermont State Archives and Records Administration, Middlesex.
    3rd Report of Lieut. Col. George B. Damon, Tenth Regiment Vermont Volunteers.
    10th Regiment, Vermont Volunteer Infantry, Records of the Adjutant and Inspector
        General (PRA 364), Microfilm Reels F26063–F26069.
    Civil War Dairy and Journal of Charles B. Putnam, 1863–1865.
    General Orders, Brig. Gen. Morris, 1 December 1863.
    Letter of Augustus H. Crown, Company D, 10th Vermont Infantry, 24 March 1863,
        Microfilm Reel F2846.
    Letter to Adjutant General Washburn from Colonel Jewett, 11 September 1862.
    Pay Roll of Vermont Volunteers for Extra State Pay, State Treasurer's Office, Record
        of State Pay, 1861–1866, Microfilm Reel F26190.
    Records of the Vermont Civil War Centennial Committee, Microfilm Reels F26220–
        26229, F2845–2850.

Virginia Historical Society, Richmond.
    Henry Klag Diary.
    Tompkins Family Papers (1800–1877), Section 24.

Woodson Research Center, Fondren Library, Rice University, Houston, TX.
    Dillingham Family Papers, 1858–1958, MS 257.

Worcester Historical Museum, Worcester, MA.
    Artemas H. Skinner Papers.

Books and Articles

Abbott, Lemuel A. *Personal Recollections and Civil War Diary 1864*. Burlington, VT: Free
    Press, 1908.
Agassiz, George R., ed. *Meade's Headquarters 1863–1865: Letters of Colonel Theodore Lyman
    from the Wilderness to Appomattox*. Boston: Massachusetts Historical Society, 1922.
Balzer, John E., ed. *Buck's Book: A View of the 3rd Vermont Infantry Regiment*. Bolingbrook,
    IL: Balzer, 1993.
Beaudry, Paul Stephen. *The Forgotten Regiment: History of the 151st New York Volunteer
    Infantry Regiment*. Cleveland, OH: InChem, 1995.
Benedict, George G. *Vermont in the Civil War: A History of the Part Taken by the Vermont
    Soldiers and Sailors in the War for the Union, 1861–5*. 2 vols. Burlington, VT: Free
    Press, 1886–8.
Benton, Charles E. *As Seen from the Ranks: A Boy in the Civil War*. New York: G.P. Putnam's,
    1902.
Berkley, John Lee. *In the Defense of This Flag: The Civil War Diary of Pvt. Ormand Hupp,
    5th Indiana Light Artillery*. Bradenton, FL: McGuinn & McGuire, 1994.
Bernard, Kenneth A. *Lincoln and the Music of the Civil War*. Caldwell, ID: Caxton, 1966.
Beyer, W. F., and O. F. Keydel. *Deeds of Valor: How America's Civil War Heroes Won the
    Congressional Medal of Honor*. 1903. Reprint, Stamford, CT: Longmeadow Press, 1994.
Bilby, Joseph. "9 July 1864: The 14th New Jersey Infantry at the Battle of Monocacy." In
    *The Monocacy Regiment: A Commemorative History of the Fourteenth New Jersey Infantry
    in the Civil War, 1862–1865*. David G. Martin, ed. 167–192. Highstown, NJ:
    Longstreet House, 1987.
Biles, Daniel V. *A Soldier's Journey: An Account of Private Isaac Bobst, 128th Pennsylvania
    Volunteer Infantry and 1st Pennsylvania Cavalry, from Antietam to Andersonville*. Get-
    tysburg, PA: Thomas, 1990.
Billings, John D. *Hardtack & Coffee: The Unwritten Story of Army Life*. 1887. Reprint, Lin-
    coln: University of Nebraska Press, 1993.
Bircher, William. *A Drummer-Boy's Diary: Comprising Four Years of Service with the Second

Regiment Minnesota Veteran Volunteers 1861–1865. Newell L. Chester, ed. St. Cloud, MN: North Star Press, 1995.

Blackford, Charles Minor. *Letters from Lee's Army: Or Memoirs of Life In and Out of the Army in Virginia During the War Between the States*. New York: Charles Scribner's, 1947.

Blackford, W. W. *War Years with Jeb Stuart*. Baton Rouge: Louisiana State University Press, 1993.

Brandt, Dennis W. *From Home Guards to Heroes: The 87th Pennsylvania and Its Civil War Community*. Columbia: University of Missouri Press, 2006.

Brockett, Dr. L. P. *The Camp, the Battle Field, and the Hospital; or, Lights and Shadows of the Great Rebellion*. Philadelphia: National, 1866.

Broyles, Michael. *"Music of the Highest Class": Elitism and Populism in Antebellum Boston*. New Haven: Yale University Press, 1992.

Bruce, George B., and Daniel D. Emmett. *The Drummers' and Fifers' Guide*. New York: Pond, 1861.

Bufkin, William Alfred. "Union Bands of the Civil War (1862–1865): Instrumentation and Score Analysis." Ph. D. dissertation, Louisiana State University, 1973.

Burnell, George W. "The Development of Our Army," In *War Papers* (MOLLUS, WI, Vol. 2) 70–80. Milwaukee: Burdick, Armitage & Allen, 1896.

Campbell, Eric A., ed. *"A Grand Terrible Dramma": From Gettysburg to Petersburg: The Civil War Letters of Charles Wellington Reed*. New York: Fordham University Press, 2000.

Carter, Robert Goldthwaite, ed. *Four Brothers in Blue: A Story of the Great Civil War from Bull Run to Appomattox*. 1913. Reprint, Norman: University of Oklahoma Press, 1999.

Casler, John O. *Four Years in the Stonewall Brigade*. 1906. Reprint, Dayton: Morningside Bookshop, 1971.

Chase, Gilbert. *America's Music: From the Pilgrims to the Present*. New York: McGraw-Hill, 1966.

City of St. Thomas Centennial. *A Century of St. Thomas Times*. St. Thomas, ND: n.p., 1980.

Clark, Walter. *Histories of the Several Regiments and Battalions from North Carolina, in the Great War 1861–'65*. Vol. 3. Raleigh: Uzzell, 1901.

Clarke, Almon, "In the Immediate Rear: Experiences and Observations of a Field Surgeon," in Military Order of the Loyal Legion of the United States, *War Papers Read Before the Commandery of the State of Wisconsin. Military Order of the Loyal Legion of the United States*. Vol. 2, Milwaukee: Burdick, Armitage & Allen, 1896, 87–101.

Cohen, Roger S., Jr. "The Civil War in the Poolesville Area." *The Montgomery County Story* 5, no. 1 (November 1961): 1–16.

Coffin, Howard. *The Battered Stars: One State's Civil War Ordeal During Grant's Overland Campaign*. Woodstock, VT: Countryman Press, 2002.

_____. *Full Duty: Vermonters in the Civil War*. Woodstock, VT: Countryman Press, 1993.

Commager, Henry Steele, ed. *The Blue and the Gray*. New York: Meridian, 1994.

Committee of the Regimental Association. *History of the Thirty-Fifth Massachusetts Volunteers, 1862–1865*. Boston: Knight, 1884.

Contant, George. *Path of Blood: The True Story of the 33rd New York Volunteers*. New York: Seeco, 1997.

Cooling, B. Franklin. *Monocacy: The Battle That Saved Washington*. Shippensburg, PA: White Mane, 2000.

Crawford, M. J. *Reminiscences of a Veteran and Translated Tales from the Spanish and French*. New York: Parsons, n.d.

Crawford, Richard. *America's Musical Life: A History*. New York: Norton, 2001.

Creekman, Charles Todd. *The 106th New York Volunteers: A Civil War Heritage*. N.p.: Creekman, 1985.

Cumberworth, Sheila M., and Daniel V. Byles. *An Enduring Love: The Civil War Diaries of Benjamin Franklin Pierce (14th New Hampshire Vol. Inf.) and His Wife Harriett Jane Goodwin Pierce*. Gettysburg, PA: Thomas, 1995.

Cummins, Simon. *Give God the Glory: Memoirs of a Civil War Soldier*. Eagle River, MI: Jones, 1997.

Davis, Burke. *The Civil War: Strange & Fascinating Facts*. New York: Fairfax Press, 1982.

Davis, George E. "Washington in Peril," *The National Tribune*, 21 August 1884.

Davis, James A. "Music and Gallantry in Combat During the American Civil War," *American Music* 28, no. 2 (Summer 2010): 141–172.

_____. "Musical Reconnaissance and Deception in the American Civil War," *Journal of Military History* 74, no. 1 (January 2010): 79–105.

De Forest, John William. *A Volunteer's Adventures: A Union Captain's Record of the Civil War*. J. Croushore, ed. Baton Rouge: Louisiana State University Press, 1974.

Delauter, Roger U., and Brandon H. Beck. *Early's Valley Campaign: The 3rd Battle of Winchester*. Lynchburg, VA: Howard, 1997.

Donald, David Herbert, ed. *Gone for a Soldier: The Civil War Memoirs of Private Alfred Bellard*. Boston: Little, Brown, 1975.

Dunkelman, Mark H., and Michael J. Winey. *The Hardtack Regiment: An Illustrated History of the 154th Regiment, New York State Infantry Volunteers*. London: Associated University Presses, 1981.

Early, Jubal A. *Autobiographical Sketch and Narrative of the War Between the States*. New York: Smithmark, 1994.

Easton, Augustus B., ed. *History of the Saint Croix Valley*. Chicago: Cooper, 1909.

Eicher, John H., and David J. Eicher. *Civil War High Commands*. Stanford, CA: Stanford University Press, 2001.

Eicher, David J. *The Longest Night: A Military History of the Civil War*. New York: Simon & Schuster, 2001.

Ellis, Edward. *The Camp-Fires of General Lee: From the Peninsula to Appomattox Court-House*. Philadelphia: Harrison, 1886.

Foote, Shelby. *The Civil War: A Narrative*. Vol. 1. *Fort Sumter to Perryville*. New York: Vintage Books, 1986.

_____. *The Civil War: A Narrative*. Vol. 2. *Fredericksburg to Meridian*. New York: Vintage Books, 1986.

_____. *The Civil War: A Narrative*. Vol. 3. *Red River to Appomattox*. New York: Vintage Books, 1986.

Foster, John Y. *New Jersey and the Rebellion: History of the Services of the Troops and People of New Jersey in Aid of the Union Cause*. Newark, NJ: Dennis, 1868.

Fox, William F. *Regimental Losses in the American Civil War, 1861–1865*. Albany: Albany, 1889.

Frank, Joseph A., and Barbara Duteau. "Measuring the Political Articulateness of United States Civil War Soldiers: The Wisconsin Militia." In *The Journal of Military History* 64 (January 2000): 53–78.

Freeman, Douglas Southall. *Lee's Lieutenants: A Study in Command*. 3 vols. New York: Charles Scribner's, 1942.

Freeman, Warren Hapgood, and Eugene Harrison Freeman. *Letters from Two Brothers Serving in the War for the Union to Their Family at Home in West Cambridge, Mass.* Cambridge: Houghton, 1871.

Freemon, Frank R. *Gangrene and Glory: Medical Care During the American Civil War*. Urbana: University of Illinois Press, 2001.

Gardstrom, Dwight A. *A History of the Fourth Regimental Band and Musicians of the Fourth Minnesota Infantry Volunteers During the War of the Great Rebellion: 1861–1865*. Ph. D. diss., University of Minnesota, 1989.

Garofalo, Robert, and Mark Elrod. *A Pictorial History of Civil War Era Musical Instruments and Military Bands.* Charleston, SC: Pictorial Histories, 1985.

George, Keith H. *George Genealogy.* Kingman, AZ: H and H Printers, 1991.

Gordon, John B. *Reminiscences of the Civil War.* New York: Charles Scribner's, 1903.

Gordon, Paul, and Rita Gordon. *A Playground of the Civil War: Frederick County, Maryland.* Frederick, MD: Heritage Partnership, 1994.

Graham, Martin F., and George F. Skoch. *Mine Run: A Campaign of Lost Opportunities, October 21, 1863–May 1, 1864.* Lynchburg, VA: Howard, 1987.

Grant, Ulysses S. *Personal Memoirs.* C. Carr, ed. New York: Modern Library, 1999.

Griffith, Paddy. *Battle Tactics of the Civil War.* New Haven, CT: Yale University Press, 1989.

Grimsley, Mark. "In Not So Dubious Battle: The Motivations of American Civil War Soldiers." In *The Journal of Military History* 62 (January 1998): 175–88.

Hall, Harry H. *A Johnny Reb Band from Salem: The Pride of Tarheelia.* Raleigh: North Carolina Confederate Centennial Commission, 1963.

Hamm, Charles. *Yesterdays: Popular Song in America.* New York: Norton, 1979.

Hansen, Richard K. *The American Wind Band: A Cultural History.* Chicago: GIA, 2005.

Harwell, Richard B. *The Confederate Reader.* New York: Barnes & Noble, 1992.

_____. *Confederate Music.* Chapel Hill: University of North Carolina Press, 1950.

Haydon, Charles B., and Stephen W. Sears. *For Country, Cause & Leader: The Civil War Journal of Charles B. Haydon.* New York: Ticknor & Fields, 1993.

Haynes, Edwin M. *A History of the Tenth Regiment, Vt. Vols.* 2nd ed. Rutland, VT: Tuttle, 1894.

Hazen, Margaret Hindle, and Robert M. Hazen. *The Music Men: An Illustrated History of Brass Bands in America, 1800–1920.* Washington, DC: Smithsonian Institution Press, 1987.

Heaps, Willard A., and Porter W. Heaps. *The Singing Sixties: The Spirit of Civil War Days Drawn from the Music of the Times.* Norman: University of Oklahoma Press, 1960.

Henderson, William D. *The Road to Bristoe Station: Campaigning with Lee and Meade, August 1– October 20, 1863.* Lynchburg, VA: Howard, 1987.

Hitchcock, H. Wiley. *Music in the United States: A Historical Introduction.* Englewood Cliffs, NJ: Prentice-Hall, 1969.

Hoehling, A. A. *After the Guns Fell Silent: A Post-Appomattox Narrative, April 1865–March 1866.* Lanham, MD: Madison Books, 1990.

Horn, John. *The Petersburg Campaign: June 1864–April 1865.* Conshohocken, PA: Combined Books, 1993.

Howell, Helena Adelaide. *Chronicles of the One Hundred Fifty-First Regiment New York State Volunteer Infantry 1862–1865.* Albion, NY: A. M. Eddy, 1911.

Hunt, Roger D. *Colonels in Blue: Union Army Colonels in the Civil War.* Atglen, PA: Schiffer Military History, 2001.

Hyde, Thomas W. *Following the Greek Cross: Or, Memories of the Sixth Army Corps.* Boston: Houghton Mifflin, 1894.

Jacobs, Charles T. *Civil War Guide to Montgomery County, Maryland.* Rockville, MD: Montgomery County Historical Society, 1983.

Johnson, Robert Underwood, ed. *Battles and Leaders of the Civil War.* 4 vols. Edison, NJ: Castle, 1990.

Keifer, J. Warren. *Slavery and Four Years of War: A Political History of Slavery in the United States.* New York: G. P. Putnam's, 1900.

Kieffer, Henry Martyn. *The Recollections of a Drummer-Boy.* Boston: Ticknor, 1889.

Klein, Maury. *Edward Porter Alexander.* Athens: University of Georgia Press, 1971.

Kuntz, Norbert. "A Brookfield Soldier's Report: The Civil War Recollections of Edwin C. Hall." In *Vermont History* 57, no. 4 (Fall 1989): 197–225.

Leeke, Jim, ed. *Smoke, Sound and Fury: The Civil War Memoirs of Major-General Lew Wallace, U.S. Volunteers.* Portland, OR: Strawberry Hill Press, 1998.

Leepson, Marc, *Desperate Engagement: How a Little-Known Civil War Battle Saved Washington, D.C., and Changed American History.* New York: Thomas Dunne Books, 2007.

Lockwood, James D. *Life and Adventures of a Drummer-Boy; Or, Seven Years a Soldier.* Albany, NY: Skinner, 1893.

Longacre, Edward G., ed. *From Antietam to Fort Fisher: The Civil War Letters of Edward King Wightman, 1862–1865.* Rutherford, NJ: Fairleigh Dickinson University Press, 1985.

Longstreet, James. *From Manassas to Appomattox: Memoirs of the Civil War in America.* J. I. Robertson, Jr., ed. New York: Kraus Reprint, 1969.

Lord, Francis A., and Arthur Wise. *Bands and Drummer Boys of the Civil War.* New York: Da Capo Press, 1979.

Lutz, Caroline C. *Letters of George E. Chamberlin, Who Fell in the Service of His Country Near Charlestown, VA., August 21st, 1864.* Springfield, IL: Rokker, 1883.

Lyle, the Rev. W. W. *Lights and Shadows of Army Life: or, Pen Pictures from the Battlefield, the Camp, and the Hospital.* Cincinnati: Carroll, 1865.

McCarthy, Carlton. *Detailed Minutiae of Soldier Life in the Army of Northern Virginia 1861–1865.* 1882. Reprint, Lincoln: University of Nebraska Press, 1993.

McPherson, James M. *Battle Cry of Freedom: The Civil War Era.* New York: Oxford University Press, 1988.

Marshall, Jeffrey D., ed. *A War of the People: Vermont Civil War Letters.* Hanover, NH: University Press of New England, 1999.

Martin, David G., ed. *The Monocacy Regiment: A Commemorative History of the Fourteenth New Jersey Infantry in the Civil War, 1862–1865.* Highstown, NJ: Longstreet House, 1987.

Messer, Timothy B. *Civil War Letters of Timothy B. Messer, Tenth Vermont Volunteers.* E. Phelps, ed. Greenfield, MA: Hall, 1986.

Miers, Earl S., ed. *New Jersey and the Civil War: An Album of Contemporary Accounts.* Princeton, NJ: Van Nostrand, 1964.

Miller, Gretchen Howe, ed. *A Young Man of Promise: The Flower of the Family: James Marsh Read, 1833–1865.* Bloomington, IN: Authorhouse, 2004.

Mudgett, Timothy B., *Make the Fur Fly: A History of a Union Volunteer Division in the American Civil War.* Shippensburg, PA: Burd Street Press, 1997.

Muffly, J. W. *The Story of Our Regiment: A History of the 148th Pennsylvania Vols.* Des Moines, IA: Kenyon, 1904.

Nesbitt, Mark. *Through Blood & Fire: Selected Civil War Papers of Major General Joshua Chamberlain.* Mechanicsburg, PA: Stackpole Books, 1996.

Nevins, Allan, ed. *A Diary of Battle: The Personal Journals of Colonel Charles S. Wainwright, 1861–1865.* New York: Harcourt, Brace & World, 1962.

Nofi, Albert A. *The Gettysburg Campaign: June–July 1863.* Conshohosken, PA: Combined Books, 1986.

Olsen, Bernard A., ed. *Upon the Tented Field.* Red Bank, NJ: Historic Projects, 1993.

Olson, Kenneth E. *Music and Musket: Bands and Bandsmen of the American Civil War.* Westport, CT: Greenwood Press, 1981.

Parsons, Phyllis Vibbard, "Drum! Drum! Drum!" In *Pennsylvania Folklife* 28, no. 3: 27–37.

Pond, George E. *The Shenandoah Valley in 1864.* New York: Charles Scribner's, 1883.

Pope, Thomas E. *The Weary Boys: Colonel J. Warren Kiefer and the 110th Ohio Volunteer Infantry.* Kent, OH: Kent State University Press, 2002.

Porter, Horace. *Campaigning with Grant.* Secaucus, NJ: Blue and Grey Press, 1984.

Prowell, George R. *History of the Eighty-Seventh Regiment, Pennsylvania Volunteers: Prepared from Official Records, Diaries, and Other Authentic Sources of Information.* 1903. Reprint, Mt. Vernon, IN: Windmill, 1994.

Quaife, Milo M., ed. *From the Cannon's Mouth: The Civil War Letters of General Alpheus S. Williams.* Detroit: Wayne State University Press, 1959.

Quint, Alonzo H. *The Potomac and the Rapidan.* Boston: Crosby and Nichols, 1864.

Rauscher, Frank. *Music on the March, 1862–65, with the Army of the Potomac: 114th Regt. P. V., Collis' Zouaves.* Philadelphia: Fell, 1892.

Rhea, Gordon C. *Cold Harbor: Grant and Lee, May 26–June 3, 1864.* Baton Rouge: Louisiana State University Press, 2002.

_____. *To the North Anna River: Grant and Lee, May 13–25, 1864.* Baton Rouge: Louisiana State University Press, 2000.

_____. *The Battles for Spotsylvania Court House and the Road to Yellow Tavern: May 7–12, 1864.* Baton Rouge: Louisiana State University Press, 1997.

_____. *The Battle of the Wilderness: May 5–6, 1864.* Baton Rouge: Louisiana State University Press, 1994.

Rhodes, Robert H., ed. *All for the Union: The Civil War Diaries and Letters of Elisha Hunt Rhodes.* New York: Orion Books, 1991.

Roberts, William H. *Drums and Guns Around Petersburg.* Bowie, MD: Heritage Books, 1995.

Robertson, James I., Jr., ed. *The Civil War Letters of General Robert McAllister.* New Brunswick, NJ: Rutgers University Press, 1965.

_____. *The Stonewall Brigade.* Baton Rouge: Louisiana State University Press, 1963.

Roe, Alfred S. *The Tenth Regiment, Massachusetts Volunteer Infantry, 1861–1864, A Western Massachusetts Regiment.* Springfield, MA: Tenth Regiment Veteran Association, 1909.

Runge, William H., ed. *Four Years in the Confederate Artillery: The Diary of Private Henry Robinson Berkeley.* Chapel Hill: University of North Carolina Press, 1961.

Schairer, Jack E. *Lee's Bold Plan for Point Lookout: The Rescue of Confederate Prisoners That Never Happened.* Jefferson, NC: McFarland, 2008.

Schank, Dennis, and Scott Schotz. *Baptism of Fire: The 151st New York Infantry at Mine Run.* Lockport, NY: n.p., 1999.

Scott, Robert G. *Into the Wilderness with the Army of the Potomac.* Bloomington: Indiana University Press, 1985.

Sears, Stephen W. *George B. McClellan: The Young Napoleon.* New York: Da Capo Press, 1999.

Sheldon, Charles LeRoy. "Diary of a Drummer." In *Michigan History* 43, no. 3 (September 1959): 315–348.

Sheridan, Michael V. *Personal Memoirs of Philip Henry Sheridan.* 2 vols. New York: Appleton, 1904.

Sherman, William T. *Memoirs of General William T. Sherman.* 2nd ed. New York: Appleton, 1904.

Simons, Ezra D. *A Regimental History: The One Hundred and Twenty-Fifth New York State Volunteers.* New York: Simons, 1888.

Small, Abner Ralph, and Harold Adams Small. *The Road to Richmond: The Civil War Memoirs of Major Abner R. Small of the Sixteenth Maine Volunteers; Together with the Diary Which He Kept When He Was a Prisoner of War.* Berkeley: University of California Press, 1939.

Smith, Brian. *Bandstands to Battlefields: Brass Band in 19th Century America.* Gansevoort, NY: Corner House Historical Publications, 2004.

Smith, Derek. *Lee's Last Stand: Sailor's Creek, Virginia, 1865.* Shippensburg, PA: White Mane Books, 2002.

Sneden, Robert Knox. *Eye of the Storm: A Civil War Odyssey.* Charles F. Bryan, Jr., and Nelson D. Lankford, eds. New York: The Free Press, 2000.

Steere, Edward. *The Wilderness Campaign.* 1960. Reprint, Harrisburg, PA: Stackpole, 1987.

Stevens, George T. *Three Years in the Sixth Corps.* Albany: Gray, 1866.

Sween, Jane C., and William Offut. *Montgomery County: Centuries of Change.* Sun Valley, CA: American Historical Press, 1999.

Swift, Gloria B., and Gail Stephens. "Honor Redeemed: Lew Wallace's Military Career and the Battle of Monocacy." In *North & South* 4, no. 2 (January 2001): 34–46.

Swinton, William. *Campaigns of the Army of the Potomac: A Critical History of Operations in Virginia, Maryland, and Pennsylvania, from the Commencement to the Close of the War 1861–1865.* New York: Charles Scribner's, 1882.

Terrill, J. Newton. *Campaign of the Fourteenth Regiment New Jersey Volunteers* (reprint of 2nd ed., 1884). In *The Monocacy Regiment: A Commemorative History of the Fourteenth New Jersey Infantry in the Civil War, 1862–1865.* David G. Martin, ed. 1–132. Highstown, NJ: Longstreet House, 1987.

Thompson, S. Millet. *Thirteenth Regiment of New Hampshire Volunteer Infantry in the War of the Rebellion, 1861–1865: A Diary Covering Three Years and a Day.* Boston: Houghton Mifflin, 1888.

Trudeau, Noah Andre. *The Last Citadel: Petersburg, Virginia, June 1864–April 1865.* Boston: Little, Brown, 1991.

United States War Department. *Revised Regulations for the Army of the United States, 1861.* Philadelphia: Brown, 1861.

_____. *The War of the Rebellion: A Compilation of the Official Records of the Union and Confederate Armies.* 128 vols. Washington, DC: Government Printing Office, 1880–1901.

Urwin, Gregory J. W. *Custer Victorious: The Civil War Battles of General George Armstrong Custer.* London, UK: Associated University Presses, 1983.

Vermont Adjutant & Inspector General Office. *Revised Roster of Vermont Volunteers Who Served in the Army and Navy of the United States During the War of the Rebellion.* Montpelier, VT: Watchman, 1892.

_____. *Report of the Adjutant & Inspector General of the State of Vermont, for the Year Ending November 1, 1862.* Montpelier, VT: Walton's Steam Press Establishment. 1862.

Vredenburgh, Peter. "Letters of Major Peter Vredenburgh of the Battles and Marches of the Old Fourteenth Regiment New Jersey Vols." In *The Monocacy Regiment: A Commemorative History of the Fourteenth New Jersey Infantry in the Civil War, 1862–1865.* David G. Martin, ed. Highstown, NJ: Longstreet House, 1987.

Waite, Otis S. R. *New Hampshire in the Great Rebellion.* Claremont, NH: Chase, 1870.

Wells, Frederic P. *History of Newbury, Vermont, from the Discovery of the Coös Country to Present Time.* St. Johnsbury, VT: Caledonian, 1902.

Wert, Jeffry D. *From Winchester to Cedar Creek: The Shenandoah Campaign of 1864.* Mechanicsburg, PA: Stackpole Books, 1997.

Whiteaker, Larry H., and W. Calvin Dickinson, eds. *Civil War Letters of the Tenure Family: Rockland County, N.Y., 1862–1865.* New York: Historical Society of Rockland County, 1990.

Wickman, Donald H. *Letters to Vermont from Her Civil War Soldier Correspondents to the Home Press.* 2 vols. Bennington, VT: Images from the Past, 1998.

Wild, Frederick W. *Memoirs and History of Capt. F. W. Alexander's Baltimore Battery of Light Artillery U. S. V.* Baltimore: Maryland School for Boys, 1912.

Wiley, Bell Irvin. *The Life of Billy Yank: The Common Soldier of the Union.* Indianapolis: Bobbs-Merrill, 1952.

_____. *The Life of Johnny Reb: The Common Soldier of the Confederacy.* Indianapolis: Bobbs-Merrill, 1943.

Wilson, Keith P. *Campfires of Freedom: The Camp Life of Black Soldiers During the Civil War.* Kent, OH: Kent State University Press, 2002.

Winik, Jay. *April 1865: The Month That Saved America*. New York: HarperCollins, 2001.

Wise, Jennings Cropper. *The Long Arm of Lee: or the History of the Artillery of the Army of Northern Virginia*. 1915. Reprint, Lincoln: University of Nebraska Press, 1991.

Worthington, Glenn H. *Fighting for Time: The Battle That Saved Washington*. 1932. Reprint, Shippensburg, PA: White Mane, 1988.

Index

Page numbers in *bold italics* indicate illustrations.